PART I

THE SQUEEZE

CHAPTER ONE

SIGNAL FIRES

PATIENTLY, the donkey trotted down the Champs Elysées. It had the run of the broad avenue. There were no speeding motorcars to frighten it. In the last five months motorcars had all but vanished from the streets of Paris. They were replaced by bicycles, or simply by shanks' mare. Occasionally a horse-and-buggy rattled by. A donkey, however, was a new means of transportation. Passers-by gave it startled glances. They were surprised that the donkey neither carried a load, nor pulled a cart. Two shiny, high boots were tied to its sides. They hit the animal at every stride. Sometimes the donkey brayed painfully. Yet it trotted on without showing the slightest sign of resistance. Only an ass could be as patient as that.

Right and left of the donkey marched a group of boys, Sorbonne students, to judge from their hatlessness, their uncombed hair, their young, furrowed faces, and their worn-out clothes. They marched in silence and dignity, as if in a funeral procession.

The day was November 11, Armistice Day, of 1940. Memorial celebrations for the victims of the first war were *verboten*. They might have led to trouble. General Joachim von Stülpnagel, Commander of the army of occupation in France, did not give the people entrusted to his protection any opportunity to get out of hand. Besides, the French people themselves did not feel like celebrating. After all, who were the victims of the senseless victory of 1918? Were they heroes— or just dead fools? Most of the passers-by on the Champs Elysées, on this November 11, 1940, at eleven A.M., were heartily glad that, as far as they were concerned, the second war was over. *Gagner la vie*, to make a living, was all they now wanted. They were resigned and patient—like the ass.

There must have been some, however, who found the donkey too patient for their taste. Why did the poor animal not throw off the empty, shining, high boots? By the time the silent procession passed the Avenue Dutuit a small crowd was following it. At the corner of the Avenue de Marigny the procession was no longer silent, and the crowd no longer small. Thousands had joined the ranks. They did not dare to sing a patriotic song. The sight of German officers strolling along the Champs Elysées terrified them. Field-gray was a magic color, and the monocle seemed invincible. Moreover, Parisians had little reason to sing. After five months of occupation the bread ration had shrunk to two hundred grams a week, and the listless children cried for milk.

Suddenly a voice burst out: "Vive l'âne!"

The call resounded a thousandfold. "Vive l'âne!" shouted the Paris street.

The ambling German officers were still smiling. "Long live the ass!" one of them translated to his comrades. Chuckling, they shook their square heads. So this was gay Paree!

Major Johann Schmidt, Infantry Regiment 344, insisted

afterward that he had been for drawing sabers immediately. He did not understand, he admitted, what all the shouting was about, but on general principles he was for drawing sabers or using service revolvers whenever a mob began to shout. His friends, however, had prevailed upon him. The chief, General von Stülpnagel, had instructed his officers to behave considerately and politely. Under no conditions must the prestige of the German army, famous for its discipline and reticence, be lowered. If there was any dirty work to be done, the Gestapo would do it. In fact, the General had issued an order that German uniforms were to disappear the moment street riots flared up.

But was this, indeed, a street riot? The people simply cheered an ass. The French were making asses of themselves. That was all.

The Rond Point was heavily policed. It is not recorded how the French police agents felt when they dutifully attacked their compatriots. Probably they did not feel at all. The rubber truncheon is not sentimental. It follows its own logic. Besides, it was well known that M. Chiappe, then Police Prefect of Paris, did not tolerate any trouble in the streets. Under the various republican governments which he had faithfully served, he had always had to curb his disciplinary measures. Now, having sold out to the Nazis, his savage instincts, perhaps a heritage from his Corsican bandit ancestors, had free rein. The chief expected every Paris agent to do his duty with the rubber truncheon.

It took the police ten minutes, all told, to disperse the crowd. The whole incident would have been quickly forgotten, and probably laughed off with the famous Paris shrug, had it not been for the donkey. In the midst of the pandemonium the frightened animal, it appears, ran amuk. It galloped—"like a race horse," Major Johann Schmidt related later —through the general brawl. "It came dangerously close to me as I stood on the pavement, entirely unconcerned in this affair between the French police and the Paris mob. The ass almost struck me with its head. A German officer can, of course, not tolerate such an insult. I drew my service revolver—"

"You cannot do that!" Robert Louis Yomais, aged twenty-six, student of philosophy, shouted, throwing himself between the major and the donkey.

Major Johann Schmidt, Infantry Regiment 344, fired. He hit the young man in the right shoulder. He did not believe, he said, that the wound he inflicted on Yomais or whatever he was called, could have been very serious. He did not shoot to kill, he emphasized, but only to get the impertinent fellow out of the way. Then, he admitted proudly, he emptied his service revolver with deadly precision into the donkey.

Robert Louis Yomais was carried off by his comrades. No police agent interfered. Dr. Maxime Rubinstein, who was subsequently sentenced to twelve years' hard labor for having aided and abetted a political criminal, bandaged Yomais's shoulder. After a few hours' rest the patient was able to walk to the Café de la Coupole, on Montparnasse, where a young intellectual belongs. The other intellectuals in the "Coupole," young and old, asked no questions about the bandage around his right shoulder. They had been sitting out the war, the debacle, the invasion, in their own café, and they were completely uncurious. Robert Louis Yomais, the first victim of the German terror in France, disappeared unnoticed among the crowd in the "Coupole."

Paris honored the donkey as the first victim. The story of the assassinated ass spread like wildfire through the city. The crime had been committed toward eleven-thirty A.M. At two P.M. two German soldiers, walking through a side street of Saint Denis, the "red" suburb, were greeted by a band of workers with shouts that sounded unmistakably like "hee-haw." It was the asses' cry. The soldiers, both elderly men and both unarmed, accelerated rapidly in the direction of their barracks. A few stones were hurled after them but missed the fast-moving targets. The soldiers reported to their commander, who, in turn, telephoned the Hôtel Crillon, Herr von Stülpnagel's headquarters.

The general received many similar calls. Paris, it appeared, was getting out of hand. Excited men were congregating everywhere in the *banlieue rouge*, the belt of Communist suburbs, and the Quartier Latin showed distinct signs of restiveness. There was a good deal of talk about a dead donkey, which the German informers could not quite make out. But suddenly also talk about the sacred significance of this day, Armistice Day, sprang up. On the Place de l'Odéon a student had exhorted an improvised meeting while the French policeman on duty listened impassively. "The English have repulsed the ferocious German air attack," the student had shouted. "The Luftwaffe is ingloriously beaten!" Then the informer "beat it" himself for fear of being recognized. But he still heard the meeting beginning, "God save the . . ." Whom God was invoked to save, the German informer could not tell.

General von Stülpnagel is an imperturbable man. He has been known to sign more than one collective death sentence for a hundred hostages without batting an eyelash. His ravenlike face remains unmoved, his lips below the dark, slightly graying mustache are pressed closely together, when he acts. He is not a man of many words. No one heard him rage, as Hitler rages, when Paris, on Armistice Day, 1940, for the first time clenched its helpless fists.

On the surface not much happened. Only the German uniforms disappeared from the streets as if by magic. But inside the barracks the preparations proceeded with clockwork precision. Mechanized soldiers donned their steel helmets, greased their rifles; each man was provided with the prescribed twenty-four rounds of ammunition. But the Parisians saw nothing but streets, their own old streets, now for the first time after five months of shame, obviously abandoned by the invader. They poured into what they believed to be their liberated streets. Instinctively, thousands of workers marched to the Boulevard du Montparnasse where they were sure to meet the students.

At four P.M. the Boulevard du Montparnasse belonged to the sovereign people of Paris—fifty thousand, the police estimated next day, packing every inch of the pavement. Lustily they sang, first the "Marseillaise" which they had been missing for almost half a year, then "God save the King!" Some groups shouted, "Hee-haw." The murdered donkey was not forgotten. It was a bacchanal of liberty.

At half past four a rumble like distant thunder came nearer and nearer. Soon it outroared the laughter, the speeches, the drunken joy. *Trap-trap*, it sounded. Heavy boots were tramping, heels were clicking, snapped commands lashed the air.

The German soldiers were in a strategic position. The lessons of the Blitzkrieg were not lost on General von Stülpnagel. His was a perfect pincer movement. His troops encircled the Boulevard du Montparnasse from both sides. On the right they advanced from the Port-Royal, on the left they grew, as it were, out of the Rue de Sèvres and the Rue Lecourbe. The students and the workers on Montparnasse were trapped.

A terrific outcry rose from the masses. Fifty thousand unarmed men and women stared into the muzzles of the Nazi guns.

The German soldiers halted.

At this very moment a young man stumbled out of the "Coupole." Robert Louis Yomais disregarded his bandaged right shoulder. Shaking his clenched fist, he flung his arm up. Insanely, he ran into the German lines. "Vive la France!" he shouted.

The volley felled him and eleven others.

Then panic broke out. It was not necessary to fire a second time. Just for fun the German soldiers crushed the skulls of a few helplessly scrambling victims with the butt ends of their rifles. Ange Dubreuil, of Dinant, who had happened into the turmoil, he did not know how, lifted his right arm to protect his head. He heard a voice barking at him in a strange language. Then he felt cold steel at his temple. When his mother came to Paris to inquire for her lost son, she was told that Ange Dubreuil had been executed for an act of violence against a German soldier.

François Cumenuer, whose family hired a lawyer with the necessary pull, one of those gentlemen who worked hand in glove with the new masters, had had, it seemed, the misfortune to be shot for insulting an officer. The twenty-two-year-old girl student Marie Plouzane was executed "for having cut telegraph wires." It was never admitted that she fell among the twelve victims of the first volley.

The whole butchery on Montparnasse was never admitted by the Germans. General von Stülpnagel, as stated previously, is not a man of many words. His communiqués are terse. On November 12, 1940, the communiqué read simply: "Paris is again under perfect control."

The next Armistice anniversary, November 11, 1941, passed in absolute calm. But as Joachim von Stülpnagel reviewed his troops on the Champ-de-Mars, his heavily armored car raced over a mile a minute through the emptied Paris streets. The windows of his high-powered automobile are of bullet-proof glass.

Four million Parisians have learned that one cannot fight machine guns with bare hands. But everyone knows that there must be other ways. There must be a thousand ways, dark ways, bloodstained ways, ways of cunning and of sacrifice, to freedom.

Again the tide was lapping the streets. Aalesund is a storm-swept town, the miniature Venice of the north, protruding into the sea. Its eighteen thousand citizens, mostly fishermen and their families, do not care to leave their houses during the time of the equinoctial gales. One is likely to get something more than wet feet.

But on this Saturday evening, late in August, 1941, no one minded a minor nuisance. The people crowded the square in front of the Freemasons Hall, packing the side streets as far as the Hotel Scandinavie, which lay in deep darkness. The Scandinavie, the only hotel in town, is the headquarters of the German staff. On this night it was abandoned. In Norway, as in France, the disappearance of German uniforms bodes ill. No one believed the German local commander, Lieutenant Colonel Fierhausen, who repeated good-naturedly, and much too loudly, that he and his staff were only leaving to spend this week end merrymaking in Oslo.

There is no merrymaking in Oslo. The girls will not dance with German gentlemen. The patrons leave the gay spots a quarter of an hour after guests in field-gray enter. This quarter-hour of polite attendance is required by the military regulations. It is forbidden to insult the field-gray uniforms by leaving the place immediately. So the Norwegians take out their watches the very moment German officers show up. Demonstratively, they lay their timepieces on their tables. After exactly fifteen minutes there is a general scramble toward the exit. Recently, the restaurant Kroll had to be closed for serving "inferior" food to officers. The sharp-eyed, weather-beaten fishermen of Aalesund knew very well that Lieutenant Colonel Fierhausen would not have a good time in Oslo. He was simply evading a worse time in Aalesund.

Mr. Lindheim was, it appeared, the only man in town not to know it. "Have a good time!" he said, making an unsuccessful effort to smile as the Colonel departed, and then he added: "Heil Hitler!" He raised his right arm in good will and complete submission. It was a wretched gesture. Norwegians cannot acquire the proper snap in giving the Nazi salute; not even the few Quislings can learn it.

"I trust all goes well!" Lieutenant Colonel Fierhausen replied. He did not bother to Heil Hitler in return. It would have been too great an honor for the creature before him. "No trouble if it can be avoided! But no weakness if a show of force is necessary!" And he added, "Can you rely on your men?"

"The police force of Aalesund is entirely collaborationist!" Mr. Lindheim hastened to assure him. "They love a little shooting!" he exaggerated assiduously.

He was only the deputy chief of the local police force. His superior, however, had been removed for failing completely to enforce the new order, and if all went well on this Saturday night he, Mr. Lindheim, member of long standing in the "Nasjonal Samling," the Norwegian Nazi party, and a personal friend of the great Quisling, was sure to be promoted to the vacant post. He was being hard pressed on account of some unfortunate gambling debts. No one would dare to remind him of them, once he was the chief of police.

The Oslo Express departed with Lieutenant Colonel Fierhausen and his staff. To tell the truth, "Express" was, under the given conditions, a slight overstatement. Norwegian trains go slowly, they no longer run on time. This is partly due to the fact that most of the country's rolling stock has been confiscated by the army of occupation and now serves for troop transports to the Russian front. On the other hand, the time-tables in Norway are constantly upset by derailments which occur with ghastly regularity.

"The only thing we are sure of," the stationmaster in Oslo replied to an inquiry as to how long it would take Gauleiter Josef Terboven, Hitler's viceroy in Norway, to get to Skien, where he planned to attend a Quisling meeting, "is that only every fifth train arrives on time. Some do not arrive at all." The stationmaster was arrested for this impertinent remark and thrown into Moellersgaden prison, where the Gestapo is raising a new breed of rats, to keep the inmates busy at night.

With characteristic German precision the freighter *Hulda,* from Cuxhaven, anchored off Aalesund the very moment the Oslo Express left with the staff of the German command. A few of the townspeople saw her approach, negotiate the difficult gale-swept harbor, and lower a boat. But no one went down to welcome the *Hulda.* The times when the people of Aalesund rejoiced at the arrival of a ship were over. Nowadays ships come seldom, and they come empty. When they weigh anchor again they are heavily laden with booty, mostly with the confiscated catch of the local fishermen. This ship, the people of Aalesund were aware, had not come to load the latest herring catch. This had already been disposed of by the business agents of the German High Command. The *Hulda* had come to swallow human cargo. She was to remove the hostages to Germany.

Her lights gleamed through the foggy dusk. Pressing one's face against the windows of the Freemasons Hall, one could see the faint beams. "She is here!" said Harald Roenneberg.

None of the seventy men who jammed the hall answered. They had been pressing their faces so often and so hard against the windows, awaiting the arrival of the ship that would carry them to Germany and to their doom, that the dreaded moment, when at last it materialized, had lost much of its horror. Moreover, the seventy hostages, picked at random throughout the town, were not used to dramatizing themselves. Norwegians are, on the whole, sober folk. They dislike scenes. And the seventy who were crammed into the Freemasons Hall, the largest one in Aalesund, were the flower of Norwegian citizenry: pastors, teachers, doctors, and a few substantial businessmen. Those whose names carried weight in the neighborhood had been fetched out of bed and dumped into the hall. The local jail could not accommodate these seventy men who were condemned to the German concentration camp in retaliation for the unrest that was spreading along the western coast.

In the summer of 1941 the system of picking out wholesale entirely innocent people and holding them responsible for acts of resistance in their respective towns or districts was still in its infancy. In Aalesund it was being applied for the first time. Herr Terboven proudly claims the invention. Of course this is a Nazi claim—a lie. In fact, the butchery of hostages was an outstanding characteristic of warfare in the dark ages. Alfred Rosenberg, Hitler's teacher of history and philosophy, now the Nazi Tsar of the conquered parts of Russia, brought the ancient trick to the Führer's attention. Jubilantly Hitler responded. "What does the Jewish Bible say?" he addressed his gauleiter, on July 17, 1941, in Munich. "An eye for an eye and a tooth for a tooth? The Bible is outdated. We will take a hundred eyes and a hundred teeth for one! A hundred for one!" he repeated, foaming at the mouth. "Go ahead, party comrades!"

Hitler's hangmen went ahead. According to a statement of the Inter-Allied Information Committee, which speaks for twelve governments-in-exile, released on November 19, 1941, at least 103,000 persons, most of them hostages, have been executed in efforts to impose the "new order" in subjugated Europe. Although in some countries (Poland for instance) the system of collective murder without trial was established immediately after the German invasion, most of this death toll of 103,000 victims was the autumn crop of 1941 alone.

The various gauleiters are engaged in earnest competition as to who may best fulfill his task of "depopulating." Today most of them decree collective death sentences without even the pretext of a cause. The process of bestialization makes rapid progress. In August, 1941, however, when the hostage system had its trial in Aalesund, it still seemed advisable to look for the semblance of a reason.

A hot summer was ending. A score of fishing smacks had escaped to Britain. The townspeople had repeatedly cheered the R.A.F. raiders. A German supply ship, hugging the Norwegian coast, while carrying Swedish ore to Bremen, had been blown up at the pier itself. Now the seventy most highly respected citizens were to answer with their lives for a change in their fellow citizens' behavior. "One more incident—and off goes your head!" Colonel Fierhausen had said as he received Harald Roenneberg. Then he smiled, watching with evident gusto the elderly gentleman being pushed out of the room and into the emergency jail in the Freemasons Hall.

He did not care, however, to watch the hostages being dragged to the prison ship. If trouble arose on the way from the hall to the pier, the local police should cope with it. Thus the honor of the German army would remain unstained, and the Nazi-controlled Oslo radio would once more have the opportunity to brag of the efficiency with which Jewish Communists were dealt with by the Norwegian police themselves.

The police executed their duty. They entered the Freemasons Hall, handcuffed the hostages, and were about to escort them to the ship. They had entered the hall unimpeded. Grumbling, but still obedient, the crowd made way for them. But when the police returned, shepherding the seventy most beloved men of Aalesund, five thousand bodies blocked their path.

"You cannot take them!" yelled some in the crowd. "They are innocent men!" a white-haired woman shouted.

The policemen looked around helplessly. There stood the trucks which were to transport the hostages to the waiting boat. But the drivers were on strike. They had taken refuge in the various bars along the waterfront and simply refused to drive. Two of them, however, were ferreted out of the "Jolly Sailor." With the policemen's revolvers digging into their backs, they crouched at their wheels. The engines were started. The people dodged the heavy lorries. The whole scene, it seemed, was over.

Unfortunately, at this moment Mr. Lindheim appeared. At this provocative sight the crowd formed ranks again. They no longer cared whether they were hit. They threw themselves in the path of the trucks, which stopped with shrieking brakes. Hell was let loose. A few sturdy fishermen tried to seize Mr. Lindheim. He dodged behind the broad backs of his policemen. "Fire!" he commanded.

The police fired. But no one was hurt. As if by agreement, they had fired into the air.

"Kill them!" Mr. Lindheim raged. "Get them all. Here, this old woman. She's the worst!"

Instead, the white-haired woman got Mr. Lindheim. Her umbrella, the deputy chief stated later, gravely injured his skull and his right ear.

It was too much for Mr. Lindheim. He retired hastily. He ran for his life. He ran toward the pier and the German ship.

The lorries started up again. Slowly, surrounded by yelling, delirious masses, they made their way to the narrow bridge, the drivers urged on by the policemen sitting next to them. But the bridge was unpassable. The people gathered there refused to budge.

They still refused to budge when they heard the sound of the goose-step behind them. Led by the agitated, wildly gesticulating Mr. Lindheim, a platoon of German marines advanced from the direction of the pier.

"Why don't you shoot?" shouted the white-haired woman, challenging the marines.

The aim of the marines was precise. They had a most alluring target. Thousands of unarmed human beings stared straight into their muzzles.

But the door of one of the trucks was flung wide open. No one could say how Harald Roenneberg had managed to open it. Perhaps the guard, fearful for his own life, had helped.

Perfectly poised, Roenneberg climbed out of the truck. He stood on the running board. "Friends!" he said. His calm voice suddenly silenced the crowd. "Do you want to help us?"

"Yes!" came the answer. Five thousand answered: "Yes!"

"Fire!" Mr. Lindheim commanded the platoon of marines. The Germans remained motionless.

"You cannot help us hostages that way," Roenneberg continued slowly. "You are only getting us into worse trouble. You don't help Norway either by being slaughtered yourselves. You must live for Norway! Save your lives for another day. Remember—" And his voice rose in the national anthem.

The crowd took it up, as Roenneberg again disappeared inside the truck, holding out his hands for the handcuffs. But the guard forgot his duty, He too, although a wretched creature of the Quisling breed, hummed the strictly forbidden national anthem.

For the last time the truck drivers started their engines. Now there was ample space. The crowd followed the trucks at a respectful distance. They sang the anthem and the Royal hymn. They sang it while the hostages were taken aboard the German ship. They were still singing as the *Hulda* weighed anchor, and as long as the departing ship was within sight. The gale roared, and the waves swept over the pier. But the people of Aalesund remained there singing until late into the night.

On the morning of October 28, 1939, Herr Karl Hermann Frank decided on a little stroll through the streets of the city. He had been rather busy in the last months. Since the German invasion he had never found time to clear his desk of its litter of death sentences, arrest warrants, and confiscation decrees. It was all his own handiwork, even if that old fool Baron Neurath had to sign the papers. It is possible that Herr Frank was sick of desk work. Luxuriously, he stretched his fat body. He yawned, and looked out of the window of his office which was installed in the Hradschin, the medieval Royal Palace, on a hill overlooking the teeming city of Prague.

It was an established habit with him to look down on the

city he loved. He fancied how easy it would be to place a few machine guns at the windows and shoot the people thronging the busy streets. At the *Bierabende,* the beer meetings, of the local Nazi group, he used to exhort his comrades: "Don't be afraid because we are one German against twenty Czechs in Prague! We are in a strategic position. From the windows of my office, for instance, I can mow them down like clay pigeons, if they get out of hand!"

Unfortunately, the clay pigeons showed no inclination to get out of hand. The population of Prague bore the first months of German terror and oppression with dignity and patience. It was impossible to break them. On the surface it appeared that they were bending back until they stumbled. No German uniform was ever insulted, although the people carefully avoided any contact with them. The decrees of the new masters were rigidly complied with, albeit they cut into the lives of the citizens in a thousand, mostly quite super-fluously cruel ways. There was no outward sign of unrest or resistance. The avalanche does not thunder before it starts to roll.

Herr Karl Hermann Frank felt bored. He had imagined a different development. He had pictured himself wading through streams of blood, his hippopotamus whip, an imitation of Hitler's famous one, in his right hand as he choked a rebellious Czech with his left. He had always loved a good fight. First, he had driven his fellow Sudetens into revolution. Then followed the sinister underground battle with Konrad Henlein, the front man, whom he successfully denounced to Hitler. Konrad Henlein, whose visit, previous to Munich, stirred diplomatic London, and who was on the point of becoming a figure on the international scene, is now a forgotten man. Herr Frank had to smile in thinking of his old comrade whom he had stabbed in the back. He smiled, too, in thinking of good old Baron Neurath, the Protector, who patiently signed on the dotted line what he, Karl Hermann Frank, "respectfully proposed." Were there no more rivals, no more antagonists, no more enemies left?

The Czechs hid in their rat holes. On this October 28, 1939, Prague was a dead city. The people's way of celebrating the sacred day, the twenty-first anniversary of Czechoslovakian independence, was to remain in their homes, thinking and praying silently, perhaps whispering to one another.

Looking out of his window on lifeless Prague, Karl Hermann Frank, Secretary of State in the Protector's administration, felt the approach of a brain wave. He would dig the rats out of their holes. He whistled for his aide-de-camp, young, pale, homosexual Dr. Peterka.

"Call the boys!" Frank shouted. "We'll have a walk. And tell them not to forget their horsewhips, either!"

"Horsewhips" was putting it mildly. When the boys, Frank's bodyguard, gathered in front of the palace, they had not forgotten their clubs, their guns, or their hand grenades. Three powerful motorcars—one of which, a few days earlier, had still belonged to Mr. Petschek, the richest industrialist and banker in Czechoslovakia—took them down the narrow streets of the Hradschin hill.

One of these little streets is the famous "Astronomengässchen," the Astronomer's Way, where the people live in centuries-old, dilapidated houses, mostly on the offerings of sightseeing tourists. One of the better known sights of this quarter was a Jew over a hundred years old whose first name was Moses; he had forgotten his family name, if indeed he had ever had one. Moses was the keenest guide in the Astronomengässchen. His rambling stories of the ancient quarter impressed the tourists, particularly the kind-hearted Americans, to the extent of rarely less than a crown. The approach of the three high-powered cars was his cue. He did not know, or could not understand, that the world had changed, and that powerful motorcars, racing down the Hradschin, spelled doom, not tips. He gesticulated, offering his services to Their Excellencies. To Moses every tourist was an excellency.

That he was killed was his own fault. Karl Hermann Frank could, of course, not tolerate an old Jew who ran after his car, gesticulating wildly, as though he were invoking Jehovah's wrath. Herr Frank related the incident in detail at the next *Bierabend*. The old Jew, he said, died of heart failure at the sight of Frank's whip. The first victim of the day of the long knives in Prague, the day that initiated (thus far) three years of terror, was simply a casual casualty.

When the three cars arrived at the corner of "Graben" and Wenzel Square, the heart of Prague, the occupants were in high good humor. A few loafers hung around. They answered the "Heil Hitler!" that assailed them from the suddenly halting cars by quietly dispersing.

Most of them escaped. Only two were hit by the hand grenades. One of the victims displayed, even in death, a humble, unobtrusive smile, as if to apologize for having been caught on the wrong corner. The other's head was blown to bits.

The hand grenades reverberated throughout Prague. The local Germans had been waiting for hours for something to happen. They heard the report of the first hand grenade. A quarter of an hour after it had exploded, Wenzel Square was overflowing with brown uniforms.

No provocation of any sort had occurred; no resistance had been offered. The ensuing outrages were due to the calendar alone. The red-letter day of Czech independence had to be marked by red blood, and celebrated in true Nazi fashion.

Herr Frank acted as master of ceremonies. The Secretary of State in the Protector's administration, personally, led the mob in Wenzel Square, which is littered with fashionable hotels and restaurants. The aim was to ferret out the rich Jews from their dugouts. Seventeen people were killed, allegedly for having resisted. It proved later that not one of them was a

Jew. Thirty-six hundred persons, most of them simply passers-by, were arrested. They were tortured in the cellars of the Petschek Palace, where the Gestapo had established their headquarters; many never returned home. Next morning the houses and apartments of the Prague Nazis were furnished with the booty of thousands of raped and looted Czech homes.

"The Czechs had an impressive Independence Day!" the *Neue Zeit*, the Protector's mouthpiece, editorialized in its next issue. "It is to be hoped that they have learned their lesson."

Indeed, they had learned their lesson. Their complacency was gone, their show of subservience broken. Collaboration was nipped in the bud. The memory of that Independence Day lingers to this moment. From October 28, 1939, until now, Prague has not had a single peaceful day, and not one quiet night. The Germans must keep half a million soldiers to police the Protectorate. Yet the flames smolder everywhere in Bohemia and Moravia. Mr. Karl Hermann Frank, it is reliably reported, has become a drug addict. He cannot sleep without dope. But even the dope offers no protection. Frank knows that he is a doomed man. He knows that he will hang. And he knows that the hangman will choose a most uncomfortable position for him when he swings from the gallows.

CHAPTER TWO

THE NEW ORDER AT WORK

NAZI Germany has invaded and completely subjugated eleven European pre-war states, and has carved rich parts out of European Russia, including the three, until a short time ago independent, Baltic states of Lithuania, Latvia, and Estonia. The eleven conquered countries are Austria, Czechoslovakia, Poland, Denmark, Norway, Holland, Belgium, Luxembourg, France, Greece, and Yugoslavia. In turn, the New Order has established three misshapen, artificial puppet states: Slovakia, Croatia, and the Italian Dominion of Albania.

The inflated body of Greater Germany and her subjugated territory form the bulk of the European continent. The rest is divided among six vassals of the Reich—Italy, Spain, Finland, Hungary, Rumania, and Bulgaria—and four countries still enjoying a precarious independence. Sweden and Switzerland are permitted to carry on because their business as usual serves the German military machine. Portugal and Turkey, both on the fringe of Europe, are constantly facing the danger of becoming the next victims of Nazi aggression.

The collapse and annihilation of a European country is usually preceded by a movie. His Excellency, the German ambassador, has the honor to invite the members of the government to which he is accredited, the ranking diplomats and generals, and the leading politicians in good standing with the Axis, to a private showing of either *Baptism of Fire* or *Victory in the West*. These two documentary films are intended to impress the audience with Germany's invincibility and to convey some idea of what happens to him who does not give the Nazi army the right of way. Both are outstanding examples of the excellence of German trick photography. Mostly the trick works. Everyone in the audience feels: "We are next!" The two pictures have won many a bloodless victory for Hitler's diplomacy. Few of the minor states cared to throw themselves helplessly into the path of the German steam roller.

The steam roller indeed has already crushed most of Europe. Hitler's blueprint is no longer in the experimental stage. It has been applied step by step to some two hundred million victims, including the population of the conquered Russian territory, and it has aroused resistance shaking Europe to her depths.

What are Hitler's further plans for Europe? One can safely conclude from the various methods which are being meted out to their victims that the plans vary according to the groups involved. Nazism is about to create three categories of European peoples: first, the fighting slaves; second, the toiling slaves; and third, the doomed nations, destined to extinction.

The prospective fighting serfs are those of the Teutonic race: the Scandinavians, the Dutch, the Flemish of Belgium, the Alsatians, Lorrainers, and Luxembourgers. When their hour strikes, the Swiss people, too, will be invited to join. These nations will be allowed to survive in such liberty as the

Nazi system permits, provided that they agree to perfect self-effacement, adopt the German language and mentality, and show their willingness to produce and bear arms for the monster that devours them, Greater Germany. Already today every expression of nationalism and patriotism in these "racially Teutonic" countries is being suppressed. The German masters castigate it as "separatism," and punish it in true Gestapo fashion.

There is an old German saying,

> Und willst du nicht mein Bruder sein
> So schlag' ich dir den Schädel ein,

which means, "If you don't want to be my brother, I'll crush your skull." This is the promise Europe's non-German, but allegedly Teutonic, nations are receiving.

Yet these peoples are still the New Order's favorite children, as compared with the stepchildren, primarily the Latins and the Balkan nations. The Latin countries, above all France, but in the end Italy and Spain as well, to say nothing of minor nations like Hungary, Rumania, Bulgaria, and Greece, are to be "de-industrialized," according to the current Nazi expression, and transformed into primitive agrarian states, into hewers of wood and drawers of water for the master race.

Hitler's policy of amiable collaboration with Vichy is full of indications that France's industry and trade shall be completely annihilated, as soon as their production is no longer necessary to the German military machine. The Nazi's way of dealing with the crucial French coal problem is characteristic. Today, rich coal mines in northern France form part of the "forbidden zone" which is blacked out and entirely cut off from the rest of the country, even from the occupied zone, and under the strictest German military rule. Its output, which used to fuel the entire French industry, goes to Germany, although the Reich by no means lacks home-mined coal and, on the contrary, is boasting overproduction. Such French plants as have contracts for the Nazi army get some of the looted coal back from the Reich, but only enough to keep the furnaces glowing as long as the contracts last. Some selected factories, among them firms with a world-wide reputation, have been annexed by the German combines, and they too are kept going. The bulk of French industry, however, is completely deprived of coal. The factories have been forced to close down, bringing mass unemployment. This result is very welcome to the German masters, since it facilitates the drain of unemployed French workers to the German labor market.

But there are other groups, too, to be annihilated—for no other reason than their geographic location. The Slovenes, inhabiting the northern part of Yugoslavia, have the misfortune to dwell in the area between the German border of the former Austrian province of Carinthia and Trieste, Italy's big seaport on the Adriatic. Trieste appears to be Hitler's next Danzig. Mussolini himself is well aware that he cannot keep the port in the event of an Axis victory. The Slovenes, forming a belt around Trieste, must, of course, get out of the way of the German settlers, who—most of them unwillingly—are being pushed forward to expand the German living space as far as the Adriatic. The extermination of Slovenes has already begun. Thus far, about one-third of the total population of 1,600,000 has been "removed."

Alsatians and Lorrainers who do not comply with the New Order are suffering the same fate by hundreds and thousands. So are millions of Polish people from those provinces of Poland which Hitler has annexed outright, not incorporated with the Government General. The biggest and most ruthless enforced mass migration is planned for the Ukraine. In this newly conquered, immense territory, Hitler has decided to settle millions of German colonists. Germany herself is by no means overpopulated. In fact, there prevails a pressing labor shortage, while the birthrate of the agrarian population shows a noticeable decline. Where then are the millions of colonists for the Ukraine to be found?

The answer is simple. It was worked out by Alfred Rosenberg, the party philosopher, who after years of eclipse is now once more riding the crest as Nazi Tsar of the conquered parts of Russia. He proposed to Hitler to use the wide Ukrainian spaces as a dumping ground for the less desirable strata of the German population. Herr Rosenberg will have little trouble in finding a few million people in his own nation who are less desirable from the Nazi point of view, which means that they are less reliable in their support of the system. He proposes to educate them by hard labor on the Ukrainian wheat fields. They shall, to quote his own words, "recover their sense of German dignity, or perish." Rosenberg, who came to Germany from Tsarist Russia, was always a great believer in the rule of the knout. He will feel no restraint in lashing the backs of his own colonists.

But what is to happen to the Ukrainian people, the natives of the colony-to-be? There are some thirty-five million of them. They are fiery patriots, irreconcilably opposed to foreign occupation. Their crops were burned, where they could not be saved before the advent of the aggressor. Their guerrillas wreak havoc behind the German lines. Even their women fight. According to German reports, many Ukrainian peasant girls have been executed.

But Herr Rosenberg, the philosophic godfather of Hitler's New Order, is equal to any emergency. "The Ukrainians?" he addressed a meeting of German geography teachers in Breslau, on October 27, 1941, "Why, we can always drive them into the Black Sea."

According to their groups different types of administration are set up in the subjugated countries. The "Teutonic" nations are to be converted into full-fledged Nazis by their own turncoats. In Norway Major Vidkun Quisling goes about this business. A recently published statement by the Nasjonal Samling (the Norwegian Nazi party) indicates that Quisling has succeeded in uniting less than one per cent of the Norwegian population in his camp. Adrian Mussert, the Dutch Quisling, failed, if possible, still more miserably. Owing to his complete lack of following, which, in fact, is confined to a few youthful hooligans, the Germans had to drop him quietly and run Holland with their own men. In Belgium, no Quisling of presentable stature was to be found. Consequently, the kingdom was saved from having to endure a puppet government. Instead, some high officials of the old regime, none of them of government rank, remained at their posts to deal with routine matters. Many of them were dismissed, and others replaced by more amenable newcomers. The real boss is General von Falkenhausen, commander in chief of the German army of occupation in Belgium and northern France. No traitor of any stature was available in Luxembourg, where the German Commissioner, Dr. Simons, runs the show. Alsace and Lorraine as well are under the control of commissioners of the Reich. France? Under the shade, and with the acquiescence, of Pétain, Laval rules; and if the system continues, in a not too distant future *Rigor Mortis* will rule.

In Denmark a middle-of-the-road solution was found. Theodore Stauning, the veteran Socialist leader and Prime Minister of long standing, decided to carry on under German overlordship. One may be permitted to doubt whether this sacrifice—which Mr. Stauning certainly considers his continued tenure of office to be—is worth the heavy blow to his prestige. His country does not benefit in any way from his having clung to his desk. Stauning simply became a figurehead, like Dr. Hácha in Prague and General Tsouderis in Athens. In Poland the few outstanding Polish citizens who were approached by the German authorities indignantly refused their cooperation. "So much the worse for you and your people," Dr. Hans Frank, Hitler's Governor General, replied. "We do not really need you. Only in tropic climates shall the natives be preserved."

The technique of occupation follows a well tried pattern. It follows three unvarying principles: First, the people get immediate reassurances that their national independence will be respected. Second, the new masters get hold of strong bargaining weapons—the classic example being the retaining of 1,800,000 French prisoners in German camps—to use in blackmail for collaboration, and for discouraging resistance. Third, the disintegration of the subjugated people's spirit is promoted by the stirring up of every latent hatred and suspicion between different sections. In France, the Paris press and radio were browbeaten into attacks on Vichy. In Belgium, the Flemish are pitted against the Walloons. In most of the Balkan states, anti-Semitism serves as a lightning conductor. The aim is, of course, the same everywhere: in the fog of local disputes the people shall overlook the real problems of German penetration.

The methods of enslavement correspond to the technique. They, too, are standardized. First comes reasonable sweetness. The German soldiers, who in the terror films had been depicted as fierce robots, are now presented as gentle giants. They share their rations with refugees; they are inveterate baby kissers. They extend the hand of friendship to the downtrodden. All day long bands play sugary Viennese waltzes on street corners; the cinemas present pictures from Babelsberg, the German Hollywood, displaying fair-haired Teuton girls and kindly old peasants in the Reich. Expressions of sympathy for the vanquished are abundant. The dictionaries with which the soldiers of invasion are equipped contain a chapter equivalent to Dale Carnegie's *How to Win Friends and Influence People*, with phrases in every European language like: "I myself am the father of three kids. . . . Don't worry, after the

war the Bank of England will pay for everything. . . . I hope
we don't disturb, but let us see your larder."

The tragedy that befalls an occupied country, the invaders
insist, is only due to its own old regime, dominated by Jews
and Bolshevists. Hitler himself set the example. When he inspected Warsaw, which his Luftwaffe had left a shambles, he
addressed Governor General Frank, for immediate publication: "Look at all this horror and destruction. Isn't it terrible?
What a shame that the Poles forced me to take such measures.
They will never be able to atone for their crime." On May 4,
1941, he added another, similarly heartfelt remark. Having a
joy ride through Athens, or what is left of it, he declared for
the evening papers: "I was genuinely sorry for the war with
Greece. To me, as a German who has always had the deepest
veneration for the culture of Greece from which the first light
of beauty and dignity sprang, it is particularly painful."

These two incidents are not accidentally chosen. The German army has ravaged practically all of Europe. But nowhere
was the destruction so ferocious, the annihilation so complete,
as in Poland and Greece.

Hitler visits subjugated countries as soon as his army has
established a semblance of order. But he is not the first German visitor to follow in the wake of the conquering army.
First come the gentlemen of the WIRU, the economic branch
of the German High Command. With clockwork precision
these hyenas arrive on the heels of the soldiers. They are members of the War Economic and Armament Board, which was
established four years prior to the outbreak of the war. Most
of them have already acted as spies in the countries they are
now looting as authorities. They know the economic structure of the countries to which they are assigned.

The *Deutscher Volkswirt*, the mouthpiece of the Berlin
Ministry of Finance, wrote about these locusts swarming over
France: "The members of the WIRU, under experienced
officer-economists, accompanied and followed the troops.

They prevented the flooding of mines and wastage of raw material, and saw to it that gas, water, and electric works did not get, or remain, out of order. Wherever stocks of matériel and goods could be traced, a sign was at once erected: 'Confiscated by the Army High Command.' Again and again secret stocks of French supplies were tracked down. Finished goods were immediately used to supplement German industrial production, awaiting proper packing and shipment. Several thousand machines, and over 160,000 tons of raw materials have been transported to Germany by these economic units."

The job of these economic units, however, is not looting alone, but bargaining as well. Some small portions of the confiscated materials went back as rewards to French factories which were ready to start immediate production for Germany. Traitors and weaklings among the French industrialists could thus gain substantial benefits. The booty of France became Nazism's prime bargaining weapon.

The next step in the policy of occupation is the establishment of Quisling governments, which, of course, are entirely shorn of influence. Their members are the front men for the German protectors, governors, and gauleiters, and particularly for the mysterious holders of the true power: the generals in command. Their only privilege is to be the drummers for Nazism. They have to rely on the assistance of the Goebbels-controlled propaganda machine.

This propaganda differs according to the plans Nazism has for the nation involved. The Danes, for instance, are to be converted to the Nazi creed. Consequently, their German-directed radio is only subject to "instructions." The Poles shall be exterminated. What they may think and feel is immaterial. Hence all broadcasts over Polish stations are in the German language, which 95 per cent of the population does not understand. The radio, Goebbels insists, is far more important than the press in forming opinion. Yet the press in subjugated countries is by no means neglected. Nazi papers, both in German, and in the local language, are mushrooming. But they cost a good deal, and scarcely sell. To counteract public indifference to its own press, the Germans hire turn-coats. They use established newspapers wherever they can lay hands on them. These are much more dangerous, since they spill their poison under the guise of their old respectability. Sometimes the change in these submissive gazettes from simulated patriotism to compliance with the conqueror develops gradually, and goes for a time unnoticed. But sooner or later the mask must drop. When the readers of the Brussels *Le Soir*, once Belgium's most influential newspaper, could no longer be fooled, they simply abandoned their old paper. Under the eyes of the German authorities, a boycott was declared on February 10, 1941. On February 11, *Le Soir* lost 85 per cent of its circulation.

Famine is an inevitable consequence of German occupation. It is due only in part to the system of requisitioning. Obviously, food disappears to provide Germans at home with unaccustomed luxuries and for laying in stocks against the winter, also to give the soldiers of the armies of occupation a good time. But to a greater extent famine, even in agrarian countries, is created through a calculated policy. Starvation among the downtrodden people serves four purposes. First, it is a powerful bargaining weapon. German authorities return small rations of the looted foodstuffs, in bribes for Quislings, as bait for collaboration, and to win victories on the "moral" front.

When Brussels had been without milk and eggs for three weeks, posters appeared on the walls of all official buildings, depicting a smiling German mother with a little Belgian refugee child in her arms. "Where would you be without German kindness?" the legend asked. The answers scribbled on the posters by nightly passers-by were so little flattering that the smiling German mother soon disappeared from the walls of Brussels.

Second, food shortage is a method of arousing the people against the British blockade; third, it has been a device to confuse American public opinion; fourth and foremost, it serves the supreme aim of German administration: to foment disunity among the oppressed. A study by Dr. Simoneit, chief of the Wehrpsychologisches Institut (Institute for War Psychology) points out the importance of food queues in the policy of disintegration, on which the German overlordship thrives. "Food queues," writes the learned Dr. Simoneit, "are the best means of fomenting jealousies and class disputes. They pit neighbor against neighbor, and disrupt society."

Finally, artificially created or accentuated famine has another by-product, most welcome to the German system. It helps to drain workers from starving countries to Germany. By means of such wholesale transfer of labor, Germany can satisfy her own pressing needs, remove potential sources of resistance, and, by the same token, hold innumerable hostages: the families of those who work in the Reich.

Starvation of course, is only a part of the economic squeeze to which the oppressed people are subjected. Drastic rationing, the requisition of raw materials, and the exploitation of industry and agriculture are means toward establishing permanent economic dictatorship. Invariably, the seizure of public utilities and of the means of transportation comes first. Thus the German overlords entrench themselves in the economic key positions. The issue of army promissory notes—worth the paper on which they are printed—and the sequestering of public funds make havoc of the country's finances. Its trade with other countries is automatically cut off. It is fully incorporated in the German economic unit.

These precautionary measures are followed up by comprehensive and systematic measures. New rates of exchange and new taxes are introduced; the banking system is subordinated to German control, frequently private banks are acquired by German institutions, at German-dictated prices. Movable wealth, including rolling stock, machinery, raw materials, and foodstuffs, is transferred to Germany. Even a rough estimate of the booty is impossible.

The New Order tends to absorb into Greater Germany all the main industrial areas in Europe. It seeks to build a nation of one hundred million with industrial monopoly. It knows well that flourishing industry means military power. Hence it plans a highly industrialized Germany with a ring of agrarian satellite states around it. This Germany would include 50 per cent of all the factory and mine workers, but only 20 per cent of the farming population of Europe. It would hold all the industrial trump cards, and exercise complete monopoly both as buyer and as seller. It would be the only purveyor of finished industrial goods and the only market for agricultural products. The industries of France and Belgium will either be fitted into the German orbit, or be dismantled and shut down. The satellite countries could scratch a living as serfs for Germany. Their standards of living would be constantly depressed, their overpopulation would find no outlet either in industrial activities or in emigration. The great industrial German Reich, containing one-third of the European population, would permanently exploit the other two-thirds.

Hitler realizes that only completely subservient peoples will accept this status. With economic means alone, however devastating, he cannot enforce this acceptance. It is necessary to break the spirit of the people, and to rear a new generation of willing serfs.

The last and most dangerous device to destroy nations under German occupation is the method of luring the children away from their loyalties to their parents and their traditions, converting them into little Nazis. The German language is being introduced in all the schools. Everywhere Hitler Youth movements are established, with uniforms, salutes, parades, and daggers of honor for youngsters excelling in brutality. A

thorough education in Nazi ideology teaches the boys a bullying toughness towards others, coupled with a blind subservience to the new bosses. Children are turned into arrogant
toughs, and at the same time into abject robots. Primitive instincts of hatred and contempt for other races are hammered
into their heads. By the same token, a doglike hero worship
of their German masters is required of them. They are being
stuffed with ready-made slogans, lest they should be tempted
to think for themselves.

This criminal corruption of youth may or may not be the
worst sin Nazism is committing under the guise of the New
Order, but it might well become the most consequential. In
Nazi circles, anyway, it is regarded as full proof of the efficiency of the system.

Nazism works with unsurpassable logic and consequence.
When it invades a country, it first seizes the goods; then it
exploits the bodies; finally it attempts to crush the souls. But
this attempt is a boomerang. The Germans have trampled un-
derfoot fifteen European nations. They have converted the
old continent into a desert of hatred. It will be a terrific out-
burst when it rebounds, and rebound it will. The resistance
of the doomed peoples, a year ago sporadic, is becoming organized and formidable. A neutral observer, the Stockholm
Morgenposten, predicted on April 17, 1941: "The German
war machine works perfectly. It is in another sphere that
Germany suffers repeated defeats—in the psychological sphere.
Germany's weakness is the mere existence of the other European nations, occupied or unoccupied. Against these weak
and always staggering outer works the enemy's death blow
will one day be struck."

The *Morgunbladid*, an Icelandic newspaper, expressed the
dilemma confronting all subjugated nations with the simple
question: "Norwegian seamen have faced terrible dangers to
escape. Would any Icelander take the trouble to try and escape from here to the German-controlled area?"

CHAPTER THREE

THE ECONOMIC SQUEEZE

It is a matter of indifference to Germany if some thousands or perhaps tens of thousands of Norwegian men, women and children starve and freeze to death during the war.—GAULEITER JOSEF TERBOVEN, September 4, 1941.

OCCUPATION is a profitable business. The subjugated countries of Europe pay to the tune of five billion dollars a year for the privilege of being "protected" by the German armies of occupation. It is by far the highest ransom any gang of racketeers have ever exacted for offering protection. The sum total of Germany's internal taxes does not exceed six and four-fifths billion dollars, so that the take from the squeezed nations represents a handsome contribution to the Nazi war chest.

France has to pay four hundred million francs a day despite all rumors of a reduction which never materialized. This is far more than double the actual cost of maintaining the German troops in France, their heavy consumption of champagne and other delicacies included. France still pays more within a period of three months than the total cost of the Allied occupation of the Rhineland eleven years after the first war. Such gigantic sums can only be raised by the ruthless use of the printing press to manufacture artificial currency wholesale. Up to the end of October, 1941, the French state had had to borrow the sum of 123,500,000,000 francs from the Bank of France. Inflation (which a rigid price control tries desperately to counteract while it actually drives business into the black markets) and bankruptcy are the inevitable consequences. The Germans, on the other hand, use the surplus of the toll they exact to acquire choice bits of French property, putting their own prices on the purchases. A large part of French industry is already in German hands, or German-controlled. Agreements in the metallurgic, automobile, cement, silk, cigar, and paper industries assure the entire output for Germany. According to an official Berlin statement, the rest of French industry is to be reduced to between 25 per cent and 40 per cent of the output in 1938—in other words, strangled.

The per capita burden of the occupation of Norway is even heavier. Norway is paying $1,870,000 a year. The Norwegian people must contribute twenty-eight kroner per week per family, more than a third of their average income. The Czechoslovak Protectorate pays approximately three hundred million dollars ransom, in addition to the normal German taxes which have been collected since the enforcement of the customs union with Germany. Moreover, early in 1940, the Reich cashed a contribution of two billion crowns (more than fifty million dollars) as a "token of good will." Shortly afterward the Czech banks were forced to subscribe a loan of six hundred million reichsmarks for the Reich government. Another four billion crowns (more than a hundred million dollars) was exacted from the Protectorate as a payment for its "defense." Besides, Berlin demanded eighty million crowns from "indirect taxation" in Bohemia-Moravia.

In the part of Poland incorporated in the Reich, the Poles (but not the *Volksdeutsche*, the German citizens) have to pay a surtax of 15 per cent, yielding some two hundred million dollars, in addition to normal taxes.

From all the occupied countries the sum total of five billion dollars yearly in tax contribution is a conservative estimate. Since the total peacetime national income of all the occupied countries—except the conquered parts of Soviet Russia—was somewhere in the region of twenty-five billion dollars, the bill for the armies of occupation would amount to 20 per cent. But the economic and financial structure of the captive countries was completely disrupted. Everywhere national incomes have dropped abysmally. It is probable that the subjugated peoples have to spend every other cent of their meager incomes for "protection" alone.

As far back as February 1, 1941, Ronald Cross, member of the British cabinet, stated that the civilian workers forcibly transferred to Germany numbered two and one-half million. In the meantime this figure has certainly increased considerably. To these chain-gang slaves at least a million working prisoners of war must be added. Their services would naturally not have been secured without strong measures of compulsion. The one and one-half billion dollars their labor is worth, and the half-billion, at least, they contribute to the German war effort, are obviously fruits of occupation. Moreover, these figures do not yet take into account the profit Germany derives from the slave work of Russian prisoners of war. Even if one does not believe the German High Command's fantastic claims, the number of able-bodied Russian prisoners certainly is large. It is an established fact that Germany, totally disregarding her obligations under the Hague convention, puts these unfortunate victims to work without pay, thus (if one can express human misery in dollars and cents) saving probably another billion in wages.

The next way of squeezing the captive nations is through the confiscation of property. A beginning was made with the seizure of Jewish property, which in the Reich itself, where it was first applied, netted close to a billion dollars. In Czechoslovakia the loot was relatively much greater, since even partly Jewish-owned companies were expropriated, and the Jews had not yet disposed of their properties when the Nazis came. The profit for the German war chest was half a billion dollars.

Then came the confiscation of state property in the conquered countries. In Poland this measure brought in approximately three billion dollars, of which the port of Gdynia, renamed Gotenhafen, alone accounts for four hundred million, the Polish state-owned steelworks for three hundred and fifty million, and the state forests for two hundred million. In Poland Marshal Göring, incidentally, discovered his financial genius. The world's most inveterate medal hunter developed an acquisitive sense in finance. The Polish steelworks were amalgamated with the Hermann Göring Werke, of which the fat Marshal is not only the name patron, but the principal shareholder. The Polish state forests were *übereignet* —handed over—to the Master of the German Forests and Hunt, who happens to be identical with the fat Marshal. Since big French, Belgian, Dutch, and Luxembourg industrial combines, to say nothing of some of the leading Austrian and Yugoslavian factories, suffered the same fate, Hermann Wilhelm Göring is today the world's biggest industrialist.

In Holland a law was promulgated authorizing the seizure of the property of "those who have promoted, are promoting, or are likely to promote tendencies hostile to Germany."

A kind of loot which proved to be of very particular use to the Reich was the gold and foreign exchange of the central banks of the occupied countries. Their rape started in Austria, where the gold and foreign exchange seized by the Germans was valued at about four hundred and fifty million schilling, or some ninety million dollars. This was spent abroad in imports essential to German armaments during the summer of 1938. Czechoslovakia, more fortunate, held most of her foreign assets in London. But some thirty million dollars' worth of Czechoslovakian gold was held by the Bank of England on behalf of the Bank for International Settlements in Geneva. Montagu Norman, Governor of the Bank of England, consented to the release of this amount to Germany, on the promise of the Nazi authorities that the treasure should be transferred to the Bank of Bohemia-Moravia. Of course, this promise was subsequently broken.

The French gold reserves were worth about three billion dollars. In spite of optimistic reports that most of this had been transferred to London or New York, the *New York Times* of June 25, 1940, estimated the amount still in Paris after the German invasion at over two-thirds of the total. This sum is today Hitler's gold hoard. He acquired the equivalent of some two hundred million dollars more by seizing the arms and military equipment of the occupied countries. Ironically, most of these arms were sold to Soviet Russia.

Such lucky strokes do not repeat themselves. Today Hitler is not likely to find a buyer for captured Russian tanks or downed Soviet airplanes. But the squeeze of the occupied countries continues unabated.

Germany "purchases" goods far in excess of the supplier's desire to sell, and pays, if at all, with manipulated currency which grossly overrates the value of the reichsmark. Already at the end of October 1940, eight hundred thousand tons of wheat had been removed from occupied France, and a million pigs and quantities of cattle had been exported to Germany in a single fortnight. It is to be noted that the wheat surplus of occupied France normally goes to the so-called "zone libre," and that France has no surplus of pigs or cattle. The entire Bordeaux grape harvest and most of the wine stocks in occupied France were taken over; cider and wine may no longer be made without German permission.

In Poland practically all crops are confiscated. All eggs produced in Bohemia-Moravia, except the produce of one chicken for every two persons, are exported to the Reich. Moreover, 60 per cent of the total Czech livestock was removed. Norway has to supply two hundred tons of fish a day, practically the entire first catch. Holland was looted of forty-three thousand tons of new potatoes within three months, whereas her normal export within a comparable period is twenty-seven thousand tons. In addition, twenty-three million out of her twenty-nine million poultry were killed for German consumption. Belgium has to deliver "all available eggs." Danish cattle were reduced from three million three hundred thousand head to about one-third. The reduction in the number of Danish pigs is from two million nine hundred thousand to eight hundred thousand.

These are a few examples, chosen at random, to prove the "healthy acquisitive instinct,"which the *Frankfurter Zeitung,* mouthpiece of the Wilhelmstrasse, claims for the German people. All told, Germany exacts from her victims five billion dollars a year in outright payments, plus additional sacrifices in the following five ways: confiscation and levies to the tune of another five billion; the working power of more than four and one-half million serfs transported to the Reich; purchases at real prices 40 per cent below those ruling on free markets; accumulation of debts by the clearing system which so far amount to two billion dollars at least; and every bit of bread out of the mouths of the starving people.

Billions have not the slightest meaning for the plain people. Few Frenchmen worry about the indebtedness of the state to their national bank, for paying the German bills. But the Germans themselves do their best to bring home to the people the frightful realities of the situation. M. François Lehideux, Vichy's Secretary of State for Industrial Production and National Equipment, has had to admit that the supply of fuel is 50 per cent below normal, and that consequently many factories will have to close down. Conditions are get-

ting progressively worse. In 1941 the production of those
mines which France still retains dropped to two million eight
hundred thousand tons from four and one-half million in the
previous years. From this meager output, France must fuel
Alsace-Lorraine, although incorporated in the Reich, and satisfy the demands of the German army of occupation.

This latter demand is particularly malevolent chicanery,
since the Germans control the departments Nord and Pas-
de-Calais, producing four-fifths of the entire French coal and
iron output. These departments are in the forbidden zone.
They are governed by the general commanding the German
army of occupation in Brussels, which means that they are
no longer considered a part of France, but are incorporated
with the Reich. Indeed, the annexation of this rich district
was already the aim of the Pan-Germanists in the First World
War.

Under such conditions the allotment of coal for public
utilities has had to be reduced to the utmost. Domestic use
of electric current and gas is almost entirely banned. The
Nazis have forbidden the use of electricity for heating, and
even for heating water. Every Frenchman feels the consequences. The two-hour lunch period, one of the most venerable French institutions, has been abandoned. Instead, workshops, offices, and stores close two hours earlier, to save light
and heating in the evening.

Passenger schedules on railroads have been reduced; most
of the trains carry freight to Germany and bring war supplies to U-boats and other German ships in French ports, and
to the army of occupation. Since it takes five trains of tank
cars to transport the oil of an average tanker, the French
railways can boast of maintaining 85 per cent of their prewar services. But accommodations for civilian passengers must
be reserved a week ahead; even then they are frequently
unavailable.

The acute shortage of raw materials in France, according

to the United States Department of Commerce, is a threat to the very life of French industry. The occupation authorities require practically all the coal and cement. No more than 30 per cent of the aluminum supply is free for use after filling German orders. Stocks of cotton are approaching exhaustion. France's raw-silk supplies have been sharply depleted. The efforts to produce substitute material ("ersatz") after the German pattern failed completely. The French are told they must wear shoe soles made of wood. But there is no wood to manufacture such soles. Many French forests were ruthlessly destroyed for the needs of the army of occupation.

Whatever trade is left has recourse to the black markets. France has become a country of bootleggers. It is reminiscent of Prohibition days in America, the difference being that not liquor, but all the necessities of life are being illegally traded. Vichy wages a relentless, but entirely helpless, war against this evil. Every day long lists of arrests, fines, and prosecutions are published. Famous restaurants have been closed for illicit food trafficking. On October 28, 1941, in Paris alone, fifty restaurants were raided. But it is not possible to raid every farm, and French farmers simply withhold their supplies, even after Germany magnanimously agreed to content herself with 45 per cent of the wheat, 75 per cent of vegetables and salads, 50 per cent of potatoes, and 30 per cent of meat, out of the French production. "We had laborious discussions with the occupation authorities," Vichy's former Minister of Agriculture, M. Caziot, declared when he brought home this agreement. M. Spinasse, another arch-collaborator, echoed him: "We are preaching in the desert." Yet the last potato crop delivered was only half of the amount in previous years. Farmers are reluctant to part with their stores; they fear to lose the seed for the next season. The scarcity of eggs, they say, is due to the lack of grain to feed the poultry. But above all, why sell their produce? For money? Everyone in France distrusts the inflated money. They call it "German promissory notes," and shrug. Wealthy people try to acquire, at exorbitant prices, old masters, jewels, anything that keeps its value. Every auction room is crowded. Postage stamps are sought as an investment, and so are race horses, unless they are slaughtered for their meat. In Bordeaux, even the famous carrier pigeons were killed and eaten.

Among the poor, thieving is rife. Petty crimes increase with the scarcity of commodities. They vary with the seasons. In winter thefts of coal and firewood and of clothing abound. Felling trees below regulation size and slaughtering cattle and lamb without permission are the practice in the countryside. In the village of Briande, in the department of Corrèze, a woman was fined for stealing two wax tapers from a church. She pleaded that she was unable to buy kerosene for her lamp.

"The situation is serious, but not tragic," Pétain declared. But André Diethelm, Free French Commissioner of the Interior, who left Paris only a short time ago, speaking of the German occupation, insists that the "prolongation of the present conditions would have a permanent effect on the population of occupied France. The French race is actually in grave danger."

This danger affects everyone. The Vichy sports commissariat instructed the French Football Federation to reduce soccer games from ninety minutes to eighty, and rugby from eighty to seventy minutes, since the ration system is weakening the underfed athletes. The increase in tuberculosis is noticeable. Other epidemics are feared as the food shortage becomes graver.

The food shortage is frequently due not only to the general poverty, but is artificially created by the Germans as a measure of punishment. In January, 1941, when Pétain had Laval arrested, the Germans retaliated by stopping all supplies to Paris. Vichy had to nourish the capital from its own depleted stocks until Laval was again set at liberty.

One cannot gauge the French food shortage by the ration cards, since these are simply not honored. Toward the end of 1941 it was still fairly easy to buy the month's ration of a pound of sugar and a pound of fats. But the meat ration of 3.6 ounces a week was unobtainable in Paris, save in the expensive restaurants. In the suburbs, butchers went for weeks with no supplies whatsoever.

Potatoes, a staple plentiful in Germany, have disappeared from the occupied zone. From the brew that passes for coffee, even roast barley has been eliminated. Cocoa and tea are gone. In the home country of cheap wine, wine cards allowing four quarts a month were introduced; but the monthly ration is scarcely obtainable. All this need and want breeds the inevitable graft and corruption. Edouard Barthe, for years one of the most powerful political figures in France because of his dominant position in the wine-grape growing industry, was placed in "administrative internment" for having tried to increase the wine shortage in order to boost prices.

Because of the serious shortage of food in Paris, infants weigh only four or five pounds at birth, and signs of undernourishment can be observed steadily as the infants grow older. The child mortality rate in Paris has increased up to October, 1941, by nearly one-half over the prewar level, the Public Health Council of the department of the Seine reports; and it summarizes the situation as one of "prolonged famine."

A few outstanding French collaborationists took the trouble to send Hitler this report by the "kindness" of his Paris ambassador, Otto Abetz. They received no answer. The *Petit Journal*, a Nazified French paper, appealed to its own masters: "There are no more weddings in Paris. In certain districts there were less than ten weddings within the last eight months. In twenty Paris arrondissements there were five hundred and fourteen weddings during the last six months of 1939, but only fifteen in the corresponding part of 1940, the first semester of occupation." The population of France drops. On

April 1, 1941, it numbered 39,302,511 against last year's figure of 42,000,000.

Marshal Pétain preaches incessantly the revival of French family life as the basis of his "national revolution." The answer is rapidly increasing child mortality, the practical abolition of marriages, the loss of two and three-quarter million lives a year in a mounting death rate.

On the night of March 14, 1939, Dr. Hácha, President of what Munich had left of Czechoslovakia, was on his way to Berlin to receive "peace terms" from Hitler. Before his sleeping car had reached the German frontier, armored Nazi troops in steel helmets were already crossing the border from their side. Their first objective was not military. They occupied Rothschild's foundries and ironworks in Moravská Ostrava and Vitkovice, the biggest industrial plants in Central Europe. The aggression against Czechoslovakia began with an act of rape.

By now the tortured country has been living three years under the iron heel. The pillage continues. The Czechoslovak government in exile assesses the loss the nation has so far suffered under German "protection" at more than a third of the total national property.

Methodically, the Germans proceeded by first taking over the highly developed Czech banking system. The "big three" among the Czech banks were affiliated with German institutes. The economic leaders were tortured to death or kept in concentration camps until they gave in. Thus Dr. Bachrach, chairman of the most important organization of Czech distilleries, died in a concentration camp. The president of the Czechoslovak Chamber of Commerce, Dr. Trebicky, was arrested, and the seventy-year-old president of the Chamber of Commerce in Brno, the country's second largest city, was kept in jail until he agreed to hand over his office to a Nazi.

Next came the seizure of Czech farm lands. Again the system of arrests worked. All the directors and leading officials of state forests and estates were jailed, both as a deterrent to the population, and to make good jobs available for Nazis. The "German land reform" proceeded under absurd disguises. Reichs Protector Baron Neurath issued a decree according to which all land and property can be seized "if special interests of the Reich are involved." Under these regulations half a million Czech peasants were driven from their soil. The regulations also justified the confiscation of the Church's landed property. The current relation between the Czech crown and the reichsmark, according to their respective purchasing power, had been four to one. The German Protector fixed the valuation on the scale of ten to one, depriving with a stroke of his pen the Czech currency of more than half of its purchasing power. The confiscation of the property of "dangerous and politically suspicious persons" netted untold millions. An emigration tax of 25 per cent was instituted, but actually emigrants were despoiled of everything they had. On October 1, 1940, the customs union between the Protectorate and the Reich was established. With this measure the German plunder of Czechoslovakia entered a new phase. The Nazis had another instrument to choke Czech economic life. The German High Commissioner of Reich Revenue in Prague superseded the Finance Minister of the Czech puppet government, whose office was liquidated "for reasons of economy." On January 1, 1941, the Czech National Bank ceased to exist as a bank of issue. The Czech currency became merely an annex of the worthless German mark. Later it was entirely abolished. Now only the German paper mark is accepted as legal tender.

The real aim of German rapacity is the highly developed Czechoslovak industry. From now on only such industries as serve the German armament are permitted to continue. Industries which compete with German interests are disappearing quickly, above all those factories which have resisted amalgamation with German combines. This amalgamation was promoted by devious means. Aryanization brought many plants under Nazi control. Another method was cartelization. The German law requiring compulsory membership in cartels was applied to Czech industries, which are now completely subject to control from Berlin. The cartels also have full control over the supply of raw materials, and use these powers for forcing the Czech manufacturers out of business. In consequence, profitable exports from the "Protectorate" had fallen 95 per cent by September, 1941. They have now ceased altogether except for arms and food taken to Germany without payment. Still another method of Germanizing Czech economy is the strict differentiation between German-owned and Czech firms, which the Reichs Protector decreed. Only the German firms receive the all-important support of the authorities. Czech mills, having exhausted their supply of raw materials, are forced to close down. The Czech stockholders of "desirable" factories are compelled to sell out at German prices. In this way the Nazis forced the stockholders of the Brno armament plant to hand over 51 per cent of the shares, giving the Germans absolute control of this important arsenal. The price was fixed at approximately five and one-half million dollars, less than a fifth of the real value. Ironically, some of the looted shareholders were notorious Nazi admirers, sympathizing with the New Order's method of handling labor questions. Now they hate the oppressor as much as the workers and wage earners do.

"In view of the present military requirements of the Reich, a long-term economic policy cannot be envisaged. It will be necesary to direct the Polish economy in such a way that the maximum resources can be got out of the country for strengthening the Reich's military power."

This sentence is from a letter Göring addressed on December 1, 1940, to Dr. Hans Frank, German Governor General in Poland. It is not surprising that Hermann Göring exercises a personal oversight over what is going on in Poland, although none of his numerous offices, dignities, functions, and titles connects him with the "Government General." His interest is a financial one. He must look after his property interests. If the Marshal decrees that the "maximum resources are to be exploited for strengthening the Reich's military power" irrespective of a long-term policy, he simply orders the timber carelessly felled and the mines robbed. Herr Göring is endowed with a certain shrewdness. He obviously senses that the exploitation of Polish steelworks and forests will not last forever. He collects hastily, while the getting is good.

Herr Göring's attitude is characteristic of the general Nazi approach to Poland. "Take it, squeeze it, then let it rot" is the slogan. Poland perhaps more than any other country exemplifies the hectic, fleeting quality of the nightmare that is Nazi domination.

Soon after the invasion of Poland, Dr. Frank, newly appointed Governor General, issued a decree consisting of but one sentence: "All private property in Poland shall be confiscated, if public security or the consolidation of the German element in the country demands it." On December 23, 1939, probably as a suitable Christmas present, a companion piece followed: "The right to confiscate private property is extended to the confiscation of Church property and the belongings of charitable associations."

In the meantime, Poland was exposed to S.S. brigandry and Gestapo looting on a scale unparalleled even in the era of the New Order. Not only individual houses were requisitioned, but whole quarters of cities and towns. Plants, warehouses, depots were sealed. Large quantities of supplies and goods were to be delivered by the population. If these deliveries failed, the retribution consisted in confiscation of the factories and shops themselves. The Polish peasants were called upon to hand over their meat, milk, and fats "to mitigate starvation in cities and industrial centers." They were not told that these cities and industrial centers lay in Germany. In every Polish town a *Kriegsbeutestelle*—war booty center—was established, where German customers, mainly officers and soldiers, could buy many things at cut rates, wheat, flour, sugar, or wine, and also the civil population's worn-out shoes and threadbare clothes, and chandeliers from synagogues or chalices and reliquaries from Catholic churches.

Trustees of the Reich were installed to direct with absolute power what was left of Poland's economic life. They settled the prices, allotted the rations, hoarded the goods. Yet the people, who tried to hang on to bits of their belongings, were labeled "hoarders." They were relentlessly persecuted. Incessant inspections were carried out in trains, on roads, on the street. Luggage, pockets, portfolios were emptied without explanation, unless the statement of Dr. Jäger, the German district commissioner of Poznan, could serve: "The Poles are racially inferior and consequently objects of exploitation. The law will have to treat them as such."

It did. The first laws, introduced by the Governor General, decreed the seizure of all bank accounts, with particular emphasis on those of insurance companies and charitable funds. They canceled the payment of pensions. They barred Polish people from all liberal professions. They permitted confiscation of factories, workshops, and all real estate. All the furniture was requisitioned with the houses, which had to be handed over to German settlers. Waves of expulsion swept Poland. The expelled people were allowed to take fifty pounds of their belongings, and money to the maximum of twenty reichsmarks with them. Up to March 1, 1941, one and one-half million people were thus expelled. Able-bodied men were pressed into German labor gangs, their families, wives, children, and old people were dumped in concentration camps in the swamps near the Russian border.

Such Polish workers as were retained to keep the armament

plants and their tributaries going, had to pay 20 per cent of their wages as a contribution to the German Labor Front, which bars Polish members. The workers of the Wspólnota Interesów, the biggest Polish steel mill, whose production amounts to 45 per cent of the country's entire steel output, remonstrated against this inequity. Since the Germans did not relish labor troubles in this important armory, Dr. Frank was ready to receive their delegation. Patiently he listened to their complaints. Then he patted the spokesman's shoulder and replied: "I admit that you are underpaid as workers." He paused, took a deep breath, smiled, and continued: "But as serfs you are overpaid. You should know that this situation will not change." Presently a large detachment of *Selbstschutz* —the Self-Protection Corps, known as the worst hooligans among uniformed Nazi bands—occupied the Wspólnota Interesów; and they remain in control. Another cut in the wages of the personnel pays for the maintenance of the gangsters.

At present, all business in the Government General is being conducted by the German Organization of Distribution in Poland. This organization was created to eliminate retail trade, which used to be almost entirely in Jewish hands, and to make the population completely dependent on the German monopoly of buying and selling. The peasants, however—the bulk of the population—were accustomed to the Jews. They refused, and persist in refusing, to deal with German authorities. A group of middlemen had to be introduced—not the old familiar Jewish traders, but at least Poles, such Poles as are expert in the fine art of greasing Nazi palms. Through their efforts the masters receive in return for some fertilizer and household articles, agricultural products for the Reich, which, in spite of all Gestapo terror, they were unable to obtain from farmers by requisitions. The system is concentrated New Order. The people of the agrarian colony are dependent on such regulations as suit the master race. The Poles do not like it. Since they have no opportunity to voice their opposition, two hundred and fifty local branches of the German Organization of Distribution in Poland were blown up by bombs or destroyed by arson during 1941.

Four hundred thousand men in Norway are leading a life of plenty. They are the three hundred thousand troops of the German army of occupation and one hundred thousand Nazi functionaries (most of them Gestapo men). Almost three million others, the people of Norway, are on the brink of starvation. The situation in southern Norway has been somewhat better than in the northern district, where poor transport facilities further hamper food distribution. But the whole country, experts agree, will be in a desperate situation, if the war, or the occupation of Norway, lasts throughout 1942.

Even in peaceful times Norway was never self-supporting. Imports, primarily food, exceeded exports by approximately six hundred million kroner. The balance was restored by the income from shipping, which netted half a billion kroner, and by the profit derived from tourist traffic and whaling. Both ceased immediately after the invasion on April 9, 1940. About a thousand ships—82 per cent of Norway's merchant marine— were cut off from the mother country. Today most of them are plying the North Atlantic lanes. This is a windfall for the United States and the United Kingdom, but a staggering blow to Norway's economic life.

The Nazis all but strangled Norway's foreign trade. Since the New Order allows the satellites to trade only with the Reich, Germany absorbed 70 per cent of Norway's exports during the first year of her overlordship, compared with 17 per cent which was her normal share of Norwegian exports. Almost all Norwegian goods going to Germany are requisitioned or simply looted. The New Order is about to establish a central clearing house in Berlin to regulate the imports and exports of the whole European continent. Its Norwegian department is already at work.

The country's industry was largely affected by the stoppage of foreign trade. Exports decreased by 50 per cent, while imports were reduced by 70 per cent. The fact that mass unemployment did not follow to the same extent is due to the large-scale military projects carried out in Norway by the German army. However, the highly skilled Norwegian workers must now content themselves with poorly paid jobs as woodcutters and road builders. At that, the number of unemployed is much larger than official figures show, since many refuse to register to avoid slave labor under the German lash. The German statistics admit that many thousands of workers were "transferred from industrial jobs to less well paid farm and forestry work." The president of the Norwegian National Trade Union stated at a meeting in Oslo on February 10, 1941, that the real wages of Norwegian labor had been reduced by at least 30 per cent. The Norwegian Employers' Association agreed to a general rise in wages. Gauleiter Terboven, however, refused his sanction. The Norwegian serfs, he explained, should not get wrong ideas in their heads.

The Department of Commerce in Washington, in a survey, concludes that "the Nazi occupation has left Norway in a desperate economic condition which is steadily worsening. Norway's natural resources are restricted to its forests, its waters, and certain minerals, its mineral fuel deposits being negligible. While the loss of her normal export trade has been an extremely severe blow to the national economy, it is, from an immediate point of view, by no means as important as the elimination of foreign foodstuff, which supplied nearly 75 per cent of the country's needs."

True to type, Nazi gangsters muscle into the last remaining profitable industrial enterprises. By special decree of Herr Terboven, Ragnald Bjelland, the "king" of the Norwegian canning industry, was arrested. The management of his vast factories in Stavanger was turned over to a German by the name of Hermann Baretz. "The Bjelland sardines have sold too well in America," Terboven smiled as an epilogue.

Berlin recently ordered the Quisling government to alter the concession laws, in order to facilitate the transfer of existing factories into German hands. On the Norwegian testing ground of the New Order the Nazis are obviously busy in making good their plan to outproduce America in a short time. They have no inhibitions. "Why should we have tender regard for Norwegian business and industry?" Herr Terboven commented. He followed up this rhetorical question with another, even more amazing: "Do you believe we do not know that all your businessmen are pro-British?"

The Russian war brought new hardships to the Norwegian people. On September 26, 1941, the German authorities ordered all civilians to surrender their wool blankets to the army. "In the event of nondelivery of blankets, German authorities will collect them," the order announced. Since then Gestapo men are actually conducting house-to-house searches for blankets.

Dr. Karl Evang, surgeon general of Norway, now in this country, termed this seizure of blankets "a hitherto unprecedented form of mass torture. The effect on the health of the Norwegians will be catastrophic," he declared.

The Nazis also take away the private skis, which are in large parts of Norway the only means of transportation during long winter months. This confiscation is termed a measure of retaliation, since lack of hickory prevented the Norwegian ski industry from fulfilling the German demands. Finally the women of Norway were asked to give up their snow hoods, socks, scarves, and mittens for the members of the "Regiment Nordland," Hitler's Norwegian auxiliary troops in the anti-Bolshevist crusade. The regiment numbers, all told, fewer than three hundred volunteers. Woolens were taken away by the tens of thousands. Where did they go? The answer is obvious. Norwegian women must freeze, for the benefit of the German soldiers in Russia.

Many other personal and household possessions are spirited away. Eight hundred thousand forms were distributed—to a population under three million—on which all metal objects in their possession had to be registered for confiscation, giving weight, worth, and the cost of replacement. Each family was ordered to deliver its silver to the state, for a silver tax is to back up the rapidly inflating currency. Employees in all offices had to turn over articles made of copper or other "war" metals, including ash trays and pencil holders. Josef Terboven's latest looting decree to date requires Norwegians to make over all tents, windproof jackets, knapsacks, heavy sweaters and ski trousers to the German army. A penalty of three years in jail is provided for evasion of this decree.

Indiscriminately, everything not clinched and riveted is confiscated. The county of Telemark had to deliver all its horses. The south of Norway is menaced by a large-scale deforestation plan, to increase Germany's lumber supply. Even the homes are in danger. The population of the districts of Tregnereid and Herlö, on the west coast near Bergen, was evacuated, to make room for German military projects, obviously directed against the British Isles. The people refused to abandon their farms and homes. Seventeen were shot. One hundred and twenty were taken to a concentration camp. These were the more fortunate. Another hundred, made homeless in winter, froze to death.

A curse lies on Adolf Hitler. In his hands life ceases. Riches turn to poverty, plenty to want and need, abundance yields to misery. Denmark is an example; an example, incidentally, the Führer himself likes to quote. He labeled the little kingdom the "showpiece in the shop window of the New Order." He might well find a friendly word for her, in return for the two billion kroner his system has exacted from the minute country in direct taxation alone. He likes to boast of the peace and order his soldiers of occupation brought to Denmark. All prominent foreigners visiting in Berlin are taken for a week-end trip to Copenhagen to see for themselves a subjugated country in which German officers may walk the streets without, as in Prague or Paris, keeping their fingers on the triggers of their service revolvers.

Visitors see a beautiful but deadly weary town which wishes nothing more than to go after business as usual; but business has been entirely disrupted by the occupation. Before the war Denmark supplied half the world with highly specialized agricultural products. The country had a virtual monopoly of the English breakfast table. Eggs and lard in London were almost entirely of Danish origin. These exports have stopped. Pigs and hens began disappearing from Denmark herself, at first because they were shipped to the Reich in great quantities, and later for lack of foodstuff to maintain them.

The normal daily consumption of pork in Copenhagen was three thousand pigs. Now only three pigs reach the market on an average day. Everything else must be delivered across the German border. During one week of last October, twenty-seven thousand head of cattle were "sold" to Germany—for those spurious scraps of paper *Reichskreditkassenscheine*, or against credits in the clearing account, which, in the case of Denmark versus the Reich, have reached the suffocating height of more than one billion kroner, and will never be paid.

The whole potato crop of the peninsula of Jutland, Denmark's mainland, was confiscated by the army of occupation, despite boasts that at home Germany is storing sixty million tons of potatoes. The reason is that potatoes are not only used as a staple food in Germany. Their starch serves to produce synthetic fuel for tanks and planes; it also serves as a solvent for high explosives. Finally, foods of the starchy group yield acetone and glycerine. One hundred ten tons of potatoes make ten tons of alcohol, freeing approximately seven tons of gasoline for aeroplane fuel. If the Danish people still refuse to understand why they must starve, it is their own fault.

Visiting Copenhagen late in 1941, Dr. Goebbels gave his Danish audience this precious advice: to switch to synthetic production, not of fuel for their nonexistent bombers but of bread for eating. "Grass," Dr. Clubfoot said, "which used to be dried as a concentrated cattle fodder, can now be used in baking. The bread tastes good, and you people should not be put off by its green color. If the Danish people live chiefly on such a vegetable diet, instead of on animal products, they will not only be able to supply themselves, but also to contribute to the maintenance of the German army and nation."

Strange to say, no cheers answered this friendly advice. But Dr. Goebbels remained undeterred. He had done his part, and now the German economic delegation, which accompanied him, could clear the tables. They brought back to Berlin a contract forcing Denmark to deliver one and one-half million pigs, seven million hens, one hundred and fifty thousand milch cows, and two hundred thousand heifers.

This was about all that was left in the Danish larder. Now the larder is empty. Denmark had nothing but her agriculture, no industry worth mention.

The single exception was the fertilizer industry. But this was taken over, completely, by the German Dye Trust.

Rats are seventy cents—the equivalent of twenty francs—apiece. The flavor is rather piquant, the people of Brussels assure you. But you had better close your eyes while you are eating. Rabbit ragout is considered a particular treat. "A cat bought at eighty francs [$2.80] was cooked as a rabbit," writes a diplomat. "It was a great feast." Newspapers carry such advertisements as "I must part with Dodo, my dear Alsatian, my companion of many years." Obviously, the advertiser could not himself devour his companion of many years.

But dear Dodo's fate was sealed. She certainly found a buyer on the meat market. A short time ago the German censorship clamped down on the many advertisements for "lost" dogs and cats. The Belgians were always great animal lovers. They still believe that dogs and cats taste better than potato peelings, their staple food.

The *Jydske Tidende,* a Danish paper, published a letter from Belgium: "The other day a ten-year-old boy became ill in school, vomiting only potato peelings. More than half the boys raised their hands when the teacher asked how many had not had potatoes for dinner. Eight out of thirty had eaten merely peelings."

In the morning small groups of children gather like animals around the garbage cans and dump heaps. They grub in the filth for something to eat. The most precious finds are potato peelings; these they take home to be made into a vague kind of soup.

Before the war Belgium was self-sufficient in potato production. But the 1941 crop was very poor. Moreover, the German Luftwaffe needs synthetic fuel. What is left of home-grown potatoes is largely used for animal consumption, because of the lack of imported fodder. Belgium has to deliver her allotted ration of cattle and pigs, which enjoy priority with the economic staff of the army of occupation. Human needs come later.

What little food is obtainable is traded at the black markets. These markets are a vital necessity for Belgium, the attorneys Lemmens-Biot and Meysmans stated before the Brussels tribunal in a court trial against hoarders. "Does not every single honorable member of the court supply himself there?" they asked. The *Nouveau Journal*, a Nazified paper, reported this trial, editorializing about the "incitement to disobey the existing laws." Instantly, the two attorneys were arrested by the Gestapo. But a week later the editor had to be sent to jail himself for transgressing the food regulations.

Prices on the black markets exceed the prewar prices ten and twenty times. An egg, previously fifty centimes, fetches five francs; potatoes rose from one franc the kilo to twenty francs. A sign of the bread shortage is the appearance, in enormous numbers, of forged bread coupons. On a single day, according to the *Brüsseler Zeitung*, the official German mouthpiece, two hundred thousand counterfeit bread tickets were discovered in Brussels.

The treatment Nazism metes out to Belgium is particularly merciless and cruel for one well calculated reason: a country, 85 per cent of whose population earn their livelihood in industry, is a thorn in the flesh of the New Order which aims at "de-industrializing" the countries outside Germany. The Belgians are among those who must return to the soil, and this means extinction and death by starvation for at least two-thirds of the eight million population. Even this return to the soil the Nazis preach to their victims is a hypocritical doctrine, as examples show. Take seed: Belgium has always been dependent on importation for seed; Nazism has stopped the natural imports, and refuses to make up for this from the "overflowing" store of German seed. Take tractors: Belgium has not yet been entirely cleared of war debris, since the necessary machines are missing; but Germany will not part even with obsolete machines to help.

Nazism's supreme infamy in her dealings with Belgium is the Belgian-Russian wheat agreement she promoted. Five Belgian officials, led by a high functionary of the German Ministry of Economics, visited Moscow to barter for wheat. Russia agreed to deliver two hundred and fifty thousand tons of grain during the summer, which would have gone far to mitigate famine in Belgium. Unfortunately, Hitler attacked Russia three days after the Belgian delegation returned home. Of course the German Ministry of Economics had been well aware of the situation. Reichsminister Dr. Walter Funk, its head, laughed uproariously, saying: "It was a good joke, and the joke was on the Belgians."

The joke is always on the Belgians: when Germany confiscated 74 per cent of their paper production, looted 40 per cent of their cotton stocks, confiscated all available shoes, allegedly for shipping to unoccupied France, or forbade the use inside Belgium of copper, nickel, cobalt, lead, tin, cadmium, mercury, and magnesium.

A few instances of German looting caused particular excitement in the country. One was the disappearance of rolling stock. When the Russian campaign rapidly increased German transport needs, Berlin requisitioned forty-five thousand Belgian railway cars. Most of the seventy-eight thousand trucks Belgium owned before the invasion went long ago. Germany uses them for transports in Italy and in the Balkans. On March 26, 1941, a case of bank robbery occurred. All bank safes were opened in the present of heavily armed officials of the *Devisenschutzkommando*. The vaults of persons who were not present (in many cases because they had escaped from the country) were broken open, and cleaned out. German greed did not hesitate even before a gift made by Pope Pius XII. His Holiness had ordered two thousand tins of Ovaltine to be bought and sent at his expense to Belgian prisoners. Only a very small amount of this donation reached its destination. The prison guards shared most of the Ovaltine among themselves.

Both figuratively and literally, the German army has a healthy appetite. Belgium had to pay five and one-half billion francs, equivalent to $144,000,000, for the costs of occupation in the last six months, whereas her ordinary expenditure was about 1,600,000,000 francs a year. Before the invasion Belgium had sent a part of her gold reserve, worth $37,000,-000, to France for safe keeping. Since this gold was stored in Algiers, Germany for a long time could not lay hands on it. With the gradual increase in German influence in the French colonial empire, the last obstacle was removed. A short time ago London was advised that French army planes had brought forty tons of Belgian government gold in forty trips—evidently at the rate of a ton a trip—from Algiers to Marignane Airfield near Marseilles, where the treasure was turned over to the German Armistice Commission.

As to the greed of the German army in its literal sense, soldiers were limited in the first months after invasion to sending home two hundred and fifty grams (one-half pound) of food. Later this maximum weight was increased to five pounds, soon after to ten. Now the limit is entirely abolished.

Not only the German soldiers but their relatives in the Reich thrive on Belgium's misery, while the population of the unhappy country suffers the direst need. Belgium was the first occupied country where the sale of tobacco entirely ceased. Ration cards for tobacco were abolished. Ration cards for bread, nominally good for 225 grams, do not buy even half what they promise.

The death rate in Belgium increased by 11.9 per cent during the period between April 1, 1940, and April 1, 1941. In the same period the number of births decreased by 16.81 per cent.

In Belgium, the New Order works according to plan.

The conquering German army paraded down the Rue du Stade, the principal thoroughfare of Athens. In the Place de la Constitution, the heart of the city, General von List, the victorious war lord, standing on a platform in front of the Royal Palace, reviewed his troops. It was a great military show. Thousands of tramping jackboots and clicking heels, the clatter of tank squads and mechanized columns, rattling sabers and clanking spurs filled the air with thunder.

Athens was silent. The people had disappeared from the streets. The more fortunate had escaped from the city, although around it fighting was still in progress. Those who were left sought to hide themselves in their homes. The news had spread from ear to ear that the invading army would celebrate the conquest of Athens with a night of looting.

The night came—and lasted a few weeks, until toward the end of June, 1941, the Germans left the Greek capital to be policed by Italian troops, retaining overlordship and supervision. But these few weeks emptied the city completely—lock, stock, and barrel. In Athens, Nazi acquisitiveness surpassed itself.

When the Germans first rolled into Greece, they were, it seemed, amply provided. But as soon as the heroic Greek resistance was broken the German army were determined to live off the country. Instantly, all food stocks were confiscated. German soldiers invaded particularly the famous Greek candy stores. At home they were not accustomed to such delicacies, but here they could "buy" them and pay with occupation marks, manufactured by the printing presses which accompany the troops. These marks bear on one side their fictitious value, on the other an inscription that their refusal is a punishable crime.

With their pockets bulging with these bills, the German officers went every day to the market place with trucks to cart away most of the food for the army. German soldiers went into the fields and dug up the unharvested crop of potatoes, a staple of the diet in Greece. These they put into enormous jars. Then Greek olive oil was poured in. Thus the methodical Germans save shipping space, and by the same token the potatoes are preserved. Next all fats were taken, particularly the olive oil with which all cooking is done in Greece. The resinous *vin ordinaire*, the worker's cheap wine, was as completely taken as were the precious vintages. Tobacco was pounced on almost at once. Without it, the German High Command explained, an army cannot fight. All the time Thracian and Macedonian tobacco, which American manufacturers value so highly, was requisitioned.

After devouring everything they could find in fields and stores, the German soldiers shouted in cafés and restaurants for food and drinks, which they had forbidden to the Greeks. They plundered the larder of every hotel, and requisitioned the hotels for themselves. For the short time they intended to stay, it was not worth while establishing camps. Hotels, villas, houses, and flats were taken over. When they finally moved out, they stripped their requisitioned homes, and sent their booty to Germany. Furniture, table linen and bedding, jewelry, clothing, silver, art objects, and antiques were carried off. The retailers had to accept worthless occupation marks for clothing, silk goods, especially women's stockings, soap, shoes, leather goods, and rugs. To transport the booty, the Germans picked up automobiles in the streets, or took them from garages. All delivery trucks in Greece were confiscated.

This orgy of looting would not have been possible except with the backing of very high authorities. It was clear that the German troops in Greece, and particularly the officers, had received a free rein to rob and to abuse the people. This free rein, intimate observers believe, was given to counteract the dissatisfaction that was dangerously, and obviously, mounting among some of the war-weary German regiments. Immediately after the initial parade on the Rue du Stade, which once more displayed the German army's unparalleled showmanship, discipline slackened alarmingly. Passers-by were astonished to see officers greeting their men with an encouraging smile, when they met them ambling along the streets of Athens. It was an unprecedented occurrence in the world's most strictly disciplined army for the soldiers to fail to salute first. The German soldiery in Athens was demoralized. They were fed up with victories that lacked nourishing value. They wanted to get something out of their conquests, or stop conquering.

The pilfering the German officers indulged in was obviously of a different color. Every monocled, spur-clanking gentleman in field gray, it seemed, had business relations at home, on whose behalf he was acting in Athens. German officers visited Greek firms. Off duty the majors and colonels proposed to buy the establishments, or the majority of the shares in profitable enterprises, for their German friends. Thus the Greek branch of the Socony Vacuum Company of New York was approached by a German major with the suggestion to buy up the company's interests in Greece. He insisted on utmost speed in concluding the deal. "The Italians will soon be here, and we do not want them to get anything," he admitted frankly. The Company in New York, consulted by its Athens manager, refused the German offer. Since the Italians did, indeed, come, the Germans were obliged to change their plans. Now they are about to establish a "German oil trust for Greece." Behind the German oil trust, every one knows, stands Shareholder Hermann Göring.

The plan that miscarried with the Socony Vacuum Company succeeded in many other cases. The Powder and Cartridge Company, the Kopais Development Company, many shipping and mining interests, and the bulk of Greek industry and trade were taken over by Germans. In every case officers acted as middlemen. There is no doubt that they received a commission for their work. Mighty generals are only little agents. Their bosses, who really profit by the wholesale purchases, are the influential Nazi politicians. The "German Office of Purchases," established two days after the occupation of Athens, pretends to act for the Reich government. But in every Athens coffee house you can hear the names of the Nazi party leaders, and other high dignitaries, who are "taken care of" by the Office of Purchases.

The food situation became serious immediately after the Germans had entered. Within a few weeks it led to an acute state of hunger. Last winter the Greek population was starving. As early as September, men and women fainting from hunger were a common sight in the streets of Athens and

Salonika. Bread, wheat, and flour were the first commodities confiscated by the Germans. Later they took all the tomatoes for the army in Libya. Dried figs and raisins, a Greek staple food, went to Germany. When the acting mayor of Athens pleaded with the German authorities to be permitted a few potatoes for his people, he received the answer: "There are twice too many people in your city. Half of them must die. I am afraid the poor will have to make a beginning." Fish, another diet staple of the Greeks, is unavailable. Fishermen are unable to go to sea because of the mine fields, the German submarines, and Nazi restrictions on leaving shores and ports, particularly at night. Moreover, many fishing smacks, commandeered for the invasion of Crete, were destroyed.

The German soldiers raided public ovens, where civilians, for lack of fuel, had their food cooked. In the suburb Psihiko the Germans let the water run from every hydrant to lower the water pressure. When they departed, there was no water left for the vegetable crops, on which Psihiko lives. In Athens the full output of the vegetable canning factories was confiscated; nothing was left for the winter. Necessary foods such as olives and cheese were robbed. No food from America ever arrived. Three ships from the Vanderbilt committee got as far as Egypt; there they were sunk.

An incident worth recording is connected with the distribution of powdered milk. The American Red Cross sent one hundred tons of powdered milk for the undernourished Italian children of Libya at the specific request of the British authorities, which was made on condition that the Italian Red Cross would ship an equal quantity to the children of Greece. The Italians fulfilled their contract obligation. However, it is reported that after the evaporated milk had arrived in Greece, the Germans announced that they were "temporarily borrowing" it for their own children. It was seized, shipped to the Reich, and neither returned nor replaced.

Since there is no milk, little children stand in queues in

Athens, waiting for hours for a little olive oil. Once a week they get a bit of meat, never enough to sustain them. The rate of child mortality increases rapidly as does general mortality. In the city of Athens alone, six hundred people a week die of starvation.

Even the restaurants de luxe are stripped. Averoff's, for instance, one of the most famous eating places in Athens, served baked locusts as the only course on the menu. Disgusted, the guests recoiled. Only one patron, an elderly man, had the courage to order the locusts. He asked for a second helping, and ate with gusto. Then he said enthusiastically to the waiter: "Athens is a gorgeous place to live in. I have not seen such good food for many months. I have just arrived. You see," he whispered, "I am a refugee from Poland."

CHAPTER FOUR

GERMANIZATION

You are embarking upon this campaign in order to win new land for the German farmer and worker.—FIELD MARSHAL WILHELM KEITEL, Chief of the German High Command, in an order to his troops on the eve of the invasion of Poland, which unloosed World War II.

THE fourth partition of Poland, the partition carried out by Adolf Hitler with the connivance of Joseph Stalin—which, today, probably no man regrets as much as Stalin himself—divided that part of Poland, the bulk of the country, that came under German overlordship into two sections.

The eastern section, with a population of eleven and a half million Poles, was formed into a Government General, an annex of the Reich, without, however, being a part of it. The Western Provinces—Pomerania, Poznań, Silesia, and portions of the departments of Warsaw, Łódź, and Cracow—inhabited by ten and one-half million Polish people, were "incorporated" with the German Reich.

This partition is remarkable in the light of following events. It set the pattern for the partition of France, and it stands out as the first example of the Nazi technique of dividing countries, after they have been subjugated, in order to play both ends against the middle. This technique is applied despite the fact that the partition, in Poland still more than in France, is all but fictitious. The Government General enjoys not an atom more independence than the provinces incorporated outright. There is only one difference between the treatment suffered by both parts of Poland. Whereas the population of the Government General is to be exterminated, the annexed part of Poland is to be Germanized. This fate is considerably worse.

The annexed parts of Poland were attached to different German provinces. Most went to the Warthe and Pomerania. Herr Greiser, *Gauleiter*—district leader—of the Warthe received his new compatriots on October 10, 1939, with the words: "In ten years there will not be a single non-German farmer left. All our living space in this province that has come home to the Reich belongs to German newcomers from the Baltic, Russia, South Tyrol, and Rumania."

His colleague Forster, Gauleiter of Pomerania, found a shorter expression. In the newly conquered city of Bydgoszcz he said, as early as November 27, 1939: "All Poles must get out of the country."

The story of the following two and a half years, the story of western Poland's Germanization, shows the attempt to oust ten and one-half million people from a country their ancestors have been dwelling in for over seven hundred years. It is not the general story of the New Order in Europe, which endeavors to enslave non-German nations. It is the story of some of the New Order's doomed stepchildren, whose land is wanted but whose existence is unwanted.

Ever since the western provinces of Poland were incorporated with the German Reich—legally by decree of November 1, 1939, published in the Official Journal of Laws (Reichsgesetzblatt)—the German authorities have used methods of terror and extermination unknown in history.

Immediately after the invasion, mass executions were ordered. It was not yet the indiscriminate slaughter of hostages, introduced in the summer of 1941 in France, Norway, Czechoslovakia, Yugoslavia, and other countries. In the Polish case, it was a calculated campaign to destroy all potential leaders of the enslaved nation. As soon as they entered Poland, and without giving any individual reasons, German troops executed large numbers of priests, lawyers, doctors, and businessmen. Hundreds and thousands were shot in every town. As a rule the executions took place publicly in the principal squares, preferably on market days. A typical case is the murder in Szamotuly, on the day of the annual fair, October 20, 1939. At a given moment, members of the S.S. closed the streets leading to the square. Five young men were stood against the wall. Before they were executed, they had time to shout: "Long live Poland." They fell, riddled with bullets. The commander of the S.S. then went from one victim to another, giving each the coup de grâce. Afterward, a priest, a doctor, and a barrister were ordered to put the bodies of the victims on a cart, and to push it to the cemetery, where the three men were forced to dig a common grave—outside the cemetery wall—and to bury the bodies. The only published reason for this execution was the German complaint that in the neighboring village of Otorowo, a Swastika flag had been torn from the communal house by an unknown person. The real reason was, obviously, to inspire terror in the hearts of the Polish people.

In the following months executions were conducted methodically, cruelly, mechanically. It is impossible to enumerate even a small part of these atrocities, but the Polish government in exile possesses a rather full record of them. Thousands of the German butchers involved are known by name, and it estimates that in the western provinces alone eighteen thousand Polish leaders from all social classes were put to death.

The population, made leaderless, was driven from the soil. The mass expulsion started on October 12, 1939, in Orlowo, a seaside resort on the Baltic near Gdynia. There, at six o'clock in the morning, posters appeared on the Town Hall announcing that the whole population had to be ready to leave their homes within an hour.

The mass expulsion in itself implies ruthless expropriation. To be legally on the safe side, however, the German administration promulgated further laws of expropriation. First, all the expelled shopkeepers of Poznań were deprived of their premises by special decree. Later, this decree was widened to include all Polish shopkeepers of the town, expelled or not. Particularly severe were the regulations confiscating bookshops, newspapers, hotels, restaurants, and cinemas. Through Nazi-appointed *Treuhänder*, middlemen, who, of course, received a considerable kick-back from the new owners, these shops fell into German hands. They are now decorated with posters reading *Deutsches Geschäft* (German enterprise) and *Polen Eintritt verboten* (Poles not admitted). A further decree makes possible the expropriation of the property of individuals or societies declared "hostile" to the Reich. This decree was largely applied for the confiscation of Church property. Owners of bank deposits are allowed to retain only 15 per cent of their savings. Estate owners, big and small, were indiscriminately expropriated. Some elastic paragraph always came in handy.

But these measures, Gauleiter Greiser stated, are inconclusive. They have so far served to eliminate only one and one-half million Poles, and have made room for no more than half a million German settlers. Obviously a German needs three times the space a Pole used to occupy. The expulsion and eradication of the native element in western Poland continues unabated. Lest the Poles lose their sense of proportion, the following rules prevail until the provinces are entirely Germanized:

1) All Poles are obliged to uncover their heads in the presence of German officers or Nazis displaying their party badges.

2) All Poles are obliged to give way to the Germans. Pavements are exclusively reserved for pedestrians of the master race. Poles must use the roadway.

3) The markets are in the first instance reserved for Germans. Only after German buyers have been served may Poles make their purchases.

4) In the shops also, the Germans, both military and civilian, are served first. They need not queue up like the Poles.

5) All Poles who have not yet "grasped" the difference between victor and vanquished, will suffer exemplary punishment.

These five points of the New Order were signed by Gauleiter Forster. Gauleiter Greiser, before affixing his signature as well, penciled the additional line: "In public buildings and offices Poles must use the servants' entrance."

The Bishop of Metz, Monsignor Heintz, is a silent man. For the time being he lives in a monastery, somewhere in occupied France. His flock is not allowed to know his whereabouts. If they tried to get in touch with their shepherd all sorts of trouble would arise for Madame Heintz, the bishop's aged mother, at present residing in the Hotel National in Mulhouse. "Residing," perhaps, is not quite the right word. Actually the lady of eighty-two years is scrubbing the floors in the hotel. Her roommates envy her this privilege. They are bored by their enforced idleness. Life in the National is no longer gay, since the hotel was turned into the local Gestapo headquarters. The wine cellar, incidentally, now harbors hostages, Madame Heintz among others.

The Gestapo fetched the Bishop from his palace on June 20, 1940, at dawn—the time at which the square-faced gentlemen prefer to work. Human resistance is at its lowest ebb in the early morning hours, Dr. Krieshammer, dean of the medical faculty of the Breslau University, and scientific expert of the secret police, discovered in long years of experimenting in Gestapo cellars.

Monsignor Heintz offered no resistance whatsoever. For months, ever since the invasion, he had known that it had to come. He was guilty of being the much beloved spiritual leader of the ancient town of Metz. To the Nazis, this was unpardonable. He had to leave the bishopric within half an hour, taking with him such belongings as he could carry in his hands, and no money at all. One hundred five Alsatian priests and 60 per cent of the Lorraine clergy had to follow him into enforced exile. The reason was obvious. Nazism is about to Germanize Alsace-Lorraine. To achieve this aim, the churches—both Catholic and Protestant—must first be Nazified.

The plan was worked out by Dr. Otto Meissner, who rarely figures in the news although he holds one of the most influential positions in the Third Reich. His title is Secretary of State, he is the chief of Hitler's personal chancellery. He is one of the few leftovers from the republican era, having already served Presidents Ebert and von Hindenburg as Cabinet chief. Dr. Meissner claims to be an Alsatian, although the Alsatians say that he hails from Saxony and only spent his youth in their country, and he is famous for what passes for Gallic wit in Germany. When he had sworn allegiance to Hitler he murmured, Berlin gossip reports: "First it was the saddler's apprentice [the Nazi nickname for Ebert], now it is the paperhanger. Well, let's embark upon another fourteen years of shame." According to Meissner's timetable Nazism should have another four or five years. The Alsatians believe he exaggerates as usual.

Dr. Otto Meissner blueprinted the scheme for Germanizing Alsace-Lorraine "with kid gloves"—to use his own term. The people are not to be destroyed, but converted. They are simply to stop feeling French, and jump upon the Nazi band-wagon. The system should only revert to mass executions and similar time-honored measures of establishing the New Order as a last resort. Meissner's is a very "human" scheme. This is how it works:

Alsatians and Lorrainers have deeply rooted religious be-liefs. The Cross is the pillar of their national existence. The Cross must fall. After the expulsion of most of the clergy, religious orders were forbidden, and religious schools closed. The sisters of Ribeauville and the Frères de l'Ecole were sup-pressed, as was the Protestant Theological Seminary in Stras-bourg. The ancient Strasbourg University was closed, and reopened as a German language college late in November, 1941. The new Nazi president, Dr. Karl Schmidt, declared at the opening ceremony that the sole ambition of the uni-versity would henceforth be "forging the spiritual weapons for the successful completion of the war." One of these spir-itual weapons is the total omission of French science in the curriculum. Medical students at Strasbourg do not hear the name of Pasteur, whose monument in the city has been de-stroyed.

Dr. Meissner assigned a number of turncoats to important posts. His propaganda chief is an Alsatian expatriate of many years, Professor Leroux from Heidelberg University. Alsatian audiences are compelled to listen to concerts conducted by another expatriate, Georges Boulanger. Gestapo agents at-tend his concerts, watching who applauds, and who does not.

But these are just the trimmings of Germanization. Its real aim is the conquest of the youth. In Strasbourg all parents of children above ten years old were called into the Town Hall, where they had to sign a double oath: first, to educate their children in the Nazi creed; secondly, to speak not a single word of French at home. There and then, the first hitch oc-curred: three-quarters of the parents refused to sign; they were even willing to incur the wrath of the Gestapo.

The older people, Nazism insists, are a lost generation. The system is bent on capturing the youth. In Alsace, another traitor named Bickler is entrusted with this task. Herr Bickler first won Nazi fame by designing a black flag with an inverted Z as a substitute for the swastika, which was forbidden under the French regime. Hitler promoted the young man to the rank of youth leader for Alsace-Lorraine. This was high promotion, in view of Hitler's notorious preference for surrounding himself with blond youth leaders.

Bickler's work is to Nazify Alsatian youth. The schools are Germanized. The teachers are transferred to the newly conquered territories in the East, and are replaced by hooligans from the Reich who cannot even spell German. Nazi gymnastics and Nazi singing are taught instead of reading and writing. School time is irregular, since the most important hours, from ten to twelve, are reserved for military training. All Alsatian boys of more than ten years have to wear the brown shirt and carry the dagger. Their parents must pay for both.

The Germanization of names is compulsory. In certain villages in the Vosges the entire population had to change their names. Indiscriminately a woman baptized Nicole was labeled Gertrud, and Alphonse became Adolf. Occasionally communities had the right to make their own suggestions in renaming streets, or inns. The keeper of the Jardin de France, a famous hostelry near Strasbourg, called his place "Zum Kirchhof" (Ye Old Cemetery), and got away with it. The magistrate of Mulhouse asked respectfully for the honor of being permitted to give the main street the Führer's name. Permission was granted. It's now Adolf Hitler Street. It was Rue du Sauvage (Savage Street) until the rechristening. The change causes much chuckling among the denizens of Mulhouse. On the other hand, Strasbourg had to tolerate the change of the name of its principal square from Place Kléber, commemorating the general of Revolutionary fame, to Karl Roos Platz, celebrating the notorious traitor whom the French had to shoot in the first month of the war. The Nazi vandals destroyed all the historic monuments of Strasbourg. In Metz the monument of the unknown soldier was blown up. Libraries, public and private, were searched for French literature. The books were burned in huge bonfires, illuminating the country for four nights, from the 15th to the 19th of December, 1940.

No memory of France is to remain. No contact exists with France, by mail, telephone, or telegraph. Travel beyond the border of both French zones is forbidden. The use of the French language is being persecuted. A decree of Dr. Ernst, Nazi Commissioner of Strasbourg, another Alsatian expatriate who returned after the catastrophe of his country, makes it punishable for a man to speak French, if he is known to understand German. Even the local patois, intermediate between French and German, is banned. In Alsace-Lorraine correct German is prescribed. It is fortunate for Hitler that he does not live in this province.

The Nazi system contradicts definitely the promise the authorities made when invading Alsace-Lorraine, that persons and property would not be interfered with. When a deputation of Alsatian citizens recalled this promise to Gauleiter Wagner (front man for scheming Dr. Meissner, who, for fear of hostile demonstrations, only rarely shows up in his beloved Alsace), the entire deputation was sent to the concentration camp, and the terror began.

The terror consists of mass expulsions, which have so far made homeless and ruined one-sixth of the total population of one million two hundred thousand people. It reached its peak on August 11, 1941, when the expulsion of Lorraine farmers started. Every day peasants were registered in the "undesirable" category, in order to make their farms free for German settlers. But here the system of Germanization overreached itself: many of the sturdy farmers of Lorraine burned down their houses and barns, rather than let them fall into the hands of German plunderers. Whole villages went up in flames.

Nazi Governor Wagner realized that he was provoking civil war. The time, coinciding with the start of the Russian campaign, was not propitious. So the expulsions were called off, and Herr Wagner even called back people who had left the country immediately after the German invasion, luring them with promises of reparation. A few did come back from Perigord. They were arrested, forced to return such goods as they had managed to get to France, and then kicked out again.

Persecutions were redoubled, and now Wagner decreed the concentration camp for anyone who, knowing German, spoke French. Even the wearing of a French beret was made punishable. Hotel and restaurant owners were requested to insure good transmission of the German broadcasts, particularly those from the Russian front. Until then, sudden, boisterous gayety among the patrons had always drowned the Berlin waves. A man with the good German name of Meier, calmly drinking his bock in a Strasbourg beer cellar, complained that a victory announcement with its tremendous ruffle of drums and blaring of victory bugles burst into his reflective solitude. Wilhelm Meier of Bombach was condemned to two and one-half years in jail.

Simultaneously, the propaganda campaign for Germanization shifted into high gear. On a single Friday in October, 1941, more than one hundred Nazi rallies were held in the district of Strasbourg alone. The principal speaker at many of these rallies was Prince August Wilhelm of Prussia, fourth son of the late ex-Kaiser. "Auwi," as both friends and deriders call him, is supposed to be the Hohenzollern brain child. History will decide whether he proved his political acumen in being the only Prince of the once ruling dynasty to join the Nazis. In spite of his demonstrative allegiance to Hitler, he has not risen in the party hierarchy higher than the

modest rank of a *Reichsredner* (state speaker), which is Nazi-
German for soapbox "orator." But now, perhaps, his career
is in the making. Auwi, it seems, wants to cash in on his
studies at Strasbourg in German Imperial days. He calls himself an Alsatian, with about as much right as Dr. Meissner.
He is obviously out to become the puppet king of Alsace-
Lorraine.

His chance of becoming this with the consent of the people is negligible. The German propaganda backfires, and the
Nazis are well aware of this fact. Party Comrade Mueller,
Kreisleiter (district boss) of Ribeauville had to admit in a
speech at Carspach on July 14, 1941: "Instead of showing
themselves grateful to the Führer who delivered them from
the nameless disorder of a rotten democracy, the Alsatians attempt to deride the advantages of Nazism and show themselves completely hostile to Germany. French flags fly everywhere. Of a population of about a million two hundred thousand barely five thousand have joined our organization. The
people should feel ashamed of themselves."

Sometimes the people lose their temper. Enrollment in the
German army and labor service has provoked numerous flights
across the French border, and beyond to join the Free French
forces of General de Gaulle. Both the escaping boys and their
parents are well aware that the families of the fugitives are put
into concentration camps. But they are willing to risk it.

Pressure only increases their resistance. The mass arrests
made in the summer of 1941 failed to subdue the people. Some
released French prisoners of war who crossed Alsace on their
way home, were greeted at the Strasbourg station by a crowd
shouting: "Vive la France! Come back soon to chase the German swine!" This happened in the presence of German soldiers who remained indifferent.

By night the tricolor is hoisted to the spires of the churches.
On the morning after Armistice Day, the celebration of which
was forbidden by the German authorities, Colmar staged a

strange parade. Hundreds of snails crept through the streets, their shells painted red, white, and blue, the colors of France.

The young men wear under their lapels the Lorraine Cross, the symbol of Free France. They greet one another with the syllable, "Elf!" which is the Alsatian V-signal, standing for "Vive la France." Hundreds serve as officers with the Free French and even with the reduced army of Vichy. Not a single Alsatian is an officer in the Reichswehr. The peasant girls still dream of going to Paris as chambermaids. True, Paris is occupied. So is Alsace-Lorraine. But both remain French to the core. No one can Germanize them, kid gloves or no kid gloves.

"Slovakia must be Germanized," Hitler bellowed to a gathering of high Nazi functionaries, on April 5, 1941.

He meant Slovenia. The Führer was getting a little mixed with all his conquests. He had just decided that it was Yugoslavia's turn. Mussolini would help with his legions of ragged blackshirts. By way of compensation the Duce would get a scrap of the Dalmatian coast. This had been agreed upon at the dictators' last meeting in Brenner Pass. That Italy, in turn, would have to yield Trieste, the vital port commanding the Adriatic, to the Third Reich, was not a part of the agreement. But Benito knows as well as any one that his big brother covets Trieste and that he is in the habit of getting what he wants.

Here is where Slovenia comes in. This northernmost province of Yugoslavia is sandwiched between the German border and the city of Trieste. It is inhabited by one million six hundred thousand devoutly Catholic peasants, who are among the most ancient, most colorful, and proudest of Slavs—at least, they were as many as that a year ago. They have been punished by Hitler more harshly than perhaps any other group. Their crime was that they had been for six centuries a stumbling block to German expansion toward the Adriatic. Under the New Order they were doomed.

"Skalka! Steindl!" the Führer shouted.

Two men in the gathering clicked their heels.

"Get me Slovakia!"

Again they clicked their heels. Neither dared to remark that the Führer had got Slovakia two years before. Gauleiter Franz Steindl chose silence as the better part of courage. Reichskommissar Skalka replied diplomatically: "Mein Führer, we will reorganize that country."

Next day the Reichskommissar dropped his diplomatic pretenses. "Party comrades," he addressed his corps. "Tear out your own heart! Throw it away! Instead, put a stone in your breast!" It sounds too melodramatic to be credible. But the Yugoslav government received a report vouching for this phraseology. Those in the know, incidentally, would not be surprised. Even among themselves the Nazis can only speak in slogans. The German language is reduced to clichés.

Instantly, the German army crossed the border, and occupied on that day the northwestern part of the small country, the district of Carniola. Military resistance was impossible. The plains of Slovenia lay wide open to German motorized columns and tanks. Wisely, the Yugoslav army retreated to their mountainous hinterland, where, to its unending glory, the battle is still raging almost a year later.

Slovenia, however, was immediately lost. The Germans occupied Maribor and Ljubljana, the two most important cities, and the country around them. They trampled down about a million Slovenians. The rest of the country, with some four hundred thousand inhabitants, went to Italy. A small slice was thrown to the dogs. The Hungarians, hyenas of this war preying on the carcasses of their neighbors overrun by the Germans, snapped up their bloody little bit.

The military conquest, however, was just the prelude, Hitler's goal being not to conquer but to Germanize Slovenia. As soon as the German soldiery had once more won an easy victory, the Corps Skalka went at it. This corps, of course, is the Gestapo assigned to clean up Slovenia. The aim was much the same as in Alsace-Lorraine, but the methods were very different. This time no kid gloves—this time the gloves were taken off.

As in the case of Alsace the first men to be crushed by the conquerors were the religious leaders. Bishop Ivan Tomasic of Maribor with his clerical staff of three canons and two secretaries was instantly arrested. So was the supreme shepherd of Ljubljana, Archbishop Rozman, Primate of Slovenia, on the very night of invasion. To this day his further fate is unknown. As soon as the Germans had cleaned up Ljubljana, the provincial capital, and the going was no longer dangerous, the Italians marched in. General Grazioli, High Commander, installed himself in the Archbishop's palace. His first utterance promised freedom for all, and particularly respect for the Slovenian language. His second decreed that all the newspapers should be printed in Italian. Then he went to attend High Mass in the looted chapel of the Archbishop, and had Monsignor Philip Tercelji, Professor of Religious History at the Ljubljana University, thrown into a concentration camp.

These contradictions in the Italian regime disturbed the Germans' highly developed sense of order. Gestapo Boss Skalka, clothed in his shabbiest mufti, called upon the resplendent Italian general (who is a knight of the Order of the Annunciation, and thus a "cousin of the king"). Their conversation ended in perfect harmony. It was resolved that the Italian army should do the policing of Ljubljana, while the Gestapo exercised supervision. Since conditions are not very much different in Italy proper, General Grazioli saw no difficulty in obliging his Teuton friend. The rumor that the bullets in Skalka's body, which was recovered from a river on November 7, 1941, fitted into Italian service revolvers, is so far not confirmed.

Unfortunate Skalka had only a little more than half a year to Germanize the country to which he was assigned. How he

died and why, is—if you do not credit the "Italian" version—
one of the thousands of unsolved mysteries of the ferocious
underground battle raging all over the continent. Justice to
a dead man compels one, however, to say this much for Skalka's memory: He did not miss a single day in carrying out
his duty.

Methodically, he visited the whole country. He was never
seen without a map of Slovenia, and rarely without three or
four revolvers hanging from a belt around his oversized belly.
He honored the town of Celje with his first history-making
visit. On May 19, 1941, toward eight P.M. he arrived. At
nine o'clock the Catholic seminary was ransacked, and most
of the furniture taken away. Awaiting deportation, the professors and students were jammed into a cattle truck, sixty
men old and young within a space intended for eight head of
cattle. An hour later Skalka and his henchmen invaded the
local gymnasium, where the Sokol was practicing. The Sokol
is the patriotic youth league, imbued with pan-Slavic tendencies. There are Sokols in all Slav countries and towns. In
Celje the group had fifty-three members. How many survived
Skalka's visit is not known. They were insulted, kicked with
Prussian jack boots, treated to blows. Their shins, hands, and
heads were hurt. The torture lasted all night. At dawn the
young people were driven to the monastery of the Capuchin
fathers, where the priests had to watch them being tormented
again. These tortures were repeated for fourteen nights. They
went on under the eyes of the German police, some of whom
showed distinct signs of disgust. But the police were powerless
before the Gestapo. After a fortnight the surviving Sokols
were taken to Germany, to join the voluntary labor service.
The Capuchin monastery was emptied. Skalka regretted having lost so much time on a comparatively insignificant task.

He returned to Maribor, his headquarters, where the barracks had in the meantime been filled with two thousand hostages, all carefully selected from the upper classes, priests,

professors, civil servants, and merchants. Every man had to
undergo the torment of the modern inquisition. Besides, the
victims had to register their property; they were forced to
denounce the political activities of their friends and relatives,
and finally they had to sign a declaration that they were willing to hand over their houses, belongings, and positions to
their German "heirs," who were arriving in droves from the
South Tyrol and Rumania.

At the slightest sign of refusal prisoners were sent to the
barrack cellar, where they were penned up at night so that
they were unable to move their bodies. In the daytime, they
had to jump to attention the moment a German uniform
showed up. If a warden did not find their carriage satisfactory, the victims were condemned to those exercises which
are meticulously described in Dr. Friedrich Gröber's *Gym-
nastic Almanac*, one of the Gestapo's most highly prized manuals.

This inferno lasted five weeks, during which the families
of the hostages were removed beyond the Serbian border.
Skalka reviewed his victims for a last time. Luxuriously he
mustered the shadow parade. He singled out an old Franciscan. "Are you sick?" he asked with the amiability of a tiger.

The old monk realized that an admission of the torture
would prevent his being released—the Gestapo do not care for
witnesses on the wrong side of their barbed wire. So he replied humbly: "I have long been suffering from phthisis."

Understandingly, Skalka smiled. He liked the answer. The
old boy was to his taste. He should have his freedom. Jovially,
Skalka patted the Franciscan's shoulder: "Aren't you fortunate to suffer for Jesus Christ?"

The guards looked amazed. This was a new tune. The
bloodhounds are dangerous even to their own master, and to
reconcile them Skalka said: "We don't care a snap for his
God, do we? Our God is a big sausage and two mugs of beer!"

Outside the barracks auto busses were waiting to bring the

released hostages to the Croatian border, where God would help them to get farther. Each bus had room for thirty people, but eighty or a hundred were packed into every one. The hostages scrambled for a little space. Suddenly a voice stopped them. Major Libius, the barrack commander, shouted an unmistakably Prussian "Halt!" and showed Skalka a letter.

"All right," Skalka chuckled. Then he turned to the hostages: "I have just been informed that you are to be filmed for the German news release. "Slovenia Enjoys Her New Freedom,' the picture is called. Smile and sing. You had better show your unconcern, your happiness," he added with a dangerous growl.

The cameramen came.

But there were no smiles left in the distorted faces of the hostages, and their voices had dried up.

"Go at it," Skalka commanded.

Sergeant Rossman and Oberwachtmeister Bovha went at it. Both are notorious sadists. The sergeant was in the habit of boxing the ears of the men in his charge, until they were deafened. The Oberwachtmeister, a learned man, had won local fame by his intimate knowledge of the human anatomy. He knew where it hurt most. In amazingly short time both had changed into mufti. The German uniform must not be disgraced. They were armed only with rubber truncheons. They raised their arms.

The scene was filmed. The cameramen could not use it for "Slovenia Enjoys Her New Freedom," but it was an excellent shot for "Slovenian Gangsters Massacre German Civilians," which was subsequently shown in every movie theater in the Reich and never failed to arouse the just indignation of the fundamentally kind-hearted German audience.

Reichskommissar Skalka visited all the prisoners in Slovenia. Where he found none, he established one. He invented the system of "groups of five" (five hostages or prisoners manacled together). They had to move like Siamese quintuplets, and were inseparable from one another. Orders were accompanied by shouts and blows. The war of nerves was ingeniously embroidered with all the malice and chicane a crank brain could devise. While thousands of lives were sacrificed in the dungeons, Skalka's men visited their homes, and took what still remained: a little money, some coffee, a bit of sugar, perhaps a cake of soap.

Thus Slovenia was softened up. The land was ripe for the second measure of Germanization, carried out between June 13 and 25, and, after a short pause, again in the second and third weeks of July. These were the "terrible days" of which the Chetniks, the guerrilla fighters, speak around their campfires. In less than four weeks, all told, two hundred and eighty-three thousand Slovenes were deported to Croatia and Serbia, despite disrupted communications, lack of rolling stock, almost impassable roads. These figures are authenticated by the Yugoslav government, which estimates that another two hundred and fifty thousand people have been expelled since. The mass expulsion continues unabated.

The abandoned villages did not remain empty more than a few hours. The Nazi precision machine saw to that. Immediately after the departure of the expelled, the German newcomers moved in. They came from the Baltic States, from the Hungarian Banat, and from Bessarabia. They were a strangely mixed lot. After centuries in foreign lands they had entirely forgotten their German heritage, of which Nazism had to remind them forcibly, as well as the German language of their ancestors. Instead they had acquired the passions and hatreds of the nations among whom they had lived. The age-old battle between Rumanian- and Hungarian-speaking people was immediately resumed in the Germanized villages of Slovenia.

Wherever some of the old inhabitants of these villages remain, they are subject to incessant propaganda. Posters in screaming colors claim that Kralj Matjaz, the legendary Slovenian king, whom the nation expects to lead her to happiness and welfare in the future, has indeed, risen. His name is Adolf Hitler. These and similar devices are carried out by the League for German Culture. But the league does not confine itself to such "cultural" activities. Having worked underground for many years during the Yugoslav regime, the members of the league know people and conditions in every village, and act as informers for the Gestapo.

In the achievement of their principal purpose of expulsion and extermination, the Germans feel themselves most hampered by the city of Ljubljana, the center of Slovenian intellectual and economic life. As related, the city had to be handed over to the Italians. But the Germans hold it on three sides in their iron grip, entirely cutting it off from the rest of the occupied country. Since the only sector open to Italian-dominated territory leaves no way out, the Germans can starve Ljubljana at will, simply by preventing the importation of food from the districts they hold. Frequently they stop the water supply. Eighteen thousand Slovenians in the city, all that are left of the nation's upper class and intelligentsia, finding an uncertain refuge behind the Italian bayonets, are threatened with complete destruction as soon as the Germans make good their threat to release the Italian garrison for duty in Libya.

It is likely that Reichskommissar Skalka had come to Ljubljana to discuss this matter when fate caught up with him. His corpse was found in the river, and buried with elaborate neo-pagan ceremony. At his bier Gauleiter Franz Steindl declared: "You did not die in vain, Party Comrade Skalka." Then he turned to the imaginary Hitler who is always with them when two or three Nazis are gathered together, and said, with emotion and emphasis: "My Führer, you ordered Slovenia to be Germanized. Slovenia is German."

CHAPTER FIVE

MONSTROUS MIDGETS

"Slovakia was the first country to enter the New Order voluntarily. She will become a state which will be a model to the others incorporated within the German living space."— HITLER to Dr. Tiso, President of Slovakia, after the latter's visit with the Führer at headquarters, somewhere far behind the Russian front lines.

HAVING devastated most of the European continent, the New Order entered the constructive stage. Two "independent" countries were established: Slovakia by Hitler, and Croatia by Adolf and Benito working in double harness. Both these undersized puppet states represent the New Order in a nutshell. They are monstrous midgets.

Terrific birth pangs accompanied the inauguration of Slovakia, the eastern province of what had previously been Czechoslovakia. On October 5, 1938, the day Dr. Beneš retired from his office as President of the Republic, a "Slovakian conference" was held in the town of Zilina. All the autonomists, separatists, and fifth columnists attended. Socialists were not invited. The conference proclaimed autonomy for Slovakia, which meant dualism for the republic. A motion to break away entirely from the mother state was voted down for a valid reason. Independent Slovakia is a permanent economic misfit, her annual expenses being three hundred million crowns, whereas the maximum of her taxable income amounts to half that sum. Hence the conferees of Zilina decided to continue mulcting the Czechoslovakian Republic as an "independent province," while enjoying autonomy under their own government, headed by Dr. Tiso.

The Tiso regime started next day. Instantly, it assumed the character of a savage dictatorship. Its first decrees ordered the arrest of all prominent Czechs in the country, and suppressed the Sokols (in Slovakia, as in all the other Slav countries, the foremost patriotic organization). The local and communal administration was taken over by commissioners. Pogroms were unleashed. They were more ferocious even than the persecution of the Jews in Nazi Germany. The Slovakian Jews were rounded up and chased across the Hungarian border. Unfortunately, the chivalrous Magyars drove the human flotsam back where they had come from. Teams of Hungarian gendarmes and Slovakian Hlinka guardsmen played soccer with their living balls, kicking them hither and thither.

The Hlinka Guard is the Slovakian counterpart of the German storm troops, and is built on the Nazi model. Even its emblem, the double cross, is a copy of the swastika. Its name patron was the late Father Hlinka, Slovak Catholic priest and for many years leader of the autonomist movement. But its organizer was the notorious Captain Manfred von Killinger, once the boss of Hitler's Old Guard, later active as a fifth columnist in many countries, among others the United States, finally German minister in Bratislava, the provincial capital of Slovakia. At present the gallant captain serves, with his old pal, Fritz Wiedemann, as German envoy to the puppet government in Nanking. He is, it seems, a specialist in bossing puppet governments.

His creation, the Hlinka Guard, is a super S.A. in which 98 per cent of the guardsmen are illiterate, 80 per cent have criminal records. The *Guardista*, its mouthpiece, is the laughing-stock of the country because of the highly original spelling and grammar of its stories. Yet the Hlinka Guard is the only force in Slovakia the German overlords have so far left alone. Nazism is lenient toward its bloodhounds.

A second wave of persecution and expulsion, which swept the country on November 10, 1938, engulfed the officials of the former regime. They were not accused on political grounds, but confronted with manufactured civil crimes. Some ranking functionaries were impeached for having sold recruits to the Spanish Loyalists, others for having forged passports. The victims were picked up by night, and thrown into filthy prison cells. There the Hlinka guardsmen beat them bloody.

It was a measure to soften up the country, and to beat it into shape for the elections which ensued on December 18, 1938. Hitler's shadow loomed over Slovakia. The country had Hitler elections. There were no booths. All the voting had to be done openly. The only question was, "Are you in favor of a prosperous future for Slovakia?" and 98 per cent of the electorate decided to be in favor of it.

The Slovakian parliament, a parody of the Reichstag, gathered in Bratislava. Dr. Tiso rode the crest. As a Catholic priest, he duly celebrated the New Year's Mass of 1939. Immediately afterward, on the holiday itself, he unloosed the next wave of terror and expulsion. Seventy thousand Czechs of the one hundred and twenty thousand living in Slovakia, most of them there twenty years, were expelled within an hour. All the Czech policemen were driven out. The Hlinka Guard assumed their duties. Unbridled looting followed. Synagogues were burned down. Terror ruled Slovakia through January and February, 1939.

Fear of the Germans restrained the central government in Prague from interfering with the rebellious province. But on March 5, 1939, the German minister in Prague surprisingly asked the shadow President Dr. Hácha and the then shadow Prime Minister Beran, why they did not stop the shameful conditions in Slovakia.

Prague was grateful for the cue. Perhaps the Nazis, after all, were better than their reputation. Four days later the government sent a few hundred gendarmes to Slovakia to restore order. This force was not very impressive, with only three or four gendarmes available for the occupation of each town, and the Hlinka Guard might have swept it away. But the Slovakian people jubilantly received the token force from Prague. In the night of March 9–10, 1939, the guardsmen disappeared from the streets, creeping into their hide-outs.

So did their leaders. Dr. Tiso fled to the Jesuit monastery in Bratislava. His henchman, Professor Tuka, was arrested and brought to the Spielberg, the ancient fortress prison in Brno. Another Slovakian gang leader, named Ducanski, escaped to Nazified Vienna. The representative of the Slovak dissidents in Prague, Sidor, jumped on the Czech bandwagon, which, it seemed, was going in the right direction. Shadow President Hácha received the prodigal son mercifully, and made him Tiso's successor as Slovakian Prime Minister. Immediately Sidor occupied the government building in Bratislava.

Two days later two ranking Nazi visitors were announced to "Prime Minister" Sidor. Dr. Seyss-Inquart, the Judas of Austria, and Gauleiter Bürckel asked His Excellency to declare Slovakia's complete independence from the Czechoslovakian state. Sidor smiled. Did the two want to double-cross him? Why, had he not himself been in Prague when Hitler's envoy had suggested that the central government take action against the Slovakian dissidents? He refused the tempting invitation. At present he acts as Slovakian Minister to the Holy See. He is not allowed to leave Rome, where he remains under Gestapo control. That is his punishment for having missed the bus.

In fact, the invitation was quite serious. The Nazis had simply once more played both ends against the middle. Czecho-slovakia was already groggy after Munch; to disunite it still further they encouraged Prague to sharp measures against Bratislava and, simultaneously, Bratislava to revolt against Prague.

Finding Sidor too naïve to take a chance, Party Comrades Seyss-Inquart and Bürckel went around the block to the Jesuit monastery. Dr. Seyss-Inquart (who as a practicing Catholic had won the friendship of the Austrian chancellor, Dr. Schuschnigg, and then delivered him to the Gestapo) had a conversation with Dr. Tiso, after having induced him to come out from hiding. But Seyss-Inquart was snubbed again. Tiso, too, knew what had happened in Prague and believed that the Nazis had còme to trap him. Most of the Slovak conspirators were too simple-minded to understand the Nazi ruses. Tiso refused the office of President of independent Slovakia that was offered to him on March 13, 1939, toward noon.

However, the Nazis do not take no for an answer. Before midnight a telegram from Hitler's chancellery was delivered to His Excellency Father Tiso, President of Slovakia, Jesuit Monastery, Bratislava. His Excellency was invited to fly immediately to Berlin. A special airplane was sent to pick him up.

At the airdrome of Staaken, near Berlin, the bewildered, middle-aged Slovakian village priest was received with all the honors due the head of a state. Was he dreaming? No, he heard distinctly a voice bellowing: "Either you declare your country's independence, or the German army will cross the Danube. We have already taken Prague. Our motorized columns are on their way to Bratislava."

The next morning, March 14, the German motorized columns stopped some five miles before Bratislava. The phony parliament was in session. It had to decide on a telegram sent by Dr. Tiso, whom a guard of honor kept safely tucked away in the royal suite of the Berlin Chancellery. This telegram read: "Either we declare our independence, or the German army will cross the Danube." Word for word, it parroted Hitler's threat.

Even the traitors and fifth columnists, assembled in Bratislava, were shocked. Fifty-four of them voted for braving invasion. But a majority of seventy-eight accepted the ultimatum, after the commander of the German troops across the river had sent a telephone message that he was not in the habit of being kept waiting.

The independence of Slovakia was declared. The first vassal joined the New Order.

While in Bratislava the parliament was still in session, in Prague the German minister called upon Dr. Hácha and demanded that he immediately order his gendarmes in Slovakia to hand over their arms to the Hlinka Guard.

"But they'll be killed," Hácha replied. "And you told me to send them."

Furthermore, the envoy continued, ignoring the reproach, Hitler wanted to see Hácha in Berlin pronto. A special sleeping car was already waiting at the station. The German gentleman clicked his heels. The noise of his patent leather shoes was drowned by hundreds of thousands of clicking heels. As Dr. Hácha stepped aboard his train to Berlin, the German army was crossing the Czech border. In Slovakia, meanwhile, a few hundred defenseless Czech gendarmes were massacred by the Hlinka guardsmen.

The Slovak gangsters believed themselves safely entrenched in power. Dr. Tiso was the figurehead. Professor Tuka, a mysterious character, acted as the power behind the throne, after the German invasion had released him from his cell in Spielberg. Alexander Mach, a professional criminal, gambler, and heel who despite his tender age of twenty-eight was already the proud owner of a rich police record, was promoted to be Minister of the Interior.

This meant that Slovakia was to be the Jewish inferno, with

Alexander Mach outdoing the German prophet of pogrom, blood-crazed Julius Streicher. The Minister of the Interior ordered all Jews of both sexes to be removed to concentration camps in the most remote, pathless, districts of the country. As long as this measure could not be completely carried out, the Jews were tortured in their home communities. The younger men were conscripted for labor service. On one occasion they were forbidden to work with their shirts off, so as "not to expose themselves to sunburn"; in fact, to hide the scars from their overseers'—Hlinka guardsmen's—lashes. The Nürnberg laws were fully introduced. All Jews and half-Jews must wear the yellow David star on their coats. They must not use bicycles or telephones. They were forbidden to leave their towns without a special permit. If they obtained this permit, they were still not allowed in trains. They had to hitch-hike. Bratislava Jews were moved to camps in Trnava, Zilina, Prešov, and Spišska Nova Ves, to "purify" the capital. All their property, including furniture and clothing, had to be left behind, to be distributed among Hlinka guardsmen. A group of these gangsters attacked the Jews' transport on its way to the camps, and robbed them of the few belongings they had been permitted to carry along.

The terror in Slovakia is particularly cruel, because it is the terror of weakness and of fear. The ruling gang is well aware of the fact that 95 per cent of the population stand against them. Unceasing propaganda drives are of no avail. The secretary general of the Hlinka party ordered local secretaries to summon "reorganization meetings." The main task of these meetings was "to remove disturbing elements and replace some worn-out functionaries with new ones." But the house cleaning did not come off, since no one appeared at the reorganization meetings.

Dr. Tiso organized a nation-wide campaign in his own favor. His personal mouthpiece, *Slovenska Pravda*, daily publishes votes of confidence in him. The voters are mostly pupils in elementary schools. The president wanted also to enlist the Bratislava radio in his personal propaganda service. But here he met with strange resistance. The manager of the station informed Tiso bluntly that the German legation did not believe in "personalized" transmissions.

The president of Slovakia heard the death knell ringing. Of course, he is entirely dependent on the German legation. But it is extremely difficult to guess its wishes and whims. The German legation in the miniature capital of Bratislava has a staff of three hundred gentlemen, each of them having his own connections, favorites, and interests. Every Nazi desk clerk behaves like a colonial governor, and every Slovakian cabinet minister is assiduously at his beck and call.

Minister of the Interior Alexander Mach enjoys the most intimate relations with the masters. He is engaged in a murderous battle against his chief, Dr. Tiso, and it is said that he has the influence of Hans Ludlin, the German minister, on his side. In fact, the two are frequently seen together in the night clubs and brothels of Bratislava. On the morning after one of those escapades, Minister Ludlin decorated Mach with the high award of the German Eagle with the ribbon. The third in this unholy trinity is Mr. Karamasin, secretary of state, representing the German minority in the government.

Recently Dr. Tiso was forced to make a pilgrimage to Berlin to save his regime, and perhaps his life. He had Professor Tuka, the mystery man, who is his pillar of power and by the same token his most dangerous rival, also come to Berlin. Together, they petitioned for an audience with Hitler. After cooling their heels in Berlin they were admitted to the All Highest's presence in his Russian headquarters. In his usual fashion he roared for two hours. He was most displeased with Slovakia. Her participation in the Russian crusade was a ghastly failure. She had not fulfilled her obligation to feed a few hundred thousand German soldiers. She was still poisoned by the Bolshevist spirit. On the whole, she was a liability to the New Order.

Tiso promised that things would take a turn for the better. Professor Tuka just smiled. His chances improve with the increasing confusion. A honeyed communiqué was published, in which the Führer paid glowing tribute to his faithful Slovakia. Moreover, an agreement was signed: The Slovakian army was to be incorporated with the Wehrmacht. All laws and decrees of the Slovakian government were to be published in the German language. The Slovak parliament was to be enlarged by twenty-four Nazi deputies, who need not be chosen by the people. Its legislative power was to be under the control of the German secretary of state, Karamasin. But this is only a temporary measure, since the parliamentary system is to be abolished January 1, 1943, so as to emphasize the complete break with the past. The border line with Germany will be made "invisible." In the end Slovakia will be another German *Gau*. The New Order devours its own children.

In the interview between Hitler and Tiso that doomed Slovakia, not one word was said about Sub-Carpathian Russia. This omission was not accidental. The small strip of land with the complicated name, at the eastern tip of Slovakia, is not mentioned in polite Nazi society. The reason is that this miniature country with an area of seventy-seven hundred square miles, inhabited by a handful of people—four hundred thousand, all told—is the first and so far the only piece of subjugated Europe which has won back its independence.

Sub-Carpathia was torn from Czechoslovakia at Munich. A puppet government was set up. Amazingly, another Catholic priest of Dr. Tiso's color, Pater Volosin, found himself ready to play Pétain to the Huzuls, the Ukrainians, the Slovaks, the Gypsies, who, together with a sprinkling of Ger-

mans, Hungarians, and Rumanians, make up the population of
the world's most picturesque puppet state. He installed his
government in a farmhouse in the village of Chust. The
schoolhouse was converted into the German legation, the
Japanese consulate was billeted in the home of the parish
priest, since the Yellow Empire was the only power that cared
to enter into diplomatic relations with the midget state of Sub-
Carpathia. The Japanese knew why they cared to do so.
They established an anti-Russian spy center in the remote
mountain village, and they paid Foreign Secretary Révay, a
former member of the Hungarian parliament, a monthly al-
lowance equivalent to two dollars and fifty cents for the right
to use Sub-Carpathian passports for their crew of spies. It
sounds like an E. Phillips Oppenheim story, but it is the absolute truth.

Sub-Carpathian Russia—an odd name, since the country is
entirely unconnected with Russia proper—became a Fascist
stronghold. Father Volosin set up his "disciplinary detachments," a kind of Carpatho-Russian S.A., called the "Sič."
With mysterious speed he collected arms, uniforms, and volunteers from Germany and Hungary—men who were willing
to give their last drop of blood for their adopted fatherland,
whose name they could, unfortunately, hardly pronounce.

The idyll lasted a few months. When Hitler's hordes invaded Prague, the Hungarian hyenas following him found
the moment propitious for a little picking on their own account. At that time Horthy, Hungary's regent, was not yet
ready to brave the British Empire. He confined himself to attacking Pater Volosin. He was sure that his Hungarian detachment in the Sič would open the gates of the country with
the unpronounceable name to him.

But the crisp air in the Carpathian Mountains, it seemed,
had worked a miracle on the mercenaries. They refused to
betray their funny fatherland. Indeed, they threw themselves
into the path of the Hungarian legions. A few detachments of

Czechoslovak troops, who had been left behind, forgotten in the general turmoil of their country's demobilization, helped. Strange to say, the mixed population of natives also assisted. The resistance of this oddly assorted soldiery lasted until the middle of April, 1939. Then the Hungarians were masters of the situation. Pater Volosin and his Foreign Secretary Révay disappeared. At present they are peddling passports among refugees in the Levant.

The Hungarian rule in Sub-Carpathian Russia was formed on the Nazi model. People were shut up in concentration camps. The hangmen worked overtime. Corpses were left swinging from the gallows to teach the people an impressive lesson. The people in God-forsaken Sub-Carpathian Russia, however, seemed too primitive to understand the lesson. They abandoned their wretched huts and took to the woods. Before long, guerrilla bands numbered hundreds of determined men. To begin with they had not even weapons. Some of them fought simply with an ax or a stout cudgel against Hungarians armed with rifles, machine guns, and grenades. They realized that they could not continue their fight without better equipment. That is why they, for a time, confined themselves to assailing single Hungarian soldiers or small groups, taking their weapons. It was the hard way of equipping an army, but the great arsenal of democracy lay far across the sea. Besides, one may doubt whether the Huzuls of Carpathia knew of distant America, and the lend-lease bill.

After a time, however, every guerrilla soldier was armed with a Hungarian rifle and a few hand grenades, and had a generous supply of ammunition. Now savage warfare started in earnest. A few soldiers from the Czechoslovakian army officered the guerrillas. Every night the hills and valleys of Sub-Carpathian Russia resounded with exploding hand grenades, barking machine guns, and blown-up ammunition dumps.

There is no military manual teaching the strategy of guerrilla fighting. It is a natural strategy. The men lie hidden in the dense forests until their scouts report the whereabouts of an enemy detachment. Under the cover of darkness the guerrillas then creep toward the enemy column and surround it. In ghostly silence they fall upon the sentries and annihilate them. Then they shoot the surprised Hungarian soldiers, who a moment earlier were snoring in bivouac. The death of a sleeping enemy is proof of a guerrilla fighter's skill and quick wit. Chivalry, it seems, has different meanings in different zones. In the Sub-Carpathian wilderness it means killing the enemy, picking up his weapon, sometimes also his food ration, and getting away before his companions recover from their shock and surprise.

Herr Hitler, too, was shocked when he heard the first reports of what was going on in the Carpathian Mountains. He expressed what he thought of Horthy, his incompetent Hungarian vassal, in a single short and ugly word, and sent the 167th Mountain Brigade, Tyrolese crack troops, to clean up the patch of land the Hungarians seemed unable to police.

The 167th Mountain Brigade distinguished itself but suffered heavy losses. Whole units were routed—inflicting, it is true, heavy damage on the guerrillas as well. But this damage was more than made up for by the fact that many Tyrolese sharpshooters felt so much at home in the Carpathian Mountains, closely resembling their own Alps, that they changed sides. Hitler had never asked these people of Austria whether they wanted to fight his war of aggression; and as long as they can live a hardy mountain life and hunt the chamois, or for that matter the enemy, they care not who this enemy may be. Besides, it is an established fact that many Austrian soldiers have accounts to settle with their Prussian officers.

A trickle of obsolete airplanes is Hitler's last contribution to the fight in Sub-Carpathian Russia. For the rest, he shows no inclination to lose another brigade. The Hungarians are on their own. In fact, they hold only the towns of Munkács and

Užhorod. The mountains are free. If the flag of liberty does not wave from their peaks, the reason is only that Sub-Carpathian Russia has no flag.

Prince Aimone, Duke of Spoleto, still drinks his customary afternoon cocktail in the bar of Rome's Hotel Esplanade. In Croatia some three hundred to three hundred and forty thousand patriots were exterminated. These two facts are intimately related. Croatian patriots refuse to accept the Italian princeling as their king, whereas the latter shows little inclination to have the number of murdered men in his kingdom augmented by one more—himself. Adolf and Benito did him a disservice in forcing the crown of Croatia on him when they were busy carving up Yugoslavia. His recently anointed Majesty has never dared to visit his country. His rule began in exile. Dr. Ante Pavelić, Croatia's little Führer, refused to assume responsibility for the comic-opera king's "very precious life," should His Majesty actually cross the border of his country.

Inside Croatia, the shadow kingdom was proclaimed by a handful of Nazi and Fascist agents when the German invaders were already on the outskirts of Zagreb, the country's capital, and the military fate of Yugoslavia seemed sealed. From the outset the regime of the absentee King has had no sort of popular backing. It is entirely dependent for its existence on Nazi bayonets, and on its own terrorist gang, the Ustachi.

The Ustachi, at present numbering about twenty-five thousand, are the counterpart of the Hlinka guardsmen in Slovakia. Their staff is composed of a gang of professional killers and gunmen who received their training in Germany and Italy. Their leader is Croatia's *pogacnik* (Duce), Dr. Ante Pavelić, the man who organized the murder of King Alexander of Yugoslavia and the French Foreign Secretary Louis Barthou, in Marseilles. Except for a very short time, during which he represented a Zagreb constituency in parliament, Dr. Pavelić has never lived in his own country. He has spent most of his life as an expatriate in Italy, partly in Mussolini's inner circle, partly in various insane asylums. His friends call him a romantic, because he invented the theory that the Croatians are not Slavonic, but the last descendants of the ancient Goths. "We fully accept the German thesis that we are only a minority," he told the *Deutsche Allgemeine Zeitung*, the mouthpiece of the Wilhelmstrasse, on assuming power, "and as such we form a part of the great German people." Unfortunately, he had to use the services of an interpreter in making this statement to the Berlin newspaper. Dr. Pavelić does not speak one word of his great people's language.

He estimated that his following in the country amounted to all of one per cent of the four and a half million Croats. Throughout their political history the Croats were almost unanimously united in the Peasants' Party, founded by the erratic genius Stephen Radić and led, after Radić's death, by Dr. Vladko Maček, whom Croat people came to revere as their nation's father. Dr. Maček (today a man of sixty-six, if still alive) was vice-premier in the Belgrade government at the time of the German invasion. He gave up his office to be among his own people during their grave test. Three times the Nazis invited him to Berlin, suggesting that he form a Quisling government, but he steadfastly refused. From his fourth visit to Germany Dr. Maček never returned. The most optimistic guess as to his fate is that the father of the Croats is held in a German concentration camp.

Croatia was declared independent. Dr. Pavelić's hour struck. He assumed dictatorship as Fascism's lackey. But the passive resistance of the only man the peasants recognize as representing them; the scarcity of food and the requisitioning of crops that followed the German invasion; the loss of all Dalmatia and of other parts of the country to Italy and the fact that even Hungary was encouraged to help itself to a slice; the continued presence of German and Italian troops in the country to which independence had been promised; and, last but not least, the natural, indisputable affinity felt by the Croatians like all the Slavonic people for their big Russian brother—all these elements led to growing discontent and outbursts of guerrilla warfare throughout the country.

Pavelić hoped to find support among the clergy, but only a few country priests actually favor him. Moreover, the Vatican does not recognize Pavelić as the *pogacnik*. At his audience with the Pope he had to line up with other Croatian pilgrims.

Pavelić has been for a long time mentally unbalanced. Now the snubs he constantly receives have entirely crazed him and have turned him into a vest-pocket Nero. But one cannot laugh him off: the Yugoslav government in London has listed hundreds of thousands of casualties due to his reign of terror.

The Serbian minority in Croatia suffers worst. A large part of this minority lives in settlements of its own. The town of Banja Luka, a Bosnian industrial center where twelve thousand Serbs dwelt before the war, was known as a Serbian island. Pavelić sent his Ustachi there for a purge. "Not a single Serbian hog survives in Banja Luka!" he boasted a few days later. His terminology is most revealing. "Serbian hog" is the term Dr. Goebbels uses for the gallant nation. It was, incidentally, a popular expression in Imperial Germany during the First World War.

When the entire Serbian population of Pihac, in Bosnia, was similarly routed, the Serbs, forming a third of the country's inhabitants, organized their resistance. Soon Dr. Pavelić complained to a reporter of the *Popolo di Roma* that his Ustachi were losing some of their best men in fighting Serb rebels hidden in the woods and throughout the countryside of Croatia. "But our men are cleaning up the forests," he continued, "and attacking the Serb rebels in their hideouts. Despite our heavy losses, final victory is near. The million and a half Serbs who live within our borders must adapt themselves to the new conditions, or disappear."

The Adriatic, the fishermen say, holds more blood than water. To assist their puppet regime, the Italian navy frequently shells the rebellious coastal towns and villages. This assistance, however, is anything but reliable. Mussolini is fed up with his imitator's definitely established inability to subdue Croatia. Violently, the controlled Fascist press assails Dr. Pavelić. There is little doubt that his days are numbered. Unless a bullet gets him first—and there are many potential assassins in his own bodyguard of sixty men, the *pogacnik* realizes—he will receive an invitation to Rome or to Berlin. There a desk clerk will tell him that he is through. Regretfully, Adolf will have to partition another country with Benito. Independent Croatia is doomed to premature death. Again, in giving birth to a state, the New Order only begot an abortion.

CHAPTER SIX

ROGUES' GALLERY:
THE MASTERS

For the Germans, those thieves and incendiaries who muti-
late infants and rape women; for the Germans who are able
to gloat over the sinking of a ship filled with innocent passengers; for the Germans who use poison gas, mercy would
be treason to one's country and to mankind. An eye for an
eye and a tooth for a tooth. A war of extermination must
be met by a war of extermination.—BENITO MUSSOLINI in *Il
Popolo d'Italia*, April 29, 1915.

IT IS no coincidence that the name of the general commanding
the German army of occupation in Yugoslavia should be
Dunkelman; rather it is a revelation. Dunkelman means "dark
man." The general could not be more appropriately named.
He boasts of having "shot bare" the mountains of the country
entrusted to his care. He is the proud executioner of some
three hundred thousand people, the overwhelming majority
of whom were, if sons and daughters of a rebellious nation,
noncombatants. He won military glory in leading seven divisions, some of them equipped with flame throwers, and a
couple of tank units, against the patriotic rebels who com-
menced their fight with a few discarded and damaged small
arms, abandoned by the regular Yugoslavian army in its retreat, and who continued fighting with the tanks and flame
throwers they wrested from the invaders. In an interview with

the *Deutscher Soldat,* a German soldiers' magazine, General
Dunkelman complained of the neglected roads in Yugoslavia,
which hampered the advance of tanks, and of the drain on the
Luftwaffe by the exigencies of the Eastern Front. "We had
only a handful of Stukas," he said. "However, they sufficed
to raze every Yugoslav town, except Belgrade." "And Belgrade?" the interviewer asked. He noted a voluptuous smile
on General Dunkelman's "sharp-cut eagle's face." "Belgrade
will follow," the general answered confidentally. "I will have
to blow up the town, if these Serbian hogs do not give in."

No doubt General Dunkelman will be as good as his word.
Let him only snap his fingers, and up goes the capital of
Yugoslavia. All the cellars of the official buildings are loaded
with dynamite. True, outside the town of Belgrade his nuisance value is less significant. In the eighth month after the
outbreak of the revolution, the Serbian guerrillas have won
back almost their entire country. They are in control of virtually the whole mountain area west of the Morava River and
as far north as the Sava River. The Germans hold firmly Belgrade alone, and much less firmly some points along the life
line of the Balkans, the Belgrade-Salonika railroad.

Actually, General Dunkelman's army suffered a crushing
defeat at the hands of the Chetniks. He can thank his stars
that bigger events on more important political and military
fronts overshadowed the liberation of most of Yugoslavia. But
the lesson should not be lost on the world. Without minimizing the superhuman effort and the total contempt of death the
Serbian fighters for freedom have shown, it is now an established fact that at least some of the German armies of occupation are second-rate outfits, led by third-rate martinets.

Not one of the monocled, spur-clinking, saber-rattling generals commanding the various armies of occupation has won
military distinction in this war. The undisputably brilliant feats
of the German army have been achieved by a few hard-hitting,
fast-scheming, mechanized-brained conquerors, wading through

streams of blood and, after every success, busying themselves instantly with new assaults. None of the commanders of occupation armies belongs to the hierarchy of the High Command. Inside their own circle they are half-forgotten men. That probably explains the boisterous, clamorous showmanship they display, once they become almighty in countries lying prostrate at their feet. They embody the German inferiority complex, one of the principal reasons for the mushroom growth of Nazism within a twisted nation. Residing in royal palaces, thriving on eight-course dinners, occasionally demonstrating their power by mass executions of hostages, they certainly try hard to forget that they are simply tolerated by those exercising the real power.

"Tolerance" is not in their dictionary, perhaps because it has an ominous sound in their ears. Within a few months General Dunkelman has signed more death sentences than probably any other man on earth, Gestapo Boss Heinrich Himmler and his right-hand man Reinhard Heydrich, the present Protector of Bohemia-Moravia, excluded. In the interview already quoted, Dunkelman complained also of the pressure of his work. "When the people of Belgrade admire me riding my white charger," he stated with becoming modesty, "to have a little exercise in the morning, they do not know that I have already been sitting at my desk since dawn, putting my signature under hundreds of — — — —." (Four words cut by the German censor.)

Dunkelman's counterpart in Norway, General von Falkenhorst, a rigid disciplinarian, maintains order among his troops with the same iron fist with which he tries to crush the smoldering revolution in the country. Falkenhorst is not exactly a run-of-the-mill Nazi general. He is the scion of one of the oldest Prussian warrior tribes, and he leaves little doubt about his contempt for what he calls the civilians in brown shirts. This, of course, by no means indicates potential hostility toward the Nazi regime. The group of ranking German generals waiting for the moment of Hitler's downfall, eager to hasten this moment a little, and ready to establish military dictatorship, has never existed except in the imagination of English and American wishful thinkers. Why should they care for politics? They despise mankind, the German portion included. To them a good batman is more important than a good Chancellor of the Reich. Besides, forming a state within the state, they have the time of their life under the prevailing system.

Advancements were never as rapid. According to German military tradition, after a victorious war a conquering war lord was made field marshal. About a year ago Hitler advanced fifteen generals at one time to the rank of field marshal, although his war was not yet quite won. Moreover, money, always a nightmare to men in uniform, is plentiful. The commander of the army of occupation exacts from the Bank of Norway a daily tribute of six million kroner for the upkeep of his troops. For his own personal upkeep, a Prussian soldier of the old stamp needs no money. Why should he? Herr von Falkenhorst paid no rent for his residence in the Norwegian Crown Prince's palace. No bills were ever submitted from the Grand Hotel for catering to his table. The hotel's wine cellar was simply confiscated, lest his bibulous excellency freeze in the cold northern climate. Heil Hitler! It is wonderful while it lasts.

But General von Falkenhorst proved his sober judgment in recognizing that it might not last. All of a sudden, in September, 1941, he washed his hands of easy living. He abandoned the Crown Prince's palace (immediately Gauleiter Terboven moved in) he gave the chef in the Grand Hotel a tip of ten occupation marks, and left Oslo altogether. His headquarters are now established in Bergen on the west coast, the center of the forbidden zone. The general, it seems, awaits the British counter invasion.

So does his army. But the German soldiery does not await the counter blow with unmixed relish. At the next encounter, they know, the odds will be heavily against them. If the reports of their own invasion are true, they had some fifty thousand fifth columnists to help them. Now they are living among three million pro-British fifth columnists, 99 per cent of the Norwegian people. They have wrought havoc in the country. But they are snubbed in return, cold-shouldered, ostracized, and driven into near insanity. They know that not one of them will get away alive, if they lose. Even their acts of barbarism are of no avail. The haphazard killing of civilians is no longer a pleasant way to let off steam. It is a short cut to Falkenhorst's wrath.

"The situation is too tense for indulging in pleasantries with the civil population," read an order of the day, released by the general on October 25, 1941. One of the soldiers of the German garrison in the village of Loding, two miles from Bodö, did not listen attentively enough. The morning after the warning to behave themselves had been issued to the troops, this man—whose name is not on record—encountered two little girls, aged ten and eleven, returning from a berry-picking expedition. Even the German monster has a sweet tooth. "Let me have your berries," the soldier demanded. Panic-stricken, the children fled. But there is no escape from the army of occupation. The soldier caught up with the younger child, and thrust his bayonet into her back. The other child got away and told the story at home. Her mother wrote a letter to his excellency the general commanding the army of occupation. Then the incredible happened: The mighty man came personally all the way from Bergen to the distant village of Loding. He reviewed the local garrison, leading by the hand an eleven-year-old girl. "No, no, no," said the child time and again, as she stared into the soldiers' ugly faces. All of a sudden she screamed. Then she fainted.

The slayer was identified. Falkenhorst had him handcuffed.

"But not too tightly," he ordered. "The fellow must be able to use his hands. He shall dig his own grave." He gave exact instructions about the grave's dimensions. Obviously, it was not the first time that Falkenhorst had given such instructions. Unperturbed, with a faint smile around his lips, he watched the execution. "Good shot," he said. The man had tumbled straight into the self-dug hole.

There were two epilogues to this affair. First, the cameraman whom Falkenhorst, like every other German general of consequence, has on his staff had to make a picture of his chief kissing the eleven-year-old Norwegian girl goodbye. Second, the local commander of the garrison in Loding, Captain Rudolf Becker, was thrown into the old Bergen fortification Bergenhus, where recalcitrant or incompetent German officers whose men get out of hand are kept in prison. At present fifty-one gentlemen of various ranks, from lieutenant to colonel, are crammed into the seven cells of Bergenhus.

There is only one retreat on the part of General von Falkenhorst on record. It happened, unfortunately, on August 24, 1941. On this evening the general and his staff entered a restaurant in Steinkjaer which was well filled with Norwegian patrons. The waiter appeared with the menu. Falkenhorst's aide-de-camp, Colonel Bomburg, ordered, not a cocktail, but that the radio should be turned on at once. It was the time for victory news from the Russian front. "The army of Colonel General von Leeb has taken . . ." the radio blared. A few Norwegian patrons called for their checks.

"Impertinence!" shouted Colonel Bomburg.

His chief quieted him. "Let them go," he said audibly enough. Falkenhorst cares neither for pub brawls, nor for von Leeb's triumphs. The two heroes have long engaged in a race for promotion. Since the latter was made a colonel general, Falkenhorst emerged second best.

The patrons in the restaurant in Steinkjaer took Falkenhorst's word for encouragement. Immediately every civilian got ready to leave the blaring radio and the boisterous officers to themselves. They did not get away easily. Colonel Bomburg, two hundred and fifty pounds of virility, blocked the exits. He had to be softly but unmistakably removed from his strategic position by the barkeeper. At this moment Falkenhorst rose to his full height of six feet four.

"Where is the telephone booth?" he thundered in the general uproar.

The fight started as a pub brawl and spread throughout the town. The German officers pursued the retreating Norwegian guests with revolver butts as far as the water front, where a few longshoremen came to the aid of the victims. This was the moment for Colonel Bomburg to call off the offensive. The German gentlemen returned to the restaurant, which was a shambles. The damage was later assessed at two thousand dollars. They arrested the restaurant owner and the barkeeper; both were subsequently condemned to long prison terms for inciting unrest. But at the moment the officers could not find their general. Falkenhorst did not reappear until perfect calm reigned in the devastated saloon. As if unaware of the havoc around him, he smiled cryptically. "Lucy must be asleep," he explained. "Her telephone does not answer."

The country does not sleep. The British raid on the Lofoten Islands brought some interesting information to light. The raiders confiscated two secret orders, both signed by General von Falkenhorst. "With the exception of the members of the Nasjonal Samling," reads the first order, "all Norwegian organizations and parties, and particularly the representatives of big business and industry, remain, now as before, pro-British and anti-German." In the same vein the second order continued: "Appearance would indicate that the temper and attitude of the Norwegian people have recently stiffened against our endeavors."

General von Falkenhorst's principal problem is not the enslavement of the Norwegian people—this he solves with his left hand—but the really terrifying deterioration of his own troops.

Listening to the radio has long been a prerogative of the officers and soldiers of the army of occupation. Now this privilege is gone. Falkenhorst discovered that many of his men listened to London, instead of paying due attention to the German victory bulletins. His military police, a small but thoroughly efficient gang, outdoing even the Gestapo, recently caught an officer saying: "Perhaps we can beat the Russians, but the Americans will lick us once more." This officer, Captain von Kugelgen, was brought to his supreme commander. After a short but animated conversation, he went back to his barracks and shot himself with his service revolver.

· The German soldiers are not quite as rigorously excluded from intercourse with the population as their boycotted officers. Among the little people personal ties develop more easily. General von Falkenhorst, a confirmed bachelor, does not care for personal ties. Living in the barbed-wire ivory tower of his headquarters, he does not like his soldiers to mingle with the mob. "I am informed," his order of November 22, 1941, reads, "that in German fortification projects, in which Norwegian labor is employed, it has been a common occurrence for the soldiers to come up one by one to Norse workers, and ask eagerly for the latest news from London. With those who are known to have committed this outrage I have already dealt. I warn German soldiers against repeating this crime." In further punishment he decreed that cigarettes should not be permitted to the soldiers engaged on the fortification projects involved for three months.

The soldiers shrugged. They have long been accustomed to buying such necessities and little luxuries as they can no longer obtain by looting the black markets. Times have changed for them, and not for the better. Only a little while ago the German soldiers were the main purveyors in the black trade, and some of them made a pretty penny out of

reselling their booty. Many of the soldiers of occupation
(who, indeed, are not the flower of German soldiery but
supernumerary oldsters) deposited their earnings in Norwegian banks, which seemed safer to them than the present German banking system. They were shocked when their beloved
general recently addressed a letter to the Norwegian Bank
Association prohibiting deposits by German soldiers. Such
accounts, he ordered, must immediately be discontinued. The
money must be returned to the depositors with a recommendation that it be transferred to Germany. The general, it
appears, was certain that such a recommendation by the Norwegian bank would impress the holders of small savings
among his troops more strongly than his own order could.
Falkenhorst is a shrewd commander; he knows the soldiers'
true nature. In conversation he likes to compare himself with
Sir Archibald Wavell.

But he is in a tougher spot than the British soldier-philos-
opher has ever been. Sir Archibald has never had to cope
with mischief such as occurred in Trondheim, where Falkenhorst had to have sixteen German soldiers court-martialed
for consistent stealing of petrol from army canisters during
a period of eight months, which they sold to eight Norwegian taxi owners and four truck drivers (arrested with them).

The toughest situation Falkenhorst has found himself in
materialized toward the end of June, 1941, when open mutiny broke out in the Kvarven fort, which dominates the
town of Bergen. General von Falkenhorst himself was in
grave danger. But he rose to the challenge. Armed only with
a horsewhip, he entered the rebellious fort, followed by his
staff officers. The gentlemen of the staff fired. A few soldiers
fired back. The general's whip lashed their backs. The mutiny was quickly suppressed. During the night, some of the
mutineers' bodies were dumped from the hill into the waters
of Bergen Fjord. Next morning a few fallen officers were
interred with military honors. Falkenhorst had to suppress

tears of pity for his gallant young comrades, the victims, he said, of a British night raid. Behind his tears, some saw him smiling. A disciple of Nietzsche although he probably has never read a word of the master's writing, he likes to live dangerously.

His men, it seems, do not share his predilection. Norwegian observers report that a terrible wail went up from the ranks of the German army of occupation when some regiments had to leave the hospitable land for the hazardous Russian front. Not all those dispatched obeyed the order. For months the whole countryside of Norway has been plastered with this poster: "It is hereby made known that no one is allowed to aid German deserters with either shelter, food, clothing, or in any other way. Whoever discovers such deserters must immediately warn the sheriff or the nearest police station. Whoever acts in defiance of this order will be taken before a German military court, and punished according to German law." It did not take Falkenhorst's flourishing signature on the poster to make the Norwegian people realize what punishment according to German law entails. No one will risk helping German deserters, who were arrogant toughs before their "morale" broke. Only those German deserters in Falkenhorst's realm who pose as British parachutists have any chance of help from the local population. The Norwegians cannot always make out whether the parachutist's English is correct. Their own is certainly not. But all three million of them know the words of "God Save the King."

There is more difference between General von Falkenhorst and Lieutenant General Alexander Ernst, Baron Falkenhausen, than one or two syllables in their names. The latter, commander of the army of occupation in Belgium, distinguishes himself by a quality rare enough among German war lords. He has a distinct sense of humor. His preferred newspaper is *La Libre Belgique*, the country's foremost underground sheet, which comes by mail and lies every morning on his desk.

Baron Falkenhausen likes to repeat the anti-Nazi jokes the *Libre Belgique* prints as a regular feature, particularly when the laugh is on Hitler. "Every family should be proud to sacrifice at least one son for the great cause," the *Brüsseler Zeitung*, the official German mouthpiece, recently wrote. "Righto," commented the *Libre Belgique*. "Let the family Schicklgruber set the example."

This silly joke is important only because Baron Falkenhausen repeated it frequently and with gusto at his convivial gatherings. His many friends and admirers find his insouciance charming. Politically, it has no significance. Alexander Ernst, Baron Falkenhausen, lieutenant general, works as faithfully as any one for Mr. Schicklgruber.

The baron is probably the most important of the German military dictators. His province includes not only Belgium but also the forbidden zone of France, the rich coal and iron district in the northwest. The harshness of the system he has established in the forbidden zone is unparalleled even in Poland. The civilian population was evacuated. Only the miners remain, and they are confined to their homes and the pits. A special guard of S.S. sharpshooters maintains order. Not a dozen people have visited the forbidden zone and returned to tell the tale. Occasionally, the general himself inspects the district. Invariably, he gets drunk on his return. Falkenhausen's is a tough job. It took an army of one million men to police Belgium with her eight million inhabitants. The Russian campaign drained off his troops. Only fifty thousand remained in Belgium. This, at least, was the report reaching London. The English very rightly suspect underground reports from Belgium. They may well have been planted to lure a small British expeditionary force into a trap.

The Belgian people, for their part, are not afraid of German secret service ruses. Their own intelligence, comprising

eight million Belgian men, women, and children, outwits the
Gestapo every day. A favorite test to ferret out the actual
strength of Falkenhausen's force is to assail German soldiers,
ambling, after dark, in the peaceful paths of the Bois de la
Cambre, the Central Park of Brussels. If the Germans are
present in great numbers, a free-for-all ensues. Otherwise, the
heroes in field gray make off.

Herr von Falkenhausen needs patience for his job. In
Liége, Belgian patriots shot at a platoon of his parading soldiers in full daylight. At dusk, posters appeared on the bill-
boards of the town—one was pasted up next to the *Kommandantur,* the German local garrison command. "Sabotage
acts have been committed in the suburbs of Liége. The anonymous perpetrators of these dastardly crimes are hereby warned
that, if such acts are renewed, the German army will see itself compelled to evacuate Belgium once and for all." German soldiers, the simpletons, were jubilant as they read the
posters. Belgian passers-by smiled grimly. They realized that
Ulenspiegel, the great patriot, the soul and the wit of resistance, whose identity cannot yet be revealed, was having another field day.

Baron Falkenhausen did not lose his equanimity. In the
Nazified *Nouveau Journal* he stated simply: "It is regrettable
that many Belgians still refuse to believe that Germany will
conclude the war successfully. They are always insisting that
America's industrial might will decide the war. I beg to dis-
agree." Off the record, but not inaudibly to the Belgian underground press, he said: "Don't kill anyone. Skin them. It
hurts longer." That was the send-off he gave to the men of
the special squads of the Gestapo, who hurriedly came from
Berlin to avenge the incidents in Liége.

The general is impartial to friend and foe. One day in September, 1941, his second in command, General Reeder, had
a brilliant idea. Why not, he suggested, dismiss all the public
functionaries over sixty? The older generation, as it is, is lost

for the New Order. If they were to be forced out of office, the most important jobs in the country would be free for younger elements, of course for Quislings. Falkenhausen agreed to test this regulation in the province of Limburg. It was a great success. Ninety-two mayors were forced into retirement for having reached the age limit, and hundreds of other functionaries had to follow them. Opportunities were open for all the turncoats of Limburg. Nazification advanced in huge strides. Much encouraged, General Reeder made a second suggestion, to extend the measure over all Belgium. "We could call it the Reeder law," he added. With these words he overreached himself. Falkenhausen, himself a modest man, does not care for subordinates who want to steal the show. "Let's call it the Reeder law," he consented, "to recall your services." Then he suddenly asked: "How old are you? Sixty-one, aren't you, old boy?"

Alexander Ernst, Baron Falkenhausen, himself has deserved a high medal. Indeed, he introduced an innovation that has spread like wildfire all over occupied Europe. He is the inventor of the system of hostage shooting. It happened this way:

One Wednesday night in April, 1941, unknown assailants shot and killed under cover of darkness the Rexist (Belgian Nazi) leader of Tournai. Three German police officers heard the shooting, and went into the street "to prevent further incidents." They did not prevent, but invited them. They were themselves shot at. The slayers escaped. One man was arrested and immediately executed, although he could prove his innocence. This barbaric measure infuriated Tournai. Two German police officers were killed during the following night. Then the Gestapo rounded up practically all the town. But even their third degree failed to persuade the prisoners to confess.

Here Baron Falkenhausen stepped in. He ordered: "Keep the twenty-five most prominent captives. Then the entire population of the Tournai district will feel forced to co-operate in clearing up the cowardly and senseless deed." But no one in Tournai felt forced to cooperate with the German bloodhounds. So the baron announced: "If the perpetrators do not report to German or Belgian officials or if an investigation now being carried out does not discover their identity within ten days, the hostages will be shot."

Thus the system was introduced. Being a careful man, Falkenhausen chose to test it a few times before recommending it to Berlin for general use. To be sure, the twenty-five of Tournai were stood against the wall. But only when another twenty-two hostages had been shot in Brussels, and a mere eleven in Liége, did the baron feel certain that his system worked. Both the mass executions, incidentally, were carried out on August 1, 1941.

The general hates Paris. Therefore he is the right man to rule it. He is not fooled by the Ville Lumière as are so many of his German compatriots, who invaded Paris as conquerors and were instantly enslaved by the great whore Babylon. Residing in the Hôtel Crillon, once the headquarters of sight-seeing American millionaires, looking out of his windows onto the Place de la Concorde, the world's most beautiful square, surrounded by French courtiers, who vie with one another for his every smile, Joachim Heinrich Otto von Stülpnagel remained unsmiling. He rarely shows his raven face to the people of Paris. Perhaps he treasures his life too highly to expose it in the restive streets. Certainly he disdains Paris too deeply. Herr von Stülpnagel, commander of the German army of occupation in France, could play the Roi Soleil. Thousands of Parisian ladies and gentlemen of easy virtue would make life pleasant to him. But he leaves such nonsense to big, fat Göring, who has established his grass-widower's quarters in the Palais du Luxembourg. For Stülpnagel nothing counts but duty. He is the typical Prussian provincial of the old stamp. He loves a mug of beer, and hates extravagance in any form. He seems ill fitted for the Nazi world of gamblers and speculators, in which every one takes while the taking is good. In their intimate circles the smart boys with the swastika deride the old war horse, whose military career has been neither brilliant nor distinguished. Actually, he owes his career to the timely death of his uncle, a retired major named Killisch von Horn, who owned the *Berliner Börsenzeitung*, the German Colonel Blimp's own paper. Having inherited the newspaper, and having proved entirely unable to cope with it, Herr von Stülpnagel put it at the disposition of the Nazis. This occurred before Hitler's advent to power. The Führer showed his gratitude by promising Stülpnagel a luscious command in the next world war.

The post of commander of the army of occupation in France was considered a *buen retiro*. Paris teems with intrigue, political and otherwise, but Herr von Stülpnagel takes no part in it. He plots neither with Darlan nor with Laval, and he is entirely unconcerned as to the future of the New Order. His is a policing job, which he carries out most efficiently. His record includes the bloody suppression of the first upflare of revolt, on Armistice Day, 1940, and the gruesome mass execution of hostages, of which there is at present no end to be seen. Modestly, Stülpnagel assessed the victims of his execution orders at three hundred and three men and women up to the end of 1941. Next year, he believed, would be a better shooting season.

Stülpnagel's total lack of political interest is only offset by his rabid anti-Semitism. Early in December, 1941, he fined the Jews in the occupied zone of France one billion francs. Questioned why he suddenly decided to take such a far-reaching measure, he replied emphatically: "Why, haven't the Jews killed our Redeemer?" He had to be informed by Otto Abetz, Hitler's ambassador in Paris, that Nazi neopaganism no longer uses such obsolete arguments. But sullenly the general insisted: "Every sergeant knows it."

And to the man who rules Paris, the bleeding heart of Europe, the sergeant is always right.

A running fight is on between the German military and civilian authorities in every occupied country. Usually, the army has the stronger arguments, the guns. But the civilian bosses enjoy the stronger backing and more pull in Berlin. For his part, Dr. Hans Frank, Governor General in Warsaw, won his round. He persuaded Hitler to abolish entirely the office of chief of the army of occupation in Poland. It is a rare event when Hitler sides against his generals. But he cannot say No to Dr. Frank. He owes him too much—almost twenty years of legal service and advice, for which the lawyer never collected a penny. He is collecting now. The Polish art galleries were pillaged to adorn Dr. Frank's palatial bachelor's home, the former Czartorisky palace in Warsaw. The estates of the dynasty of Habsburg in Galicia were confiscated to provide Dr. Frank with a spacious summer residence. Since he is a bookish man, he had six thousand volumes from the library of the ancient University of Cracow transferred there.

Hans Frank and Hitler first met in the winter of 1923, after the latter had been condemned to five years in "honorable prison" for his abortive Munich beer-cellar putsch. Hitler had defended himself in court, and had brought the reactionary jury to their feet. "You will never need legal counsel, you excel all of us," Dr. Frank, then a Munich shyster lawyer, assured the prisoner on a visit to his comfortable quarters in the fortress of Landsberg. Hitler understood the offer. "But I have no money," he hesitated in the bashful manner that stood him in such good stead during his formative years. The deal was closed, and celebrated with a few mugs of beer. (Although Hitler is a notorious teetotaler, he considers beer not as alcohol but as a sleeping remedy; and his painful sleeplessness causes him to gulp it in an endless stream.)

Throughout this time the Führer and his legal adviser were closely associated. They were involved in more cases of libel, slander, and blackmail than any other two crooks in Germany. But they always scored in court. German judges, churchgoing and Hohenzollern-minded, could not resist the pied piper's charm. Dr. Frank was a formidable second.

Today, after two decades of untold crimes, "Hänschen klein," as Hitler affectionately calls his oversized friend, looks like a fat, overgrown boy. His cheeks are inflated, which makes his shoe-button eyes appear even smaller. His thick lips are voluptuously curved. When they open slightly in one of his cannibal smiles, they uncover two rows of yellowish teeth. His double chin extends so far that it almost meets the protruding belly. Dr. Hans Frank, it appears, is nothing but flesh.

He is the devil in flesh. The record of the massacres he has instigated, of the mass executions he has ordered, of the new varieties of atrocities he has devised, is unparalleled even in the hell of the New Order. Admiringly, Major General Riege, his police chief, called him "truly a fertile brain."

His friendship with Hitler still holds, probably because Frank knows too much about Hitler's beginnings. To commemorate the second anniversary of Frank's assumption of the office of Governor General, the Führer sent him a unique token of appreciation: a rhinoceros whip modeled after his own.

One day in the autumn of 1941, Baron Neurath, then Protector of Bohemia-Moravia, sent for General Eliáš, the puppet premier. General Eliáš, however, failed to appear. Indignantly Baron Neurath threatened to prosecute him for the crime of lese majesty. But he was too late. Instead of General Eliáš, a shabby, rough-looking civilian appeared in the Protector's gilded reception hall. He sat down on the historic oak desk which once had served Charles V, His Most Catholic Majesty, stretched his legs, and boomed: "Hello, Neurath!"

No man on earth had ever said: "Hello, Neurath!" But Reinhard Heydrich has no peer on earth. He is Gestapo Boss Number Two, second in rank, but not in power, to Heinrich Himmler. "You need no longer protect good old Eliáš," he laughed. "We took him into our own protective custody. At present, the general is enjoying the hospitality of the Petschek palace."

"He had telephoned every day to London. He spoke with that damned Beneš, didn't you know it?" Heydrich continued. "Did Toussaint, your military adviser, not warn you? Of course not, you didn't know a thing. It's time you started protecting yourself. I am taking over the Protectorate."

As unceremoniously as that, Constantin, Baron Neurath, a cavalier close to seventy and Germany's last gentleman, was dismissed.

Unflinching, he took the blow. He kept his poise. "May I still speak to the delegation waiting for me?" he asked.

Heydrich grumbled something like consent.

The door opened, and a committee of professors from Prague University was ushered in. "Our gracious Lord Protector," the spokesman began.

Heydrich cleared his throat. But the desperate look the old courtier gave him reminded even Germany's bloodhound Number One that other people at least have hearts. "Proceed," he said.

The delegation begged permission to give a few courses at the university, which had been closed for two years on account of a students' demonstration. "Do not let our youth grow up entirely uninstructed," the spokesman implored the man in whom he still saw the Protector.

Again Heydrich cleared his throat. Neurath trembled a little, but he rose to full stature and said in his softest voice, with his most engaging southern drawl: "Even elementary schools are more than the Czechs deserve." With inimitable grace he nodded slightly in Heydrich's direction. He had made his last obeisance to Hitler.

He left Prague the next day with Baroness Neurath. Stored in his private car were twenty-seven cases of goods.

"Open the windows!" shouted Heydrich when his predecessor was gone. "This house needs a good airing." He personally smashed, with his jack boot, the stained glass of the window through which Emperor Charles V had peered on Prague.

Not very long afterward, however, Reinhard Heydrich stood in the Cathedral of St. Vitus. The atmosphere of old tradition had caught up with him. In token of Czech faithfulness to the Reich, Dr. Hácha handed over to him the seven keys to the iron shrine in which the crown and the coronation jewels of St. Wenceslaus are preserved.

Again Heydrich cleared his throat, and said: "I return four of the keys to you as a sign of my confidence. Take these three and keep them safely. The Führer trusts you." Indeed he handed two keys back to Dr. Hácha. He can open the iron shrine just as well with five keys. Besides, the Gestapo has a large staff of expert locksmiths.

Reinhard Heydrich introduced himself with a "thorough house cleaning" as Protector of Bohemia-Moravia. The expression was his. The Czech people were startled when the familiar red posters with the swastika suddenly altered their language. They had been accustomed to the grave dignity of Baron Neurath's archaic officialese, which politely called the gallows an abode of execution and the concentration camp a place of enforced confinement. Suddenly the red posters—the Protector's only means of communication with his nation—

used terms every one could understand. The lingo of the Nazi gangsters poured down on the Czechs. "House cleaning" was just a beginning. Soon authoritative decrees promised to wring the people's necks. Orders in council spoke about burning in oil all rebels. "I will rub you out" is the accurate translation for what the new Protector announced he would do to the people entrusted to his care.

Reinhard Heydrich did not stop at the announcement. In the last week of September, 1941, immediately after his predecessor Neurath's departure, he proclaimed a curfew for the entire country. Theaters and movies as well as most of the pubs were closed. German troops in steel helmets paraded the streets of all major cities. It was healthy exercise and gave the soldiers an excellent opportunity to practice sharpshooting on living targets. Gestapo agents, many of them newly imported, swarmed over the country.

On November 3, 1941, Heydrich took a deep breath, wiped his narrow forehead with his famous red silk handkerchief, coughed a little, and made the portentous statement, "Ouf!" indicating that the purge was successfully concluded. Except for the four biggest towns in Bohemia-Moravia, which must remain chained as long as the system lasts, the curfew was canceled. The theaters were rededicated to Viennese operetta. The German troops received rounds of beer on the house; every innkeeper was delighted to stand them a few drinks.

In the meantime, Heydrich boasted that he had killed three hundred and ninety-four Czechs. On second thought he admitted that he had forgotten to include twenty Czech criminals involved in the arson case in Vienna. The list rose, consequently, to four hundred and fourteen victims. They had been liquidated fifty-fifty, he divulged in his racy Gestapo slang, which means that half of them were hanged, and the other half shot. Besides, Heydrich insisted, the purge had crushed the revolution.

The Czech government in London doubts the accuracy of

both these statements. The four hundred and fourteen victims should be multiplied by five, Dr. Beneš believes. On the crushing of the revolution, he is entirely uninformed. He still speaks every day by the two-way radio with his followers at home. Herr Heydrich, for his part, continues hiding himself behind droves of bodyguards when his duties force him to leave his castle.

He prefers, however, for valid reasons, to execute his duties within his palatial residence. After the purge he decided to resume friendly relations with the population, based on mutual trust. He was particularly bent on winning over the working class. Perhaps his personal charm would influence them to abandon the endless sabotage that transforms Czechoslovakia, supposed to function as Greater Germany's armory, into an economic cemetery. So he invited a delegation of Czech labor leaders to come and see him in the Hradschin.

His guests were a select group of idlers, loafers, and jailbirds, a handful of isolated, boycotted, cold-shouldered turncoats without any influence whatsoever on the great body of Czech labor. Voluptuously, they smoked the pipe of peace with the persecutor of their fellow workers. Tobacco and cheap cigarettes were gratis at the Hradschin party. In a country bled white there are always a few ready to sell their souls for such miserable bribes. Like the Führer, Reinhard Heydrich is allergic to smoking around him. It makes his chronic cough worse. But he knows when he has to sacrifice for the cause. Through clouds of blue smoke he smiled at his visitors.

The personal charm worked. "You certainly are a great man," Mr. Delivec, boss of the Nazified miners' union, flattered him. "I never met a greater one; and, in my time, I have met all the big fellows. You see," he explained, "I did time in Pankratz—fifteen years." Pankratz is the old Prague prison for incorrigibles.

Reinhard Heydrich smiled good-naturedly. "Pankratz."

He pondered for a moment. Then he burst out laughing. "How is old Chlapotnik?"

"Our good chief warden," the jailbird replied with a suppressed tear in his voice, "passed away." In a country of the New Order it is cautious to refer to death in polite terms. The killers are rather touchy.

"Oh, yes, I remember," Heydrich recalled suddenly. "I saw his name on one of my lists. It was his own fault: I had warned him seriously enough not to serve me lukewarm dinners all the time, fifteen years ago—or was it sixteen?"

Reinhard Heydrich's memory, as well as his physical strength, suffered gravely during his adventurous youth. He is still comparatively young; but at thirty-eight he has already completed twenty-two years in crime.

The story of his life is a telling one because it is the story of Germany's lost generation. At the tender age of fifteen young Reinhard, the son of a respectable surgeon, joined the Nazi party, then a gang of some two hundred Munich hoodlums. He is a veteran follower of Hitler, one of the handful among the old guard who escaped being purged on one occasion or another. Heydrich was always among those who did the purging. At sixteen a juvenile court sentenced him for homicide. He served a year and broke jail as he was being transferred to an asylum. At twenty-six he used to introduce himself in the best brown-shirt manner, with a stiff, rectangular bow and the words, "Reinhard Heydrich, forty-nine scalps." The much coveted fiftieth was captured when he assassinated Melitta Braun, the Hitler-girl who proved to be a Jewess. His record of fifty was now complete. Heydrich kept a lock of her dark hair.

In the Gestapo he rose from the ranks. He was already a member of the then secret brotherhood when he joined the navy. A smart youngster, he was attached as orderly to the purser of the armored cruiser *Scharnhorst*. After six months he was dismissed for irregularities in the ship's cash, although he insists he was fired for organizing the first Nazi cell on a German man-of-war. The matter was never entirely cleared up. There was no trial, since the armored cruiser *Scharnhorst* herself was contraband, forbidden by the peace treaty. Her mysteries could not be aired in public.

Heydrich, by then a full-fledged Nazi, worked subsequently in many countries. He trailed through Austria, Czechoslovakia, Holland, France, and a few South American republics. Everywhere the police pursued him. As often as not he slept in prison cells. This, he explains today, is the pride of his life. He never accepted as much as a red cent from the movement. He had to live on petty thievery, assaults, robbery, and preferably on marriage swindles. But he lived for Hitler.

He tells a colorful story of having been discovered and inducted into the intelligence service by Colonel Nicolai, the German espionage chief during the first war and one of Hitler's earliest collaborators. Nicolai, for his part, knows nothing of his alleged discovery. "I used to surround myself with sharpshooters, not with assassins," the old colonel explains. He made this statement a few days before the outbreak of the second war. Instantly he lost his job as the director of the Reichsarchiv in Hamburg, a center for Nazi espionage in the United States. Heydrich had in the meantime become a mighty man in the Third Reich.

As Gestapo Boss Number Two, as Hitler's personal confidant, and as the general inspector for security, he still looks very much the young hooligan he once was. With incredible energy he manages to keep his well polished appearance. He is tall, bony, and pale. His eyes still show that flicker, shrewd and insane at once, which made observers speak of them as "cobra eyes."

Although now resplendent with the title of Lord Protector, he does not care for dignity. His toughness is exuberant. "The horse-and-buggy days are gone," he ridiculed departing Baron Neurath. "Full steam ahead into the new millennium."

Reinhard Heydrich will not see much of the new millennium. His constant cough is tubercular. He is well aware that he will have to go soon. Hence his mania for killing. He wants company on his way. From Hitler down, all along the line, each shudders at his solitude.

Dr. Arthur Seyss-Inquart is the softest of them all. He is almost an albino. His cheeks are pink. He speaks with a melodious Viennese accent. He never raises his voice. Inaudibly, he snaps his fingers. Every one knows this means another execution.

Some twenty years ago, when I first met him, Seyss-Inquart had just hung out his shingle as a lawyer in a modest house in a suburb of Vienna. It was after the first war. Two thousand members of the bar were starving. What was left of the imperial city deteriorated rapidly. The legal profession became a racket. No one deplored the barbarization more than young Seyss-Inquart. Every day he went to church, praying for the advent of better times. He spoke of taking the vows, of entering a monastery. He established an intimate friendship with his father confessor, another of whose penitents was Dr. Kurt von Schuschnigg, the last chancellor of Austria.

Seyss-Inquart slid on his knees into politics. Schuschnigg made him his right-hand man in the government that was pledged to fight to the last breath for Austria's independence. Fifteen minutes after the first German airmen had descended on Vienna, Seyss-Inquart, handing Schuschnigg over to the Gestapo, shrugged, folded his hands, and said: "The ways of Providence are unfathomable."

The Austrian Nazis suffered bitter disappointment. Hitler pushed them aside, and put his own henchmen into the positions of power. Seyss-Inquart alone was singled out for a spectacular career. "Learn Dutch," the Führer advised him.

"The Dutch will have to learn German," Seyss-Inquart replied courageously. It is his only wisecrack on record. But for the Führer it was proof enough of brilliance. After the invasion of the Netherlands Seyss-Inquart moved to The Hague.

Today, the shyster lawyer from the Vienna suburb resides in the Binnenhof, the ancient Royal Castle. He still exercises the art of the law. In violation of the conditions for surrender, he had the commander in chief of the Dutch army, General Winkelman, arrested a few months after the invasion, with the excuse that the latter's subordinates thought evil about the German masters. The paragraph, legal minds were agreed, was a new one.

However, it proved a most useful one. Winkelman's removal to the fortress-prison of Troppau deprived the demobilized Dutch soldiers of their leader. They were a body without a head. Their resentment was no longer dangerous. Still the tension in the air disturbed the sensitive, susceptible Seyss-Inquart. He asked General Friedrich Christiansen, the commander in chief of the German army of occupation, to honor him with a visit in the Binnenhof. The general, it is reported, murmured something about a shabby civilian's insolence in not presenting himself when he asked for an interview. But in the best Prussian fashion he came and clicked his heels in front of the "shabby civilian"—whose intimate connection with the Führer was, after all, well known.

"Permit me to give you your next order of the day." The shyster lawyer smiled in his grandest viceregal manner. He handed the general a typewritten sheet. Christiansen looked at it, and his interest was arrested. Every time he came to the words "will be shot," he nodded vehemently. It was more difficult to read the phrase "who by their very ideology hurt the feelings of German soldiers." The word "ideology" was a stumbling block. Seyss-Inquart had to repeat it several times before it penetrated the general's head.

Next morning the general commanding the army of occupation issued his order of the day. It was called, "Measures to Secure the Military and Economic Interests of the Occupation Forces." He read it over the broadcast. The complicated sentence with the word "ideology" went swimmingly. Still, Christiansen shook his graying head. "Their very ideology . . . will be shot . . ." he afterwards repeated to himself. There was doubt in his voice. Then an idea struck him: "Couldn't we shoot those who boo German teams at football matches instead? Their crime is—how shall I say?—more palpable."

Graciously the viceroy consented: "We will shoot them all."

There was but one category of Dutchmen whom Seyss-Inquart wanted to exempt from the general shooting order. Himself a veteran fifth columnist, he understood the plight of those who had helped the German parachutists ravage Holland, but whose wages, a few months after the invasion, had decreased 25 per cent while living costs had risen 50 per cent. This unfortunate coincidence estranged most of the Dutch fifth columnists—there had been more than a fair number of them—from the new system. Their bread had been buttered on the side they had betrayed. Most of them fell in line with the overwhelming majority of the Dutch people who prefer death to Nazi rule.

Among the martinets, the racketeers, the killers who run the New Order, Dr. Arthur Seyss-Inquart undoubtedly is Pervert Number One.

Tsarskoye Selo, the Tsar's resplendent marble palace near St. Petersburg (no longer is the city called Leningrad), has opened again its gilded gates though, for the time being, only its image has been revived. The throne has been replaced by a desk. But when Alfred Rosenberg sits down at the inlaid desk he is Peter the Great. A dream still wilder, still more fantastic, than the paper hanger's dream of sitting on top of the world has come true. To Alfred Rosenberg the Tsar's sacred throne is the highest peak on earth. It stands on a little hill. From this hill he sent the thundering message that was intended to outroar the Sermon on the Mount. "The Jewish Rabbi Jesus, popularly named Christ . . ." it began.

Alfred Rosenberg is the inventor of neopaganism. His book *The Myth of the Twentieth Century*, although not much more than a rehash of the crazy English renegade Houston Stewart Chamberlain's *Foundations of the Nineteenth Century*, became the Nazi Bible after Hitler, then a Munich rabble rouser, had turned over the leaves—not quite grasping what it was all about but carried away by its secular impertinence, couched in a strange semiscientific gibberish. Today *The Myth of the Twentieth Century* is a highly prized library rarity in Nazi Germany. It had to be withdrawn from sale because it was competing dangerously with another tome, Hitler's own *Mein Kampf*. But the two authors remained closely associated.

Hitler had learned from Rosenberg what he calls his philosophic conception. Moreover his first stumbling steps on the international scene were guided by his worldly-wise, hard-bitten friend. Besides, Alfred Rosenberg is probably the only man on earth who could outwit and outsmart the Führer for twenty consecutive years. After having dethroned Jesus Christ, at least for the benefit of overcrowded, sweaty, smoke-filled Nazi beer-cellars, Rosenberg taught the gospel of the German world mission which Hitler is carrying out in his own inimitable fashion. Since no one understands Rosenberg's balderdash anyway, the fact that he preaches it in a heavy Russian accent makes little difference. Actually, the world prophet of Teutonism remains, like Hitler, a mongrel from a nationally mixed borderland, with the mongrel's craving for racial purity. The difference between the two is only that Hitler means to be a German, whereas Rosenberg pretends to be German, while in his heart of hearts he is a Russian. Most of Nazism is his invention—although the Führer alone had what it took to put it over on the German people—and anti-bolshevism was for a long time Rosenberg's monopoly. He hates Russia as violently as Hitler hates Austria. Both suffer from the same overriding desire to castigate the country that refused to give itself. It is a hatred-love complex in both cases.

Alfred Rosenberg comes from the Baltic, the once Russian seacoast. The common people were Latvians, Estonians, Lithuanians. They were used to being treated like swine. The Jews were the traders and formed the intelligentsia. Russians exercised the administration and constituted the ruling class. But the real power was in the hands of the Baltic barons, feudal landlords and owners of large estates speaking an archaic German, descendants of the Teutonic Knights, lazy, degenerate, and in some cases, like many decadents, oddly fascinating. For generations their elder sons had lorded it over the land, while the younger ones went to St. Petersburg and rose rapidly as courtiers and generals. When the First World War started, many of Imperial Russia's highest dignitaries were Baltic barons.

To belong to their class was to dwell with the demigods. Alfred Rosenberg definitely was not one of them, although he craved admission. His name indicates Jewish descent, albeit he ferociously insists on being the only Aryan in the world by the name of Rosenberg. This might well explain his becoming the prophet of anti-Semitism. He may have to outcry the voice of the blood. His father was a modest artisan, his mother an Estonian peasant girl. Of course the German upper class in the Baltic shunned him. An exclusive fraternity at the University of Reval, now Tallinn, refused to admit him. Smarting from the rebuff, young Rosenberg betook himself to St. Petersburg. Again he was disappointed: Tsarskoye Selo did not open its gilded gates to him. He was forced to content himself with a small job with the Ochrana, the Tsarist secret police.

The job expanded as the first war broke out. Rosenberg

was sent on a confidential mission to Paris. His activities there are not on record. Under Nazism, however, curious people by the score were executed for asking on just which front Alfred Rosenberg served in the first war.

After the war he bobbed up in Munich, then the hotbed of international espionage. The German *Frei-Korps*, predecessors of the Nazi gangs, had made Bavaria their secret armory. An Interallied Military Mission tried, mostly in vain, to ferret out the hidden stores of arms, which, according to the Armistice, were to be handed over to the Allies. Many German officers and soldiers who complied with the terms of the Armistice were denounced to their reactionary superiors, then already dreaming of the war of revenge. Stool pigeons denouncing their law-abiding comrades could make a pretty penny. One of them even made a remarkable career: he became the Führer. But Adolf Hitler does not like to be reminded of the days he bowed and heel-clicked his way into German history.

Even before they knew each other, Rosenberg went Hitler one better. Whereas Adolf still acted as a shabby informer, Alfred was already Dr. Jekyll and Mr. Hyde. In the daytime he studied at the University of Munich, making friends among the patriotic, arms-hiding students; by night he was frequently seen coming out or going into 7 Gärtnerplatz, the home of the famous Major Rollet, the head of the Interallied Military Mission. Rosenberg was still on the side of Germany's enemies when he saw the light shining in Hitler's bird-of-prey eyes.

Hitler, then at the very beginning of his career, had used the few thousand marks he had obtained from the cash of the Munich garrison command to buy a moribund anti-Semitic weekly, the *Völkischer Beobachter,* and to convert it into the mouthpiece of the incipient Nazi movement. He was looking for an editor who could do the spelling for him (in those days he still tried to comply with the bothersome grammatical necessities of the German language). He met Rosenberg, and offered him a bargain. His words are on record: "If you can make a go of the sheet, you can earn a living. But first I must make my living as the publisher. That is all I want."

It seems not to have been difficult for Rosenberg to quit Major Rollet and become spokesman of the German counter-revolution. What did the frustrated Russian care about the Germans or the French? His bread was buttered on the German side. The layer of butter grew thicker and thicker. Hitler made him his *Kulturprophet* (cultural prophet), and then chief of the party's foreign department. The other Nazi bigwigs loathed Rosenberg. His constant witticisms and cynicisms disgusted them. His heavy foreign accent repelled them. His undisguised Russian obsession seemed like a mania. But he knew how to make this obsession palatable to Hitler. Russia must be destroyed, he insisted, in order to assure German hegemony on the "Eurasian" continent. Actually, he always wanted to use Nazi Germany's dynamic strength to crush the Russia that was, and to build, on its ruins, the Rosenberg Russia—a kind of new Tsarism with emphasis on the knout. Many suspected him of such tendencies, a few knew of them and were silent, Ribbentrop spoke out.

The champagne agent proved the stronger of the two. Rosenberg was shelved. His name remained on the banner-head of the *Völkischer Beobachter*, but he was forbidden to write editorials. Finally, the Moscow Pact dealt him, it seemed, the deathblow.

But Rosenberg saw through the hollowness of the Hitler-Stalin alliance. The ink was not yet dry on the pact when he established the Russian Bureau that has now been turned into the Reichsministerium für den Osten (Reich Department for the East). He surrounded himself with the last pillars of White Russian emigration in Berlin. To this day, he keeps a few grand dukes, some Ukrainian hetmans and gouty Tsarist ex-generals on his pay roll. The language spoken in the newest Reich Department is strictly Russian.

Rosenberg rejoices in the feeling that his realm is twice as large as Germany was before the war; but in the whole vast territory hardly one stone remains on another—the fields are burned, all industrial enterprises have been destroyed and disorganized. Moreover, Rosenberg's empire shrinks and dwindles almost as fast as it grew. A windfall brought it into being, a hurricane may destroy it. Never since he acquired so much of her has Rosenberg visited Russia. He has a thousand excuses, and one reason. The reason is the cholera, rampant in Russia. Herr Rosenberg does not care to endanger his precious life. He runs Russia by remote control. Letters to him are actually addressed to Tsarkoye Selo, the Palace near St. Petersburg which is also engraved on his own letterhead. His correspondence cannot go astray. The German post is so efficient that his fancily addressed mail is delivered correctly in Berlin, 9 Voss-Strasse.

CHAPTER SEVEN

ROGUES' GALLERY:
THE LACKEYS

Just handfuls and cliques of wicked men and their military and party organizations have been able to bring these hideous evils upon mankind. It would indeed bring shame upon our generation if we did not teach them a lesson which will not be forgotten in the record of a thousand years.—WINSTON CHURCHILL, December 11, 1941.

"PLUS ÇA CHANGE, plus c'est la même chose," the old French truism, was never more true than when applied to the French collaborationists of recent vintage. They have not learned the lesson of defeat. It is the same old stale wine they are pouring into new barrels. The rejuvenation of France, led by an octogenarian, claims to be a "national revolution." It is, actually, the revival of the old play. Some roles have changed hands, but the cast remains the same, on the whole. The plot of trickery, of double-crossing, of corruption that undermined and finally broke the Third Republic goes on, unabated, in the sorry farce of Vichy. It is, in terms of the Hellenic drama, the satyr play following the tragedy.

Some fallen stars await the hour of their comeback. Undaunted even by the Gestapo, Edouard Herriot has never left his occupied city of Lyons. Some understudies have advanced to the parts of leading men. Admiral Darlan is no longer confined to the ministerial anterooms in which he made his republican career. He is Admiral of the Fleet for life. But whose life, one feels tempted to ask.

Some men on the flying trapeze manage to sit on both sides of the fence at the same time. When Camille Chautemps appeared in Washington, he traveled as a special envoy of Vichy, richly endowed with funds which, it goes without saying, must have passed the Hitler control; and he was conspiring with Henri-Haye, once the official greeter of Versailles, a glorified Grover Whalen, one of the last Axis conspirators left behind on the banks of the Potomac. But, coming to America, M. Chautemps did not forget to emphasize his record as a republican ex-premier. He proudly boasted his dignity as a grand-something-or-other of the lodge of the Freemasons, membership in which means, in Vichy, 1942, the concentration camp. He tried to establish friendly relations with the Free French. His posterior, indeed, had to be tough-skinned to stand the kick the Free French gave it in return for his wooing.

But M. Chautemps is just an insignificant equilibrist of all-round collaboration. Pierre Laval and François Darlan are the two arch-collaborators. Today M. Laval is back at the head of the government. He wields more power than he ever exercised as a Republican Prime Minister. But he is an old man, beyond his years. He has not quite recovered from the two heavy blows he received. The first was his dismissal from the government and his imprisonment just as he was on the point of staging a coup d'état which was to put himself in place of Pétain as chief of the French puppet state. The day he was arrested, December 13, 1940, was one of jubilation for all France. But the joy was short-lived. Hitler wrested him from his bailiffs. Laval settled down in Paris. He conducted a vicious slander campaign against Pétain, "the man who has long survived himself and still refuses to die"; and, while he was campaigning, he started another campaign enlisting recruits for Hitler's antibolshevik crusade. He was hit a second time. Paul Collette, a young man from Brittany, where the most fiery French patriots grow, registered, only to have an opportunity of emptying his revolver on Laval. Unfortunately, his revolver was an obsolete weapon. Its five bullets did not miss, but could not kill Laval, who—physically as well as politically— has the nine lives of a cat. After a few weeks in the hospital, Laval was able to return to his Château Châteldon in unoccupied France. On April 15, 1942, he moved on another 18 miles to take over Vichy. At present he seems to be at the pinnacle of power. But this time power came late to him. His latest photographs show a human derelict with haggard cheeks and glazed eyes deeply sunken in their sockets.

Again he has his photographs taken for publication, he still wears his proverbial white tie, and now he has his definite chance to sell out France for a modest consideration. He has done more difficult tricks in his time. The modest considerations he amassed since he entered politics in 1914, shortly before the start of the First World War, amount to the equivalent of five million dollars. He is the only millionaire in France, he boasts, who was not "affected" by the measures of German requisitioning. His string of newspapers flourishes. So does his mineral water concern, which, next to the overextended span of Pétain's life, was the main reason why Laval hated Vichy, another mineral water supplier, until Hitler installed him in power.

With a renegade's white-hot hatred, he loathes bolshevism, after having started his political career as a Communist deputy and mayor of one of the red suburbs of Paris. With a veteran conscientious objector's sovereignty he derides the uniform, at least the French uniform. He vituperates Pétain's generals and Darlan's admirals, but he kotows before every field-gray noncom. During the first war he was on the list of the politically suspicious. Only his friendship with Briand, whose cabinet colleague he was in a few governments, saved him from the military tribunal. Gratefully, he stabbed Briand in the back when the time was ripe, and was instrumental in bringing about the downfall of the elder statesman. "More room for Laval" was already then his creed. When he had all the room he wanted, being prime minister of the French Republic, he signed the Hoare-Laval pact, flashing the green light to Mussolini for the rape of Abyssinia. A storm of outrage in England and France felled Laval.

Laval held England responsible for his fall, and for the five following years he had to spend in the political desert. He was always a good hater, but his acrimonious detestation of John Bull dwarfs all his other piques and grudges. "Let Great Britain boil in oil," he advised the United States in his last interview with American correspondents. For a time, it was his swan song. Once more he mustered all his powers of persuasion, which had swayed innumerable parliaments and governments, to bring America into line. "If I were younger, I would go to America myself," he said. "I would make my fortune there. Perhaps I should be elected to the Senate." Then he explained that America and France were fundamentally alike; but when a reporter, taking up the cue, spoke about the two great republics Laval cut in sharply. "France is no longer a republic. Monsieur Hitle-e-er—" He interrupted himself. Probably he realized that it was too late. He could not deliver the United States, too, to Monsieur Hitler. Washington did not deem his trial balloon worth an answer. And when, a few months later, he muscled into Vichy, appeasement was finally and definitely shred to tatters.

Admiral François Darlan is still heir presumptive to Maréchal Pétain, at least on paper. But the Admiral of the Seven Seas, it appears, is all washed up. Even his next of kin seem to realize it. His wife never shows herself with him in public. His son recently relinquished the naval service to become an insurance salesman, entering a business in which Darlan senior will probably embarrass junior less and certainly be able to help him considerably more.

The last time I met the then Vice Admiral Darlan was shortly before the outbreak of the war, in Portsmouth, where the British navy passed in parade before King George VI. The representative of the allied French fleet was seated close to the King. Everybody had been advised to neglect his outward appearance—he looked a little ridiculous in his ash-stained dress uniform—and to treat the little great man with all due honor. To be sure, he richly repaid the compliments with which he was showered. "The British navy is invincible," he told me. "There are only two big fleets. The other one is ours. Or would you call the Japanese barges a navy? Or the American nutshells? Non, monsieur. The Americans will never have a navy, in spite of that crazy landlubber Monsieur Roosevelt's naval complex. They are not really a seafaring nation."

About three years have passed since this memorable interview. In Oran, the British were compelled to put out of action some of the "other big fleet's" most formidable units. Darlan enriched the collection of Japanese barges with a few obsolete French gunboats which he left behind in Indo-China. His fingers itch to test his metal against the ships of the crazy landlubber Monsieur R.

The Admiral has little reason to mock at others as landlubbers. For a short time he commanded a small French flotilla in Chinese waters; after that his entire naval career was spent at desks. He won renown as a gunnery expert, but had occasion to prove his expert knowledge only as a teacher in the naval college. For the rest he was a political admiral. Darlan, son of a small-town politician who was a short-lived Minister of Justice under the Republic, owes his career and his rapid advancement to his godfather Georges Leygues, the well known Paris chain-store millionaire, who was Minister of

Marine—minister for life, he was jokingly called—in every cabinet that wanted his financial support at elections.

François Darlan early learned the mysteries of French parliamentary corruption and graft. He was always with the majority. Since the majority of the French Chamber was generally leftist, he himself showed pink inclinations and a constant tendency to democratize the navy. This consisted primarily in appointing his personal friends to important naval jobs.

Admiral Darlan's naval dictatorship was only marred by the indisputable fact that the crews did not join in his plotting. The French sailors are incorrigible. Not that they are remarkably pro-British. With the exception of a slight sprinkling of De Gaullists they are indifferent toward Albion. They shrug when they are reminded of the Oran incident. Most of them admit that Churchill was forced to do it. The heart of the average French *marin* belongs neither to Darlan nor to De Gaulle, but to Stalin. The French rating is wildly class-conscious. He was taught communism by the *cellules rouges*, the red cells, which thrived aboard every French warship in republican days—and which still exist in all the units of the Darlan navy. It must be difficult to induce French sailors to give up their passive resistance to another war. Not even Hitler has been able to work the miracle. He coddled the few thousand sailors among his one million eight hundred thousand French prisoners of war. They were the favorite sons in every Prussian camp. Many were released, although one million and a half soldier-prisoners are still retained. Those French sailors who were released from imprisonment in Germany and sent to Toulouse showed no gratitude whatsoever. Immediately, the red flag waved over their barracks.

Sadly, Darlan shook his head. He does not understand such consistency. No one could accuse him of this attribute. He is, indeed, most self-contradictory. Was he not a trusted friend of England? Did he not, in the fateful days of Bordeaux, still oppose the surrender and advocate the continuation of the fight against Nazism with the fleet and the resources of the empire? When he heard that Pétain had taken over the power, he coined the ominous phrase, "Défait accompli," and retired to a hearty dinner in the Capon Rouge, Bordeaux's most celebrated eating place. There, it appears, he saw the light some time between the third and fourth bottles. The next day he put himself and "his" fleet at Pétain's disposal. Today England has, with the exception of Pierre Laval, no more spiteful enemy.

Two of the most prominent Nazi lackeys in France, who have personal accounts to settle with Stalin, are Messrs. Paul Marion and René Belin. Both were Communists from the first hour, but both quit the party early, if not quite voluntarily. Belin decided to assume the role of the moderate, antibolshevist union leader, as a sort of French Sidney Hillman. But his allegiance to democratic unionism was short. He used the first opportunity to switch over to the swastika. Now he is the pro-Nazi labor leader of France. His organization has all of two hundred and seventy-six members, not one of them a workingman. His fellow traveler, Paul Marion, left the ungrateful labor camp entirely. He tried his luck as a writer, a newspaperman, and as a politician. After three failures he went to Vichy, where he acts as the appointed agent for Laval and Doriot. He does not object to being called the French Goebbels.

If there is, in fact, a French Goebbels, it is Marcel Déat. The world has heard twice about him: first, when he coined the slogan "I don't want to die for Danzig," the second time when, with Pierre Laval, he was shot at on August 26, 1941. He recovered quickly enough to resume his editorial writing in the Paris _Œuvre_ which explains every day to the French nation why she must join in the war against the traditional Anglo-American archenemies.

Even in his own camp many sympathizers smile at assiduous

Marcel Déat who works so hard for his money. But no one
was ever seen smiling at M. Barnaud. The difference is that
the latter has not to work for his money at all. It comes to him
as if by itself. It flows in torrents through his hands. He does
not have to pay for publicity. Instead he pays to keep his
name out of the news. M. Barnaud, general manager of the
not entirely Aryan Bank of Worms, is now acting as the chief
banker for the collaborationists. He has not been long in politics. Indeed, his political interest did not awake until the advent of the Front Populaire government. Then he invented
the phrase "Better Hitler than Léon Blum," which made him
immediately the *enfant gâté* of French high finance. During
the war he organized a conspiracy, on Laval's behalf, to overthrow Paul Reynaud and to conclude a separate peace with
Germany. The plan miscarried, but the armistice opened new
and untold possibilities for M. Barnaud. From the collapse at
Bordeaux to this very day he has represented the big bankers
and industrialists of France in the Nazification of the country.

The old guard surrenders but does not die. The hyenas
who hounded France until she gave up her soul are now busy
gnawing the carcass. *Plus ça change, plus c'est la même chose.*

The Belgian government in London valiantly aids the
Allied war effort. Its forces in the Congo hold a key position
in Africa, the continent that may well become the next decisive theater of war. Its legions of volunteers, composed of
Belgians from all over the world, and of young men by the
thousands who braved death and worse—the Gestapo—to escape from their oppressed country, as well as the Belgian air
force, linked with the R.A.F., indeed, revive the glory that
was "heroic little Belgium" during the first war.

In occupied Brussels, however, a group of traitors have
formed what they themselves call a shadow government. They
are aware of their precarious position. Even the joint power
of the Gestapo and the German High Command was unable

to impose its rule on the defenseless nation. General von Falkenhausen, the German commander in chief, did his best by forcing the King to receive the self-styled Premier of the shadow government. He could, however, not prevent the "prisoner of Laeken" from turning his back when the shadowy gentleman appeared, and refusing to converse with him.

The worthy's name is Léon Degrelle. The name is not quite unfamiliar to students of the European scene. M. Degrelle attracted a good deal of international attention in 1935 and 1936 with his "Christus Rex" movement, a copy of Fascism with an allegedly Catholic background. The Archbishop of Malines, Primate of Belgium, however, called the self-styled Rexist Catholicism "blasphemous." This statement by the foremost prince of the Church in Belgium broke the movement just as it was about to endanger the unity of the kingdom seriously.

The soap bubble exploded. But Degrelle was not the man to give up a fight. He was too sure of his assets: his youth (he was twenty-six and twenty-seven in his heyday), the appearance of a slightly overweight gigolo, and the romantic forelock which brought him into competition with Hitler. Indeed, when he visited the Führer, about a year before the outbreak of the war, the dictator and the would-be dictator, it is credibly reported, discussed, above all, the art of keeping one's hair in trim and the pomade each preferred.

There must have been other topics of discussion, too. On his return from Berchtesgaden, Degrelle established the fifth column in Belgium. He disappeared from the public platform to devote himself to plotting and conspiracy, which did not go unnoticed by the authorities. Unfortunately, the authorities before the war were no less lenient in Belgium than in other democracies. They did not crack down on handsome Léon until the morning of May 10, 1941, the day of the German invasion.

Degrelle was dispatched across the border and dumped in

the French prison at Caen. On his release immediately after the fall of France, he complained of having been physically mistreated. In consequence he is deaf in his right ear, he insists. Later events proved that this deafness came in handy. Furthermore, he had grown a beard in prison. The gigolo was transformed into a martyr.

His new pose did not help much. Degrelle's return to Belgium was far from the triumphal march he had expected. He published his memoirs under the unassuming title: "Degrelle Was Right." But the authorities of occupation disagreed. In spite of his service to Hitler, the Nazis treated him with the unconcealed contempt with which they treat all the traitors in their service. He was permitted to edit the *Pays Réel*, a rag which licks the Prussian jack boot, but nothing was heard of his political career.

Persistently he pestered the German authorities until he was allowed to campaign throughout the country. He told bewildered Belgians that the Führer had saved Europe, and his speeches invariably ended with the words, "Do not be afraid to shout '*Heil Hitler!*'" Unafraid, the audiences shouted, "*A bàs Degrelle!*" In the end, the Gestapo put a stop to Degrelle's meetings, which had to be heavily policed and failed to pay any political dividends. He was asked to confine his activities to giving interviews to the foreign press. Permission to capitalize on his faded fame was the last contribution to be got from the blunted instrument.

A provincial Italian paper was ordered to send an interviewer to the man whose every utterance had once made European headlines. Quickly, Degrelle grasped the opportunity to bask once more in the limelight. He did not care that the lights were dimmed, and that he was only speaking to the limited audience of the small Italian town of Cremona. He was Hamlet again—Hamlet in Kalamazoo. He delivered a violently patriotic and independent statement. "Rex has never been in the service of Germany, and never will be," he declared. "Rex never received a cent from Germany before the war or during the war, and will never receive anything in the future."

General von Falkenhausen, it is said, nodded gravely as he read the last line.

"Of course," Degrelle continued, "a National Socialist Germany or, for that matter, a Fascist Italy and a Falangist Spain are closer to us than the Brussels plutocracy. But Rex exists only to serve Belgium and its King."

Whereupon Rex ceased to exist altogether. The German overlords do not care even for a semblance of independence among their creatures. The very show, even if it is only to disguise slavish dependence on Berlin, is forbidden. The extremist parties who since the invasion of Belgium have openly admitted their connection with Nazism received the order to merge. It was a large order in view of the fact that, in Belgium as elsewhere, the traitors and turncoats are engaged in murderous cutthroat competition. Desperately Degrelle tried to counteract the order. He mustered all his courage to utter, much against habit, a few truths, actually addressed to a meeting in the Cirque Royal in Brussels, but directed to the attention of the German masters. The real situation in Belgium could not be more adequately described than in the words of Turncoat Number 1: "At present, not fifty first-rate men, whether industrialists, businessmen, professors, or lawyers, would dare to assert their allegiance to our cause in public. Yet, to meddle in politics today involves assertion, choice, even gambling. Whoever takes sides, even in the most cautious way, is immediately labeled. Any prominent man who would choose, at this time, to adopt an attitude not strictly in conformity with the spirit of pro-British, anti-German, and sabotage tendencies would immediately be branded as a traitor and incur the execration of nine-tenths of his family and business relations. In a month's time, his life would be positively poisoned."

Degrelle deduced from this, to him, sad state of affairs (which reveals more clearly than any patriot could do the real state of the Belgian mind) that "it would be futile to consider, at present, a vast union on a daring political basis, of men who because of their social position would never venture to confront the general hatred. The blackmail of some circles," he concluded, "would immediately stop the coy drive of honest political starters who cannot even rely on their family, and would certainly not risk mixing in the daily fights."

Every word was reasoned. But Herr von Falkenhausen had but one answer: "It is no coincidence that this address was delivered in a circus."

After his chastisement, Degrelle made another desperate attempt to regain the favor of the masters. He made an appeal to all young members of the party able to drive a truck to form a unit of truck drivers to "hasten German victory." Among the young members of the party only two volunteered.

He pointed out his merit in having organized all of two truck drivers for Germany. In the opinion of the overlords, however, truck driving is not sufficient sacrifice. General von Falkenhausen gave Degrelle a last chance of rehabilitation. He should organize a Belgian legion for the antibolshevist crusade. Degrelle went at his task, but the legion never materialized. To atone for his failure, Degrelle personally enlisted. But his deaf right ear forbids him to go to the front. He is still hanging around the Brussels gambling dens and night clubs. However, when he enters these joints he never takes off his blue legionnaire's cap. Officially, he is in Russia.

For the duration of his "absence," Victor Matthys has been appointed leader of the Rex movement. He is assisted by two lawyers in the service of the German High Command, Messrs. Pevenasse and Van de Velde, and his political counselor is José Streel. The post of party secretary is vacant. Jean Ouderke, who held it, was killed by a bomb which had been smuggled into his office. No one cares to take over the empty desk although it shelters Degrelle's precious correspondence with General von Falkenhausen. A stenographer, the office's last occupant, wanted to get rid of the compromising mail. She wrote to Degrelle to remove it. It was addressed to "His Excellency, M. Léon Degrelle, Prime Minister of Belgium, c/o Madame Valentine."

All Belgium listens to the broadcasts from London by Pierlot and other members of the government in exile. But the voice of Belgium, now compelled to speak from London, does not utter the one name that sounds like a curse to the country. Henri de Man is unspeakable. Among the rogues in Hitler's service he is probably the most contemptible, and certainly the most vicious, stooge. He had a good name to lose and, indeed, he lost it utterly.

Once Henri de Man was among the few men on whom the hopes of Europe were pinned. His importance far outweighed his little home country. As an active peacemaker—not to be confused with appeaser—he was equally welcome in London, in Paris, in Geneva. A professor, he had held a chair at the University of Frankfort, then Germany's most liberal institution of higher learning. At home, De Man was a moderate, right-wing member of the Socialist party. But he derived his particular authority from the common knowledge that he spoke on behalf of King Leopold. This tall, dark blond man, looking like Flanders incarnate, spoke in a soft, persuasive voice, which sometimes appeared ill matched with his heavy build. Very few people heard the false ring in his voice. Göring was among them. In 1938 he said to the stunned Belgian ambassador in Berlin: "Henri de Man? Excellent. He is as much a Nazi as I am. Perhaps even a little more."

Another Göring folly, the diplomatic world agreed. Henri de Man's reputation was not impaired by the compromising praise of Germany's fat playboy. On the contrary, as the clouds of war darkened the horizon, Henri de Man, the King's man, as he was frequently called, appeared to many as one of the last spokesmen of sanity.

Personally, I always believed that he was not sane. His studied calmness appeared to be the overcompensation of a restless, twisted brain. His hail-fellow-well-met attitude arose from the insecurity of a man standing with a leg in each of two conflicting camps. His Flemish, almost Dutch, physical heaviness embodied a bundle of restless nerves. He was a man who always took a run, yet never dared to leap.

Hitler knows how to make his creatures jump. The Swastika was hoisted above the royal castle in Brussels. After a few days of unavailing resistance the King surrendered. Every one expected to see the King's man sharing his sovereign's tragic lot. But Henri de Man raised his bulky hand in the Nazi salute. Then he greeted his old friends from the Nazi camp with his old, soft smile. "Hitler is unifying Europe," he declared. "As soon as my Führer's victory is completed, the ferocity of his system will give way to the emanation of the German spirit. In the meantime we Belgians must prove ourselves worthy of becoming members of the greater German brotherhood."

Belgium lay in shambles, destroyed towns were still smoking ruins, harassed refugees by the hundreds of thousands were crowding the country's roads, when Henri de Man published his volume *After the Putsch*. The confessions of a traitor had been written in time to appear at the kingdom's deadline.

"Adolf Hitler has the almost superhuman task of educating Europe to brotherly cooperation," Anton Mussert, returning from a visit in Berchtesgaden, addressed his followers in Groningen, on May 24, 1941. The little Führer of Holland would very much like to facilitate personally big brother Adolf's task, at least in his own Netherlands. But the Dutch are proverbially stubbornly pig-headed. They won't listen to his exhortations. It has become the custom to surround Mussert meetings with trucks and motorcars. All the drivers blow their horns in unison, while the dentist of Amsterdam, whom his people do not recognize as their God-sent leader, tries in vain to outroar the din. When subsequently motorcars were confiscated, thousands of bicycle bells replaced the horns. Mussert meetings are rather amusing shows. They usually attract from twenty to thirty of his Dutch brown-shirts, uniformed on the German storm troopers' pattern, and, depending on the size of the town in which he happens to speak, up to a few thousand hecklers. Yet Holland's little Führer feels perfectly safe among the hostile crowds. No one takes him seriously, which is a sort of life insurance.

Not all his henchmen, however, were similarly insured. As early as May 13, 1940, immediately after the German invasion, Captain van Heuvel shot the Dutch Nazi leader Noordendorp—"like a mad dog," he later explained. Afterward, a score of Dutch Quislings went the same way as Noordendorp. On October 2, 1941, the German High Command revealed in a communiqué that a member of the Nazi party was stabbed in the back because he had attended the burial of another Dutch Nazi, who, in turn, had "died from unexplained causes."

The Dutch are about to purge their country of the Quisling breed. They have a dangerous enemy to contend with. After the open street battle betwen Netherlands Nazis and their opponents that took place on September 8, 1940, in Amsterdam, the Dutch police chief E. van der Mey was replaced by Public Security Commissar Rauter. Rauter, who has long been a personal friend of Seyss-Inquart and comes from Austria, was known then as "The Animal," pure and simple. The Dutch promoted him to the rank of "The Beast." He richly deserves his nickname. He is an oversized, herculean ruffian with a primitive mind. He does not believe in the newest, streamlined devices of the Gestapo. He prefers to liquidate his victims with his own hands. He enjoys, he boasts, a charmed life.

For three years he was Hitler's personal bodyguard, and not a hair on his head was touched. In the second year of his assignment in Holland, however, he is growing bald. Thousands of Dutchmen have an appointment with Rauter.

Even miniature Luxembourg has her midget Quislings. As in certain other countries, they work in double harness. Gauleiter Gustav Simon, an expatriate who, at the head of a large column of German police, returned to Luxembourg on August 7, 1940, started his assignment with a round-up of officials at the grand ducal court, priests, and other dignitaries. He had spent most of his professional life as a schoolmaster in the Saar district during the years of French occupation and had learned the elements of the underground battle as Hitler's first envoy to the Saarland. Under false names he used to appear at Nazi meetings in the Reich. He was rewarded by being appointed a Nazi party official. In this position he embezzled party funds. Instead of being investigated, he was promoted, and became Gauleiter of the Koblenz-Trier district. He owed this favored treatment to the fact that he had acted as an intermediary receiver of French subsidies, which, in the early twenties, found their way from the pockets of French heavy industrialists via the Saar into Nazi accounts. Hitler, of course, tried to hush up this awkward episode. But the pertinent facts are revealed in documents at present in the possession of the Luxembourg government in exile.

As Gauleiter of Koblenz-Trier the honorable Gustav Simon again committed felonies, which enabled him to build an extravagant country house. To dissipate ugly rumors, he let it be known that this had cost "only" fifty thousand marks. In front of his residence appeared the following poster: "Tell us, Simon, where did you take the fifty thousand marks from?" Outraged, the Gauleiter announced a reward of one thousand marks for the discovery of the perpetrator. Three days later his sumptuous mansion was smeared with the question: "Tell us, Simon, where did you take the fifty-one thousand marks from?"

This man is now engaged in the unbridled looting of Luxembourg—despite its small size one of the richest industrial areas of Europe. The days of felony and embezzling, of course, are over. Luxembourg is being squeezed in strictly legal fashion. What the German army and the Gestapo do not liquidate, the V.D.B. is seizing. "V.D.B." stands for *Volksdeutsche Bewegung* (German Racial Movement). But the population uses the alternative terms of *Verein der Banditen* (bandits' association) and *Versorge dein Brot* (secure your bread) for the gang.

The gang is headed by a Luxembourg Nazi of German extraction, Professor Kratzenberg, who is surrounded by a choice selection of ex-criminals, opportunists, and turncoats. To broaden this basis, Kratzenberg decreed that first the soldiers of the Luxembourg Volunteer Company, later the small police corps, and finally the public employees must join the movement as a body.

On Hitler's last birthday Professor Kratzenberg reviewed his adherents in parade. Being in great good mood, he singled out a fireman who wore his swastika with particular dash. "Tell me, party comrade," the professor asked. "To whom do you people owe your allegiance? Be frank about it!"

"Frankly," the man replied, "one-third, I should say, is still following the priests."

"But the other two-thirds?" asked Kratzenberg.

"Well," the fireman answered, getting visibly embarrassed, "another third are De Gaullists."

"Remains one-third," the professor said tensely.

"Communists," the man admitted.

"Are there no Nazis among you?" Professor Kratzenberg burst out.

"*Mais ça va sans dire,*" the fireman comforted him. "Of course we are all Nazis."

One could not say that all the Danish people are Nazis. At the elections of 1935, the National Socialist Workers Party, Hitler's spearhead in the kingdom, polled 16,257 votes. This number increased to 31,032 votes out of a total of 2,159,356 cast at the polls of 1939, when the big neighbor, the Third Reich, seemed at the peak of its might. In its heyday, Danish Nazism mustered about 1.5 per cent of the constituents. Since the Danes' experience of the blessings of German invasion, it has decreased almost to zero.

Only two Nazis are left in Parliament. One of them is the representative of the German minority, the other is Frits Clausen, M.D. He is a stout, overgrown fellow, more famous for gulping down beer than for his political achievement as the leader of the Danish Nazi movement. Of course he is a German by birth.

On May 31, 1939, Berlin signed a nonaggression pact for ten years with Denmark. April 9, 1940, German troops were smuggled into the harbor of Copenhagen. The good-natured Danish people laughed. It was an irresistibly funny show. A paunchy fellow in a brown shirt much too tight for him stood on the water front and bawled his commands to the invading troops. "Shut up," a German sergeant barked at him. Obviously, the noncom did not know that the invasion of Copenhagen had been blue-printed, to the last detail, by the paunchy fellow in the much too tight brown shirt.

Today, Dr. Frits Clausen is a shattered front-man. The power behind him, however, remains unbroken. This power is embodied in the sartorially impeccable Erik Scavenius, Denmark's Foreign Minister. Mr. Scavenius is a man of sixty-five, but looks twenty years younger. He is Hitler's tool number one in Denmark. The son of a high Danish court official, he served his diplomatic apprenticeship as a dashing attaché in Berlin. At the age of thirty-two he was for the first time appointed Danish Foreign Minister. A colleague sent congratulations, which were, as if by misunderstanding, addressed to the Imperial German Minister in Copenhagen. Since then Scavenius has been Danish Minister to Italy, Austria, and Sweden, acting everywhere as a German agent. His intimate friendship with Ribbentrop, it is related, is not based entirely on unselfish and idealistic considerations. Abandoning his diplomatic career, Scavenius entered Parliament as the leader of the pro-German Radical party. In the coalition government he formed with Stauning, he brought the veteran socialist leader entirely under his nefarious influence. His first act as Foreign Minister was to declare his loyalty to the "new European order." Yet his conduct of office did not go undisputed. His cabinet colleagues refused to ratify the customs union with Germany, which Scavenius had secretly negotiated. Denmark's formal adherence to the anti-Comintern pact was achieved only after Scavenius' reminder to his colleagues that Hitler does not take No for an answer. It was, incidentally, watered down by the official statement that the pact involved Denmark in no political obligations.

Mr. Scavenius will not escape his fate. Three million Danish people, the gentlest in the world, are waiting for the moment they can tear him to pieces. No tears will be shed for him. But Theodore Stauning, his official chief and actual prisoner, had a good and honorable name in European politics to lose. The Danish people shrug when his name is mentioned. To them he is guilty of cowardice. However, the old man will be a much regretted casualty on the long list of victims who are digging their own graves by aiding and abetting the enemy of the world.

Three heavily armed bodyguards protect Vidkun Quisling by day, four by night. The fourth man in the night shift is equipped with a syringe. Now and then, always more frequently as time goes on, the Major needs an injection. Ordinary soporifics no longer help. Quisling cannot sleep. He does not try to conceal this affliction. He is proud of it. He shares it with Hitler.

It is the only thing they have in common. For the rest, the man whose name added a new word to the English language, a synonym for "traitor," has been cheated out of the prize for which he sold out his country. He was promised a place in the Nordic Valhalla, but he receives the treatment of a colored slave. His people hate him with a cold fanaticism. In his own gang, palace revolutions are constantly brewing. He does not dare to go to Germany any longer. Every time he ventured to visit Berchtesgaden, he was lashed with the whip.

Two years ago he was a proud man—too proud, he confessed, to be patriotic. To him Norway was an all but bolshevist state, not only geographically the closest neighbor of Soviet Russia, but a voluntarily disarmed land of pacifist dreamers, ruled by a red government under a shadow King. His virility, Quisling explains, revolted against such conditions. His virility, he insists, made him betray his country's poor defense secrets, conspire with a handful of other dissatisfied martinets, and finally invite the mechanized monster to take over. Vidkun Quisling is the prototype of the Nazi stooge to be found everywhere: the frustrated superman.

Virility, Nazi style, is a contradictory quality. It is not afraid of war. On Friday September 5, 1941, Vidkun Quisling delivered a speech presenting practically an ultimatum to the Swedish neighbor. "Eleven million inhabitants of Denmark, Norway, and Finland," he argued, "are now all members of the New Order. Sweden's six million cannot hope to remain outside, if the Scandinavian peace is not to be endangered."

Receiving a message of congratulation from Ribbentrop, an honor which he had been missing for some time, and which was never to be repeated, Quisling announced a rehash of his address for the next day. His entire following and, in order to bolster up its numbers, all the German soldiers of the Oslo garrison off duty were gathered at the Skansen open-air restaurant, next to the harbor. Quisling was due to make his ceremonial entry at six o'clock. But on this particular Saturday the skies over Oslo darkened earlier than usual. The setting sun was blotted out by a squadron of American-built flying fortresses on their first visit to Oslo. They dropped high explosives on German shipping and military establishments along the east side of Oslo Fjord, uncomfortably close to Skansen's. The aim of the British pilots was accurate. They wrought havoc on ships and plants, but not a single person in the crowd near by was even scratched. Trusting in the unerring British marksmanship, the gathering of turncoats and German soldiers stood out the raid. Gramophone records were played to fill in the time, although the tunes were drowned by the high explosives.

After two hours the R.A.F. had achieved its aim: the port of Oslo was in ruins. The flying fortresses turned homeward. The news of their departure was received in a deep air-raid shelter. Out came Quisling. "Forgive my delay," he shouted, arriving breathless on the platform. "The pressure of business, you know . . ."

"Shabby comedian," a German officer standing in the crowd could not help yelling.

Norwegians call him Macbeth. According to intimate observers, he paces his apartment at night, in tears and violent hysterics, the blood of treason and murder on his hands. Sometimes he throws himself down at a table, burying his head in his hands, and shouting confused words. The only echo is the monotonous footsteps of his guard.

Quisling is, incidentally, not the only one of the band of Nazi-appointed State Councilors who can no longer stand the strain of their cursed lives. At least four of his inner circle have broken down. "Councilor" Kjeld Stub Irgens had to be sent to a Danish sanatorium after a nervous collapse; there he tried to commit suicide. Birger Meidell of the Social Department tried unsuccessfully to convert the Fishermen's Association to Nazism. On his return from the expedition he went on "indefinite sick leave." So did Councilor Skancke of the Church Department, after having been banished from religious services for his dismissal of two Protestant bishops and four pastors. The most interesting case of illness was that of Gulbrand Lunde. On August 8, 1941, he was taken to a hospital in Oslo, where it became known that he had tried to take his own life with poison.

Lunde is not the next best man, and certainly no weakling. He is Propaganda Minister in the traitor-government, and plays at being the Norwegian Goebbels. He would not mind replacing Quisling, either. He is a grand master of the double cross. He had stamps printed with Quisling's likeness on them. "The people will spit on the wrong side of the stamp," he confessed to an intimate, who conveyed this bit of information to London. Quisling himself had to forbid the distribution of these stamps. He was forced once more to restrict his overzealous follower Lunde when the latter ordered that Quisling's pictures should be hung on the classroom walls of all the high schools and of the University of Oslo. The pictures were displayed for two days. They had all been smeared, or torn down, when Quisling ordered their removal. A heated argument ensued: "Do you want to expose me to public ridicule?" Quisling asked menacingly. Lunde shrugged. "The Norwegian nation is difficult to manage, and very stubborn," he replied.

Quisling number three is Jonas Lie, Minister of Police, whom his people have rechristened "Judas." He is not accustomed to receiving tokens of his popularity, but resounding cheers bade him farewell after he had inspected the police force of Trondheim and taken his leave with the words: "Only six of you fellows, I understand, are members of the Nasjonal Samling. You are not worth my interest. This is the first time I have talked to the police of Trondheim, and it will be the last time."

Sverre Riisnaes, acting Minister of Justice, however, went his colleague one better. An old Norwegian law stipulates that certain cases may be heard by arbitrators outside the courts. Riisnaes perverted this fundamentally democratic ruling by appointing Quislingites as arbitrators throughout the country. Norwegian justice was struck out with one stroke of the traitor's pen. The people retaliate by settling their differences among themselves, with neighbors acting as magistrates. Some Nazi-appointed judges are completely ostracized. Judge Mohr, for instance, appointed to the new Nazified Supreme Court of Norway, confessed in a moment of weakness that he "found himself about as popular as a garlic-eating skunk." Not only did he have a whole subway car to himself when riding to Oslo from his suburban home, he complained, but the members of his own family will have nothing to do with him since his appointment by the Nazis.

Other Quislings thrive on their perfidy. Each of the "Constituted State Councilors" ("Prostituted State Councilors," the people call them) serving in the puppet government receives forty-eight thousand kroner yearly from the German overlords, if only in the form of a check on the Bank of Norway. Only eighteen thousand kroner appear in the budget as being paid. The rest is camouflaged as "expenses." These salaries have cost the white-bled country a total of some three million kroner so far. But the money is not entirely wasted. The wife of Nazi-appointed State Councilor Hustad was able to buy thirty-six dresses and coats plus a generous supply of underwear within three months, which is the equivalent of seven thousand and sixty coupons, whereas the whole family was entitled to only four hundred and twenty coupons for this period of time. Such peccadillos might go unnoticed in normal times. Under the rigid rationing system, however, which restricts the entire population to utter self-sacrifice, injustices like this foment more dissatisfaction than great political decisions.

If possible, the Quisling brand, although few, are greater masters in the art of crushing private lives than even their Nazi models. There is no private sphere left in the oppressed country. Sports, tremendously popular in Norway, have been coordinated where possible. It is not always possible. Birger Rudd, the world-famous ski champion, who should be remembered in America as the winner of the 1938 ski-jumping contest, expressed the feeling of thousands of Norwegian athletes when, in answer to the Nazi sports dictator Reichborn-Kjennerud's insistence that it was his duty to compete in Germany, he said: "When the day comes on which it is my duty to participate in such a contest, I will burn my skis."

An amusing side-show is offered by the fact that the Nazis distrust their own creatures. They hand-picked Berhard Askvig as the chief of police in Oslo. While he still held this elevated position, his radio was confiscated by the Gestapo. Chief Askvig complained. Were not members of the Nasjonal Samling, to which he proudly belongs, exempted from the general seizure of radio sets? "Certainly," the Gestapo replied. "But only if the majority in a household are members. Your wife and daughter are not. At home, you are a hopelessly outnumbered one-third minority." The radio had to be delivered.

This unconcealed contempt of their German masters menaces the band of Norwegian turncoats more dangerously than the hatred of their own people. Ironically, the Nazis call the Quislings "traitors" and "double crossers"—not, of course, for having sold out their country, but for having failed to deliver the goods. Aside from three or four big businessmen, only some groups of job hunters have joined the Norwegian Nazi movement. Their brown-shirts, the Hirdmen, number one thousand, all told. This figure includes the Norwegian version of the Hitler Youth. Three hundred Hirdmen live in the

Oslo district. Formerly the membership consisted almost entirely of high-school boys and jobless white-collar workers. Lately recruits have been found among the criminal elements. They receive nominal pay, but the attraction lies in their immunity from the attentions of the police. The Oslo police recently captured a gang of boys who were responsible for a wave of theft in the capital. When the young lawbreakers proved to be Hirdmen, they were immediately released.

The principal and most coveted income of the Hirdmen is derived from the betrayal of loyal Norwegians. The prizes are not high. The secretariat of the Nasjonal Samling pays five kroner (one dollar) for a scalp. Only in the town of Skien, where an unsuccessful assault was made on Quisling's life, are informers paid at the rate of twenty-five kroner.

But despite handsome bribes the Nasjonal Samling, the only legally permitted party, suffers one setback after another. With the total population close to three million, only 30,871 have joined. This figure became known through the "indiscretion" of one of the party's leading functionaries. The Quislings, it seems, are not even safe in their own house.

They certainly are not safe from Gauleiter Josef Terboven's wrath. In private life Herr Terboven appears as a jolly good fellow, bibulous, speaking with the soft accent of the Rhineland, and as a God-fearing Catholic into the bargain. However, the picture changes rapidly when he is aroused; and he has good reason to be aroused at every turn. The heaviest blow his system received was the successful British raid on Ostvaagö, one of the Lofoten Islands off northern Norway. Punishment followed immediately. Terboven betook himself to Svolvaer, the town on the island of Ostvaagö. He had all the houses set on fire and all remaining inhabitants imprisoned. No Quisling minister was permitted to have anything to do with the matter. "You had at your disposal for many months all the tools and propaganda, and the entire government machinery, not to mention the bayonets of hundreds of thousands of German troops," Terboven yelled at Quisling, who stood rigidly at attention while being dressed down. "What did you do with all this power? It is astounding how little you have been able to influence your people. Our patience is exhausted," Terboven fumed. "We will have to apply other means."

Heinrich Himmler himself came to Norway on a two days' visit to apply these "other means." He stabbed the Nasjonal Samling where it hurts most: the pocket. The Gestapo boss left behind him a letter to the Quisling Minister of Finance, not abolishing corruption in the Quisling party but making it less profitable.

Usually it is Heinrich Himmler's habit to use more bloody measures for his purges. Revolutionaries are executed. But crooks are robbed. They understand it better.

Caught between two millstones, Quisling tried a last desperate appeal to Hitler's magnanimity and forgiveness. It is incredible how low the once proud superman was able to bend in his effort to ingratiate himself with his master. Frantically he searched for scapegoats in his own circle. He answered the snub of not having been admitted to the Anti-Comintern Pact with a servile whimper: "If Norway had been permitted to keep its government of April 9"—meaning his own position on invasion day—"then her signature would not have been missing from this epochal agreement. Instead of being able to fulfill wholeheartedly this historic and sacred mission we are compelled, due to the intrigue of traitors, to stand by as unnoticed spectators. Meanwhile we are represented in our hearts in Berlin, and we regard ourselves morally as a signer of the pact."

Quisling published this lament in *Fritt Folk*, his official mouthpiece. It prompted no answer from Berlin, nor was it reprinted in the German-controlled press.

Immediately another Quisling editorial appeared in *Fritt Folk*. The little Führer called upon the population to take revenge upon all Jews, even upon families who had lived in Norway for six hundred years. Followers were encouraged to wreak destruction on Jewish property at night, to smash windows, and to write obscenities on the walls of non-Aryan shops.

Simultaneously Quisling embarked upon another campaign, directed against a curious combination: King Haakon, whom even the most vicious traitors had not so far dared to mention personally, and the English language. "King Haakon speaks English," Quisling raged, "because he is the son-in-law of King Edward VII. But William the Conqueror, a Norwegian, spoke English with a Norwegian accent, and we will force those English people to speak with a Norwegian accent again. A Norwegian-German alliance will rule Europe. Only mentally unbalanced Norwegians desire an English victory."

The word "mentally unbalanced" was the clue for Quisling's doctor to forbid him further public utterances. The nervous strain, he explained to his patient, was too great.

The Nazis did not even listen. They do not use a blunted tool. At present, Quisling is kept only to carry on "ideologic propaganda," maintaining the shoddy Norwegian front. Behind it, the power of administration is steadily slipping out of his hands—he has even had to hand over the embezzled seal of state to a German petty official. Condemned to death by his betrayed King, and abandoned by his masters, he faces the abyss both ways.

His fate causes grim satisfaction among Norwegians. They do not even mind the ever increasing number of German secret police and civil servants flooding their country. To them even a ruthless, bestial enemy is less contemptible than the traitor within. Besides, they cling to their conviction that the days of foreign occupation are numbered.

Unperturbed, the Oslo city council received the order to evacuate the two biggest office buildings in the capital, with all equipment to be left intact, for the use of the German newcomers. Quietly, also, they accepted Terboven's command to establish three new swanky night clubs reserved for lonely Germans. Only one alderman ventured to ask: "With air-raid shelters?"

Terboven nodded violently: "Make them deep!"

The Czech Quisling is the most inscrutable fellow on earth. Indeed, in many cases it is not quite certain whether he is a Quisling or not. Does Dr. Emil Hácha, the shadow President of the "Protectorate," belong to the honorable guild? He is an old man, suffering from a progressive heart disease. On that "terrible day" when Hitler blackmailed him into asking for German protection, he suffered one collapse and breakdown after another. He had to be doped and treated with injections to survive the day.

Does such treatment produce genuine Hitlerites? Before he debased himself to accept the position as the Führer's Czech lackey number one, Dr. Hácha had a wide reputation as an authority on international law. He was a member of the Supreme Court in Prague, and a well known delegate to the International Court in The Hague. He was generally respected for his devout Catholicism. His subtle conscience was proverbial in his country.

Perhaps he is a conscientious traitor. He perhaps believes that he must endure the sacrifice of sitting at table with the German mass-murderers, of eulogizing the Führer in stammering after-dinner speeches, of spreading poisonous lies about the common welfare of the Czech and the German people. Perhaps he thinks that God has singled him out to carry this burden, in order to ease a little the crushing burden borne by his martyrized nation.

If so, his efforts are in vain. The lower Dr. Hácha bends, the harder the jack boot lands, trampling on Czechoslovakia. His every compromise is a defeat, his complacency only invites more ruthless persecutions.

Perhaps he does not know it. Perhaps we for our part do not know how much horror he accepts, in order to stave off a little longer more horrors. Dr. Hácha is no fighter, no leader of men. But he is the victim of evil more than its perpetrator.

At heart, I do not take him for a Quisling. The aged President of the Protectorate is Nazism's whipping boy.

General Eliáš, his former Premier, was a horse of another color. Bristling with newly acquired Nazism, overflowing with assurances of loyalty toward the tyrants, executing with poorly copied heel clicking the most vicious orders from Berlin, he seemed a vassal after Hitler's own heart. One day in August, 1941, however, he refused to carry out an order from Berlin. The matter was insignificant enough. Prague was to change the names of its streets from the Czech language into German. "Shall history remember me for having been the first Czech Premier to introduce German signposts in this city?" he asked a confidant. History would remember him for worse things, the two-faced confidant pondered. Then he wrote a letter to Berlin.

September came. Reinhard Heydrich arrived in Prague. The big purge came. It started with the arrest of the Premier. General Eliáš was accused of having spoken every day of his Premiership by telephone with Dr. Beneš in London. He was condemned to death. A few days later this death sentence was commuted to life imprisonment. Mitigating circumstances had been discovered. Did General Eliáš double-cross Dr. Beneš? The great leader of the Czechoslovak nation is silent on the subject. Nor will this author venture an opinion. Whatever one says will aggravate the situation of Eliáš in his German prison—if he is still alive. If not, the general may have been beheaded as a spy. Whom did he spy on? The era of the New Order is full of impenetrable mysteries.

They are all doomed to death. They know it. There is not a single Quisling, from the North Cape to the island of Crete,

who does not live in constant fear for his life. But the first to
go, it is a safe guess, will be the Yugoslavian traitors. "We
have their goings and comings on record," wrote a ranking
Serbian patriot in a circular letter (his name, of course, cannot yet be revealed). "We have our watch set on them. We
shall probably lose a few men in the attempt to get them, but
we will get them."

The first on the Serbian patriot's fatal list is Milan Stojadinović. For a few years Premier of the Kingdom, he sold out for
cold cash to Adolf Hitler. Stojadinović, whom his fellow
Serbians call the arch-corrupter, threw himself on the mercy
of the British when his country rose against him. As long as
the prison in Kenya shelters him, his life is not menaced. But
the legal Yugoslav government leaves no doubt about its determination to court-martial him in due time and put his
pomaded head with the smooth epicure's face and the Hitler
mustache where it belongs: on the block. He will be followed
by Dragiska Svetković and Pinkar Marković, the signers of
the short-lived Axis pact, as soon as they are ferreted out. At
present both are in hiding.

There is but one man among the poor mighties in Croatia
to dare the bullets of potential assassins and the assaults of an
infuriated population. His name is "Vancha"—Ivan—Mihajlow, which means nothing to the outside world, but has
spread for thirty years or longer untold terror all over the
Balkans. For many years Mihajlow has worn a steel waistcoat,
he boasts. Yet his formidable body has been riddled with some
twenty bullets, none of which, to quote the hero again, could
"entirely finish him off," although he has only his right arm
and walks with an artificial left leg. He is an illiterate but a
philosopher, resigned to taking punishment in the pursuit of
his profession. Professionally he is a *komitaji* chieftain. The
komitaji are the bands who since time immemorial have fought
under any flag in any war disrupting the burning Balkans.
There are Serbian and Greek *komitaji*, but the main body

consists of sturdy Bulgarian mountaineers. Mihajlow's political affiliations vary. He was credited with having blasted the
Sofia Cathedral on behalf of the Comintern, but later he evidently made his peace with Tsar Boris III. However, the Tsar
found it opportune to prescribe a prolonged rest cure in the
central prison of Rustschuk for his loyal subject.

Mihajlow was a forgotten man when the ordeal of the New
Order swept neighboring Croatia. It is related that Mussolini
was the first to remember the prisoner of Rustschuk. Here
was the man to build up the new order. Diplomatic conferences ensued. Mihajlow was released, and assumed the role of
"coordinator of defense" in Croatia. He was Boris III's first
lend-lease gift to the Axis. His second contribution Tsar
Quisling made in declaring war on the United States—an act
that went all but unnoticed in this country.

Boris of Bulgaria was the only sovereign in Europe who
voluntarily submitted to the New Order. Indeed, he not only
submitted, he craved acceptance in the fold. The reason for
the sell-out of his country is as convincing as it is simple. The
house of Coburg, from which the Tsar of Bulgaria descends,
still owns a number of castles and immense estates in Germany as well as in Bohemia-Moravia, Slovakia, and Hungary.
It was simple prudence to avoid the inevitable confiscation
of these properties which would have taken place had Boris
heeded the wishes of his people, who are 98 per cent anti-
German and 95 per cent pro-Russian.

Boris was not willing to endanger the family fortune. He
knows too well the meaning of poverty. For many years,
even as Tsar of the Bulgars, he did not receive a single penny
of the income of the rich Coburg fortune. His father, the
"Old Fox of the Balkans," ex-Tsar Ferdinand, who had to
resign the throne after having led Bulgaria into the disastrous
alliance with Germany during the first war, keeps the money
together. He is a thrifty paterfamilias, not above accepting

an annuity equivalent to thirty thousand dollars from the Nazi regime. In return, the old man, now eighty-one, runs his son's puppet empire by remote control from his exile in the Bavarian town of Coburg, which prides itself on having been the first Nazi-administered town in Germany.

For a long time the father's stinginess was the crowned son's despair. His situation was further complicated by the refusal of the Sobranje (the Bulgarian parliament) to raise the Tsar's civil list beyond a mere pittance. Boris's disgust with democracy and parliamentarism is well founded. The struggle for life has made him tough. He was not always so.

In the early twenties Boris of Bulgaria was widely adver- tised as a dream prince, ruling in solitary melancholy. If he never quite achieved the international popularity of his cousin King Carol of Rumania, the sole reason was that he avoided amorous scandals. His court was managed by a respectable dowager, Mme. Tery Furholzer, the widow of a Viennese coffee-house owner, who, in her position as mistress of cere- monies, saw to it that the audiences the youthful Tsar granted to ladies never lasted too long. The reason for this display of propriety was the search for an American heiress. Boris of Bulgaria, unique in many ways, is probably the only Tsar who was ever offered on the marriage market. On May 19, 1929, his then Prime Minister André Liaptcheff startled the world with the following declaration: "His Majesty will never marry an American heiress for her money alone. Wealth, splendor, pomp mean nothing to him. He prefers to drive an old German car, since he cannot afford a brand-new Ameri- can model. He is only happy when he can share the company, the fortunes, and the trials of his own humble people. What American heiress would care to share this simplicity with him?"

This invitation in reverse brought no answer from Amer- ica. But Mussolini grasped at the opportunity which Newport neglected. Bulgaria, after all, like Paris, was worth a Mass.

The Duce decided to bind the stronghold of the Balkans with marital ties to his own growing Empire. The time was 1930, the aim to keep German penetration out of the Balkans.

King Victor Emmanuel's eldest daughter, Jolanda, was shown a picture of the lonesome Tsar. The dreamy eyes, the bushy hair, the classic profile impressed her. Besides, she was told, she would live among roses. In fact Boris is an avid gardener. He cultivates roses and tobacco in alternate rows, thus, he claims, producing rose-scented cigarettes and roses with a faint suggestion of a man's lip. Besides he is an authority on herbs. Of the three hundred varieties science recognizes, about half, he insists, grow best on Bulgarian soil. Using the slogan, "For every ailment God has provided a herb," he made a flourishing trade out of his production, far outdoing, in Sofia at least, both Mesdames Rubinstein and Elizabeth Arden.

Small wonder that Princess Jolanda could not resist the temptation. "I will," she said. But when her fiancé came to Rome to celebrate the announcement of the royal engagement, which was eagerly awaited by two great nations neither of which had ever cared for the other, it proved that his fascinating photograph was at least fifteen years old. In the flesh, Boris was indisputably bald; his hair receded alarmingly, his nose protruded, and both his ears stuck out. Princess Jolanda coined the phrase that Greta Garbo later immortalized: "I think I shall not get married today." But the scandal was quickly hushed up. Dutifully, her younger sister, Princess Giovanna, filled the gap. Fascism's children have not much choice. Princess Giovanna is today Tsarevna Ioanna. Her life is embellished by the presence of her two spinster sisters-in-law in Euxinograd Castle on the Black Sea. The huge brownstone building in Sofia, the official Tsarist residence, is not safe enough for the mother of the country.

Boris III did not settle down after his wedding. Now he had to fulfill his part of the marriage contract. He had to make Bulgaria fascist. It did not prove an easy task. The Bulgars, despite their high percentage of professional assassins, are stanch lovers of liberty. Besides they are imbued with a Russian complex which contributed little to their willingness to go either Italian or German. Boris was soon commonly dubbed the "traitor-Tsar." Innumerable assaults were made on his life; on the 15th of August, 1940, no fewer than three within as many hours. Although the assaults miscarried, they were a definite warning that the nation did not want to be forced into the Axis camp. The memory of the first collapse at Germany's side was still fresh in every one's mind.

Boris got his unfortunate people against such heavy odds into their suicidal war by a masterpiece of cunning. Undoubtedly the fine hands of his father, the Old Fox of the Balkans, pulled the wires. The betrayal of Bulgaria began on November 17, 1940, when Boris was the first Balkan ruler to be admitted into the privacy of Berchtesgaden. Hitler demanded the right to occupy Bulgaria. He expected stiff resistance. Indeed, Dr. Meissner, the chief of his personal chancellery, admitted later: "We were prepared to pay a sack of gold. But Boris is an unselfish crook. He consented gratis." He just asked for a few more months' time to prepare his country "morally." His moral preparation began by his calling the British Minister to Sofia, Mr. George Rendel, to his palace, and assuring him that the visit in Berchtesgaden had been nothing more than a social call without the slightest political significance.

Months passed in silent preparation. On March 1, the Sobranje was forced to ratify Bulgaria's adherence to the Tripartite pact. Boris hailed this event in a message to Hitler. Hitler, in turn, cabled back his "deepest wishes" for Bulgaria. Prince Konoye did not miss the opportunity to voice Japan's "great satisfaction over the splendid German success in the Balkans." The choir of joy was only disturbed by Mr. George Rendel's call on the treacherous Tsar. Exactly what was said during their two hours' conversation will be up to the British minister to divulge in his own time. Sofia court functionaries were pale and shivering when Mr. Rendel, reversing all diplomatic ceremonial, terminated the audience. "Never has a man spoken as plainly to a sovereign," was the unanimous comment. But probably no diplomat ever had to speak so plainly. In the face of obvious facts, Boris dared to assure the British envoy that he had entered into no commitment whatsoever with Hitler, and that his heart glowed with friendship for England. A week later, Mr. Rendel and his staff left Sofia. The Bulgarian camarilla retaliated by accusing British press attaché Norman Davis of having led a spy ring which was distributing explosives and fostering revolution in Bulgaria. He was condemned to death *in absentia.*

They had barked up the wrong tree. The spy ring that still endangers the Bulgarian dictatorship was by no means headed by a foreigner. Anton Proudkine was outraged when Mr. Davis was accused of deeds for which he himself proudly assumed the responsibility. Proudkine is a professional revolutionary of old and honorable standing. In a long adventurous life he has been poet, writer, fisherman, sea captain, and intermittently Police Commissioner of Sofia, until he had to be dismissed for having blown up a theater in which his political enemies were gathered. The old man challenged Tsar Boris to a duel with any weapon His Majesty might choose. But Boris, at fifty-two, is no longer a fighter. He had rather his people did the fighting for him. He set the Gestapo, a few squads of which he had imported, on Proudkine's trail. So far, they have not got the old fire-eater.

Sofia was flooded with German agents. The most important visitor was Grand Admiral Erich Raeder, officially the First Lord of the Nazi navy, actually Hitler's personal confidant among his otherwise not too reliable marshals, generals, and admirals. The German minister was replaced by Herr Bekerle, the head of the Fifth Column in Bulgaria, who now assumed official responsibility. Field Marshal Siegmund Wilhelm Walter List asked on the telephone whether his visit would be agreeable, and whether Bulgaria was prepared to defray the costs of room and board for his entourage, about one million men. He would like, he indicated, to be received by his old friend Lieutenant General Konstantin Loukoff, who was immediately promoted Bulgarian chief of the general staff. Premier Bogdan Filov shaved his beard, keeping nothing but a Hitler mustache. This was the last indication of great events to come.

But it remained for the Old Fox of the Balkans, who outlives and outsmarts them all, to flash the green light. On June 5, 1941, he received his son Boris in Vienna.. Hitler had just raised the ex-Tsar's annuity to the equivalent of fifty thousand dollars. He never bought a country as cheaply as that. "*En avant!*" said old Ferdinand.

Boris clicked his heels. "The unification of all Bulgarians has been achieved by the Axis," he stated, returning to Sofia.

Unwittingly, he spoke the truth. All Bulgaria is unified—against the Axis.

The staircase leading to the Presidential Palace in Bucharest is adorned with two rows of lions in stone. It is against this background that General Ion Antonescu prefers to have his pictures taken. His staircase is the equivalent of Mussolini's balcony. Here he exhorts his people; here he declares his wars. Conversely, the "Head of the State"—to use the self-fashioned title Antonescu shares with no one but Pétain—receives his own orders in a less glamorous surrounding: two blocks down Victoria Street, in a modest office of the German Legation.

Ion Antonescu is a veteran stooge of Hitler. His allegiance dates from the Führer's assumption of power in the Reich. "Jean le Beau," as many of his friends, particularly his lady friends, used to call Rumania's chocolate soldier number one, was among the first well-wishers to hurry to Berlin when the marauders in brown shirts were let loose on the streets of the German capital. Obviously, he was deeply affected by the pogroms and parades that initiated the rule of Nazism. On his return to Bucharest a reporter asked the general for his impressions of Germany. "It hurts terribly to be born in a second-rate country," Antonescu replied. Today still, the state he heads is only a second-rate country to him. His conduct proves it. The Rumanian auxiliary troops lost scores of thousands in besieging, and finally helping to take, Odessa. After sufficient time for cleaning up the streets and mopping up the guerrillas had elapsed, Antonescu on his white charger made his triumphal entry into Odessa. His flag was hoisted on City Hall. Not the colors of Rumania—the swastika.

He has chosen the white charger as his symbol. Jean le Beau rides no other horse. It reminds him of his glorious start. A white charger carried him to his first victory.

It was back in 1907. The Rumanian peasants' revolt gave the young, dashing lieutenant, then fresh from the officers' school, an early opportunity to prove his cunning. He was sent to a district in southern Moldavia, where the ordeal was worse. Lieutenant Antonescu arrived with machine-gun squads and artillery. The peasants were armed with pitchforks and scythes. Yet they awaited him undaunted.

Antonescu scored his first bloodless victory. Perhaps his white charger impressed the simple people. Perhaps he did the trick by shedding a few tears as he adjured the people to listen to reason. He would take their spokesmen to Bucharest, where all their complaints would be settled. The people dropped their pitchforks. They cheered His Excellency, the dashing cavalry lieutenant. Their delegation followed him to Bucharest, where every one of them was shot. Ion Antonescu's persuasive gifts were duly rewarded. He was appointed to the general staff. His career was assured.

It was a career of crime and double-crossing. The first war provided no milestones along the way. He sat out the four long years in a hospital. But he could not sit out the world revolution of Nazism, whose appeal was irresistible. He founded the Legionnaires, Rumania's first organized fascist movement. The Legionnaires were smart and fashionable, they protested their allegiance to their King and received subsidies from Mussolini. But a rival gang soon bested them. The "Iron Guards" were clad in ragged black shirts. They mocked His Majesty. They received their pay from Nazism. For a short time Antonescu was on the wrong side. He helped King Carol break up the Iron Guards. Their leader Codreanu and twelve of his henchmen were shot "while attempting to escape," after their arrest. Rumania was at the brink of open revolution.

The Iron Guards swore to avenge Codreanu. But they did not get Antonescu, who had planned the murder. He simply disappeared. All Bucharest buzzed with rumors that Jean le Beau had committed suicide. After two weeks he emerged again. He had spent these two weeks in the Bistritsa convent, waiting until the country was once more quiet. Now he rode his white charger again down Calea Victoriei, Bucharest's main street. His reappearance led to new outbreaks of violence. The Iron Guards assassinated Antonescu's bosom friend, Prime Minister Calinescu. On Antonescu's advice stern repressive measures were taken. Nine Guardists were shot in full daylight, in the center of Bucharest. Their bodies were exposed on the road. The population was told to come and enjoy the spectacle. For three days the bodies of the murdered gangsters lay in the streets in full view of the public. Candy and soft drinks were sold from booths alongside the place of execution. Every morning and every evening the man on the white charger rode by, stopped to survey the gruesome spectacle, smiled, and lit another of his perfumed cigarettes.

Such perfect poise impressed Carol II. On September 5, 1940, the King asked Antonescu to form a government, pri-

marily to protect his anointed head from the popular wrath.
The same day a distinguished stranger arrived in the Grand
Hotel. It takes only two hours by air to come to Bucharest
from Istanbul, where Herr von Papen entertains in his palatial summer villa. Papen persuaded Antonescu that Hitler was
a better bet than Mussolini. Of course, the German Jack-of-
all-trades happened to know a few of the Führer's faithful
followers among the Iron Guards. He volunteered to establish personal contacts. Why not talk it over?

Antonescu, indeed, formed his government to protect the
King from the Iron Guard with the help of some of the
guardsmen's leaders. Hore Simia, the assassinated Codreanu's
successor, became his Vice Premier. When the King received
his new government to accept their oath, Antonescu said:
"Your Majesty, I can give you just one hour to abdicate. I
am afraid I cannot keep the masses under control any longer."
Indeed, the square around the royal palace was crowded with
a mob, Legionnaires and Iron Guard in brotherly concord,
blood-crazed and shouting for the scalp of "the Jewess,"
Madame Lupescu, the King's common-law wife.

The story of King Carol's fantastic escape with her, a
dozen pets, and most of the Rumanian crown jewels, in his
bullet-ridden, armored de luxe train, has frequently been told.
Less accurate are the published reports on the suppression of
Iron Guards in Bucharest, which followed immediately. One
single sentence of Antonescu's is on record: "They have outlived their usefulness." Outlived, he meant literally. What
happened to Hore Simia is uncertain. Some reports are that
he was killed; more pessimistic accounts are that he is in a
German concentration camp.

Herr von Papen sent a message of congratulation. Hitler
cabled his appreciation personally. He welcomed the general
as a recruit to the New Order. Soon thousands of Rumanian
peasants were slaughtered on the Russian battlefields. They
had to do the dirty jobs in the hazardous Crimean campaign. As

prescribed, they died with a cheer for Antonescu on their lips. That is, at least, his conviction. "Ever since the beginning of the world men have rejoiced when they lost their liberty," he declared. "Mortals passionately love only those who put them in chains. Adam was a sergeant major. Recognizing this, we understand that Rumania has never been in such dire need of irrational activity as today. Do not be surprised if our country soon passes through a phase of orgies, fanaticism, and irrationalism."

The words are General Antonescu's. Lest he stutter in delivering them, his ghost writer, Emil Chioran, wrote them carefully on the general's manuscript.

In Poland the German authorities of occupation made the flattering suggestion to Professor Jan Kupnaczewski that he form a puppet government. The old professor, it appeared, would be amenable for two reasons. First, as the author of the once famous book *White and Red Tsars in Russia*, he was well known for his flaming anti-bolshevism and for his equal contempt for Tsarist Russia. Second, he had already been Prime Minister of a German-instituted Polish shadow government during the years 1917 and 1918, when his country was occupied by Imperial German troops.

Pointing out the difference between Nazism and old-style imperialism, Professor Kupnaczewski refused the offer. When he was threatened with what Governor General Dr. Hans Frank termed the "inevitable consequences of failing Adolf Hitler," the professor replied: "I am close to eighty." That settled the matter.

Dr. Frank's second choice was another aged professor, Dr. Stanislaw Estreicher, the country's foremost savant, whose life work, the *Bibliografja Polska*, already begun by his father, Karel, is comparable only with the *Encyclopædia Britannica*.

Professor Estreicher accepted. But he made three conditions. First, German troops must evacuate Poland immediately. Second, all Polish military and civilian authorities should be reestablished, the requisitioning of Polish property must cease instantly, and payments must be made for goods already requisitioned. Third, all Polish prisoners of war must be released immediately.

For having stipulated these conditions, Professor Estreicher was taken to a German concentration camp, and tortured to death.

The job, offered to both men, is still vacant.

Poland has no Quisling.

CHAPTER EIGHT

TERROR

If God exists it must have been He who chose Adolf Hitler to exterminate the mob nations.—GAULEITER GREISER, Kalisz, Warthe, October 5, 1940.

TOWERING above subjugated Europe, listening to inner voices and inspirations, Adolf Hitler, like the Pythia, sits on a three-legged stool—the Gestapo, the concentration camp, and the system of hostages. These, next to the bayonets of his armies of occupation, are the three pillars of his power over some two hundred million desperate and, if he wills it, doomed people.

Since his self-created advancement to the rank of supreme war lord the paper hanger has indulged in the use of military simile. "The Gestapo," he told his assiduously listening high command, "are my shock troops. They are the spearhead of every advance. They hit hard and fast. In the concentration camps my battles of attrition are being waged. All we want is a little barbed wire to put out of action three million enemies. And where, in military warfare, I would put the Luftwaffe to supreme service, political warfare demands the hostage system. It is cheaper, and just as effective as razing a few cities."

The *Deutscher Freiheitssender* (German Freedom station), the fearless pirate of the German radio waves, acquainted the nation with Hitler's flights of speech by broadcasting the contents of his address to his generals, delivered in "the Führer's headquarters somewhere on the Russian front," actually at Berchtesgaden, on December 5, 1941. The broadcast was repeated on five consecutive days. Of course, the German Freedom station does not disclose its sources. The responsibility for the report remains with it. But its information has frequently proved accurate. Perhaps some orderly or some bodyguard in Berchtesgaden listens in when the Führer thunders. It is by no means impossible that some member of the German High Command informs the "black" waves. The generals hate the Gestapo. Not for any moral reasons. It is simply a matter of competition.

For some time the jealousy of the generals kept the Gestapo chiefs out of the oppressed countries, while the Secret Military Police cleaned up the invaded countries. This Secret Military Police, although little known to the world, is a formidable body, led by Admiral Canaris, whose name it is strictly forbidden to mention in Germany. Its rule is no less brutal and terroristic than Gestapo rule. Yet the people recall it nostalgically when the Gestapo muscles in, which happens sooner or later in every country under the jack boot.

In the words of Peter Krier, the Luxembourg Minister of Labor and Social Insurance in exile, who, before escaping, had shared his little country's ordeal for a long time, the Secret Military Police, with all its strictness, was mainly concerned with discovering and preventing espionage and sabotage. The Gestapo, which came afterward, had according to its nature political functions and purposes, and the network of its spies and agents intruded into the private life of every one. The civilian administrators who took the places of the officers were either fanatical Nazis or shady characters with dubious records. While the military police confined itself to maintaining military security and strict order in Luxembourg, the Gestapo pursues the aim of "bending the people politically to the will of the Reich."

In Luxembourg, incidentally, the Gestapo established its headquarters in the Villa Pauly, which was soon to become notorious througout the country for the cruel maltreatment of prisoners in its cellars. Arrests made by the Gestapo were abundant. Vague denunciations were sufficient; often arrests were carried out without any stated reason at all. The prisons were crowded with people against whom not even the German police could charge any offense. When they were eventually released, they had to promise not to speak of their experiences. Yet the stories of the abominable tortures soon got about. Among those arrested were, in spite of his infirmity, the aged court marshal of the Grand Duchess, the castellans of the two Grand Ducal castles, the administrator of the Grand Ducal revenues, and many gendarmerie officers, Catholic priests, technicians, students, and workers. No section of the population was spared. Spying and informing was systematically organized. Block wardens, after the German model, were introduced for rows of houses to watch the inhabitants.

Firmly entrenched in power, the Gestapo unloosed a renewed wave of arrests. The Luxembourg Administrative Commission, which had hitherto collaborated with the German military authorities, was dissolved by the new masters; the chairman was arrested and deported to Germany. Industrial life was similarly "cleaned up." "Arbed," the immense European steel combine with headquarters in Luxembourg, was forced to accept as general manager an "economic expert" of the Gestapo named Bernhuber. The director of the "Arbed" selling organization, Columeta, was arrested for no other reason than his alleged anti-German tendencies. Herr

Max Meier (a name which sounds too commonplace to be anything but the nom de guerre of another Gestapo-expert) took over the management of the Hadir group. Luxembourg's other important factories were swallowed by private German interests, among which the Hermann Göring Werke did not forget to exercise its customary priority. The De Wendel works and the UCPMI works in Hagondange are now producing for the fat Marshal's benefit. The Gestapo has deserved well of German heavy industry, which, in turn, showed its gratitude. Herr Himmler received a small matter of ten million marks from the *Rheinstahlverband,* the organization of the big industry in the Rhineland, for having displayed his patriotic zeal in Luxembourg.

In Brussels, the Gestapo established sumptuous headquarters in an office building on the Avenue Louise, opposite the Abbaye de la Cambre. The monks say that they can no longer sleep at night: the tortured screams from the cellar opposite hound them. Besides, the brothers of the abbey find themselves in a strange society when they venture on the streets. The Gestapo building opposite is constantly besieged by sinister characters. Streetwalkers, thieves, dope addicts, the whole assortment of human derelicts surrounds closely the house of terror, where information about neighbors fetches prizes up to five thousand francs.

Almost the whole activity of the Gestapo in Belgium is mobilized against the Anglophilia of the population. Such centers of resistance as are known to the Germans—restaurants, clubs, halls—are constantly combed. Incessantly the Gestapo is on the search for Belgian creatures who would accept an assignment to mingle with private society in which Mr. Churchill's good health is being toasted. Its agents in disguise watch the graves of the British dead in the first war, which are frequently decorated with flowers and laurels. Any donor whom they catch is doomed. The Gestapo has a cleaning-up squad of its own. Five hundred charwomen are on its pay roll to scrub off the *V* signs from the walls on which they appear nightly. Another special squad is hunting more or less well known patriots, who enlist Belgian youth to fight for freedom and make contact with the British parachutists descending frequently on the country, partly to supply the revolutionaries with arms, partly to escort the volunteers to Belgian camps in England. Much of this secret traffic goes on along the border of France's forbidden zone. This frontier is littered with Gestapo posts—in mufti, of course. Every night shootings occur, in which the Gestapo and the army's military police compete in head-hunting.

A rare case of frictionless cooperation between Germany's military and civilian authorities was the control established over the Belgian prisoners who had returned from captivity. The Brussels Ortskommandatur had asked the Gestapo for a list of their names. They were the obvious hostages, if continued sabotage should make internment advisable. This time, the Gestapo outdid itself. Not only were all the returned prisoners listed. Herr Klammerstein, Gestapo chief in Brussels, was delighted to offer General von Falkenhausen a list of a million and a half names including all the more or less prominent citizens of occupied Belgium, from which His Excellency might make his choice of potential hostages. The letters "PB" after a name indicated the pro-British attitude of its bearer. Almost all the names were marked "PB."

Herr von Falkenhausen returned the file angrily. "It is no good," he said. "I cannot take a million and a half hostages, and shoot them."

"Why not?" Herr Klammerstein asked innocently.

Heinrich Himmler's own Gestapo in Vichy France is largely French-manned. The bosses, of course, are Germans: They sit in all the ministries, departments, offices, and agencies of the Pétain administration. The economic and the political life of both the occupied and the "free" zone is supervised by Gestapo agents. At least one hundred of them have their desks in the Paris police prefecture. Their head man is Commissioner Richard Schlutter, in charge of the special section engaged in ferreting out the perpetrators of attacks on members of the German army of occupation. Gestapo bosses and French ace-detectives work hand in glove. Their harmony is perfect, their aims identical: the ruthless suppression of the French people.

A most interesting case of Nazi infiltration into the fine network of French secret service was the "coordination" of the *Deuxième Bureau*. Every reader of prewar espionage fiction knows the name. To espionage fans the Deuxième Bureau was the opposite number of Scotland Yard, the hallowed scene of every detective thriller before the homespun American mystery story came into its own. But the Deuxième Bureau was more than the background of innumerable yellow-bound *romans policiers*. Before the decay of France, it was, indeed, the world's foremost spy center. The Germans took it very seriously; they had good reason to do so. Hence one of the many secret clauses of the Armistice of Compiègne provided for the abolition of the Deuxième Bureau. General Huntzinger, the late Vichy War Minister, who was France's chief negotiator at Compiègne, tried frantically to save the remnants of the famous and time-honored institution. In a way he succeeded. It proved impossible to cut off its thousand tentacles. The Deuxième Bureau's agencies and branches were dispersed all over Paris, all over France, all over the world. Moreover, the Germans displayed their magnanimity. Officially insisting on the liquidation of the octopus, they shut their eyes to its continued functioning. They even encouraged it. There was but one small condition attached to their tolerance. The Deuxième Bureau had henceforth to work for the Axis.

Vichy gladly complied. All military secrets in their possession, not only their own but also the British—confidential information on aviation and armament production, new devices for combating the U-boat menace, strategic plans—were traded to the Germans. The information was made mostly obsolete by the surrender of France, but it was a new proof of Vichy's determination to play its role in the New Order, and as such was highly appreciated by Hitler. The Deuxième Bureau had signally proved its usefulness, and it now enjoyed the particular protection of the protectors.

Vichy, with a noose around its neck (to use Pétain's own phrase), almost completely shut off from foreign contacts, is, amazingly, again the spy center of the world. Foreign ambassadors, who do not use ugly words, call it "a window onto the world," and are reluctant to leave their observer post, although Vichy-France herself admits that she is no longer a sovereign country. Her old virtues persist. Next to China, whose secret service has accurately predicted all the major events of this war, including their precise timing, enchained France is leading in the field of international espionage. The Deuxième Bureau is going strong once more. Of course, it derives much of its regained strength from an infusion of German blood. Its *fiche* (file), of which Marcel Peyrouton once boasted that it "covers every man worth while in the whole world, and does not forget his mistresses, either," piles up sky-high. Most of the new reports, however, are written bilingually, with the German copy frequently the original.

The lower ranks of the Gestapo in France are about equally divided between German and French jobholders. Of course, the French collaborators are admitted only as informers, not as members of the staff. That hundreds of Darlan's naval officers are cooperating with the Gestapo was pointed out previously. Vichy's newly instituted secret state police also receives its orders from Heinrich Himmler's headquarters. The collaboration is intimate in Paris, where, in his unassuming office at 9 Rue de Presbourg, Dr. Grell lords it over the secret service, as well as in Marseilles, where the German Armistice Commission has built up an information center covering the Mediterranean coasts of both France and her North African empire.

Latin America, however, provides the most tempting opportunity for the Gestapo and its French subsidiaries to work in double harness. Since the entry of the United States into the war, German tourists and traveling salesmen lie low in the countries of the Western Hemisphere, although numerous incidents prove that they have by no means abandoned their activities. Yet Herr Himmler had to call off some of his dogs. When Baron Thermann, the German ambassador, was forced to leave the Argentine, a large fifth column lost its jobs. They were quickly filled by a number of convinced Darlanites, who cash in on the great respect most Latin-Americans still feel for immortal France.

Colonel Kurt Meisinger assumed his Polish assignment on the strength of an ordinance of October 29, 1939, signed by Governor General Dr. Hans Frank: "In all matters of principle the commander in chief of the S.S. and police will act only with my approval. But he is authorized on his own responsibility to take any action he may consider necessary for the maintenance of security and public order."

This rubber paragraph made the Gestapo independent of the courts. Colonel Meisinger was not bound by any laws. The great majority of executions, arrests, and deportations were based exclusively on his own, or his henchmen's, decision. Only death sentences ordered by the courts received publicity. But these were the smallest fraction of all the cases. For the rest, murder and execution in Poland were shrouded in the deepest secrecy.

During the first year of the Meisinger regime more people were put to death than had been killed by the steamroller of war that passed over Poland in September, 1939. The Polish government in exile has exact reports of the wholesale butchery in Bydgoszcz, where ten thousand Poles were massacred. They know every detail of the mass executions in Wawer, Łuków, Częstochowa, Starachowice, Skarżysko, Inowroclaw, Opozno, Bochnia—indeed, in almost every town in Poland and in thousands of villages. In one place, Palmiry near Warsaw, five thousand people were murdered and buried in ditches; in an attempt to hide the crime these ditches were filled in, and roads built over them. The gardens of the House of Parliament and the square in front of the citadel of Warsaw are cemeteries without tombstones.

The purge of Poland, conducted by blood-crazed Colonel Meisinger, originally aimed at the extermination of the upper classes. Large numbers of priests, lawyers, professors, doctors, and businessmen were shot. Later, as the resistance of the Polish people increased, the Gestapo changed its tactics, directing them primarily against citizens of known patriotic sentiment. The pretense is always the same: that the doomed men—and women—participated in "persecution of the German minorities" before the war. It is now the third year since these alleged crimes—time enough, one would believe, for the superefficient Gestapo to have cleared up all the cases demanding German vengeance—but trials in 1942 are still dealing with offenses of the years 1938 and 1939.

Colonel Meisinger boasted that he had thoroughly cleaned up Poland before departing. At a farewell dinner, given in his honor by the Governor General, he recalled with relish the slaughter of two leading statesmen, Professor Casimir Bartel, former Prime Minister of Poland, and Maceji Rataj, the former speaker of the Polish parliament. He reminded his boon companions that he had had his "little personal share" in these "tragicomic incidents."

The perpetrator of all this horror is gone. (He acts, at present, as go-between for the German embassy in Tokyo and legation in Nanking.) But his system is being carried on. After the German assault on Russia the Gestapo terror in Poland increased enormously, with extensive arrests and thousands of executions, and all the jails in the country are overflowing. The accused are not brought to trial until many months after their arrest, and the treatment of prisoners is undescribable. In Warsaw, two priests, arrested for preaching patriotic sermons, were chained to the wall, and the guards shouted at them: "Now you can bark as much as you wish, if you still feel like it."

This terror had but one effect: it increased resistance and sabotage, long rampant in Poland. Railroad lines used for the transportation of reinforcements and supplies to the Eastern front are constantly being damaged, and bridges are blown up. The most serious case on record was the dynamiting of the big bridge near Białystok over which almost all the trains from the Reich must pass. This offense brought Heinrich Himmler personally to Poland. The Gestapo boss went to Białystok to conduct the investigation. Three hundred "suspected" people were arrested immediately on Himmler's arrival. Indiscriminately, thirty of them were shot since the guilty men could not be discovered.

Heinrich Himmler issued his "decree of Białystok" which makes a fine difference betwen collective and personal responsibility for offenses committed. Personally responsible, according to this decree, are all leading citizens. Wherever disturbances of public order occur or anti-German sentiments are displayed, the mayor of the community involved, the local priest, and former Polish functionaries or officeholders must answer with their heads. Collective responsibility, on the other hand, is another expression for the system of hostages. No less than 10 per cent of the population shall be shot or hanged as a measure of "collective repression" to punish what Himmler terms "outbreaks of lawlessness."

The decree was immediately translated into action. In Zerun eighty-one men and five women were shot after the

German district commissioner had suffered an "unexplained accident." In Ozarow, near Warsaw, two German gendarmes were killed. In retaliation, the entire population of the village of both sexes and all ages, was assembled in the market place, and machine-gunned.

The same terror devastated innumerable villages. Terror is rampant everywhere, but it is worst in Warsaw, where the "show cases" are handled. In the capital, they have the greatest educational value. The victim of one of these "show cases" was the shopkeeper Golaszewski, whose store in Grochowska Street was fairly well known to the public. In the back room of this shop a radio was found which Golaszewski had failed to deliver. The Gestapo came, surprising the old man with the order that he should pick up a few old newspapers. "They'll keep you a little warmer while you are growing cold," one of the men informed Golaszewski. Then he had to summon his children, a boy of eighteen and a girl aged sixteen. "Let's get going," the Gestapo boss shouted. Golaszewski was marched to the street, and shot. His clothes were confiscated as a prize. His children, forced to watch their father's execution, had to wrap the body into the sheets of newspaper. They were strictly forbidden to remove it before dawn. "We want to give our dear Warsawers an impressive lesson," the Gestapo boss said. Next morning both the children were spirited away. In spite of all its exertions the Gestapo regretted that the kidnapers could not be found.

Late in November, 1941, the Gestapo raided a house in Lwowska Street, in the heart of Warsaw, where, according to confidential reports, patriotic meetings were held. The first of the raiding party to enter, Sturmbannführer Heimerle, was received with a rain of bullets. He fell. In retaliation all present at the gathering, numbering two hundred, were shot on the spot. Eight thousand more Polish men betwen the ages of fourteen and forty-five were arrested as "accomplices," and sent to concentration camps.

Heinrich Himmler signed another decree. It was called the decree of Warsaw, and announced that henceforth a thousand Poles would be executed for every single German killed or wounded. Then he returned to Berlin.

Few prisoners return from Polish concentration camps; those who do, remain marked men for the rest of their lives. Hundreds of thousands of Polish citizens are still detained; they are dying a slow death. In Warsaw alone many tens of thousands of people have been captured and deported to these camps. The same thing has happened at Lublin, Łódź, Piotrków, Radom, Kielce. Every town and every village has had its share of captured and deported. Each visit to Poland by a Nazi boss, each renewal of German military preparations, each day in the calendar commemorating an event in Polish history means fresh arrests and fresh deportations; in fact, fresh death sentences. When merciful death finally comes, the family of the murdered victim is informed of the fact by a telegram from the Gestapo, and asked to send seven marks as the price for the ashes of the deceased. Catholic burial is denied to the Polish martyrs, most of whom were devout Catholics throughout their lives. In Poznań a crematorium was constructed where the bodies of those who died in concentration camps are burned. Disposing of the dead bodies in this manner erases all evidence of brutal beating and torture.

The most sinister concentration camp is in Oświęcim, near Katowice, on the western border of occupied Poland. The camp is surrounded by a "neutral belt," two to three miles wide, separated from the world by electrified barbed wire. The camp "accommodates" thirty thousand inmates, but, as a rule, only eight thousand are Poles. The rest come from other occupied countries. To be sent to Poland means, all over Europe, aggravation of punishment. The prisoners are divided into three groups. In the first group are the political offenders; in the second, the criminals; in the third—the flotsam of the camp—are Catholic priests and Jews. Youthful S.S. officers between the ages of eighteen and twenty-one act as commanders. The wardens are Gestapo noncoms. In addition, every dormitory has its own boss, selected from among the inmates. These bosses are mostly criminals serving life terms, the favorites, frequently the pals and partners, of the wardens. Invariably, they are degenerates, abusing their practically unlimited powers of discipline with gusto. They are not taken to account for beating and kicking their less privileged fellow prisoners. They relish their task. Some have developed the technique of injuring their victims so artfully that a single blow incapacitates a man for many days.

Prison rules are strict; punishment even for unwitting violation is savage. The violator gets twenty-five to seventy-five lashes with the whip, while his fellow prisoners must watch. Since the food is entirely insufficient, minor thefts are common in the canteen. The special penalty for such petty larcenies is tinged with Teutonic humor. First the "glutton" who stole an illegal crumb of moldy bread has to run the gantlet between his comrades. Those who do not beat him hard enough must join him. If he crumples, he is hauled up by the wardens, and made to run on. He is pursued as far as the gates. Now he becomes an "escape case." The gayety is uproarious when the guards hustle the victim to the crematory. There he is thrown into the furnace where the as yet unburned bodies lie. Ever good-humored, the wardens warn the stokers to be careful in separating the "living" bones from the dead ones. These treacherous Polish bones, they add, are so unreliable that they can get mixed after death. A man exposed to such treatment awaits death as a salvation. But he is cheated out of even this last hope. When he wakes up in the hospital, he is horrified by the sudden shock of finding himself once more condemned to life in Oświęcim.

Life begins at five A.M., the reveille being announced by kicks and beatings. Three men have been sleeping—as far as they can sleep—on the same straw mattress: they are so tightly crammed together that all three must move if one wants to get up. The dormitories are never heated. In winter the melting snow drips in through the windows. Three minutes are permitted for washing and dressing. Then comes breakfast: two hundred grams of moldy bread. Lunch is the same, enriched with a bowl of malodorous soup and two potatoes. Dinner consists of another two hundred grams of the same ersatz bread, and a cup of brown water which passes for coffee. All meals must be swallowed in a hurry. There is no time to chew.

Between meals the inmates of Oświęcim work. They are forced to perform the most senseless tasks. Twenty times the same hedges and walls are built up, destroyed, and erected again. The men at work stand with naked feet on stony paths; this is to make escape still more difficult.

Most terrible are the tricks to which the third group are exposed. Much of their work consists in carrying heavy stones around the courtyard. Wardens on bicycles accompany them and lash them if they do not run fast enough. They maintain that a fellow can bear twenty-five such lashings before he collapses. If a man rubs his frozen hands, he is required to stretch them out and keep them up for a whole hour. The men dig snow with their bare hands for shovels. Breakdowns and sudden deaths during the work occur frequently. But only 38 per cent of the sick, statistics reveal, are admitted to the hospital. Minor diseases lead right to the penitentiary cells from which there is only one exit: to the crematory.

Late in November, 1941, when all the Polish hospitals were requisitioned for the benefit of wounded German soldiers from the eastern front, a few thousand syphilitics with open wounds were dumped in Oświęcim. In the absence of any hygienic precautions the contagious disease spread rapidly. Some Polish patriots can estimate the mortality rate in the camp by keeping an eye on the telegraph office in Oświęcim. Between the 5th and 9th of December, in Warsaw alone, a few hundred families received telegrams informing them that their imprisoned relatives had died of "heart trouble." On December 13, four hundred of these messages were dispatched. The fatal heart trouble, it was soon established, was not of the usual variety. It was neither torture nor syphilis. A hunger strike had broken out in Dormitory 6. The warden appeared, and had the strikers horsewhipped. In the ensuing free-for-all, two wardens were killed. The four hundred prisoners present at the riot—only a few of whom had been actively involved—were taken into the forest and shot.

The latest addition to the network of concentration camps in Poland is the institute recently established east of Białystok, near the Russian border. It was founded by special demand of the German *Sicherheitsdirektor* (director for public security) Fischer, who argued that the "very conditions of the uninhabitable marshland east of Białystok will help to wear down the resistance of the prisoners, who will no longer be dangerous if and when the tide should turn against the German liberators." Herr Fischer suggested making room in the new camp for the sixty thousand most stubborn among the detained. Indeed, they poured in by the thousands. Since not the slightest move of the oppressors remains unobserved—or will go unpunished—in occupied Poland, track has been kept of every single transport. From Pawiak and Dzielna came four hundred men and one hundred women; all of them had first undergone a mock medical test and were declared fit to stand the rigors of prison life in the swamps. A batch of two hundred and ninety-three persons from Pawiak were spared similar medical niceties. From the Warsaw prisons came six hundred and eighty-six men and three hundred and sixty women. Mass transports from Tarnów and Novy Sacz included mostly priests, professors, and students. The exact number could not be established.

A shooting wave also emptied the hospitals in Polish prisons. Hospital beds in the occupied countries are a rare commodity since the Russians began to take their toll of German cannon fodder. Moreover, the Nazi creed firmly believes in the survival of only the fit. Both these facts were good reasons for the hospital purge conducted last autumn. In Chełm four hundred "nervously diseased"—people, obviously, who had been too long exposed to the prison's hospitality—among them a good many children, were shot. So were several wardens who would not stand by as they were told. The Gestapo occupied the building. Subsequently they refused to release it even for the wounded German soldiers, on whose behalf the hospital had been confiscated. Similarly, the asylum for the aged in Płock was purged. It was not a matter of great consequence. Only forty-two inmates had to be rounded up and stood against the trees in the wood. In Zakopane, the Polish Davos, the chief of the German military hospitals in the district of Cracow arrived with a large entourage of S.S. guards. The luxurious sanatorium of the Academic Union and the Sanatorium Renaissance were evacuated. So was, since Nazism knows no class differences, the hospital for tubercular poor children, Na Bystrem. Dr. Schaefer, the chief of the military hospitals of Cracow, was humane enough to permit Christian burial. Personally, he delivered the funeral oration. "His Holiness the Pope," he declared, "does not believe in euthanasia. I hope the poor people we have relieved from the sickness of their lives will rest in peace. Of course, if they care to, they may complain in heaven."

No funeral speeches are delivered in Poznań, Fort VII. Death is a matter-of-fact business there. The old Polish fortress was converted into a Gestapo school. Pupils get their instruction in the cellar. It is instruction with living and dying models. Newcomers among the guinea pigs are instantly beaten unconscious, then refreshed with a stream of cold water from the fire hose, and beaten again. The whip lashes throughout the nights. The prisoners must "play dog" in ice-cold courtyards and corridors. Sometimes the game is rabbit chasing. A rubber tube is introduced where it is anatomically possible (not in their mouths). Streams of hot and cold water flow through it, until the tortured man's intestines burst. "Hands up, and keep them up for twenty-four hours!" is a much favored command. If the hands drop in convulsions, the horsewhip sends them up again rapidly. Twenty-four hours of incessant torture precede the formal inquisition. To soften up the accused, their limbs are broken, their eyes and teeth smashed, their nails torn out. Other physical torments, particularly those applied to women, are unprintable. The end is invariably the same: if the prisoner does not die during the hours of torture and inquisition, he is brought into the gas cell.

No victim lives to tell the tale. But information comes from wardens who have deserted. There are a handful of them who fled from Germany and addressed themselves to the Polish authorities in exile. A few had gone mad. Only three or four could give a coherent report. Their own experience is limited. The wardens in Fort VII only last four weeks. Then they are regarded as skilled. They get certificates from the Gestapo school and are distributed over all the other prisons and camps. Most of them, incidentally, are Berliners or men from East Prussia.

There is no end to the horror. The worst fate, a fate beyond description, is reserved for those Poles who have been transported to concentration camps inside Germany. Count Alfred Chlapowski, former Polish ambassador in Paris, died "from exhaustion" in Sachsenhausen. Among many others, fourteen professors from the University of Cracow perished in the same camp. Monsignor Fulma, the Bishop of Lublin, was "detained" in Sachsenhausen, and with him his entire staff of coadjutors and numerous prelates. Monsignor Goral, Auxiliary Bishop of Lublin, with ten professors of theology died in the same camp. Their ashes, sent back to Poland, are revered as the relics of martyrs.

At present six thousand Poles are held in the concentration camp of Mauthausen on the Danube, in Upper Austria, and three thousand more in Dachau, the camp near Munich, cursed all over the world.

The Red Cross inquired after the fate of the prisoners in Castle Kuestrin, in Neubrandenburg. The answer came: "Stop writing. Do not send visitors. There are no detained left in Castle Kuestrin."

By the time the Red Cross made its inquiry, all the prisoners of Kuestrin had been tortured to death.

It is painful to admit, but there would be no excuse for concealing the fact that France trails Poland closely in the horror of prisons and concentration camps. There is one fundamental difference. The camps in Poland are German institutions, enforced on the crucified country, filled with martyred Polish people. The prisons and camps in unoccupied France, on the other hand, are French establishments, for which not Gestapo boss Himmler but Vichy boss Pétain bears, and assumes, responsibility. Actually, it is true, the Vichy jailers are only Nazi serfs. But as long as they pride themselves on being voluntary collaborators, they condemn themselves to share the curse and the execration of all free peoples aroused and revolted by the inferno of the twentieth century.

Conditions in the Vichy camps are scarcely less infernal than they are in Sachsenhausen or Dachau. The confusion is even greater. The victims of Vichy's secret state police, the twin of the Gestapo, are a mixed lot. There are anti-Fascists of almost every country among them and particularly a great number of German and Austrian refugees. Many have already been delivered to the Gestapo. The others are awaiting the day they will be handed over. A handful of British prisoners, not prisoners of war but civilians whom the French debacle caught unaware among the faithful allies, are still expecting the same fate. One of them is Mr. Amery, son of the British Secretary of State for India. Sooner or later the young man will be a prize catch for Himmler. After these, a great many anti-Fascist Frenchmen at present experience the horror of God-fearing Marshal Pétain's abodes of detention. And then, of course, there are always the Jews.

The management of the Vichy camp is—one shudders to use the word—French. Supervision and control are purely Nazi. *France Speaks,* the excellent Free French mimeographed news sheet, recently published a letter dealing with conditions in the German camps in France. It reads, in part: "I visited Camp St. Nicholas at Nîmes and saw two thousand Austrians and Germans living like animals on the ground. They have been sleeping on the earth now for seven months. It is a place revolting in its degradation and filth; the dining room of the Commandant's own house was appalling with fleas and dirt. Everywhere desperation marks the faces of these interned refugees; they have nothing to do between meals but hold their heads in their hands, and wait and wait. There are six thousand of them at Camp St. Cyprien near Perpignan, all waiting for the German commission to come and select the ones they want for trial at the hands of the Gestapo. The women are huddled together at Gurs in the Pyrenees—husbands and wives separated. Some of the men are distinguished physicians, lawyers, research students, and bankers."

Not all of them are still waiting for the German commission to come. Rudolf Breitscheid, the leader of the moderate Social-Democrats in the old Reichstag, and Dr. Rudolf Hilferding, once Minister of Finance in the German republic, have been picked out of French camps by Gestapo agents. They disappeared into Germany. Both men—each over sixty —have probably been executed.

Among the distinguished French men and women in the Pétain camps are Jean Lebas, former deputy of the department of Nord and Labor Minister in the Blum Cabinet. With

his son, who had never taken any part in politics, M. Lebas
was arrested toward the end of last June. No information has
been released about him, beyond the general hint that he may
be in some concentration camp. Another ex-member of the
Blum Cabinet, at present detained in a camp, is M. Henri
Sellier, Senator and Mayor of the Paris suburb of Suresnes, a
former Public Health Minister. General Cochet, one of the
few French army chiefs who protested against the surrender
and betrayal at Bordeaux, was arrested for having signed and
distributed pamphlets voicing his disapproval of the collaboration policy. M. and Mlle. d'Astier de la Vigerie, son and
daughter of the former commander-in-chief of the Northern
African air force, are detained for having disseminated De
Gaullist literature. Marshal Pétain's verbose Catholicism did
not prevent him from interning in the concentration camp of
Vals the Father Superior of the Franciscan Order and head
of the Medical College in Beyrouth, who refused to bless
General Dentz's arms, when the latter pitted his troops in
fratricidal, if abortive, strife against the De Gaullists who
came to liberate Syria.

In vain one asks oneself why the Vichy government is
wreaking such hardships on the anti-Fascists who are its victims. In Germany the prevailing Nazi mind is ample explanation for all the tortures. But for what reason are the French
authorities and police as deliberately barbarous in their treatment of their prisoners? Only one explanation offers itself.
Every French collaborator is anxious to impress the Nazi masters favorably. Assiduously he tramples on the underdog, to
fawn the more shamelessly on the—very temporary—upper
dog. This serf psychology explains conditions in the French
concentration camps.

In all of them the mortality is heavy. Yet there are several
types of camps. There are the ordinary camps (which form
the majority), the penal camps (where foreigners suspected
of political intrigue are imprisoned), and the *prestataire* camps

(reserved for the more favored prisoners, foreigners who enlisted as volunteers in the French army). The camp of Argelès is built beside the ocean. Here ten thousand unfortunates are huddled in wooden cabins, which cannot be heated, and through which the wind sweeps in icy gusts. At the Gurs camp twenty thousand persons are housed in flimsy wooden barracks, with roofs that provide no protection against the rain. These vast shacks cannot be heated. Sixty people are crowded into a single building, and have to sleep on straw-filled sacks, set in close rows on the floor the length of the room. There are no chairs, no tables, no adequate space for eating. Each inmate is restricted to the narrow circuit of his pallet. The sanitary facilities are appalling. The death rate mounts steadily, with several people reported dying each day. Children born here have to be wrapped in old newspapers, because there is no linen. Old men and women simply die of cold and hunger.

In the prestataire camps the conditions are somewhat better. The internees have a little more liberty. But there are other drawbacks. There is the German Commission. It is feared that all the prestataires of non-Jewish descent will be obliged to return to Germany.

During August a German Commission called at the camp of Argelès, and asked for volunteers to work on road and fortification projects. Some of them went, but soon the word was passed around that they were sent to Cherbourg or Brest, and that many of them were killed during the British bombardments.

Foreign prisoners are always under the threat of transference to labor camps in the African desert, to build the Trans-Sahara Railroad. They are divided into twelve camps of two hundred men each. Thirty-two European nationalities are represented among them. There are many neutrals—Turks, Swiss, etc.—who served in the French army, and who have been rewarded by being shipped into these African infernos. These men violated the neutrality of their countries by volunteering in the French army, and their consuls can do nothing to rescue them from their fate. The members of the famous French Foreign Legion have also been drafted for this grueling task.

The project involves the laying of tracks. All the work is done by hand. The daily pay amounts to one and one-quarter francs (approximately three American cents) and food. Every morning about two pounds of bread is doled out for every eight men. Lunch consists generally of unseasoned lamb and beans; supper, of the same allotment of bread and some malted coffee. Each man has about two quarts of water a day, which has to suffice for drinking, washing, and laundering clothes. The prisoners live in dugouts covered with canvas. They receive neither soap nor clothing.

Along the first subsection, which extends from Bou Afra to Meughomb the men are treated fairly well. The second subsection, stretching from Meughomb to Menabha, is a strip of hell on earth. It is stark desert, without a leaf or a drop of water. When the tankers from the first cannot make the trip, the men go for hours or days without any water whatsoever.

There are ten European camps set up in this part of the Sahara (with about ten thousand men, of whom three thousand are Spaniards), and the inmates are treated like beasts. For the slightest "insubordination" the wretches are consigned to the Merja camp, in the burning center of the Sahara. After a few weeks there most of them go insane. Physical punishment is the rule.

Recently some hundred prisoners from Jewish concentration camps in France have been sent to North Africa to work on the Trans-Sahara Railroad. They are, it appears, the vanguard of great numbers to follow. Thus ends the tragic epic of the Jewish persecution in France. It has won honorable admission for France—the France of Pétain and Laval—into the New Order.

Three friendly little towns in Norway are spoken of with shudders: Grine in Baerum, Ulven near Bergen, and Hakadal. They are the sites of the largest concentration camps in Norway. According to the Stockholm newspaper *Social-Demokraten* they hold some two thousand prisoners; and they are overcrowded at that. After the first British-Norwegian raid on the Lofoten Islands, on March 4, 1941, the demand for what Gauleiter Josef Terboven called "detached space" increased rapidly. The inhabitants of the Lofotens had to be punished for welcoming the raiders. The neighboring coastal districts should be warned. A fourth concentration camp was set up in Bredtvedt, just outside Oslo. Ten fishermen from the Lofotens and the well known sports leader, Bjorn Heger, were the first to be ushered in.

The warning went unheeded. Instead of being curbed by the menace of the new inferno, popular resistance was further aroused. The inhabitants of Oslo answered the latest measure of terror with a shrug. "Well, we won't have to go so far, if they fetch us," was all they had to say.

Sure enough, they *were* fetched. Three hundred citizens of Oslo were arrested in a single week, and even the newly built camp could not devour them all. Nor was the Oslo police station spacious enough, although three men at a time were herded into cells for solitary confinement. The hard-pressed Germans took over a reform school and a court building in Oslo and converted them into jails. But the tide of arrests rose. "There is not one large factory and not a single firm in this town which is not represented in the local prisons," a Swedish observer remarked. He soon found out the explanation. Every Norwegian citizen regarded as "politically undependable," a ranking Nazi authority told him, might now be thrown into prison by any Gestapo agent and kept there, without trial, for the duration of the war.

To facilitate the policing of Norway—a job that is getting

more and more out of hand—prisoners have recently been denied the right to legal counsel. The Nazis themselves shied away from assuming responsibility for this decree, which renders void all conception of civilized law. Quisling's acting Minister of Justice Sverre Riisnaes had to sign on the dotted line. To make matters worse he issued a warning that henceforth political prisoners would not be released when their terms expire, unless they proved to the satisfaction of the authorities that they had undergone a "healthy change of mind." Recalcitrants would be confined in concentration camps after having served their time, he added.

The camps, however, were filled beyond capacity, and so another outlet had to be found. Gauleiter Terboven, never at loss for a remedy, decreed that all political offenders sentenced to more than three months must serve their terms in Germany. There they are forbidden to send home letters or to receive mail from their families. They are to be entirely uprooted. Even the Bible is forbidden reading to them.

Here, finally, is a report from a civilian in the German-occupied zone of western Russia, transmitted by an official Soviet source. It testifies to the bestial cruelty rampant wherever the swastika waves. It is a shocking document of neopagan savagery and a full explanation of why the peoples of Europe will never accept the thousand deaths of the New Order. It reads, in part:

I was captured by the Germans after being wounded and was thrown into a concentration camp near the town of Golovanevskoye. I was there about three weeks with other captives, residents of occupied districts.

We went through all imaginable and unimaginable ordeals. In the first four days we were given neither food nor drink. On the fifth day they brought us some stinking soup made of concentrates, tainted with kerosene—two spoonfuls for each of us. People died from this poison. Thirty to forty persons died daily.

We received no medical aid. The wounded removed worms

from their wounds with spoons. Nina Fastovets, an army nurse who was with us, asked the commander of the camp for bandages to dress our wounds. For this she was caned on the spot until she lost consciousness.

An old doctor imprisoned with us, whose name I do not remember, tried to help the wounded as best he could. Learning of this, the commander ordered him to the courtyard and began beating him with a cane. "Dance, Russ!" the commandant ordered, flailing the sixty-two-year-old doctor. The old man refused to dance, and the blows became heavier. When he could no longer endure it, he danced. Then they forced him to stand motionless all day long under a scorching sun.

The people of Golovanevskoye tried to help us. They threw us food and fruit through the wire fence. But all this food was taken away by the Germans.

After nineteen days I was taken to another camp. We were driven without halting, those who lagged being shot down on the spot by our guards. On the road the Nazis invented a bloody game: one of them would order us to march by fours, while another ordered us to form by sixes. This naturally resulted in disorderly movements, and for "disobedience to orders" the guards opened fire with their automatics. Thus, on the twenty-four-hour march to Uman, sixty-four of our comrades were brutally murdered.

The concentration camp in Uman was still more terrible. This camp was known in all occupied districts of the Ukraine as "Uman pit." We were herded into an enormous clay quarry about three hundred yards in diameter. The vertical quarry walls were fifteen yards high. They were guarded by numerous sentries who fired their automatics at random when they noticed the slightest movement in the pit.

Many railwaymen from the Akkerman area were kept there. We were given orders through loud-speakers. Every morning they would order one group to line up near Wall No. 1, others near Walls No. 2, 3, and 4. Wall No. 2 often meant death, as those who for one reason or another displeased the guards were shot near this wall.

Here we were starved worse than at Golovanevskoye. Those who starved to death were buried right in the pit. There were so many of them that we had no time to bury them all. Besides, we had nothing with which to dig graves.

In an effort to keep warm some of us dug holes in the walls with our hands. One day a wall slid down and buried thirty-six people.

Once they hurled a wounded horse down to us. When we set about slaughtering it, a cameraman appeared above to perpetuate this scene. Obviously they were preparing some kind of photographic fake. Too many of us gathered around the horse, which annoyed the cameraman. Soldiers with automatic rifles came to his assistance, killing several in our midst.

Often the Nazis unleashed dogs in the pit and set them on us. Many of us had arms and legs bitten. The Nazis also practiced the following torture: They stretched men, including wounded, on the ground and played water on them from a hose. I remained only a few days in the Uman pit, but I shall never forget that experience.

From Uman I was driven to another camp in Vinnitsa. On the way we stopped over at Gaisin camp, which resembled the other two camps, the only difference being that instead of canes the guards used rubber clubs. At Gaisin I managed to escape.

When I told peasants in a neighboring village that I had been imprisoned in the Uman pit, they looked at me as if I had risen from the grave. The peasants were extremely kind. They gave me food and clothing and showed me the way.

Proceeding farther on territory captured by the Hitlerite bandits, I saw everywhere the same horrible scenes of outrages and torture. I remained in Nazi clutches for more than one and a half months, and every day I thought that Nazi captivity was worse than death.

The system of taking and killing hostages in barbaric times, the most cruel expression of savagery, was reintroduced into modern history by the German Imperial High Command during the last war. It was used to combat resistance in Belgium.

Adolf Hitler, always a copyist, followed the lead. Unfortunately he is in the habit of exaggerating whatever he copies. In this war he applies the hostage system on a Europe-wide scale. The phrase substituted for it is "collective responsibility." The aim is to cement German tyranny with blood. The advantage of the method, as compared with Gestapo rule and concentration camp terror, lies in the fact that these can deal only with individuals—if with millions of them—whereas no human being is exempt from his share of "collective security." It is an all-embracing measure, leaving no loopholes.

The execution of hostages—people arrested indiscriminately without being accused of any offense—the Nazis insist, is a measure of retaliation taken only if it is impossible to find and punish the individual perpetrators of attacks on German soldiers and those who have insulted the German army, state, or race. This excuse is contradicted by the facts. The first big-scale round-up of hostages was carried out on the day after the outbreak of the war, long before any sort of resistance had materialized among oppressed people. The scene was Czechoslovakia. Five thousand prominent Czech men and women were seized—among others Dr. Frantisek Soupuk, President of the Senate, and Dr. Markovich, Vice President of Parliament. These two and many others were subsequently killed, none being confronted with any accusation. For the first time the ominous expression "hostages" was used, and its meaning illustrated.

Up to this day Czechoslovakia has had to bear the brunt of the system. Its "base was broadened," to use a phrase coined by Karl Hermann Frank, Nazi State Secretary in the Protectorate, when in the winter of 1939, a German policeman was shot in the mining town of Kladno. The Gestapo arrested the mayor and the whole municipal council and tortured them in order to obtain the names of the assailants, who were presumed to be Czechs. Mr. Doubek, the mayor of Kladno, was driven to "suicide" in the Gestapo prison in Brno.

Herr Frank explained the system. "The Gestapo can never err," he declared. "Even when innocent persons are interrogated the hope is always justified that their evidence will incriminate some one."

Many Czech hostages were executed for offenses committed during the time they were in prison. Reinhard Heydrich, recently promoted Police General—a newly created dignity—started his purge of Czechoslovakia by announcing martial law on September 28, 1941. Two days later the six chief troublemakers, whose activities had brought about the announcement, were caught and summarily shot. Once more the Gestapo had vindicated its fame as a fast worker. It soon proved, however, that four of the "culprits for the recent trouble" had been in prison for two years, and the remaining two, the Czech generals Bily and Vojta, had been languishing for twenty months in the Gestapo cellar in the former Petschek Palace. Manifestly, they could not have been involved in the actions for which they were condemned and killed.

The total death roll of Czech hostages cannot be even approximately assessed. Official German statistics admit some eight hundred cases. The Czechoslovak government in London insists that this catalogue of horror mentions only a fraction of the executions of innocent people. It is, however, determined to conduct a strict investigation of every single case brought to its attention after victory is achieved.

In France two hundred and fifty civilians were shot by the Germans alone between the middle of September and November, 1941, including the fifty hostages shot in Nantes and fifty shot in Bordeaux. These also are official German figures. There is no way of checking the innumerable other murders which have been committed by the Nazis in France—of hostages, of individuals sentenced under false charges (or under no charge at all), or of those who have been condemned to death for minor and major acts of sabotage.

On September 15, 1941, a curfew from nine P.M. to five A.M. was imposed on the Paris region. This resulted in the arrest of two hundred Frenchmen found in the streets after nine o'clock. It was then announced that these two hundred would form a pool of hostages from which numbers would be taken and shot in the event of further attacks on German military personnel. It is interesting to note that the hostages, arrested at random, have since been described by the Germans as "Communists" or "De Gaullists."

Many months earlier, however, the German policy of collective punishment in occupied France took the form of heavy fines which were imposed on towns or localities for crimes whose perpetrators were never discovered. It is impossible to give a detailed list of all these fines.

Not all punishments take the form of fines Thus one town in the north of France, where there were numerous demonstrations on Joan of Arc Day, was threatened with the withdrawal of its ration cards. In Sarrebourg, in annexed Lorraine, the Nazis punished a recalcitrant population by deporting one member of each family in town. In Paris fines have been imposed on owners or tenants of houses on which a "V" had been marked, without any effort to prove that the tenants were personally guilty. In a town in Normandy, when students covered the walls with De Gaullist placards the whole population was deprived of meat for forty days. In Hochfelden, Alsace, after demonstrations on the 14th of July one hundred and sixty young men were arrested at random and sent to concentration camps.

Twenty French railway workers were shot by the Germans at Lille on September 26, 1941, when high explosives disappeared from an ammunition train. Toward the end of October, following the shootings in Nantes and Bordeaux, a six P.M. curfew was imposed on the whole of occupied France. This curfew is still in force. Meanwhile, all over France, great black, red, and white posters announce in French and German the names of persons executed for sabotage or "Communist" activities.

In Greece, the method of taking hostages was first applied by Italy during the Albanian campaign. According to official figures, fifteen hundred Greeks were taken as hostages from Klisura by the retreating Italians; over one hundred from the Pogonias region; forty-nine from Argyrokastron and a number of the leading citizens of Goumenitsa, in which town the Italians shot a number of the leading men before retreating. It is not known what happened to the hostages.

The Germans have proclaimed their intention of punishing innocent hostages for the acts of other people. For example, a proclamation was posted in Salonika, officially under German occupation, stating that for every offense against the occupation authorities, punishment would be inflicted upon the whole area in which the offense took place. On the 24th of September, hostages from the village of Kerasiasa were executed in Salonika. On the 31st of October, thirteen Greek hostages were hanged after two German soldiers had been killed in Salonika. The exact number detained by the Germans is unknown.

Greece under the occupation of the enemy has been divided into three zones. Western Thrace and Eastern Macedonia up to the river Struma was handed to the Bulgarians. Central Macedonia with Salonika, and Crete, are under German occupation. The rest of the country was transferred by the Germans to Italian occupation.

The Italian army in Albania carried away on its retreat eleven hundred twenty-six hostages of Greek nationality, either Greek or Albanian subjects. They came from fifty-four towns and villages in Epirus, and included leading citizens, priests, old men, women, and children. Part of those hostages were taken to concentration camps in northern Albania. Others, including the leading citizens, were shot by the Italians at Goumenitsa and Chimarre before they retreated. The fate of the rest is not known.

In the regions of Greece under German control, the German authorities officially proclaimed the principle of "collective responsibility," with retribution to be inflicted on the innocent. When the Germans occupied Crete, the German High Command proclaimed, "Localities near which attacks against German soldiers take place will be burned, and the population will be held responsible." Following this proclamation, six hundred and eighty-five persons were shot in Crete—most of them completely innocent hostages.

The Bulgars took hostages from practically every town in western Thrace and eastern Macedonia, the two Greek provinces under Bulgarian occupation. The night of September 30, three hundred were seized in Kavalla; four of them were shot on the spot; the fate of the rest is unknown. In the Bulgarian zone of occupation, the principle of "collective responsibility" has received its most ruthless application.

On the pretext that in the last days of September Greek armed bands killed nineteen Bulgarians, Bulgarian bombers were sent out on a punitive expedition on the 30th of September to destroy the small Greek towns of Doxato, Nea Ziini, Aghion Peneuma, Prostostani, Gazaros, and Pontapolis, all under Bulgarian occupation. After the bombing, in which Doxato became a complete ruin, a Bulgarian motorized force exterminated the survivors. Fifteen thousand people are believed to have lost their lives in this massacre.

The wave of terror and the ruthless punishment of innocent persons which is now sweeping Europe began in the Netherlands shortly after the invasion, when the Dutch East Indies authorities, in conformity with their rights under international law, interned German residents. The Germans immediately retaliated by arresting six hundred innocent Dutch subjects and dragging them away to concentration camps, where a number of them have since died. The pretext was "reprisals for the inhuman treatment of German nationals in the Netherland East Indies."

Under the legal-minded Seyss-Inquart the Germans in the Netherlands have generally preferred to find a pretext for

their arrests or to camouflage them under the false description
of "reprisals." Thus, soon after General Winkelman of the
Dutch Army had been dragged to the concentration camp of
Troppau in Sudetenland, the Germans arrested Dr. C. Gosel-
ing, the former Dutch Minister of Justice, whose only crime
was that he had adopted energetic measures before the German invasion. He died in Buchenwald concentration camp
"of pneumonia."

Other prominent members of different Dutch cabinets who
have been arrested at various times without specific charges
being brought against them are: Dr. de Wildo, former Minister of Finance; Mr. van Dijck, former Defense Minister;
and the Grand Old Man of Dutch politics, Dr. Colijn, who
was arrested with sixty members of his party.

In Norway the practice of taking hostages was applied later
than elsewhere. But for some months the Germans in Norway, too, have resorted to this method. Hostages were first
taken in revenge for the Lofoten raid in March 1941, when
relatives of young people who had volunteered to go to England were taken to Oslo and put into the neighboring concentration camp at Grini. Vague threats were made of the
infliction of "severe penalties" on hostages if there were any
further raid. In April, Reichskommissar Terboven informed the
mayor of Stavanger that, owing to repeated acts of sabotage
against the cables and telephone wires of the *Wehrmacht* in
Stavanger in the county of Rogaland, three citizens of Stavanger had been imprisoned as hostages—against further sabotage. In the summer, the Germans introduced the general
practice of arresting as hostages the fathers of young people
who escaped to England. These hostages number several hundred.

In August, 1941, the Germans applied the system of hostages against sabotage. The factories engaged on German
war production were told to establish corps of industrial

guards, to prevent any interference with production in the factory. If saboteurs could not be discovered, the guards themselves would be made responsible. Later, this practice was extended to railways in the neighborhod of Oslo. Following attempts to blow up railway lines, all young men between the ages of twenty-one and twenty-five in the districts bordering on the lines betwen Oslo and Eidsvold, and Oslo and Kongsvinger, have been ordered to join a "railway guard," which has the duty of watching the lines and preventing sabotage. Here again each "guard" is required to sign a declaration that he recognizes he is "responsible with his own life for keeping watch on the section to which he is posted."

Toward the end of October, 1941, the institution of "protective guards" was expanded to cover the whole of Norwegian industry. Everywhere factory defenses were set up. Their members were made personally responsible for every real or alleged act of sabotage occurring on the premises.

There remained one last line of resistance which Quisling had to take: the schools. The year 1941 ended in Norway with a thorough purge of schoolboys between the ages of six and sixteen. Many children were dismissed, others brought to the juvenile courts, frequently not for their own misbehavior but along the line of collective responsibility, for outrages committed by their classes.

This war against schoolboys is the only one Major Quisling has ever won. He had to take much punishment from Hitler. But on the German New Year honors list of 1942, he figured as General Quisling.

The practice of killing hostages in enemy-occupied Yugoslavia has been applied in a particularly barbaric manner by the Germans since the Chetniks embarked on their open war of liberation. Almost daily German-controlled newspapers in Yugoslavia announce "reprisals." In most cases fifty people

have been shot following the assassination of one German
soldier. Thus the *Donauzeitung* in Belgrade, published the following official communiqué of September 4, 1941: "This
morning a German soldier was shot in a street in Belgrade by
Communist bandits. As a reprisal for this cowardly murder,
fifty Communists were immediately executed."

A report the Yugoslavian government received from An-
kara disclosed that fifteen hundred hostages were seized in
Belgrade on a single day in November. The Germans officially announced that for every soldier killed, they would
shoot one hundred hostages, usually described as "Communists."

Yugoslav official quarters in London have confirmed that, on
October 13, two hundred Serbs were executed as a reprisal for
the death of a German soldier. Another instance is given by
the *Donauzeitung*, the German official newspaper published
in Belgrade, which states that fifty Serbs were executed by a
firing squad in Belgrade as a reprisal for the mere wounding
of a German soldier. Referring to the punitive expedition
which Germany undertook against the Chetniks, W. Gruber,
soldier-correspondent of the *Donauzeitung*, stated on September 13: "We shot every tenth man in the village—and occasionally the whole village was burnt."

On November 5, 1941, the Yugoslav government in London
charged that Axis forces had slain more than three hundred
thousand Serbian men, women, and children, including virtually the entire population of some towns in a campaign to
exterminate the Serbian race. The Serbian Orthodox Church
informed the government in exile that the massacres were
continuing on a large scale. The town of Skela, the Metropolitan reported, had been razed, and all the inhabitants but
fifty machine-gunned. These fifty were carried away to be
hanged. Dive bombers and tanks were sent to burn and destroy other districts, including the town of Sabac, forty miles

west of Belgrade, and the surrounding villages of Valjevo, Uzice, and Arhandjelovac. All the inhabitants of this district were shot, hanged, or deported for forced labor.

Particularly dreadful is the fate of the Serbs who live in "independent" Croatia. The Archbishop of the Serbian Orthodox Church has made a report of their extermination. One copy was sent to the Archbishop of Canterbury, another to the German commander in Croatia. Hitler's general did not deign to answer the head of the Serbian Orthodox Church. At this writing the massacres are still going on.

The Serbian Archbishop's document covers events only until the early part of August, 1941. By then one hundred eighty thousand Serbs had been killed in Nazi-invaded Croatia. Giving what is described as "only a pale picture" of the ghastly reign of terror, the document says that at Korenica hundreds of persons were killed, but before they died many of them had their ears and noses cut off and then were compelled to graze on grass. The tortures most usually applied were beating, severing of limbs, gouging of eyes and breaking of bones. Cases are related of men being forced to hold red-hot bricks, dance on barbed wire with naked feet, and wear a wreath of thorns. Needles were stuck in fingers under the nails and lighted matches were held under noses.

Among many specific instances of individual torture the Archbishop describes how four men were first crucified on the doors of their homes, then mutilated with knives.

Priests' beards were pulled out, and their throats cut.

In one case a priest was forced to dig the grave of his own son, a student, who was tortured to death before his eyes. Then he was ordered to read the burial service. During the ceremony the father fainted three times, but was revived each time and forced to continue. When he had finished he also was tortured and killed. The document adds that both the priest and his son were killed by an Ustachi agent, Ivan Scheifer, a teacher by profession.

Families of some of the victims had to pay large sums of money for return of bodies for decent burial, the Archbishop said.

The wanton destruction of ancient parts of Europe, the clamping down of an atrocious police rule on every man, woman, and child over practically all of the continent, the razing of historic towns, the indiscriminate murder of hundreds of thousands of people, the wholesale extermination of entire parts of nations—all this, Europe has suffered under the New Order. All this, however, is only a preparation. The supreme ordeal is still to come. It will come at the moment when Adolf Hitler realizes that he is cornered. He has sworn that he will bring down all Europe in his own downfall.

Yet there is good hope that the last crime he undoubtedly plans, the blitz destruction of Europe, will not be carried out. No one knows when Adolf Hitler will go down, or how. But whenever the day comes, under whatever circumstances, the agony will be short, and the collapse sudden. There will be no time for stroke and counterstroke. An earthquake without precedent will shatter the New Order.

PART II

STROKE AND
COUNTERSTROKE

CHAPTER NINE

THE FIGHTING CHURCH

The world is too small to provide adequate living room for both Hitler and God.—PRESIDENT ROOSEVELT in his address on the State of the Nation, January 6, 1941.

Ecclesia militans, the fighting church, is reborn. The church was crucified in Poland, martyred in Czechoslovakia, desecrated in Slovenia, persecuted in Norway, Holland, Belgium, Luxembourg and through the Balkans. All over Europe cathedrals and chapels have been devastated, monasteries and convents pillaged or liquidated. Hundreds of members of the clergy have been killed, thousands are in concentration camps. The church in most of the countries of the New Order has been spared no insult, no desecration, no blasphemy. Although the Catholic Church has had to bear the brunt of the savage attacks, Nazism's pagan crusade is not directed against it alone, but against the very institution of religion.

On the spiritual field, however, Nazism has suffered its first and crushing defeat. Alfred Rosenberg, the prophet of neo-paganism, himself had to acknowledge it. Choosing the day tactfully, he presented the German nation at Christmas, 1941, with his plan to abolish every Christian creed, and substitute a German National Church. *Mein Kampf* was to replace the Bible, and the sword the cross.

Remarkably, Rosenberg confined his plan to the German nation. It was the first time that the subjugated nations were exempted from a measure of "coordination." This omission is certainly not caused by mildness, but by a combination of the two fundamental elements of Nazism: hatred and fear. Christianity, Rosenberg insists, softens up humankind. He does not object to the captive nations being softened. The weaker they are, the better he likes it. But he is well aware that Christians, soft as they may be, would fight desperately, unmindful of sacrifice and death, rather than worship *Mein Kampf* and Hitler's bloodstained sword. While Nazism shows no inclination to placate its victims, it cannot at present afford to drive them into a religious war. Hitler is engaged on too many fronts. Besides, the toll Nazism has already exacted from Christianity is heavy enough.

The persecution of the church was fiercest in Poland. It began with Hitler's letter to Gauleiter Greiser, which decreed:

The church in Poland ceases to exist in the legal sense. Religious associations are not allowed to have central headquarters, or to maintain relations abroad. Germans and Poles are not allowed to assist at masses in the same churches. All religious education is to be suppressed. Spiritual associations are not allowed to accept donations or to own buildings or other establishments. They are forbidden any kind of relief work, which henceforth is a privilege of the Nazi party. All the convents and religious foundations are to be suppressed. Every priest is to have a secular job. Their activities, parish work included, can only be carried out in their spare time. German officers and functionaries are not allowed to join a religious community in Poland.

An excerpt from a report to the Vatican, in which Cardinal Hlond, Primate of Poland, summed up the religious situation in his country, shows how these instructions have been carried out. The report reads in part:

Churches and Catholic cemeteries are in the hands of the invaders. Catholic worship has ceased to exist. The word of the Lord is not preached. Sacraments are not administered even to the people on their deathbeds. In many places, religious confession has been forbidden. In other parts of the country, churches may be opened on Sundays only, but for no longer than a few hours. Marriages between Poles have been forbidden for many months. The Catholic Action has been suppressed; the Catholic press and charity organizations have been destroyed. No initiative pertaining to religious life is permitted.

Religious houses both of men and of women have been methodically liquidated, as well as all the flourishing organizations they had created, such as schools, hospitals, charitable and social institutions. Their buildings have been occupied by the Nazis. Many of the friars have been imprisoned, the nuns have been dispersed.

Cathedrals and Episcopal palaces, theological seminary buildings, the residences of canons, endowments of Episcopal sees and of ecclesiastical chapters, funds of the *curiae* and of the seminaries, farms and forests belonging to the Church, churches and their equipment, parochial mansions with their furniture and the personal belongings of the curates, even archives and diocesan museums—all have been plundered by the invaders. Robberies have been committed for the profit of the German State or for the benefit of individuals. Everything that could be carried away was transferred to the Reich. The rest was left for the newly arrived German settlers. Ninety-five per cent of our priests have been imprisoned, expelled, humiliated before the eyes of the faithful.

Most gruesome was the treatment inflicted on the clergy. Almost all the bishops in the "incorporated" provinces have been interned or imprisoned. In Poznań and Pomorze four-fifths of the priests were arrested. Most of them were deported to concentration camps in Germany; to Dachau, Oranienburg, and Mauthausen. Later, all priests under sixty years of age were deported to German camps by special decree. Up to February 7, 1941, more than seven hundred Polish priests had been executed by the Germans; and on that day three thousand were imprisoned in the German camps.

On February 3, 1941, the Governor General ordered: "Poles are required to possess special permission cards to enter churches on Sundays and holidays. The clergy, celebrating the Masses, are obliged to inform the German police at least three days prior to the Mass." Simultaneously, theological seminaries were forbidden to admit new students. The teaching of philosophy and church history was banned. Only pastoral theology and liturgy were approved. The aim of these restrictions was obviously to lower the level of education.

A large number of priests, particularly those of advanced age and higher ecclesiastical rank, were sentenced to labor service. Many of them were held as hostages. In Poznań, priests were ordered to attend mass executions of their compatriots, to dig the graves, and to bury the executed. Similarly, the Polish clergy is constantly subjected to blackmail. Scores were arrested in retaliation for the refusal of the peasants to deliver over their crops. Only those priests who were willing to speak from their pulpits on the duty of delivering the requisitioned harvest were released. At present the Catholic priests in almost all the communities are compelled to assist in the requisitioning. Many were arrested because, in the judgment of the Gestapo, they did not encourage young people strongly enough to volunteer for chain-gang labor in the Reich.

A report made by the Eastern Orthodox Bishop George Sava to the Archbishop of Canterbury divulges some of Hitler's ruses to Nazify the Eastern Orthodox Church. Two Ukrainian émigrés living in Berlin, who had never had any connection with the Orthodox Church whatsoever, men named Illarian Ogipenko and Palladinius Rudenko, were raised to the rank of Bishop by the Führer on condition that they would take an oath of loyalty both to himself and to Dr. Frank, the German Governor General. The God-fearing Ukrainian peasants were so aroused by this blasphemous comedy that they ran Ogipenko and Rudenko out of the country. Hitler was then preparing the attack on Russia— which, he hoped, would be considerably facilitated by a Ukrainian revolt against atheist Moscow—and at first he did not punish the rebellious worshipers of the Eastern Orthodox Church in Polish Ukraina. He sent them a new redeemer of his own making: St. Serafin.

St. Serafin was wrapped in a veil of religious mystery. He had been ordained, Nazi propaganda spread, in the "Living Church" in Kiev, and there he would establish his personal heaven, after the fashion of Father Divine, as soon as Kiev was occupied by the Germans.

Subsequently Kiev was, indeed, occupied. But St. Serafin never established his personal heaven there. The Patriarchs of Istanbul and Moscow debunked him: he had at one time been a priest in a White Russian village, but had been ostracized for polygamy; moreover his priesthood was a part of his career as a swindler. Actually Hitler's Ukrainian Saint is a German named Lade. Some twenty years ago, before being promoted to the saints, he used to be a barber-shop assistant in Munich, and his favorite client, later his pal, was a paper hanger with a romantic forelock.

The persecution of religion has driven the church in Poland underground, but it has failed to affect the nation's devotion. On the contrary, Poland, always a deeply believing country, has lately developed a conviction of having been chosen to share the Lord's martyrdom. Polish people speak of themselves as of the "nation of Christ." In their feeling, religion and nationality are one. From both these sources of strength, now so harmoniously united, they derive a unique capacity for resistance.

In Czechoslovakia, too, the Nazi persecution of the Churches has resulted in a very strong religious revival. The Czechs lack the mystic touch that so deeply permeates the Poles. In Czechoslovakia the Church was never identified with the nation. Masaryk's republic was polite to religion and would have abhorred any infringement of religious liberties. But the national flag was not hoisted on the cross.

Today the Premier of the Czechoslovak government in exile is Monsignor Jan Srámek, the veteran leader of Czech Catholicism. He was chosen for his position as an elder statesman as well as for his clerical garb. However, the development is characteristic. All suppressed people feel a little nearer to God.

The religious terror began after the tragedy of Munich in the ceded territories. Most Czech priests were expelled from the Sudetenland. Those who remained were forced to do hard manual labor. When the rest of Czechoslovakia fell, the Gestapo went at it. Their agents supervised Masses and other religious services, listening carefully to the sermons. Hundreds of priests were denounced and punished, with the usual insults and tortures. The declaration of war brought a wave of persecution, and a year later there was a second wave. On September 1, 1940, very early in the morning, the Gestapo arrested four hundred and eighty-seven priests, among them high ecclesiastical dignitaries such as Monsignor Stasek, canon of Byserad—who was subsequently transferred to Dachau and there, although a sick man, employed in road building—and Monsignor Tenora of the chapter of Brno, a man of eighty years in frail health. Together with the members of his chapter Monsignor Tenora was taken to the notorious prison in the fortress of Spielberg near Brno. They were crowded with other prisoners in a subterranean cell, and compelled to sleep on the bare floor. Father Karel Fandrla of Brno, in this unfortunate group, did not hesitate to answer the question why he had been arrested: "Because I am a Czech and a Catholic priest." He was mercilessly beaten.

In the concentration camps, whether in Germany or in the Protectorate, priests have not the right to wear their soutanes. Only when they are building roads is an exception made. Many passers-by have seen priests, dressed in the rags of their religious habits, exhausted, pulling a cart, and guarded by a seventeen- or eighteen-year-old brown-shirt with a horsewhip.

The confiscation of church property continued without ceasing. In December, 1941, word reached the Vatican that the Nazi authorities had finally seized all the property of Czech bishops and dioceses, including not only their landed estates, but also the schools, orphanages, and other charitable institutions. This action was accompanied by the arrest of another seventy priests. According to the *Osservatore Romano*, the mouthpiece of the Holy See, four hundred Czech priests are at present imprisoned.

The Protestant churches in Czechoslovakia are no better off. They are particularly hated by the oppressors because they remind the Czech people of Hus, whom Protestant Czechs claim as their religious liberator, and in whose time violent battles were fought against the Germans. Consequently, strict censorship was clamped down on Czech Protestantism. One pastor who had been bold enough to apply the teachings of the Gospel to present times was warned that in future he would have to submit his sermons to the Nazi censor. However, a few hours later he was arrested. Today he is forced to work as a woodcutter in the Sumava forests, living on a piece of bread and a cup of black coffee a day. His wife and year-old child were left without means of support. Yet she is being compelled to pay twenty crowns a day for her husband's living expenses. "Otherwise," the Gestapo commissioner told her, "your husband will probably die of hunger."

In Czechoslovakia, too, the Christian religion is driven underground. Clergymen wear civilian clothes in order not to attract the attention of Gestapo agents. Worshipers meet in secrecy. Perhaps they do not simply pray when they congregate. Religious feeling and nationalism tread the same road to resistance.

Both German and Italian intriguers were promoting a religious war between the Catholic Croats and the Orthodox Serbs as a diversion and a means of bringing about the extermination of both. The master minds of the Axis believed that the persecution of Orthodox priests would be a bait for the Catholics. Twenty-four members of the Orthodox Synod were brought to Zagreb, accused of having fostered espionage, and condemned to death. Then the Catholic Archbishop of Zagreb, Monsignor Stepinetz, was asked for his blessing. Instead, the head of the church of Croatia, suffering under a self-styled "Catholic dictatorship," replied unmistakably: "It is impossible to use Catholic priests for the purpose of creating a wider gulf between the Croats, the Serbs, Bosnians, and Herzegovinians. I do not recognize the temporary system as long as terror and persecution last."

Amazingly, the prince of the Catholic church is still alive and residing in his palace.

Whether his opposite number in Athens, the head of the Greek Orthodox Church, Metropolitan Chrysanthos is still alive, is unknown. The Metropolitan has not concealed his steadfast opposition to the Axis-instituted puppet regime. General Tsolakogli, the local Quisling, who wisely only calls himself "head of the government in Athens" (realizing that his authority does not even reach as far as the suburbs), at last replaced the Metropolitan. His successor was a man named Damaskinos, who four years ago was expelled from the Greek Orthodox Church for "irregularities."

The State Church in Norway, aided by all the other Christian organizations and denominations, is openly defying the New Order. This opposition is the gravest threat among the many dangers to which the Quisling system is exposed. It has not been overcome, although the Nazis and their lackeys have applied their customary pressure, including police terror and rigid censorship, to break the opposition.

But the system has not been able to prevent the recent establishment of the "united front" by all religious groups in Norway. The front is led by Bishop Eyvind Berggrav of Oslo. Paradoxically, Bishop Berggrav is the one man in Norway whom the Nazis courted and flattered to bring him into their fold. Even Gauleiter Terboven, many incidents prove, was impressed by the fighting Bishop's transcendental personality. He would have liked to swap his own Mr. Quisling for him. But the Bishop of Oslo, of course, refused to compromise with the Nazis.

The seven bishops of the Norwegian Church have signed a document that will survive as a new *magna charta* of religious liberty when Nazism is only a nightmare memory. This document took the form of a declaration addressed to Ragnar Scancke, the Quisling Minister of Church and Education. The bishops stressed his transient power by persistently referring to him as the "acting" Minister. Their document was a solemn indictment of the New Order in Norway. It lashed out at the "systematic rule of terror by the Nazi Storm Troopers"; it pointed out the enforced resignation of the Supreme Court of Norway which caused "grave insecurity" in the country; and it rejected the interference of the police with the clergyman's oath of silence.

The turncoat Scancke's reply was evasive and menacing. He brushed aside the complaints about the terror exercised by the storm troops. "In these times of pioneering and ferment," he pleaded, "things may happen which are regrettable and which we deplore. This is understandable. But there are many instances when the oath of silence cannot be observed. The oath shall not be generally canceled, but newly interpreted. We warn the Church against any acts which might increase the unrest of our people. Thoughtless action now may result in serious consequences for the Church." Simultaneously, Quisling's Church Commissioner ruled that henceforth circular letters from the bishops to ministers or congregations must be forwarded in triplicate to the Department, obviously to be censored.

It was an open declaration of war on the Church. The bishops accepted the challenge. They continued to send their circular letters, and their language grew bolder. "When the authorities permit acts of violence, and exert pressure on our souls," the next letter read, "then the Church becomes the defender of the people's conscience. A single human soul is worth more than the entire world. . . . The church can never be silenced. Whenever God's commandments are deposed by sin, the Church stands unshaken and cannot be directed by any authority of the State. In our congregations we now perceive a ferment of conscience, and we feel it our duty to let the authorities hear clear and loud the voice of the Church."

Such frank language had never been heard in any oppressed country. Gauleiter Terboven raged.

The deathblow against the Norwegian Church was finally aimed at Bishop Berggrav. After some hesitation Quisling decided to have the great church leader arrested. His whereabouts are at present unknown, but it is widely believed that he is in the concentration camp at Grini. His six fellow bishops resigned in protest, and a general church strike ensued. Among 77,000 Protestant Ministers less than forty carry on under Quisling's orders, half of them not without apologetic explanations. At this writing open religious revolution rages in Norway. The issue is: Quisling or Christ?

The Belgian clergy is constantly being attacked by the Nazi-controlled Brussels press for leading the resistance against the invaders. Expressions like "scoundrels in cassocks," or "cassocked accomplices of the British murderers," "valets of Roosevelt and Churchill," and "believers in the Atlantic gospel" enjoy the indulgence and encouragement of the Nazi censors.

The fury of the turncoat press is a plain indication of the influence the Church exercises in preserving Belgium's will for independence. Léon Degrelle's *Pays Réel* claims: "Certain priests are much more concerned on Sunday mornings with the proclamations of Mr. Churchill than with the gospel." The same paper advises an unnamed reverend father, who gave his first Lenten sermon at the Institut des Dames de Marie in Brussels, to join the staff of the B.B.C. On another occasion it attacks priests who, announcing a collection for the reconstruction of the Louvain library, began their sermons with the words, "The same causes always having the same effects, the Louvain library has been destroyed a second time." The *Nationaal-Socialist*, a Flemish counterpart of the *Pays Réel*, complains bitterly that Nazism is making no progress in Malines, the seat of the Belgian Primate, because "the shadow of the Episcopal See falls on everything."

This complaint is not unfounded. The whole country looks up to Cardinal Joseph Ernest van Roey, Archbishop of Malines, Primate of Belgium, as its God-sent leader and spokesman. Born in Vorsselaer, a village of the Campine, the flat, dry land of northern Belgium, he comes of sturdy Flemish peasant stock. He studied theology at the University of Louvain and was assistant, as well as principal adviser on matters of theology and church law, to Cardinal Mercier of First World War fame. Indeed, many of Cardinal Mercier's immortal pastoral letters during that time were drafted by Monsignor van Roey.

The present Cardinal is a soft-spoken, rather silent man

with a reputation for taciturnity. Only one anecdote about him is on record. Embarking on a trip to Rome, one of his assistants said, "I think it is going to rain." When the party arrived in Paris the Cardinal replied, "Maybe." But on their arrival in Rome he added, "Everything said was strictly between you and me."

But when he decides that something has to be said the Cardinal speaks plainly and directly. After repeatedly having warned his clergy not to read the Nazi-controlled press and after having attacked the paganism of Nazi philosophy, Cardinal van Roey spoke out to members of the Catholic Action at Wavre-Nôtre-Dame, near Malines. His speech, suppressed in his own country, was smuggled out and into the United States. Here is a short excerpt from it, indicating that the Belgian Church will never make peace with the oppressors:

One often hears it said that it matters little what a regime is. The Church, it is said, can adapt itself to any regime. But we must distinguish. The Church can adapt itself only to those regimes which safeguard liberty and do not violate conscience. How, for instance, can the Church adapt itself to the regime at present imposed on . . . the Grand Duchy of Luxembourg, where seminarists are imprisoned and convents closed? No, the Church cannot live in climes that suffocate it. Catholics are obliged to "collaborate." But to collaborate with those who seek to impose a regime hostile to the Church is forbidden, as it is forbidden to Catholics to favor a regime of oppressors.

Twilight shrouds France, and a heavy cloak of fog almost blacks out the actions and movements of the French Church. Since the powers that be largely follow the trend of contemporary history instead of endeavoring to make history, the Church, powerful in the Pétain set-up, tries now to avoid taking any clearly defined line. Moreover, the Catholic hierarchy in France—to be sharply distinguished from the plain French Catholics, the overwhelming majority of whom hate Nazism and pray for an Allied victory—is disunited. The only possible general statement is that the French hierarchy and clergy sympathize with Pétain, but are suspicious of Darlan and Laval and reluctant toward collaboration.

There are, of course, extremists on both sides. Henri Marie Alfred, Cardinal Baudrillart, Archbishop of Paris, a man of Pétain's age, is a regular contributor to the Paris Nazi press. This remarkable prince of the Church out-Darlans Darlan in his almost hysterically professed allegiance to the New Order. He baits England and attacks America, and he caused both laughter and outrage among his own adherents when he blessed the arms of the poor devils who were either bribed or shanghaied into the French anti-Soviet legion. He called this wretched cannon fodder in the German uniform "the best sons of France."

Emanuel Célestin, Cardinal Suhard, is much more cautious in public although he, too, appears to be a sworn enemy of democracy. Observers are at a loss to find a sufficient explanation for this subservience to Nazism on the part of two ranking dignitaries of the very Church whose total extermination is patently one of Hitler's ambitions. It is true that the Church was anything but coddled by the Third Republic. Personal resentment may not even end at the republic's grave. The vociferous Communists of Paris may have had much to do with driving Cardinals Baudrillart and Suhard to an extreme. However, burning, boiling, revolutionary Paris, which suffers most under the daily provocation of a terrorist occupation, is not only the center of Nazi propaganda in France, but the seat of the hottest hatred of Germany in the country, and probably in the world. The gap between the feelings of an overwhelming majority of Parisians and those of their two archbishops can hardly be bridged.

The openly collaborationist cardinals are practically isolated in their own camp. Professor Le Fur of the Law Faculty in Paris, and two or three newspapermen who would like to start a "Catholic" pro-Nazi sheet in Paris with German money, are their only followers of consequence.

More important are the two go-betweens of the high clergy and Nazi headquarters. Both are unknown to the public, and both have good reason to conceal their activities. The German in this combination is Dr. Kurt Reichel. He is acting as German emissary to the high dignitaries of the Catholic Church in France, endeavoring to win them to collaboration. He calls himself "envoyé officiel du Haut Commandement Allemand." Unfortunately he is completely unable to speak French. An interpreter with the resounding name of Colonel Mancio must always accompany him.

His counterpart on the French side is the Jesuit Père Débuquois. He is better known as the "gray eminence"—a part Father Débuquois seems to perform with relish. Officially he is director of the Action Populaire, which is active mostly among working people. Until the betrayal of Bordeaux, Father Débuquois was known as leftist and was believed to be stanchly democratic. He has been active in national and Church politics ever since 1919, and established excellent relations with many influential prelates who were surprised by his conversion to outspoken Nazism and the warmest advocacy of rapprochement with Hitler.

However, these influences and maneuvers do not sway the French Church to any degree. Above all, its attitude is cautious. The sympathy of many prelates for Pétain's playing of Hitler's game does not blind them to the fact that there are important differences to be bridged between the Church and the French State.

For a long time the outstanding grievance of the Catholic hierarchy was the fact that Church schools received no help from the State and at the same time had to pay taxes and all other imposts levied on commercial enterprises, whereas State schools were supported from public funds and not taxed. Church schools have an aggregate roll of one million two hundred thousand children. There is much money at stake, and the impoverishment of France under the German system forces budget makers to squeeze every sou.

But since religion regained an important place in the Marshal's system, and a number of privileges were restored to the Church, the school problem has been largely solved by sacrifice on the part of the State which only Pétain personally was willing to make.

Of his heirs the French Church feels a healthy distrust. This is due not only to the impossibility of reconciling the Catholic masses to the notorious traitors but also to the Church's fear of totalitarian ambitions.

Catholic youth and labor are both firmly opposed to a merger with totalitarian organizations. Although under German pressure the French Confederation of Christian Workers had to be dissolved, its whole organization, the trade federations, the regional labor groups, and the local unions continue to function. They find strong support among the high clergy. The Archbishop of Toulouse declared in a public address that France could not be reconstructed without respecting the workers' rights and that he was "hoping and praying for free unionism." A fortnight later Cardinal Gerlier, Archbishop of Lyons and Primate of the Gauls, took up the same cause.

Next to Cardinal Gerlier, who has repeatedly preached courageous sermons in his Cathedral Saint Jean stands Monsignor Delay, Bishop of Marseilles, in his refusal to compromise with the intruders. Monsignor Saliège, the Bishop of Toulouse, had frankly anti-Nazi prayers read on the Feast of the Sacred Heart. Monsignor Théas, Bishop of Montauban, declared: "Naturally, we cannot collaborate when this involves confusion between the spiritual and the temporal powers or, worse, submission of the spiritual power to the temporal. France, yes and heartily, but God first." On another occasion, addressing his clergy, he said that Marshal Pétain merited the highest esteem, but that he was badly advised. "I will not make any allusions," he declared. "I wish to say directly what I know, and I have irrefutable witnesses for my statement. Admiral Darlan is the man fatal to our country."

The Archbishop of Toulouse was still more explicit. "The dignity of man and the rights which his Creator has conferred upon him, the dignity of work which is not regarded as a mere article of trade, the dignity of the family which is not deemed simply a breeder of children, the dignity of the fatherland formed by God, but not set up for idolatry—none of this will vanish."

This is the true answer of Catholic France to Hitler's challenge.

CHAPTER TEN

FAILURE OF A CRUSADE

Accept my most sincere congratulations on your sixtieth birthday. My best wishes for your personal well-being and a happy future for the Soviet people.—HITLER to Stalin, December 20, 1939.

A FEW months before Hitler's relentless war against Christianity was climaxed by the Christmas message of 1941 that replaced the Bible with *Mein Kampf*, and the Cross with the sword, the Führer organized the crusade to save Christianity in Europe from Bolshevism. This, however, did not mean a respite for the Church. Its persecution in all the occupied countries continued unabated. But while priests were tortured in Poland and arrested in Norway; while cathedrals and chapels were blown up in the Balkans; while believers all over the Continent were driven underground into new catacombs, all the suppressed nations were summoned to rally around the Swastika to help annihilate the great atheist in Moscow.

The contradiction was so absurd that it went almost unnoticed. The normal mind simply cannot grasp it. Students of the Nazi mind, however, were by no means surprised to see the archpagan in the white knight's shining armor. From its very beginning Nazism has thriven on self-contradiction. Hitler roused the Germans in promising higher rents to the landlords and lower rents to the tenants, more profit to the capitalists and higher wages to labor, perpetuation of their large estates to the Junkers and just distribution of the soil to the landless farmers. Attacking Russia, he again used his time-honored technique of playing both ends against the middle.

But even in the hour of deepest despair Europe was not blind. Hitler's call for allies went unheeded. For the first time the overlord of the Continent saw, in stark reality, the limit of his power. He can force the subjugated peoples into slavery, but he cannot force them to fight for him. He dared not give the hostile masses guns. Inevitably, they would have backfired. It would have been arming his own murderers. Strange experience for Hitler, there was no compulsion possible. To be sure, every device of propaganda and high pressure was applied to enlist selected volunteers. Yet, among the countless millions of Europe only a few thousand "volunteered." Some were criminals, others professional soldiers, the great majority consisted of Quislings for whom life in their own countries had become more dangerous even than the hazards of the march to the Russian slaughterhouse.

The total failure of the abortive crusade was a silent but overwhelmingly eloquent plebiscite. It deserved more attention in the free world. Perhaps attention was not drawn to it because, from a military point of view, the whole crusade did not count. Strategic experts could safely neglect the insignificant incident. But it is possible to gauge the further development in Europe from the example of this short and inglorious interlude.

Enlisting began, of all countries, in France. Pétain was at his lowest, which is very low, on November 6, 1941, when he wrote this letter:

By joining the crusade, French soldiers have acquired rightful title to the gratitude of the world [meaning Berchtesgaden], and thereby you will protect your country, while at the same time saving the hope of a reconciled Europe. For these reasons Admiral Darlan and myself wish you good luck in the accomplishment of the noble duty which you have chosen. For my part I shall follow you in your trials with all my solicitude until the glorious day of your return to your homeland.

The letter was addressed to Colonel Jean Labonne, commanding the Legion of French Volunteers Against Bolshevism. Of course it implied a plea to Hitler to make good his promise to release some of the two million French prisoners of war in Germany, since Frenchmen were now fighting at the side of the Germans.

No answer came from the Führer. Little news was heard of the French crusaders, who were to fight in German uniforms, only retaining the blue beret to distinguish them from real Nazis. In true contemporary French fashion most of the Russian war was fought on the Paris home front. While Colonel Labonne trained his first four hundred men in Poland, Jacques Doriot, ex-Communist and at present most rabid Nazi stooge in Paris, claimed the command, insisting that the Legion was due to his exertions alone. Former Comrade Doriot addressed recruiting meetings in the biggest halls of Paris, at which there were no audiences.

The French die-hards, whose antibolshevism had contributed as much to the catastrophe of France as Communist sabotage, gathered around another crusader. The retired Colonel Eugène Deloncle's appeal was stronger. He was one of them. A veteran chief of the Cagoule, he had been a fanatical foe of the defunct republic. After the downfall of France he was among the first whom Göring invited to lunch in the Luxembourg. Gossip had it that the gallant Marshal insisted that the colonel bring his niece and secretary, Mlle. Marie Masse, along with him. Mlle. Masse was, in her way, a fascinating woman. Crusading with her uncle, she appeared as the new Jeanne d'Arc. She—not the retired colonel—was the attraction, packing the halls of Paris with the curious and the hysteric; the bored and the blasé: the French collaborators. Her uncle forgave her for incessantly stealing the show. She was indeed irresistible in her field-gray uniform, the Swastika pinned on her bulging bosom, and, for good measure, a ribbon with the Tricolor in her hair. Her argument was invariably the same: "France must play her historic role in saving Europe. Jacques Doriot says so, too. But his men only receive twenty-four hundred francs a month, whereas the Regiment Deloncle pays three thousand for participating in the Russo-German war."

Sometimes she had to deal with hecklers. Most persistent was Marcel Gitton. He did not oppose the crusade, but he loathed the commercialization of a sacred idea. He had once been a Communist deputy, and the clung to his anticapitalistic purity when he switched over to the Nazi camp, accepting a modest job as a translator in the offices of the German High Command. The job, it appeared, did not entirely satisfy his ambition. So he, too, mingled with the crusaders, endeavoring to form a third legion.

For a short time the people of Paris watched the strife in the camp of the Nazi apologists. Then they made their choice. On September 5, 1941, Marcel Gitton was shot by a passing cyclist as he strolled through the suburb of Saint-Denis. One month later, on October 7, the body of Marie Masse was found in the Seine. She had been strangled. In neither case were the police able to ferret out the culprit.

Disgusted with the French disunity, the Nazis wanted to entrust the antibolshevist legion to an expert. General Denikin, the former commander-in-chief of the White Russian armies, had been an exile in Paris for more than twenty years. He was already an octogenarian, but his name still spelt glorious memories. It would be effective, the Nazis speculated, both in Paris, where every boulevardier had come to know the old white-bearded gentleman, and in Russia as well, where he was unforgotten. General Denikin was invited to visit General von Schaumburg, the commander of the German garrison in Paris. When he heard that he was supposed to lead a legion of French turncoats against his own Russia, he turned away without a word. But the door behind his back was locked. At present, Denikin is locked up in a prison somewhere in Germany.

The total strength of the French Legion Against Bolshevism has never been given. The Nazis pretend that the number is nine thousand. But the Legion's own publicity department has regularly chronicled enlistments, which Free French observers have put together, arriving at the total of 1,802 volunteers. To this number, "Germanized" Alsace-Lorraine contributed all of one hundred men; Brittany, not one. Those who enlisted were deceived about their pay. Instead of the promised twenty-four hundred or three thousand francs a month, the actual pay of a legionnaire was only fourteen hundred. The much advertised rapid promotion to officer's rank failed to materialize. The French Legion is officered by Germans.

The only French ranking officer is the titular commander Colonel Labonne. In the first days of November he sent to Paris a message for help from his training camp somewhere in Poland. His men, he reported, were getting out of hand. They would not take the daily beatings from the German subalterns in their command. Moreover, they refused to depart for the front.

Again Marshal Pétain intervened. He sent Fernand de Brinon, a self-styled "Count," once a professional racetrack gambler, afterwards Laval's confidant, and now Vichy ambassador in Paris, to the camp in Poland to exhort and inspire the recalcitrant troops. M. de Brinon did as he was told. He spent only two hours in the camp, and excused his precipitate departure by pleading an important appointment with Göring. On his return to Paris he told the press: "It was elating to see the pictures of Hitler and Pétain hanging jointly on the walls of a French barracks." That was all the information he gave. To Pétain, privately, he may have disclosed more. The recruiting for the Legion was discontinued. Whether this occurred in consequence of Brinon's report or because the inmates of the Santé, the Paris prison for incorrigible criminals, had just refused to join up, was never established.

Finally, the German officers in the French camp in Poland forced their men at the points of guns to take the train for the front. The Legion, forming two battalions, was attached to the 255th infantry division in Marshal Siegmund Wilhelm List's army. The Marshal, who had already proved his dislike of foreigners in Athens, dispatched them to his rear guard. But when the German death toll rose rapidly, the French allies were ordered to the advance firing line and exposed to the ferocious attack of Soviet General Antonoff's tanks and cavalry. Retreat was impossible on account of the five hundred German military police at their backs.

The French Legion was routed. Some prisoners who fell into the hands of the Russians insisted they had changed sides during the combat and helped to kill the German military police. But the reports of prisoners of war should always be taken with a grain of salt, particularly if they originate with French crusaders.

The Spanish "Blue Division" was freezing and starving to death before its first engagement. This was the contents of a radio message from the commander of the division, General Grandes, to the German corps commander Colonel General von Leeb, imploring him to send warm clothing, vodka, and bread. The Russians picked up the message, as well as Leeb's answer. The German commander sent nothing more tangible than his heartfelt sympathy. Shrewdly the Russians concluded that the Spaniards were not feeling comfortable on the north-western front, where Hitler had dispatched them to make up for tremendous German losses. The Russians attacked immediately, and the Blue Division was broken up. It lost at least thirty-two hundred men, the Soviets say. "Most of the men," Prisoner of War Sanchez Vasquez, of the 269th Spanish infantry regiment, stated, "died for lack of medical assistance." The division had to be withdrawn from active combat. For Spain the crusade was over after the first fight.

Similarly, the Hungarian troops returned from the Eastern Front, unsung and unheralded, "because of insufficient winter equipment and a widespread outbreak of pneumonia in their ranks." This was the official explanation. Jacob Kovac, soldier of a scouting battalion of the 1st Royal Hungarian motorized brigade, offered an additional explanation when he threw up his hands. "Hungarian soldiers have no desire whatever to fight against the Russians for German interests," he stated. "We were forcibly driven to the front. A driver in our battalion did not want to go any further. He damaged something in his engine to make his truck useless. Our officers started an inquiry. The driver was sentenced to death. This incident made me think a great deal about the reasons for which Hungary is fighting Russia. I arrived at the conclusion that Horthy had sold us wholesale to Hitler. Well, here I am."

The Czech legion was organized by four retired officers. Former Colonel Libor Vitez, a Hungarian of Czech citizenship, drafted the plan for the enlistment of volunteers in Prague. In appreciation of his loyalty, Hitler gave him the rank of general. Instead of joining his troops, however, the newly appointed general retired to the country and wrote a book about the invincible Germany army, which had to be published by the official Nazi-owned press, since no Czech publisher was willing to print it.

Another pensioner, former General Kalal, spent six months,

from the day of the assault on Russia until the end of 1941,
trying to enlist retired service men and invalids. He could not
find a single volunteer, and finally gave it up. His colleague
Colonel Cetkovski, on the other hand, insisted on being permitted to march with the Germans, even if no Czechs would
follow him. He was a fugitive from justice, having embezzled
the funds of the Czech Invalid Association. Escape into the
firing line seemed wise.

The top man of the Czech legion was Colonel Otto Blaha.
He offered to raise a corps of volunteers for the "holy war
against Jewish Bolshevism." Indeed, a few dozen members of
the Vlajka, the Czech storm troops, enlisted under duress.
When they came to the German arsenal in Prague for their
weapons, a Prussian noncom received them. He said three
words: "Czechs? Arms? Scram!"

In "independent" Slovakia the Germans proceeded less cautiously and consequently much less wisely—perhaps because
their decision was not made by a simple noncom, but by the
Führer himself. A few days after he had attacked Russia, Hitler received President Tiso in his headquarters. The meeting
between the two heads of states was most ceremonious. Hungary, Rumania, and Finland had not yet joined up. Slovakia
was to set the example for the vassal states. Flanked by his
two ranking generals, von Brauchitsch (who has since been
fired) and Keitel, Hitler shook hands with Tiso, who was escorted by his Premier, Dr. Tuka, and War Minister Catlos.
It looked like a meeting of monarchs. Hitler declared that the
Slovaks had never disappointed Germany, and that all confidential reports he had received about their attitude were
favorable. He wanted to pay tribute to the gallant Slovakian
nation and to the pious President. In return, Father Tiso
modestly compared Germany's greatness with the smallness of
Slovakia, while he did not dare to mention the Führer and
himself in the same breath. However, Slovakia would once

more do her duty. Two of her divisions were already fighting on the Eastern Front. More would follow.

The first Slovakian contingent numbered forty thousand men. Only eight thousand of them deserted to the Russians. The rest had to be withdrawn. Berlin was furious. Two important members of the Reich government, Dr. Goebbels and Dr. Funk, journeyed to Bratislava for an inspection. Despondent, Father Tiso received them. He swore he would have committed suicide, had he not been a Catholic priest, so badly ashamed was he of the behavior of his soldiers. He asked for one more chance to rehabilitate the glory of Slovak arms.

The German emissaries drove a hard bargain. They insisted on a new contingent of a hundred thousand men. It would receive German equipment and be under the command of German officers. Slovakian pilots—one hundred, all told— would no longer fly their own machines, but be dispersed among the German Luftwaffe. This measure was advisable because both General Viest, chief of the Slovakian air force, and his chief of staff Colonel Ambros, had piloted their planes to London.

Tiso agreed to all the conditions. If his religion forbade him suicide, his horse sense told him that a German concentration camp would not be much better. Indeed, midget Slovakia mobilized a hundred thousand men for Germany. It was necessary to force them into service and to bribe their families in order to keep the country from revolting. War Minister Catlos decreed that the families of mobilized soldiers should obtain assistance for their field labor according to the number of prisoners taken by each unit on the Russian front. The Slovakian soldiers believed they would send home as unpaid farm hands such prisoners as they captured. Probably this was the reason why the second Slovakian expeditionary force behaved well. They fought ferociously. But they fought in reverse. They attacked the Hungarians who held the sector next to them. For centuries the Slovaks had been the Magyars' slaves, and the Slovak legionnaires sought revenge. Had they not King Hitler's permission to send their prisoners home and make them work? Indeed, some of the fiercest battles on the Russian front raged between Slovak and Hungarian contingents. The Slovaks were man-hunting. By tradition the Hungarians were enjoying a massacre of Slovaks. The German officers were powerless. Finally, German troops had to be wedged between the fighting allies.

The Slovaks felt vaguely that Hitler had cheated them of their prize. Their fun was spoiled. A new wave of desertions mounted. General Catlos, commander in chief and Minister of War, broadcast that every attempt at desertion would be punished by the firing squad. The broadcast came from Bratislava. General Catlos had had to return to his capital to set up a supreme military court. Perhaps he, too, had not enjoyed life on the Russian front.

Finally, the contingent had to be withdrawn. At present, according to a German statement, the Slovakian fighting forces consist of one infantry battalion and one artillery battery. The others are used to police southern Poland and what is left of the occupied Ukraine. There the Slovak soldiers fraternize with the Communist population.

Not even the nightingale of Nazism could lure Norwegians into the Russian deathtrap. In vain Kirsten Flagstad of faded Metropolitan fame appeared at a gala performance in the Royal Opera in Oslo for the benefit of potential crusaders. Very few were interested in benefiting. Equally few availed themselves of a promise made by Mr. Henry Johansen, who happens to be Madame Flagstad's husband, and, by the same token, Quisling's chief financial backer, that he would give a job to every hero who returned alive from the Russian front. The men of Norway need all their heroism—and they have it in plenty—for home consumption and in their daily lives.

Every attempt to enlist young Norwegians for German military service miscarried. Nazi press and radio flooded the country with stories of the heroism of the Regiment Nordland, Norwegian volunteers, who had been fighting for many months with the regular German army. It proved, however, that this legendary Regiment Nordland had never existed. Actually, the handful of young Norwegians pressed into the German army had been thinly distributed in various regiments so as not to build cells of resistance. The example was not alluring when the German drum beat a second time, calling for volunteers for Russia.

Again the Church was in the front line of defense. A meeting of the seven Norwegian bishops dealt with a great many matters, but it completely neglected to encourage would-be crusaders. *Fritt Folk*, Quisling's own mouthpiece, raged:

We felt entirely certain that no meeting of the bishops could be held without the main theme being a settling of scores with the deadly enemy of Christianity. But we were wrong. Norwegian churchmen are undermining our country's future in the new Europe; they are almost Bolshevism's best friends. The time has come to let these gentlemen take the consequences of their decisions.

Indeed, the bishops took the consequences. Bishop Berggrav, Professor Hallesby, and Arnold Oevern sent a letter to the clergy to arrange for prayers in which no mention was to be made of the crusade. This silence on the part of the State Church in Norway was as significant as the Pope's refusal to endorse the crusade, which the Holy Father maintained against the heaviest diplomatic pressure from the Axis. In fact, instead of making cruel sport of Christianity, as Hitler planned, his mock crusade resulted in bringing the Christian churches closer together.

The Nazis realized that they would have to rely entirely on their own appeal for volunteers, since no spiritual or popular support was forthcoming. Gauleiter Terboven issued a pompous declaration. The Führer, he announced, had "permitted" the formation of an independent Norwegian legion to fight against Russia. Those who joined would be rewarded with government jobs after one year's service and with farms after two years. As additional bait German citizenship was offered.

Terboven had two large barracks built to accommodate the recruits he expected. For a few weeks they stood empty. Then they were turned into concentration camps for "those dangerous Communists who sabotaged the enlistment campaign." Norway has practically no Communists. In the last Norwegian Parliament there was not a single Communist. The campaign for the crusade was frustrated from a different quarter. King Haakon addressed his people in one of his rare radio speeches from London. "Every impartial observer knows that the attack on Russia is above all a part of Germany's struggle for world domination," the King said. "If Germany should be victorious, it would mean oppression and serfdom for Norway and for the rest of the world. The way in which the Germans have secured a foothold in our country in all fields of life and the brutality with which they trample on our most sacred possessions is sufficient proof of this. With this clearly in mind it is not difficult to see that any one helping Germany in her fight against Russia is assisting Germany in her fight against the liberation of our own country. We are at war with Germany. The Germans are our enemies."

The King's address found a resounding echo. It was distributed in thousands of leaflets, and avidly read, although every reader realized that his head would be in a noose if he were found with the royal address. A second leaflet made the rounds of the country. It was not backed up by any authority, but it contained the impressive sentence: "It is the Germans, not the Russians, who have stolen our country." The phrase became a battle cry. One night it was smeared all over the front of the Crown Prince's palace, the present residence of Terboven.

The central recruiting office in Oslo, 14 Parkveien, remained deserted but for small groups of young Hirdmen listening to German agitators who told them that they had first to capture Moscow, then London. Then the Hirdmen sang their regimental song, "Through London's streets we march in serried ranks." And then they decided to stay at home. They were, their spokesman declared, needed in Norway to maintain order.

Quisling saw his system breaking down before his eyes. In Berlin he had given Hitler his word that he would muster at least three thousand men. He had scarcely three hundred to offer. To fill up the empty ranks he decreed that fifteen-year-old volunteers should be allowed to enlist without their parents' consent. As a bribe the boys were promised free travel in busses, trains, and trucks throughout the country until they departed.

With these and similar measures he brought all of one thousand fellows together. Their subsequent parade was a pitiful show. Quisling reviewed his thousand ragamuffins. A man in a brown shirt patted his shoulder. "Say," he asked with all signs of unconcealed disgust, "is that the regiment I'm to take over?"

"You?" Quisling retorted.

"Of course." The brown-shirt clicked his heels. "My name is Sturmbann-Obergruppenführer Daum. I was sent by the Führer to release you from the command of the Norwegian Legion."

For Vidkun Quisling it was a blessing in disguise. The first battalion of the finally formed Regiment Nordland deserted to the Russians immediately on the legion's arrival in Finland, and helped in the defense of Murmansk. The second and third battalions were routed by Timoshenko's troops somewhere

west of Rostov. Only Vidkun Quisling's uniform has not
been as much as wrinkled.

Belgium with almost three times the population of Norway has contributed the same number of men to the crusade.
Among the thousand who joined were fifty White Russians
living in the country, all at least sixty years of age. Even this
meager number of enlistments was obtained only by use of
the general misery, which made the offer to the volunteers
seem enticing. Their pay was fixed at twelve and one-half
francs a day outside the combat zone, and twenty-five at the
front. Parents, wives, and children were to receive allowances
amounting to 85 per cent of the wages received by the volunteers before joining the "anti-Russian brigade." Furthermore
the heroes were officially assured that no harm could come to
them from the hazards of war. The recruiting pamphlet reads:
"Of course, the brigade will not be used in offensive action.
Modern attack formations need long and specialized training.
Therefore it can be assumed that the brigade will be placed
in the second line." Moreover, the medical services of Professor Frans Daels of the University of Ghent were assured
for the anti-Russian brigade. Professor Daels is a famous ob-
stetrician. What sort of service he could render on the Russian front was a matter of much speculation.

In the Walloon part of the kingdom threatening letters
were sent to Rexists who had announced their intention of
joining the brigade. Léon Degrelle complained that he had
received hundreds of such letters. Undaunted, he said at a
meeting attended by a German general: "It will be glory or
death. Little we care. Before we embarked upon the crusade
we admired the Führer. Now we love him." A few days later
at a mass meeting at Liége, however, Degrelle had other reasons for crusading. "It is not Germany we are helping," he
declared. "We are only fighting for the future of Belgium and
its king. . . . I go," he continued, "as a simple soldier. The chief

should show where duty lies. I do not know whether I will come back from this expedition, but I think it is better to die well than to live badly."

He had thought the same when he went to Mexico to join the revolution. He wrote a book about his adventures there. Later it was proved that he had never set foot in that country. His record in the Spanish civil war was along the same lines. After boisterously announcing his departure for the front he had to admit that he "somehow never got there." Léon Degrelle has now had the same misfortune the third time. He is still crusading in Brussels' cafés. Perhaps Hitler's Christian crusade failed everywhere so ingloriously because the Quisling breed are not really fighting animals.

CHAPTER ELEVEN

THE BATTLE OF
PROPAGANDA

One must only repeat a lie often enough. It is incredible what people will believe.—ADOLF HITLER, in *Mein Kampf*, first unexpurgated German edition.

FRENCH journalists, like waiters in America, used to live on tips. A few shining examples to the contrary notwithstanding, the French press was the most venal in the world, and found it, consequently, easiest to jump on the Nazi bandwagon. All over Europe the Nazis have suppressed or taken control of the independent press and radio. Everywhere their creatures continue to publish respectable old journals as organs of Goebbels propaganda. In all the subjugated countries the Hitler gospel is spread in the national language and under the threadbare cloak of national independence.

But France supplied the biggest contingent of voluntary helpers. The Nazification of the French press was supported by some writers of international reputation, by publishers of enormous means, and by the government of Marshal Pétain. Soon the helpers realized that they were the dupes. Even prophets of collaboration among the writers were silenced, publishers cheated out of their "coordinated" property; how Marshal Pétain is treated by the Nazified Paris press will presently be told.

The volte-face of the larger part of the French press was intended to go unnoticed. The German system anxiously preserved the fiction of freedom of opinion. Captain von Grothe, once the correspondent of the official German news agency in Paris and leader of a Nazi spy ring, now the Goebbels-appointed press dictator in occupied France, decreed: "The French press is to be completely reorganized on the principles developed by the authoritarian state. The system of censorship is outdated. It is to be replaced by the method of holding the journalists themselves responsible for what they are writing." The old hand in the spy game goes most carefully about his business. Personally inaccessible to his own French underlings, he gives to anonymous "official spokesmen" the outlines of his orders. "These outlines," he insists, "should form the subject of intensive oral instructions to editors. In no circumstances must the instructions be made public, nor must the fact that such instructions have been given become known in any way. Editors should, however, make copious notes in their own handwriting while receiving their oral instructions."

By far the most important source of news for the French press, both in the occupied and unoccupied zone, is the Agence Havas, the official news agency. Under German pressure Havas had to be reorganized. The agency was divided into three sections: publicity has its headquarters in Paris, whereas news service and Télémondial (the international service) are centralized in Vichy. A financial operation cut down the value of the Havas shares to 250 francs, but their number was increased to 648,000, representing a capital of 162,000,000 francs. The Vichy government reserved for itself the majority of 438,000 shares for which it paid 109,000,000 francs. As the holder of the majority of shares, it controls the news service as well as the foreign service and assumes responsibility for both. The management was completely re-formed —"in a manner," Vichy admitted, "to include German gentlemen in important positions." Indeed, the government-owned official French news agency is controlled by four Germans. Werner Klatten is director of publicity; Fritz Sohn, technical expert; Oscar Mohring, legal adviser; and Hans Seydel, business manager. The office of the four men is in Paris at 5 Boulevard Raspail. Their powers expire—provided Hitler lasts that long—at the end of 1946.

Marshal Pétain celebrated the conclusion of this bargain, which allows France to sanction German dictatorship of the French press with her own money by uttering the words: "A great example has been given. The transformation of the Agence Havas sets the model for the reorganization of all the important big industries, banks, insurance companies, and leading business enterprises in France."

The radio was partitioned along simpler lines. Radio-Paris is admittedly a branch of the German Reichsrundfunkgesellschaft. Radio-Vichy is "independent." It is directed by Paul Marion, a henchman of Laval who spent most of his time in Paris, where he attacked Pétain as "unreliable" toward Germany, and by Benoist-Mechin.

The Paris press serves a double purpose. First, it had to push Vichy into further submission to Germany; secondly, it lets itself go in attacking England and the United States. Strangely, there is scarcely a word to be found against De Gaulle. The general's followers in Paris, it appears, are so numerous and so hot-tempered that prudence cautions against irritating them. Invectives, name calling, slander, blackmail, and abuse were always prominent features of the Paris press. Under Nazi domination, however, the pamphleteers have lost much of their dash. Many articles are written in halting, ungrammatical French, divulging clearly the fact that they are poor translations from the German. All the morning papers reserve a column for advertisements in the German language.

Many newspapers preferred to close down, among them the Catholic *L'Aube*, the patriotic *L'Epoque*, and the socialist *Populaire*. Others moved to unoccupied France. *Paris-Soir*, which once had the largest circulation in France, leads at present a shadowy existence in Limoges. A fake *Paris-Soir*, printed in the building of its old competitor *L'Intransigeant*, is published by the German Lieutenant Weber, the notorious fifth columnist who had had a job as elevator boy on the paper. On the day of the German invasion he dropped his mask and took over the *Paris-Soir*.

Le Matin of one-time world fame is at present the choir leader of the Nazi press. The many grammatical mistakes in its columns—most of its stuff is simply German translations—make this paper the laughingstock of Paris. Its vituperation of the Allies in oddly mixed German-French, however, is unsurpassable. Not even Wladimir d'Ormesson, once a pillar of the alliance with England and an outspoken admirer of America, can compete with these execrations, although his *Figaro*, which moved into the "zone libre," claims to be the most violent enemy of the Anglo-Saxons. The royalist *Action Française* also thrives on England-baiting, while it considers America as "unspeakable." *Gringoire*, the weekly which already in republican times held the world record for journalistic depravity, is a distinguished anti-Allied companion piece.

Interesting is the fate that befell *La Victoire*. Gustave Hervé, its editor, long a crackpot of French political life, was the first noisy advocate of Hitler in France. He did not hide his violently antidemocratic feelings; he is pro-Nazi not by opportunity, but by the innermost inclination of his twisted mind. He used to be the stormy petrel of Paris, until he was laughed off and half forgotten. Jubilantly, he welcomed the Nazi invaders. But he retained independence enough to warn against the unjustified press campaign against England. Immediately the Nazis clamped down on him. *La Victoire* was suppressed. One does not know exactly what happened to Hervé. In any case the fact was established that Hitler has no use for independent admirers.

Others, less independent-minded, thrive on the opportunity of betraying their country in every edition. Jean Luchaire, editor of *Les Nouveaux Temps,* and his colleague Jean Boissel, who had to spend the last year of French independence in prison, have long been on the German pay roll. They were traitors in peacetimes. Luchaire was a Nazi spy during the war, now both are pillars of collaboration. The once famous leftist *Œuvre* has sold out to Goebbels. *L'Illustration,* the weekly magazine which was to be found in practically every French-speaking house, both in France and abroad, had a remarkable experience. Its publisher hastened to affirm his collaborationist zeal. He did not object to having German partners. He hoped he could retain at least a small share of his property. He did retain it for a few months. When the German partners felt sufficiently at home in *L'Illustration,* the turncoat proprietor was told that his assistance was no longer necessary. He had to leave without any compensation. Yet this unfortunate man was still lucky in comparison with others of his color. The traitor Jean Fonterroy, who had a respectable name in the world of letters to lose, lost both his name and, probably, his life. He disappeared without a trace. No one knows whether the Gestapo or French patriots got him. M. de Châteaubriand, also a widely known writer, lives in constant fear of assassination. At least he complains in every article of being threatened with death, only because he finds Nazism acceptable and once wrote a eulogy of Hitler, admiring even the Führer's mustache.

The turncoat papers are popularly called *la presse vendue:* the press that has sold out. Their contents were largely praises of the "correct behavior" of the German army of occupation and eulogies of the Nazi system in all its aspects. Since Laval's return to power they are almost exclusively devoted to open war-mongering. A special group of weeklies tries to interest working-class readers. *Au Travail!* (To Work) supports the national revolution and intimate collaboration with Nazism on the field of labor unionism. A similar publication in the unoccupied zone is *L'Atelier* (The Workshop). The daily *La France au Travail,* another paper for the laboring class, had to suspend early in November, 1941, because its last readers were deserting it. It was replaced by *La France Socialiste* which began publication with the banner headline "A Warning to America."

These French-language Nazi papers with pink varnish indulged in attacks on the "reactionary" and "clerical" system of Vichy. It was the only permitted way of letting off steam and of feigning independence.

L'Œuvre, itself a *journal vendu,* remarked melancholically on the Paris press: "Most of our editorialists, having in former days adopted an attitude to which they cannot remain faithful, are today obliged to write the opposite of what they wrote yesterday. The more talent they possess, the shorter and the more infrequent are their articles."

Sometimes readers are surprised to find articles by great French authors and scientists who, it is commonly known, have emigrated and despise Nazism and its creatures. The explanation is simple. It is a habit of yellow journalism in contemporary France to make up such articles and to steal the names of honorable men. No law protects respectable and sincere French writers against this offense.

The readers fall away in droves from the *presse vendue.* But the mushrooming anti-Semitic sheets have created a new reading public. The notorious Nürnberg *Stürmer* found its counterpart in *Au Pilori!* (To the Pillory!). Other anti-Semitic rags hide their purposes under such patriotic titles as *La Vie Nationale* and *Notre Paris.*

Another desperate method of keeping or attracting readers is the prize competition. For a few days all Paris papers asked the same question: "Who is the author of the following ten anti-British or anti-Semitic quotations? . . ." After a fortnight Radio-Paris transmitted the correct answers. The names of the winners were not given. The prize, incidentally, amounted to ten francs, the equivalent of a dime.

The political books published in Paris keep in step with the papers. Drieu la Rochelle, pro-Nazi editor of the *Nouvelle Revue Française*, recently published a book "Ne pas attendre" (Don't let us wait!) in which Hitler, "one of those outstanding figures only periodically revealed to mankind," is praised for his "foresight and wisdom, his almost supernatural intuition." Similarly, Bertrand de Jouvenel, in his *Après la Défaite* praises his Nazi friends for allowing the French to collaborate with them in constructing a better Europe. To all these writers Vichy minus Laval was the eternal whipping boy. The bourgeoisie and the army, the two strongholds of Pétain, were made to appear responsible for all the weakness, the indecision, the half-heartedness condemning France to slow death.

Tired and cautious, the Vichy press sometimes ventured to reply. It was merely inviting new criticism. The *Matin* attacked it for its "abundance of English information." The *Figaro*, at present in Vichy-France, was sharply censured for having attacked the actor Sacha Guitry, who fawns upon every German uniform. The *Jour* and the *Temps*, in their Vichy exile, attempted occasionally to speak out against giving the Germans more than the armistice demands. But these voices have long been silenced. There is an atmosphere of general uneasiness in the Vichy press. Only *L'Effort*, the mouthpiece of a few socialist turncoats, is openly for full cooperation with Nazism. The other papers have learned to smile ironically. Some complain discreetly about the "hard law of silence."

The Catholic press is an exception. The attitude of *La Croix*, the organ of the Catholic Youth movement, and of the

Semaine Religieuse, once a parochial weekly which now enjoys nation-wide circulation, toward the government is prudent. Both stress the universality of the Church over nationalism. They crusaded gallantly for the refugees, and disapproved of chauvinism and anti-Semitism. They resist the tendency of the state to impair the independence of Catholic associations and schools. Agreeing to "cautious collaboration," they refuse, on behalf of the Church, any identification with the existing system. They remain faithful to the Christian ideas of universal liberty and humanity.

Two other Catholic magazines, the *Temps Nouveaux* and *Esprit*, dared openly to express their opposition to the Pétain regime and maintained an uncompromising democratic and anticollaborationist viewpoint. Both magazines were originally in a strong position. The weekly *Temps Nouveaux* was the successor of *Sept*, founded in 1934 by a group of Dominican Fathers loyal to the doctrine of liberal Catholicism. *Esprit*, a monthly, was from its foundation in 1932 one of the most significant French periodicals, widely discussed in Catholic circles both in France and abroad. It had fostered study groups in Paris, in rural France, in Switzerland and Belgium.

Both magazine were a pride, perhaps the only one, of contemporary French political writing. Toward the end of 1941 both were forbidden by Marshal Pétain, the God-fearing churchgoer.

In the midst of all this decay, however, French spirit and valor rise to new heights. The beautiful French language, abused, prostituted, sold out for a pittance, is still a powerful weapon in the fight for honor and truth. The old adage of the pen being mightier than the sword is fully vindicated by the uncanny influence the underground press is exercising in France.

Valmy was the first clandestine newspaper to appear. Late in December, 1940, a picture was distributed throughout

France showing two tense hands against a dark background, one slipping a scrap of paper with the imprint *Valmy* into the other.

The Gestapo was forewarned. They searched every corner of France. The omnipresent secret police only forgot to inspect the mail. When the New Year's mail was distributed, many French families received with the conventional holiday greetings a most unconventional message. *Valmy* made its appearance. "There is only one enemy—the invader," its bannerhead read. The editorial, under the heading "Assurance," made a violent attack on the collaborators:

The cooperation of all the forces of the Anglo-Saxon world, of Great Britain, the Dominions, and the United States, will become manifest. They have joined in union with many other powers, all of whom are determined to liberate hundreds of millions of people, to eradicate tyranny, and to give the tormented peoples new hope for a world habitable for human beings.

The Germans, the Japanese, and the Italians will not break up this enormous power in the making. You, Frenchmen, have no choice. Do you want to accept a share in the defense of a New Order which is nothing but the disorder of misery? Do you want to accept as definitive a defeat which was transformed into surrender by men greedy for power, who are the sworn enemies of liberty? No, that is certainly not what you want. You realize that democracy is not dead. One could betray and blemish her. But from now on no one will attack democracy unpunished. She is forging her weapons in the world's most powerful arsenal.

With its visionary ring, its merciless contempt of the traitors, its accurate prediction of the ultimate line-up, and, above all, with its unshakable faith in America, this appeal sounds like Winston Churchill at the beginning of 1942. In fact, it was conceived by an unknown, anonymous French journalist —a year later, after his escape to London, disclosed as M. Simon—at New Year, 1941, when Hitler was at the height of his successes, Japan, to all outward appearance, still sitting on the fence, and America woefully undecided. It may also be added that the phrase "arsenal of democracy," later made proverbial by President Roosevelt, first appeared in this mimeographed, illegal French sheet.

Like a torrent the voice of *Valmy* swept France. There was no problem the courageous paper did not tackle. It fought with editorials, with personal disclosures, with quotations, anecdotes, with the sharpest weapons of truth. It confronted the famine rampant in France with accurate figures of French agrarian production, omitting any comment, but forcing the conclusion on the reader that the German army of occupation was stealing all. It published the daily arrivals of foodstuffs at the Paris market to make the readers see what an infinitesimal fraction of them was left for civilian consumption. Who was raiding the bulk, *Valmy* asked. Perhaps the R.A.F. or the British blockade?

Valmy joined the fight against anti-Semitism in telling the story of the Archbishop of Bordeaux who decided to send a sick old woman of seventy years alms of fifty francs. When he was told that the woman was Jewish he doubled his contribution. "Give her my thanks," the prince of the church added, "for her confidence in Christian charity." Phrases like "Pétain's *Rassemblement National* is the dupes' market," coined by *Valmy*, immediately found their place in popular parlance. When Radio-Vichy announced that Eve Curie had been expelled from the United States, *Valmy* disclosed that she was at the time of the broadcast staying as a house guest at the White House. Admiral Darlan was christened: "Peter Darlahn, Grossadmiral der Flotte." *Valmy* was not taken in by the old guard who feigned resistance while they were betraying the cause. How is it, the paper asked, that all these over-age French heroes have German names, viz: Weygand, Huntzinger, Dentz? What sort of Frenchmen are they?

Valmy fought valiantly for a year. When the Gestapo, finally, laid hands on it, it was even surpassed in its appeal to the plain people by the tabloid-sized *Les Petites Ailes de France* (The Little Wings of France), whose bannerhead carries no patriotic slogan, but the sane advice: "Read carefully, copy copiously, and circulate cautiously." Opposite appears the proud claim of "the largest circulation of any underground paper in the world." The paper is available in literally every hamlet in France. In London it is sold in Piccadilly Circus, although, it is true, the delivery across the Channel is not regular.

During the last year a score of other underground papers—printed on toy presses or regulation presses, mimeographed or copied by hand by courageous groups of women and men—began publication. *Peuple de France* and *Vériste* are received in England with great regularity. Next in importance are *Pantagruel,* an anticollaborationist newspaper printed and published in Paris, and *Résistance.* Others are *Humanité, La Voix de Paris, Le Feu, L'Ordre Nouveau, La Liberté,* and *Le Papillon* (Butterfly), a comic paper whose cartoons are signed with pen names like "Ribbentrop" and "Goebbels."

Early in January, 1942, both the occupied and the unoccupied zone of France were flooded with handbills announcing that a new underground publication, *La Libération,* was about to start. Most characteristically this announcement, disdainfully inviting the Gestapo to play hide-and-seek, was made the day after R.A.F. pilots had "bombed" Paris, Lille, and the rest of the occupied zone with two million of the "United States Leaflet No. 1," which conveyed President Roosevelt's speech expressing his confidence that the United Nations would win the war. Within ten minutes, Free French reports affirm, this leaflet became France's preferred reading matter.

The French underground press is courageously assisted by the Radio Inconnu (Unknown Radio), an illegal station operating somewhere inside France. Every day this station broadcasts the most violent attacks on all traitors, particularly against the "boche radio" in Paris. Here is an excerpt from a transmission as it was recorded by CBS in New York:

"The Russians won't stop at the precise line where Generalissimo Adolf would like them to. The Russians have been attacked in a cowardlly way. They will go into Germany. They will carry destruction into German cities. The Russians will feed Hitler his own medicine. But not only the Russians will invade Germany. The English, the Americans, the Dutch, the Poles, the Norwegians, and even the French will be with them. The Free French who will show the Germans what war means. . . . The boches will lose the war, and the Nazi regime of terror and oppression will disappear. Their new Europe is nonsense." This illegal French station concluded with the identification: "You were listening to the known voice of the Unknown Radio station somewhere in France." It was an understatement. Listeners had been hearing the voice of France.

The Agence Dechenne, the Belgian counterpart of the Agence Havas, and until some time ago owned by this institution, went the same way as the once great French news service. At present Herr von Balusek, formerly an employee of the German Library in Brussels, controls Dechenne, which is in charge of news gathering for, and the distribution of, forty daily and one hundred and fifty weekly and monthly publications. Some thirty newspapers—the underground press —do without the Nazi poison that flows through the channels of the official Belgian agency.

Occupied for almost two years, Belgium's economic situation is desperate. Business has practically come to a halt, only the newspaper business enjoying a veritable boom. During the happy days of the freedom of the press, the number of publications was never anywhere near as high. At present, Belgium has not only the world's densest population per square mile, but also the largest number of newspapers. Unfortunately, their prosperity does not equal their number. But a large part of the Belgian press has learned to be extremely modest. Publishers, editors, and contributors, as well as the news venders and most of the readers, feel that they are lucky if they get away with their lives. That goes not for the underground press alone, but perhaps even more for their rabid enemies, the Quisling press, which has to dodge the wrath of a population near the point of explosion.

Yet there exists a great variety of Quisling papers. The explanation for this prodigality is the disunity in the camp of the traitors. There are at least half a dozen different groups engaged in the race for Hitler's favor—which, incidentally, the Führer does not lavish on his foreign creatures. Outside the conflicting camps, without any party affiliations, stands the lone wolf, Henri de Man, the renegade Socialist. His Brussels paper *Le Travail* appeared as a daily with the special permission of the Nazi authorities, who hoped it would help to win the Belgian workers for collaboration. But the paper was boycotted by Belgian labor. The Nazis, their ears to the ground, cut *Le Travail*'s subsidy down to 10 per cent. Henri de Man is today no longer the King's confidant, but the publisher of a moribund weekly, harassed by his printer's bills.

Le Soir used to be Belgium's most influential newspaper. It still carries on in its traditional trappings. Print and make-up are as of old, and only the contents have changed; but the circulation has disappeared. A law case recently conducted at the Tribunal of Commerce in Brussels revealed how *Le Soir* was Nazified. A Quisling named Raymond de Becker seized the paper during the absence of its owners Melli Rossel and Lucien Fuss. When the publishers returned, De Becker showed them a decree signed by the chief of propaganda—Staffel B, the German propaganda office for the district of Brussels—which nominated Raymond de Becker editor and manager of the paper with a provision for his immediate dismissal if his services should be found unsatisfactory. De Becker was to receive fifteen to eighteen thousand francs a month, drawn from the profits of the paper. Of course, the Nazified *Le Soir,* successor to the biggest moneymaker in the Belgian press, makes no profits. The louder De Becker beats the drum for the New Order, the more rapidly circulation drops. There is, he insisted at court, but one solution for the problem: the introduction of enforced subscriptions to *Le Soir* by all people depending on the state.

In a totalitarian state there are a goodly number of such people. Unfortunately for De Becker, they have already been snatched away by a competitor. The *Nouveau Journal* was founded after the German invasion. The money came from Germany—not from Goebbels' Propaganda ministry, but from the Franz Eher Co., Hitler's own publishing house. The general manager of Eher's, Herr Amann, betook himself to Brussels to assist at the christening of the newest product of his fertile combine, which has "acquired" the best-selling papers of every town, in Germany and in the occupied countries. Departing, he half promised and half threatened his Belgian collaborator, Paul Collin, "Behave yourself, and I will let you alone."

Collin is one of the most unsavory creatures in the malodorous Quisling world. Before the war he was spiritual leader if not the chief of the Fifth Column in Belgium. He escaped arrest during the war only by diverting the suspicions of the authorities to his accomplices. In fact, he acted as an informer. For good measure he violently attacked Germany. "The German aggression," he wrote, "constitutes a crime. It will open the eyes of the world to the hideousness for which the Reich stands." Moreover, he fawned on every member of the Belgian cabinet. Today, Collin calls the same men, Pierlot and his government in exile, traitors, and his eulogies of Nazism are only surpassed by his deification of Mussolini. "Italy, the master of the Mediterranean, will soon annihilate the English Fleet in the Mare Nostrum, and chase the British from Egypt and the Near East," he predicted a year ago. Evidently, Mussolini's cash was speaking.

The *Nouveau Journal* is constantly involved in the feuds between the various traitorous cliques. Collin asserted "with disappointment" that many who collaborated with the power of occupation had been "converted by false motives: ambition, flattery, uneducated ravings, and vulgar hopes of profiteering." He did not conceal that he was pointing out the Rexists and their chief Degrelle. In turn, he was rapped on the knuckles by the super-Nazi Flemish Nationalist *Volk en Staat*. He was asked whether he wanted to be denounced once more to the occupation authorities, or why else he was misinterpreting the statements made by other papers.

The Belgian people have their fun with these unending feuds. They feel the same hatred and disdain for traitors of all brands, and they have devious ways of expressing their feelings. Sighing, Collin admitted in his sheet: "A heavy task lies ahead of us. Insults and contempt await us. . . . Yet a German victory is very probable."

These words were his undoing. The *Brüsseler Zeitung*, the German language mouthpiece of the army of occupation, took him to task for having called German victory only "very probable." These words, the *Brüsseler Zeitung* maintained, proved a deplorable lack of confidence. The Belgian chief propagandist of Nazism, it is reported, escaped the concentration camp only by promising that he would never again commit a similar faux pas.

Incredible as it may seem, the Flemish traitor press bends back even further than the Walloon. The principal papers are *Volk en Staat*, which instigated the pogrom in Antwerp, and *Hier Dinaso*. The editor of the latter is Pol Le Roy. His job is to create anti-British feeling, blaming the blockade for the "suffering from empty stomachs," although he admits that "all Belgian property owners want a British victory, and the people are stupid enough to curse not the blockade but those who want to give them a new order." His deepest hatred, however, is not directed against Albion, but against his own country, Belgium. This traitor shouts that there is no Belgium:

We are people of Flanders, Brabant, and Limburg: There is no such thing as a Belgian people or nation. By following our former democratic leaders we have lost the right to help decide what political order is to be established. The *Dietsch* state will perhaps have fewer rights than the German people. But we realize and accept the limitations of our own sovereignty and liberty within the German community. We no longer acknowledge a Belgian fatherland, people, nation, soul or spirit, history, custom, culture, nor, above all, a Belgian honor. We have finished with all that was Belgium. Our greatest duty is to destroy clericalism. The Belgian clergy is a hideous monster, stinking of death, hell, and the devil.

The *Brüsseler Zeitung* represents genuine authority. The Gestapo purge of November, 1941, was preceded by the paper's complaint:

Belgians are drawing up lists of Quislings. Many people feel that the journalists who now edit the Belgian newspapers are traitors. But future generations will recognize the noble conscience they felt in fulfilling their national duty. The surrender of May 28, 1940, brought liberty to the Flemish as well as to the Walloons. It showed them a better future which is already taking shape.

What shape the future—a very short-lived future, to be sure —is taking was best exemplified in the treatment of the Belgian Catholic press. Father Fernand Morlion had established the International Catholic Press Service, which worked in fourteen European countries and carried complete and regular information across the German border. Its famous news letter was published in thirty European and American countries. The editors using it did not know where their material came from. It proved, however, so excellently informed and so meticulously accurate that it was widely considered as the best inside information. Suddenly the quality and the reliability of the news deteriorated. The letter still came in the same language and went to the same papers, and the underground service to Germany was not neglected; but it contained strange and disturbing expressions like "Hitler's is the new type of the New Order—it has to be judged by other standards than the old accepted ones."

One of the few men in England who had known Father Morlion's whereabouts sent, via grapevine, a Belgian friend to his office. The Belgian go-between found himself in the propaganda section of the Gestapo. A man in a stained cowl, introducing himself as an "irregular Trappist monk," received the visitor and presented him to Father Leonard. Father Leonard in turn pretended to be a Jesuit and explained that he was carrying on Morlion's work. The Belgian go-between took no time to ascertain whether the Jesuit's soutane was also faked. He was lucky to get away.

Is the Catholic press in Belgium indeed strangled? The *Brüsseler Zeitung* complains that a great number of Catholic anti-German pamphlets are still circulating in Belgium. The German paper admits that a mascot is being widely distributed. It represents Joan of Arc in armor, kneeling, and bears the inscription: "Joan of Arc, protect the city of London." *Pays Réel*, Léon Degrelle's sheet, attacks His Eminence Cardinal van Roey for "his secret collaboration with clandestine newspapers."

By far the outstanding underground paper in Belgium—probably the foremost of its kind on the entire European continent—is *La Libre Belgique*. It is a paper with a battle-scarred and honorable tradition. *La Libre Belgique* was published secretly in Belgium in World War I. It was started again, its front page says, on August 15, 1940, two and one-half months after capitulation of the Belgian Army. Its address is marked, humorously, "Oberfeldkommandantur, 1, Place du Trône,

Brussels." The "publisher" is Peter Pan, whose statue stands in the Egmont Garden of Brussels.

Quotations from speeches by personalities prominent in the first and second periods of German rule emphasize that Belgium suffers and resists for the second time in a quarter of a century. King Albert, Burgomaster Max of Brussels and Cardinal Mercier kept Belgian hope alive from 1914 to 1918. King Leopold, P. J. van de Meulebroeck, whom the Germans deposed as Burgomaster of Brussels, and Cardinal van Roey are cited today.

La Libre Belgique discloses that strikes broke out in the mining and metallurgic districts of Belgium early last summer. The workers wanted more bread, more meat, more potatoes. The present Belgian rations give only 1,400 theoretical and 1,000 actual calories daily to each Belgian, according to the paper, while the minimum needed by adults not engaged in manual labor is 2,200 calories. A delegation of workers went to Brussels and was received by the Belgian authorities. The latter said that better rations could not be granted without an order of the German commandant. The commandant refused to receive the strikers.

La Libre Belgique, starting as a mimeographed sheet, is today a well printed daily newspaper of six pages. Its circulation is one hundred thousand, and it is obtainable practically everywhere. Its editors are polite enough to send complimentary copies to all the important German authorities. If the Gestapo gets hold of a batch, the newspaper in some unaccountable way usually hears of the mishap and replaces the confiscated copies, so that the subscribers suffer no loss. Of course they receive their issues gratis. It would be too difficult to collect subscriptions. It is difficult enough to distribute the paper. Only the fact that practically all Belgium is united in a single conspiracy explains it.

Following *La Libre Belgique* in importance are two other clandestine publications, *Le Belge,* and *Tenir* (Hold Out).

Whereas *La Libre Belgique* publishes three editions for different parts of the country, *Le Belge* appears in two, and the others in one. All told, there are more than thirty underground papers mocking the Gestapo.

Two more publications of a similar brand are *Het Vrije Woord* (Free Speech), a Flemish-language paper which specializes in fighting for the rights of the workers who are sent to Germany or for those who have to work in the regions which are usually attacked by the R.A.F., and *La Vérité et le Peuple* (Truth and People), a Communist sheet which, in the bygone days of the Stalin-Hitler pact, used to attack Hitler and Churchill equally ferociously. This sin cannot be forgiven by the other underground papers. They will have no truck with former vituperators of Mr. Churchill. Outlawed, driven underground, desperately striving for their lives, Belgians remain respectable.

In Norway, too, the Nazi system began by disclaiming any intention of interfering with the freedom of the press. There was just one little reservation attached: any editor who was "misrepresenting historic events" would be removed.

This rubber paragraph served to liquidate many papers, and their writers as well. A number of well known Norwegian journalists are held in the concentration camp at Grini. Among them is H. Neese, the political editor of the Oslo *Aftenposten*. The editor of *Folkebladet* at Molde, Jakob Bolstad, was released after ten months in prison. He was never told why he had been arrested.

Two distinguished journalists named Christian S. Oftedal and Fridtjov Lundh who, together with eight others had been sentenced to death on February 24, 1941, allegedly for having conveyed military information to England, were submitted to a particular ordeal. The R.A.F. had bombed the aluminum plants at Hoyanger. After the raid, four unexploded bombs were discovered by the Germans. The Nazi commander sent for the ten condemned men who were awaiting their execution in prison. Pointing out the unexploded bombs, he said: "We can of course not jeopardize German lives to remove these infernal machines. You have forfeited your heads, as it is. Would you do us the favor?"

The Norwegian prisoners had had not the slightest experience with bombs. But they went at the job which the highly trained German experts were too cowardly to tackle. No incident occurred. No mercy was granted. The rescuers were shoved back into the death cell.

Also condemned to death were the journalists Fredrik Ramm and Olav Gjerlöw. Ramm had won an international reputation when he accompanied Roald Amundsen on his polar flight in the dirigible *Norge* in 1926, and sent back an unforgettable dispatch to the New York *Times*. Gjerlöw was the chief editor of the *Morgenbladet*, a consistent opponent of his country's Nazification. The condemnation to death of two such popular and widely beloved men aroused such a state of excitement throughout Norway that Gauleiter Terboven found it prudent to commute the sentence to life imprisonment; and Gjerlöw has been released since.

Quisling's own paper is *Fritt Folk*. It recently launched a campaign to increase its circulation. The person who signed up the largest number of subscribers was to receive an autographed photograph of Vidkun Quisling. The second prize consisted of a similarly autographed copy of the Little Führer's book "Quisling Has Said So." The winner of the third prize was to have the singular honor of spending a whole day with Vidkun himself. This third prize was won by a careful man carrying water on both shoulders. To be sure, he did his best to solicit new subscribers. But when he was told that his day with Quisling would include a stroll through the streets of Oslo, he begged to be excused from accepting the prize. He offered a dozen reasons which prevented him, from a cold in the head to a sudden heart attack on the part of a mother-in-law at whose bedside he had to remain. The real explanation was, of course, his fear to be seen in public with Norway's dictator. *Fritt Folk* used this sad example of hesitation to publish an editorial regretting that "90 per cent of the Norwegian people are politically undecided."

There is, however, no indecision in the underground press, which circulates almost freely. The muzzling of all Norwegian newspapers last summer, and the fact that since then the Nazis and their Quisling lackeys have been in control of all the accepted instruments of propaganda—a change that began with installing German "political collaborators" in the Norwegian Telegraph Agency—has only stiffened the attitude of the free and secret, or not so secret, press. Handwritten, mimeographed, and even printed sheets are widely distributed among patriots. Their very titles show what they stand for— for instance, *Freedom, We Want Our Country*, and *All for Norway*. All told, there are as many as twenty. Two things about these free papers are significant: first, that they result from the financial, editorial, and practical cooperation of large groups of people from all walks of life; and second, that their tone is free from revenge or incitement to lawlessness. It is by plain facts and skillfully wielded irony and satire that this patriotic press counteracts the ravings of Quisling and the oppression carried out by the Nazi authorities in Norway.

Two unlicensed Norwegian newspapers which are very widely read are *The Free Labor Movement* and *Tidens Tegn*. This last ceased to come out openly some months ago as it refused to renounce the rights of a free press. It now appears, practically without change, as an underground paper, carrying on a clandestine campaign as a result of which all over Norway there are appearing two parallel arrows chalked up side by side, one pointing down and meaning "Down with Quisling," and the other pointing up and meaning "Long live King Haakon." It took the Germans a long time to guess what they meant.

The Germans were hammering at the port of Leningrad, the Shah of Iran abdicated and fled, Kiev was in flames. But the Czechs bought no newspapers. For the whole week between September 14 and 21, 1941, they abstained from buying their Nazified press, as the radio in London had advised them. Thus Czechoslovakia celebrated the anniversary of the death of Masaryk, the founder of the Republic. Circulation of the principal morning papers dropped to practically nothing. The subscribers did not bother to fetch them from the news stands. Evening papers, lacking subscribers, disappeared from the streets. The newsboys were playing soccer. In tramcars and trains the people read well thumbed volumes, mostly Czech classics. Guests in coffeehouses refused papers brought to them, as is customary in Central Europe, by their waiters; soon the waiters refrained from bringing the papers. Whole parcels of papers were left unopened with the news venders. Those who bought copies proved themselves traitors. The venders—who were recompensed by getting the price of the papers without handing them over—passed secret lists of such "scabs" to the strike committee. A few readers, obviously *agents provocateurs* of the Gestapo, were publicly beaten up. The boycott was carried out throughout the country. The two most vocal Nazi papers in the Czech language never recovered from the losses they suffered during the week of strike. *Ceské Slovo* lost permanently two-thirds of its former circulation and the Nazified, once rabidly anti-German *Vecer* dropped from forty thousand to nine thousand. *Der Neue Tag*, the Nazi mouthpiece, declared angrily that if the Czechs would not read their newspapers it would be better not to waste good German newsprint on them. A large crowd gathered in front of its editorial office. For the first time the police did not have to protect *Der Neue Tag* from mass hostility. The Czech crowds cheered the Nazi suggestion. They are deadly sick of their turncoat press.

Since the establishment of the Protectorate no fewer than

nine hundred newspapers and magazines have been suppressed, including the famous scientific review of the Prague museum, the foundation of which, in the early nineteenth century, was enthusiastically saluted by Goethe, and *Malý Čtenář*, the weekly for children between the ages of six and ten.

Baron Neurath, the former Protector, explained the suppression of the first batch of four hundred periodicals by a paper shortage. His successor, the Gestapo boss Reinhard Heydrich, was more direct. Soon after the beginning of the Russian war he forbade another five hundred and twenty publications with the frank declaration that an inferior race must not read. Czech papers are compelled to publish furious denunciations of the nation's own historic and political traditions. Frequently, the editors publish such articles as they come from the German Press Department—with linguistic mistakes and misprints that betray their character at the first glance. Another ruse in the battle of wits is to exaggerate German victory claims in order to expose their falseness. When the Germans claimed to have reached Kiev, the Czech press reported that Moscow had fallen. When Berlin announced the crossing of the Dnieper, in Prague it became the Volga. The official figures of Russian prisoners captured by the Germans were supplied, at least on unprotesting paper, with an additional naught. In consequence, German bulletins were exposed to general ridicule, but the Nazi press chiefs could only thank their assiduous press slaves for their zeal.

The five daily broadcasts from London in the Czech languages and Slovak have, indeed, been the fountainhead of resistance. It is impossible to exaggerate the B.B.C.'s influence on the thinking and the actions of the Czech nation. The *V* campaign was probably nowhere so enthusiastically carried out, and so meticulously observed in all its detailed directions, as in the Protectorate. When Colonel Britton, its leader, made a passing reference to Colonel Emanuel Moravec, the chief traitor in Prague, and a frequent broadcaster, the latter left his microphone panic-striken, retired into a hospital, and had to be coaxed for many weeks to resume his broadcasts.

The traitor Emanuel Moravec realizes that he is a doomed man. All those of his color are on the proscribed list. Some names are already marked with a cross. The day before Heydrich's arrival, five Nazified Czech newpaper writers were celebrating with a banquet the advent of their new boss. The next day one of the boon companions, Karel Laznovský, the foremost Quisling writer of Prague, died of poisoning in the German hospital. Having denounced a colleague, Manrich by name, editor of the *Ceské Slovo*, who was subsequently killed by the Gestapo, Laznovský well deserved his fate. His death was not unexpected, least of all to the victim himself. He had openly complained for months that people meeting him on the street made characteristic movements around their necks, symbolizing hanging, particularly since his denunciation had been rewarded with a highly paid job. Hundreds of letters had threatened him with death. He and his family had been socially ostracized. On his deathbed, a nurse overheard him murmuring: "At least, I am relieved." Relieved in the same way was his colleague and accomplice in treason, Vladimír Kryčtálek, who died a day later from the same poisoning. The other three guests at the banquet recovered, but never regained their health.

In the relentless struggle on the Czech press front, death, of course, strikes both ways. Last September, Karel Skálda was executed in Berlin. He was the founder of *V Boj* (Into Battle), Czechoslovakia's leading underground paper. Publication did not cease with his death. His staff is carrying on. *V Boj* is still printed every Thursday and distributed every Friday, as it has been during the last two years, although its office is moved after the publication of every issue. Most of its contents, incidentally, is news picked up from the B.B.C. broadcasts.

The underground press has a mighty ally in a secret Czech

radio station that began broadcasting on Sunday June 1, 1941, exactly at the hour a radio address by the Protector was announced. The new station calls itself Nazdar (Hello). Although chiefly serving Czech listeners it is also clearly to be heard in England. Its reports consist of attacks on the Germans and, especially, denunciations of their Czech creatures. Among a great many other feats, Nazdar is responsible for the solution of the Melantrich case, which stirred all Czechoslovakia. Melantrich is the largest publishing house in the country, and one of the largest on the European continent. It was controlled by Herr von Wolmar, assistant chief of the German press service in Prague, but the actual management was in the hands of Director Jaroslav Salda and Editor-in-chief Ludek Stránsky, two Czech turncoats. Strangely, the patriots only mildly objected to their serving the German masters. This benevolent attitude of an otherwise highly impatient and vengeful public was explained when Herr von Wolmar sent his two henchmen to a concentration camp in Germany (where they, presumably, were killed), accusing them of being indeed turncoats. Although they feigned to be collaborators, they were actually in daily contact with Dr. Beneš in London.

How did the German chief discover their double game? The somewhat threadbare reputation of the Gestapo in Prague seemed brighter. But here the secret station Nazdar came in. "The Gestapo," it broadcast, "is as inefficient as ever. They had not the faintest notion of what was going on in the Melantrich house. The denunciation was an inside job. A minor employee of Melantrich's, Dr. Emanuel Vajtauer, was responsible for it. We spell his name: V, for victory; A, for . . ." Nazdar did not forget to give his address. It was Braník, a Prague suburb.

An hour later an outraged crowd stormed the house in Braník. But Dr. Vajtauer, the super-traitor, himself had been listening to the illegal radio. As soon as he heard his name on the air, he fled from his house. At present he lives in "voluntary confinement" in the police prison in Smíchov, in the heart of Prague. The Czechs say it will not take another storming of the Bastille, but simply a suitable opportunity, to get him out.

The case was widely discussed all over Prague. Obedient to their orders, the newspapers tried to hush it up. Only *Vlajka* (The Banner), the mouthpiece of the local Nazis, featured it in order to affirm its own loyalty to the German masters. Immediately these masters clamped down on *Vlajka*. The paper that for two years had been a stench in Czech noses was suppressed for a breach of discipline.

Nazdar continued its revelations. It never gives the time of its next transmission, but promises that it will be heard as usual some time the next day. It always warns its listeners to take the greatest precautions. "Do not fear for us," it assures them. "The Gestapo is much too slow for us."

The Gestapo, evidently, could not take this provocation lying down. Its agents combed Prague from cellar to ceiling. Upon special information, a raiding party entered a house on Václavské Namiěstí, the main square of Prague. Shots were heard, and two men were seen descending by a rope from a window. The Gestapo agents, following the fugitives rapidly, found a dead man and a radio transmitter. The other man escaped. A rich reward was promised for the identification of the corpse. But no citizen of Prague cared to earn the thirty pieces of silver.

However, in the search for Nazdar, the Gestapo discovered a few other things. One of them was a secret radio station in the Prague insane asylum. Dr. Kafka, the director of the institution, was immediately shot. Among other findings was that many German officers from the Prague garrison were regular listeners to the London broadcast and the Nazdar station. A number of them were court-martialed. The trials, however, stopped as soon as it pleased Nazdar to end them.

The secret broadcast addressed itself to the Protector directly. "Listen, Reinhard," the voice from nowhere said cordially. "We know you are curious. We will tell you two things. Both will interest you. First, we are not alone. We have competition aplenty. At present, fourteen secret radio stations are operating in your realm. So what good is it to single us out in your futile manhunt? Second, we have a list of five hundred and sixty-seven German officers, who are our—shall we say, regular customers? There are enough witnesses against every one. We would prefer not to publish our list—we rather like our listeners. But if you force us—well, you can have your purge of the German officers' corps."

Heydrich called off the search for Nazdar. So far the Czech broadcasters have not involved the five hundred and sixty-seven German officers in a scandal that would blow sky-high the reputation of the almost invincible German army. The men at the transmitter have no reason to be unfriendly. Undisturbed, all fourteen stations operate in day and night shifts. The hostage system, they proved, works also in reverse.

In the Government General of Poland five newspapers are printed in German, and seven Nazi newspapers in Polish. The aim of this press, according to German statements, is repetition of official announcements, declarations in the Polish language, and the printing of propaganda material. All newspapers printed in Polish are directed exclusively by Germans; Poles are used only for translation. "The press in Polish is to demonstrate and impose upon Poles a new point of view, as well as to teach them that Germans are the element of order in Europe," Governor General Dr. Frank declared, enumerating the Nazi papers. He forgot—or was ashamed to mention— *Neu Polen,* a new German weekly edited by Edward Sykes, the former editor of the English-language *Warsaw Weekly,* who pretends to be an American citizen although, he admits, he is "making no use" of his citizenship "at present."

Much more important was the omission of the one hundred and forty-six underground papers flooding the country and mostly instructing the people in sabotage. Poland, indeed, is the most prolific producer of clandestine publications. They range from single-sheet mimeographed papers published daily to thirty-two-page quarterly reviews.

The news in the Polish underground press is never more than four or five days old. One paper even apologized for the belated printing of a picture that had appeared in London six days earlier. "But you see," the editor explained, "our offices have to be hidden in forests, paper has to be brought from great distances, and our staffs are small. The contributors to one paper are not known to the others, so that if one is captured he will not be able to reveal the identity of his colleagues. This condition causes occasional confusion. For all these reasons, delay in our news service is sometimes inevitable," he concluded in the polite Polish manner.

Unlicensed publications first appeared in Poland a few weeks after its occupation by German and Soviet troops. At first they were very brief, containing mainly short slogans. As early as the fall of 1939 posters bearing such slogans as "Long Live Poland!" and "Long Live Liberty!" could be seen in Warsaw, Cracow, and other cities. About the same time unlicensed publications carrying information made their appearance. They filled the gap created by the German confiscation of radio receiving sets. The most popular was the bulletin "I Listen to the English Radio!" In November, 1939, the "Manifesto of Freedom," one of the first programmatic publications, giving the political platform of Polish democracy, was issued. It was later reprinted in this country. Throughout 1940 the Polish underground press steadily expanded its activities. In the first year of the war, more than a hundred unlicensed periodicals, as well as many pamphlets, booklets, and leaflets have been published.

The German authorities consider the editing, printing, circulation, or even possession of unlicensed publications as a crime subject to capital punishment. The severity of the punishment testifies to the indomitable courage and self-sacrifice of the underground fighters, and to the efficiency of their organization. It is hard for any one outside to imagine the difficulties in obtaining a printing press in occupied Poland, of bringing it to a safe place, of procuring paper, printing ink, and other materials. But that is only the beginning. The underground publications must be distributed. Thousands of people meet regularly under the very eyes of the Gestapo, to insure the regular circulation of the papers. The least disturbance, the least slip in the execution of the arrangements would cause the entire system to collapse. But the underground movement could not achieve the regular printing and distribution of illegal publications without the active support and sympathy of the general masses. The masses are behind the movement.

Many of the unlicensed periodicals in Poland are mimeographed, but most are printed. Despite the tremendous difficulties the printing is remarkably good. Even photographs often appear in them. One weekly was able to print a photograph of Mr. Churchill visiting a Polish military camp "somewhere in Scotland" in the company of the Polish Premier, General Sikorski.

Most of the publications are small, for convenience in transportation and handling.

One can judge the importance and effectiveness of the underground papers only by realizing that they are read with an emotional attitude which is lacking for any freely published newspaper; also that every copy of an unlicensed paper is much more widely circulated and read than that of a freely published paper, so that a publication of but a few thousand copies actually has a far wider influence than an ordinary paper with a larger circulation.

The role of the underground press in molding public opinion and disseminating new ideas cannot be underestimated. Every shade of public opinion finds expression in it, although the liberal and progressive papers are the strongest. They stand for democracy both in Poland and in international relations. The European problem is frequently and thoroughly discussed. Political democracy and social justice are advocated as the basis of the future organization of Europe. That the democratic and progressive publications today constitute a decisive majority of the clandestine press indicates that Poland has undergone profound ideological changes in the course of the war.

Polish political life is thus developing in a progressive direction. There is no trace of romantic conspiracy in Poland today. The Polish leaders insist the movement and its press are politically mature, developing and expanding under the very heel of Nazi terror, growing stronger despite oppression, and resolutely determined to destroy it.

The people make tremendous sacrifices to keep their underground press alive. Here is a brief testimony. The man who made it was obviously too modest to relate it in the first person. He invented an imaginary "friend" as the hero of his short story. The Polish authorities vouch for its contents, however, as well as for the narrator.

At the factory [the witness begins] my friend goes into his shop, and puts on his overalls. In his pocket something rustles. He smiles to himself. They have done it again. For the moment he feels quite happy. His comrades, actively engaged in spreading secret communications, have already got a new leaflet through to him. He will read it tonight. And he must not forget, before leaving the workshop, to leave in his drawer his contribution to the publishing fund. This money will be secretly collected by some unknown person and handed to an equally unknown treasurer.

The money is urgently needed. The Germans have requisitioned all stocks of paper. They have even stripped the stationers' shops of nearly all their books and sent them to the paper mills for repulping. That is where the Germans get the paper for their noisome publications. So the "underground" workers have to send a long way for their supplies. The cost runs into large sums. Then the presses must be moved from place to place constantly.

Recently the Germans discovered one such place in Warsaw. When they knocked and received no reply, they threw in hand grenades and machine-gunned the house. Two comrades were killed, and a woman was wounded and died later. But there was a fight, and the Germans didn't have it all their own way.

Since all other methods have failed, the Germans now attempt to spread confusion among the population by means of pseudo-underground papers. They produce these false publications and distribute them widely through Gestapo agents, especially among peasants on market days. The crowd is then immediately surrounded by police and hundreds of people are arrested as a warning not to accept any illegal material. Often these pseudo-underground publications are planted in homes, leaflets pushed through windows and under doors, and Gestapo raids follow.

In Lublin a Gestapo agent, formerly well known as a Communist leader, printed and distributed news from the British Broadcasting Company and delivered to the Gestapo the names of the recipients of the bulletins. Three hundred people were arrested; many were shot, among them a seventeen-year-old girl. Their deaths were quickly avenged. Soon afterwards the agent was found dead with four bullets in his body.

The most important underground paper is *Free Poland*, printed and published in Warsaw. So far, the Gestapo of the Polish capital has been unsuccessful in suppressing it. The Warsaw sheet prints cartoons, and one of its latest was suggested by the German confiscation of all toy soldiers and toy guns. The cartoonist shows a gloating German officer watching the edict being put into effect.

Headlines on the upper half of the cartoon run: "Stop Press. Great Victory for the German Forces. 10,000,000 dead, 10,000,000 prisoners. Germany is invincible."

The artist completes the satire by inserting below his drawing a reference to the Nazi edict: "All wooden or cardboard figures of soldiers, toy weapons such as guns, armored cars, planes and toy fortresses, and also reproductions of same without regard to the uniform they are wearing, must immediately be handed over."

The Polish underground press is undaunted. Even the establishment of a new concentration camp near Radzymin exclusively for those who are suspected of distributing papers or leaflets ridiculing the Germans for their defeat in Russia —lately a common offense—failed to deter them. The Jewish underground press is just as courageous as the rest of the secret papers. Recently a propaganda drive was started in the Warsaw ghetto with the purpose of persuading the Jews to go to the country as farm workers. The underground paper of the General Jewish Labor Union opposed this drive violently.

A clandestine calendar, printed in very small type on pages one and one-half by one and one-quarter inches, is in every house. It contains apt quotations for every month of the year, quotations that stir the blood of patriotic Poles and keep up their courage. Here is one: "To be a Pole means freedom. To be a traitor, a renegade, a coward is worse than Prussian slavery. Learn to be free in bondage." And another: "Have you sown your fields? When you think of the harvest, think also of what you owe Poland—not remnants, nor shreds, nor alms, but everything you have: your possessions, your children, your blood."

There is one paper that thrives on and flourishes in this war: *Deutsche Soldatenzeitung*. Its circulation is millions, it is published "somewhere on the Eastern Front," and its editor-in-chief signs himself Adolf Hitler. Every morning this paper is thrown in heavy bundles all over the German fighting lines. It is avidly read, and frequently cheered, by the soldiers. In its comic section it claims astronomic successes for the German army, ten million Russian prisoners and so on; strangely, its editorials predict imminent revolution and the collapse of the Third Reich. Adolf Hitler, it must be explained, is only the pen name of the editor, an exiled German writer, at present in the service of the Soviet propaganda. Millions of copies actually are dropped on the German lines, daily. The newsboys pilot Red bombers and fighters.

The nightmarish picture the European press today presents is rounded off by a small group of newspapers which one can read from cover to cover without finding a single word about the war. The Gestapo, exercising strict control over these publications, feels too tender toward the readers of this group to let them be excited by reports of war. The Jewish papers in the countries in the New Order must deal only with affairs of their own organizations and charities. There are five of them. *Information Juive*, issued biweekly in Paris since April 19, 1941; *Yoodsche Wachter* (Jewish Guardian) in Holland; *Gazeta Zydowska* (Jewish Gazette), appearing thrice weekly in the ghetto of Warsaw; *Zidowske Listy* (Jewish News) in Prague, which Gestapo boss Heydrich pretends to read regularly, because he gets a good laugh out of it, and, finally, *Vestnik Ustredni Zidow* (Jewish Weekly), whose modest building stood in Bratislava until December, 1941, when it was blown up by the Hlinka guards.

SLAVE MARKET

At this moment Berlin is the principal slave-market of all the world.—President Roosevelt to the delegates of the International Labor Office, November 6, 1941.

America's entry into the war meant something more than a new lease on life for the suppressed peoples. To all of them this turning point in history conveyed the assurance of rebirth. By the scores of millions, people became aware that their life-and-death struggle, this pitiful yet titanic underground war, must now end in the triumph of liberation.

But the underground road to victory is paved with sacrifices, as are all the approaches to freedom on land, on the seas and in the air. The subjugated peoples, too, have had to suffer their Pearl Harbor. At the same moment he declared war against the United States, Hitler loosed a ferocious attack on labor all over Europe.

It has now become his supreme necessity to outbuild and outproduce the arsenal that is America. We know that his hope of achieving this aim is delusive. But Hitler does not know it. Dr. Funk, his economic sub-dictator, recently bragged that Germany and Japan together command an industrial man-power of sixty million, 20 per cent more than America. Moreover, he added, American labor works an average of 2,000 hours a year, whereas German and Japanese labor is toiling ten hours a day, seven days a week, which adds up to 3,650 hours. Characteristically, Dr. Funk entirely omitted Italy's contribution to the Axis labor total. However, he stressed the necessity of stepping up the "follower nations'" productive capacity. "The swastika rules over another two hundred million Europeans," he declared in his Breslau speech, "most of whom are fit for manual work, women and men, professors, priests and unskilled farm hands alike. Many can be put to work in their own countries. But for a greater number, the doors of Germany are still wide open."

The gates of Germany have, indeed, long stood wide open to European serf labor. The latest German official statistics on the employment of foreign slaves in the German market are obsolete, since the numbers given have been surpassed by the new drain of forced labor into the Reich, the results of which are still guesswork. Nevertheless, one figure remained stationary. Despite Hitler's repeated promises to Pétain, one million five hundred thousand French prisoners of war are still slaving in Germany. So are approximately five hundred thousand Polish prisoners, most of whom are in the fields, and an unknown number of Russian captives, whose usefulness, however, is limited, since not even the methods of persuasion current in Nazi camps can break Ivan's passive resistance.

The Nazi labor boss Robert Ley contemptuously calls the Russians "the unskilled barbarians." But the complex problem of skill is one neither he nor his comrades care to discuss. They hate to admit that the American worker can work fewer days and shorter hours than the German, to say nothing of the unwilling serfs of Nazism, and yet produce more. It is a competition between the highest paid, most independent body of labor in the world and a proletariat, despised and abused by its own masters, that has been overworked and underfed for nine years. Moreover, a certain percentage of German labor is anti-Nazi, and has little interest in stepping up production. Perhaps still more important is America's mechanical superiority. American labor is backed by a much larger amount of machine power than serves even the streamlined German armament production. This factor alone assures the victory of the United Nations in the battle of productive man power.

Hitler's only hope of tipping the scales is in the forced labor of subjugated Europe. If he can obtain this Nazism can indeed outproduce its opponents for a time. To prevent such a development is our own vital concern. To prevent it, is vital also to a free Europe. Here, in the labor problem, above all, the shooting war and the European underground war are one. It would be fallacious to minimize the danger. Already before America's entry into the war, the foreign civilian workers in Germany numbered one million Poles, close to a million Czechs, a quarter of a million Jews, and a trickle of French, Belgians, Dutch, and Norwegians. The six hundred thousand Italians are in a different category. They like to work in Germany, it appears, where conditions, poor as they may be, are better than those in their own famine-stricken country.

The workers from the subjugated countries, on the other hand, prefer starvation at home to labor at starvation wages in Germany. The overwhelming majority had to be forced across the border—many after losing the dole in their own country. Their treatment in Germany is not much better than that accorded to prisoners of war.

The manual of the Deutsche Arbeitsfront (the state-controlled German "unions") has this to say about the comrades from abroad:

Foreign labor will offer no undue competition to German workmen. The slave workers will be mostly employed in northern and northwestern Germany. They are forced to work during air raids. Cripples are drafted into munition factories and assigned to such jobs as they can manage despite their physical handicaps. The ages of the men range from fourteen years up. The slave workers are under constant supervision exercised by our comrades from the Labor Front.

The serfs are recruited by German labor agencies in Nazi-dominated or pro-Nazi countries. Hence it is made to appear that every one has come to Germany of his own volition. There are many thousands of cases, however, in which this fiction is being brushed aside. This goes primarily for the Jews. Whether they came "voluntarily" or under compulsion, foreign workers of either sex are trapped the very moment they arrive in Germany. Their contracts run mostly for a year, but contain a clause according to which they can be renewed by the management for the duration of the war. Very rarely, well authenticated illness, incapacity through an accident at work, or manifest unfitness bring about a worker's return to his own country. Women workers used to be released in case of pregnancy; but this is no longer allowed. The most widespread illness is genuine or feigned homesickness which affects the working capacity. A worker who shows signs of this particular disease is subject to severe punishment and is sure never to be released; yet homesickness as a physical affliction is rampant in the foreign labor camps in Germany. The workers affected will go to any lengths, and endure any hardships, to get out of their contracts. Attempts to escape are the rule rather than the exception. But the Nazi camp guards have methods to prove that this is "the wrong way home."

Except for those herded together in armament plants, the labor serfs are mostly distributed in groups of twenty, guarded by brown-shirts. They work a thirteen-hour day from six A.M. to eight P.M., with one hour off for lunch. Their food is strictly rationed. They get half a pound of bread a day, meat twice a week, and some potatoes, margarine and marmalade in varying but always insufficient quantities. The men and women work in pitiable rags. They are forced to wear identification badges; those of the Poles are red, those of the Jews yellow.

Men and women get the same wage for the same class of work. Depending upon the type of labor, the wages may be up to ninety pfennig an hour, nominally equivalent of twenty-two cents. In actual purchasing power it is a fraction of this amount. To check and step up the individual performance the Bedaux unit system is used, including premiums. Few workers, however, care for these premiums, since they cannot obtain anything for their money. The only possible way is in purchasing through the Nazi commissar, who much more often than not embezzles the small funds he is entrusted with. Theoretically, the serf worker can send to his family overtime wages beyond his thirteen prescribed hours; but he is never certain whether the remittance will actually be transferred. Moreover, the arbitrary exchange rate in the subjugated countries, largely overvaluing the reichsmark, almost nullifies the pittance a man in a German labor camp can send home, since prices in francs, kroner, and zloty have risen three and four fold since the German occupation.

The "aristocrats" among the slaves are those working in armament plants. They are the "trusted" among the outcasts. But the faith their German masters place in them is best illustrated by the large numbers of uniformed *Werkpolizei* (factory police) with which all German armament plants teem— particularly those having many foreign workers among the personnel. Mostly these factories are spread out, covering areas up to fifty miles, and are located far from the big cities. In the more modern factories the buildings are set some distance apart, isolated by high, grass-covered banks of earth, so that an explosion or an outbreak of fire in one workshop cannot damage the next one. The bomb shelters are deep underground, but most of the machine shops are on the surface of the earth. Thousands of men and women stand beside seemingly endless rows of lathes. Yet each appears to be strictly isolated. All are under constant guard. The specter of sabotage is ever present.

According to reliable reports foreign serf workers in Germany are not prone to acts of sabotage. They are too deeply intimidated. Dr. Ley complained in a speech to the Krupp workers, delivered on November 22, 1941, that the Poles, although "minus-men" and really not human beings, are more reliable than some German racial comrades who are "getting ideas in their heads." It was, however, probably not dissatisfied racial comrades but the foreign workers forming the great majority of the shifts who caused three explosions on two consecutive days—December 1 and 2, 1941—in the *Gute Hoffnung Hütte,* one of Germany's foremost pits, interrupting regular production for a fortnight.

It is also reported that foreign workers are restive over the dispatch of large groups to the Eastern Front, where they are employed in clearing Soviet mine fields. Ironically the German central labor exchange in France was moved on September 25, 1941, to the Quai d'Orsay, world-famous as the address of the French Foreign Office. Richelieu's desk is occupied by a brute named Kaffer who enjoys forbidding any French plant to function whose skilled labor he covets for jobs in Germany. His heyday was the two weeks in mid-December, 1941, during which all French plants had to close down, officially for lack of coal. Only the French aircraft industry, producing German models such as Messerschmitt, Focke-Wulf, Junkers, and Dornier, was exempted from the general shutdown. They are reported to have a total of slightly over two thousand German machines on order, the completion of which was not to be retarded. Actually, the Nazis are about to replace the completely broken-down Italian aircraft production with the French productive capacity, which made such a miserable show as long as France was independent but is now stepping on the gas under the German lash.

Outside the aircraft industry, however, the drain of French labor to Germany overrides all other considerations. After the enforced work stoppage last December, Herr Kaffer stated jubilantly over Radio-Paris: "The hundred thousandth French laborer has just left Paris to work in Germany. His departure was made an occasion for a ceremony with patriotic speeches describing the great possibilities awaiting French workers in Germany."

The French workers can gauge these great possibilities from the sad lot of the French prisoners of war in the Reich. Few families in France are without a close relative among these. That, perhaps, is the main reason why French labor maintains such an uncompromisingly hostile attitude toward the Germans. The fallibility of some of their fellow-Frenchmen notwithstanding, labor in France is unanimously anticollaborationist, despising Vichy, and ferociously hating Nazism.

The struggle of labor developed into the national fight for liberation. Resistance is mounting among the workers, and they are indifferent to threats and coddling alike. They persistently refuse to take part in official ceremonies. The Socialist party is gradually regaining ground. It continued its party work uninterrupted even in the bleakest days. Its stronghold is the "forbidden zone"—the mining district in northern France where the German military terror is worst. Few reports trickle out of this zone. It is impossible to guess how strongly the production, all of which goes to Germany to satisfy vital needs of armament production, is affected by passive resistance and sabotage; but it is not likely that the German exploitation goes unopposed by the sturdy French miners. During the last war production in the coal region—which then too was occupied by Germany—dropped to 8 per cent of the peacetime output.

Another stronghold of labor resistance is Paris and its belt of suburbs. Little hampered by the Gestapo, the Socialists hold their secret meetings almost daily. They decide on, and carry out, propaganda campaigns, such as the marking of all the houses in Paris with anti-Nazi slogans. Politically, they are working closely with other groups—Catholics, De Gaullists, republicans, and democrats. Only two camps are excluded from the renascent French unity: collaborators and Communists.

Among the various political parties only the Communists have been able to keep their propaganda mechanism going without heavy interference since the occupation. At any rate they started immediately to disseminate literature, and soon *L'Humanité* appeared in mimeographed form.

The first change of attitude became apparent in September, 1940. At that time Communist secret literature revealed a new tendency: a supreme indifference toward the fight between the two "imperialisms"—the English and the German.

The impossibility of maintaining this stand was realized in international Communist circles, influenced by French members of the party. However, since relations and contacts with Moscow had slowed down, it was not until December or January that a new change of direction became evident: to fight against Germany's despotism, but not to have any truck with England. And, naturally, an anti-Gaullist position at the same time.

This stand was held for quite a while, and widened the rift between the Communists and other opposition forces.

Finally, at the beginning of June, a new transformation took place: the Communist party reaffirmed that there was no choice between British and German imperialism. It decried the Gaullist illusion.

But at the same time it proposed the formation of a national front against Germany, with the Communist party as its central point. It claimed for itself leadership in the struggle against Germany. Simultaneously, and in the same leaflets, its leaders advanced another proposition. This was that they were ready to support any government inclined to join the fight to drive out the Germans.

The outbreak of war between Germany and the Soviet took the Communist party by surprise and left it in a very awkward dilemma. There was no new attitude available. Near the middle of June, while the Soviet Union was at death grips with Germany, the Communists were still sowing leaflets around proclaiming that British imperialism and German imperialism were brothers under the skin.

Paradoxically, the only support Communism finds in France comes from the German hangmen. In labeling most of the hostages they shoot and most of the activists attacking German officers and their collaborationist creatures "bolshevists," the Nazis do their best to foster a revival of Communist sympathies among the French people. It is, however, limited. The French workers have had their fill of Stalin. Unanimously they admire the Russian feats of arms. But for themselves they almost unanimously prefer the tricolor to the Soviet star.

At the end of August, 1941, one million Belgian wage earners (in a total population of eight million) were out of work. "It is quite natural that we are taking advantage of this vast unemployment to drain off Belgian man power to Germany," the *Brüsseler Zeitung*, official organ of the army of occupation, admitted. The Nazi paper omitted the simple fact that the mass unemployment in Belgium had been artificially created by the power of occupation in order to force the shift of labor to the Reich.

By now, the number of Belgian workmen transferred to Germany has passed the two hundred and fifty thousand mark. An additional twenty thousand Flemish workers were moved into the forbidden zone of France, where they participate in the construction of new coastal defenses. The Flemish are regarded as the least anti-Nazi among the conquered peoples. Consequently they were selected for a job which could be entrusted only to reliable workers. It seems, however, that the German authorities miscalculated. The work of the Flemings failed to reach the prescribed standards; soon their efforts slackened, and flare-ups occurred frequently. Finally the five thousand Flemings who were at work on the port of Brest in Brittany had to be returned. They were not sent home, but dispatched to Poland, where, according to reports reaching London, a new Siegfried line is under construction at a distance considered far enough from Moscow.

The fate of most of the Belgian workers in Germany or in other occupied countries is largely unknown. No contact with their families is allowed. The people at home only see, month after month, further contingents of twenty-five to thirty-five thousand workers disappear over the German border.

Only a few come back. Recently, five thousand workers escaped from Germany and reentered their country. The stories they told were appalling. They had been employed in every sort of craft, but only in sections subject to constant R.A.F. raids. For the Belgians who were fed up with slavery in the Reich these raids proved a blessing in disguise. The Germans, apparently, could not take it. They lost their heads as soon as the raiders appeared, and engaged in a mad scramble for the shelters. "To the accompaniment of British bombs," a returned Belgian said, "it was not difficult to walk out on the Germans."

There are two methods by which Nazism has pressed one and one-half million Poles (a conservative estimate) into labor gangs in Germany: tormenting prisoners of war until they volunteer for labor service to escape the hell of their camps; and man hunts in the Polish towns and rural districts.

Since the Hague Convention to which Germany pretends to adhere forbids the enforcement of work on prisoners of war, Nazism had to cajole the Poles into themselves offering their services. The tender wooing began with a radical worsening of conditions in the prison camps.

A few thousand Poles were sent to Norway to repair damage caused in Oslo and Bergen by R.A.F. raids. Approximately a hundred thousand are helping construct the eastern Siegfried line. But most Polish prisoners of war are put to work in German fields and mills. They are treated like cattle. Their employers pay the German authorities for their transportation, their board in the labor camp, and a hundred reichsmarks insurance for every man. After the promise of high wages the men get, if they are lucky, twenty-five reichsmarks a month; but frequently even this small sum is retained as compensation for their food. Polish serfs may have no social intercourse with the German population. They are even prevented from going to church. Their working hours are at the pleasure of the boss or the overseers. Talking on the job is *verboten*. Sundays and holidays are abolished. Physical punishment is frequent. The men have only one hope—the hope that the insufficient food, the lack of clothing, and the general hardships will make them so gravely ill that they may be returned as invalids to Poland.

On April 10, 1941, a poster appeared on the official buildings in Warsaw, signed by the Governor General, Dr. Frank:

Since Poland cannot satisfy the needs of her own economy, Germany must subsidize and feed her. Germany cannot do this for nothing. Hence the Reich has the right to impose enforced labor on Poles who will be sent to Germany. If Poles seek to dodge this obligation, they will be taken by force, and deported. Those working in Poland for the benefit of the German army or industry are exempt. All other Poles of both sexes above sixteen years of age are included in this labor draft.

Immediately S.S. squads and police detachments swept over the country. The man hunt was on in towns and villages, in trains and on roads, in fields and forests where many "draftees" were hiding. Every town and district had to yield a quota. But even when this quota had been filled the hunt continued. In towns it was mostly conducted during the rush hours. Armed squads combed the streets. Although the Governor General's decree conscripted only those over sixteen, boys and girls of fourteen years were taken. All were pushed into trucks and driven immediately to the railway stations. Frequently coffeehouses were raided, churchgoers were picked up, trains were stopped and searched; and the homes were no safer from the Gestapo.

At the close of 1941, Dr. Hans Frank could proudly state: "One million of Poland's best skilled workers have found new homes in Germany. Now let us get the next million!"

The lives of Polish workers are held cheaply, and many of the leaders have been executed. The *Reichsarbeitsblatt*, the German official labor journal, published a decree to the effect that the bodies of foreign workers who die in Germany may be shipped back to their countries of origin—except those of Polish laborers.

Polish labor, however, does not take this treatment lying down. Its hatred against the Nazi system is elemental. The methods of combating it are coolly calculated. In all the Polish factories producing for Germany the "Go slow!" slogan is accepted. The dangers involved do not discourage the Poles. A German decree provides heavy penalties, not only for bad workmanship but also for "failure on the part of the worker to show good will." Yet all day and every day the workers court the risk. It is not their intention to deliver good workmanship. They make as fine a show of work as they can. But all the time they are wasting precious minutes: adjusting machine parts which need no adjustment, overscrupulously examining materials, repeating, as though unconsciously, the same operation, dropping their tools and retrieving them slowly, and generally delaying the work effectively, yet unostentatiously. Thus the German effort at intensification fails. The workers have become skilful in this form of sabotage, and even the German supervisors can find no tangible proof of it.

From time to time the Germans become infuriated and choose at random a number of workers whom they send to concentration camps, or even execute. But no such action has the slightest effect. Every worker does his bit and does it with thoroughness and gusto.

Not least active in sabotage are a number of workers who have been brought to Warsaw from Gdynia. These highly experienced dock workers must do unskilled work in the capital for a miserably low wage. Ill as they can afford it, the other workers have assisted the families of these men with small contributions to save them from starvation.

The war on the Eastern Front provided a great opportunity for the unknown soldiers of the Polish underground struggle. Today they are engaged in unceasing sabotage behind the German lines.

Transport and communication, which are of vital importance, have become a constant target of sabotage. The International Transport Federation has issued an appeal to all transport workers in German-occupied countries to sabotage transportation—an appeal broadcast in every European language through the B.B.C.

In addition to innumerable acts of sabotage, the Polish working people staged hunger demonstrations and strikes. In Krosno, an important industrial center, the inhabitants, driven into despair by the shortage of food, demonstrated in front of the house of the German garrison commander. Troops opened fire. Seventeen people were killed, and forty-seven wounded.

In December, 1941, the turmoil in Poland caused Heinrich Himmler to make an unannounced visit to Warsaw. He reviewed the situation and showed his men how to tackle it.

Had most of the "accidents" occurred on the railways? Well, Himmler had the first four railroad porters he met in the station of Warsaw arrested and shot "for being obnoxious to German travelers." The same day he signed sixty death warrants, choosing the victims indiscriminately from the lists of the politically suspect, on which all the well known names in Poland figure. Where Himmler spent his week end, the Polish underground movement could not discover, although few incidents in the lives of the German masters they are constantly shadowing escape them. Presumably, Himmler had done some hard thinking. On Monday morning, returning to the Hotel Europejski in Warsaw, he produced a plan, blue print of the location, manual of regulations and all, for the establishment of a new concentration camp near Jaslo to be reserved for saboteurs. "The climate in Oświęcim is too mild," he explained. "But Jaslo will not be a hellish den, either," he continued. "It will do if we shoot ten inmates a day." Assiduously those about him nodded. But their servile assent did not do them much good. Before leaving Warsaw, Himmler purged his own Gestapo in Poland. About half the functionaries were replaced for their proven incompetence.

The Gestapo chief rode home to Germany in the governor general's private de luxe train. When Heinrich Himmler unfolded the timetable, he found, sandwiched into it, a copy of *Free Poland*, the underground paper. "Heinrich, dear Heinrich, do not exert your mind," the editorial began. "The vision of an independent Poland will sweep away the slavery and transform our country into the motherland of freedom."

The Protectorate of Bohemia-Moravia, with a population of about eight million, has nine thousand unemployed, all of them unemployable. The New Order has solved the crucial problem of enforced idleness. Incessantly, Nazi propaganda drives home this fact to all who listen. Until America's entry into the war, all the economic societies, groups, and institutes in the United States were flooded with pamphlets harping on the abolition of unemployment in the Protectorate; the signal success of Hitler's economic policy. Both conscious and unwitting American Nazi tools resorted to this supreme argument in explaining that, after all, one thing must be said for Nazism, deplorable as it might otherwise be. The thing to be said was, "Look at Czechia." Even the most ardent onlookers could not always pronounce the name.

Well, look at Czechia. The fact is clear. There are only nine thousand unemployed. The reason is simple: Half a million Czech workers have been drained off to Germany. "Drained off" is a very polite expression. The transfer of workers from the Protectorate to Germany began on April 1, 1939, two weeks after the country's occupation, and has not yet stopped. Three reasons make the Germans continue this transfer with increased ruthlessness: first, the fear of sabotage which is rendered more difficult if suspicious workers are removed from familiar and sympathetic soil to a factory where they are controlled by colleagues of a different nationality; second, the lack of industrial man power in Germany proper; third, the desire to Germanize Czech districts out of which native labor is expelled to be replaced by German newcomers.

Living conditions for Czech workers in Germany are meticulously regulated. The workers receive one loaf of bread each for two days; black coffee in the morning; white cheese in the forenoon; pea soup, sweet pudding (made of fruit otherwise uneatable) and some vegetables with a piece of meat for lunch. They have two meatless days every week. On two other days only one meal is served.

The average wage of a man working ten hours a day six days a week, is 21.60 reichsmarks (about $5.00) weekly, food and lodging paid. The worker is unable to exercise his legal right of sending his earnings to his family in the "Protectorate." In some districts, workers employed in cities receive

one and one-half reichsmarks daily; in the country they get
one reichsmark, nominally the equivalent of a quarter. Like
their Polish fellow serfs the Czech workers are barred from
any social intercourse with the German population.

In the meantime the persecution of Czech workers in their
own country continues. The heaviest blow was dealt to them
when the Protector dissolved all the twenty-six trade unions,
replacing them by a Nazified syndicate ironically called the
Czech National Center, which forms a part of the German
Labor Front. A German Nazi named Köstner was made commissioner. His first act was to issue a May Day message expressing adherence to the New Order and pledging Czech
labor to "untiring work for victory."

Czech labor responded. It is indeed working untiringly for
victory—for the victory of the United Nations to which it
proudly belongs, and for the complete destruction of Nazism
that has no more determined enemy in the world, inside or
outside the New Order. The weapon of Czech labor is sabotage. If this is a serious threat to the Nazi system in Poland,
it is Nazism's undoing in Czechoslovakia. Hitler selected the
Protectorate to become Germany's second armory, ranging
in importance next to the Rhineland-Ruhr district. Actually,
it not only proved impossible to step up the industrial production of Bohemia-Moravia to the sky-high ceiling Hitler
demanded, but, according to German admission, the production in 1941 fell by some 40 per cent. "The curse of sabotage," Göring called it in an unguarded moment.

Czech sabotage affects the German war effort so much the
more dangerously, because its prime targets are the armament
plants. The first large-scale inside job occurred in the Skoda
works—after the Krupp works in Essen, the largest armament
factory on the European continent. A vast caldron of molten
lead was suddenly overturned. An unfortunate accident? A
flaw in the crane apparatus? No, in the Skoda Works in Pilsen
there are no such flaws in the crane apparatus. And as to the

probability of an "unfortunate accident," the caldron overturned at the very moment when twenty-two members of
a German Army Commission were walking underneath it.
Fourteen people lost their lives on this occasion—no, fifteen,
because the crane worker, old Vaček, immediately after the
"accident" jumped down from a height of sixty feet and
smashed his head on the concrete floor.

Fourteen Germans were killed—officers of the General
Staff and the engineers who had come to take delivery of
air bombs. The rest suffered more or less serious burns. Of
course, the Pilsen Gestapo immediately started an investigation to find the culprits. It also goes without saying that they
found none. Of old Vaček, the only one whose guilt was
established, they only found the shattered body.

About a year ago the war on the "Third Front," as the
Czechs proudly call their underground battle, began in earnest. It is a heavy drain on the German military power.
Czechoslovakia alone engages three hundred thousand soldiers of occupation, one hundred and fifty thousand elite
guards and policemen, and fifty thousand Gestapo agents.
Yet this imposing array of German force and brutality is
fighting a losing battle. Returning from the Protectorate, a
neutral witness in the Swedish *Göteborgs Handels- och
Sjöfartstidning* observed that, despite the German terror and
firing squads, the production of war material in Czechoslovakia is steadily declining. In the Skoda Works, he continued,
the output in November was lower than in October, and this,
in turn, was already 35 per cent lower than the September
figures. Trains passing through the Protectorate, the Swedish
visitor concluded, must be closely guarded since they have
an uncanny tendency to collide.

The attack on German food supply is just as important as the
sabotage of armament plants. Moreover, *Der Neue Tag*, the
Nazi daily in Prague, complained that the milk production in
Bohemia and Moravia has fallen off. This is not the fault of the

cows, observes the editorial writer in the Nazi organ, because the German and Czech cows, according to his information, are racially the same. The striking difference in the quantities of milk delivered to the authorities from Czech districts, he says, is caused by sabotage and by the passive resistance of the Czech farmers. *Der Neue Tag* threatens, therefore, confiscation of all Czech farms.

Pandemonium is let loose in Czechoslovakia. In Prague, Brno, and other industrial centers, handbills are distributed secretly calling upon the Czech people to abstain from open fights against the Nazis but to continue sabotage. Czech farmers, butchers, grocers are being executed because they withheld food from Germans, thus reserving it for the Czechs. The secret Czech wireless station Nazdar announced that strikes had broken out on account of a shortage of food in Walter factories in Jinonice, Loděnice, Prague, Hradec Králové and in textile factories of Hradec Králové, Upice, and Polička. Members of workers' committees have been arrested, but the workers did not allow themselves to be intimidated by threats that their arrested comrades would be executed if they continued to strike. The Gestapo was powerless against this resistance.

The incredible happened: Reinhard Heydrich, the butcher of Prague, softened up. He invited representatives of Czech labor to a week-end party in the Hradschin. In the previous week he had exacted a death toll of two hundred and eighty victims. About 70 per cent of the sentences had been for so-called economic sabotage; for failure to surrender grain, for secretly slaughtering cattle and pigs; for selling meat without ration cards or grinding corn without permission. Before Heydrich's arrival such offenses had been punished by a fine of a few thousand crowns or a short prison term. The death sentence for what is considered everywhere as petty larceny was Heydrich's invention.

But when the Czech labor leaders—every one of whom,

Heydrich was well aware, was engaged up to the hilt in "crime against the state"—gathered in his palace, the butcher of Prague turned sentimental. With a sudden gesture of the arm, as if he wanted to invite all and sundry to shake hands with him, he said: "I was always a friend of labor. Why, my Führer, your Führer, our Führer, belonged himself to the working class. Let's call off the feud. Why be incorrigible? Why can't you see which side your bread is buttered on?"

"I haven't seen any butter since 1939," one of the guests grumbled.

"Always witty!" Heydrich replied amiably. "What is your name, my friend?"

"Soukup," the heckler obliged.

Soukup is a name as frequent in Czechoslovakia as Jones is in these parts. Next morning all the Soukups in Prague were rounded up by the Gestapo and every one was told: "The Protector wants to see you. It appears he has a little account to settle with you."

The heckler Soukup was the only one of the name to escape. He had fled the country as soon as he left the Hradschin. After weeks of wandering, he arrived in London. He did not even take time to shave. He rushed to the B.B.C., asked when the Czech hour was on, shouted, "Give me the air!" and indeed, thundered an hour later to his fellow Czechs: "There is no appeasement with the butcher of Prague. . . ."

Reinhard Heydrich is quite right. These Czech workers are incorrigible!

CHAPTER THIRTEEN

YOUTH

Giovinezza, giovinezza,
Primavera di bellezza.

Youth, O youth,
Springtime of beauty.
—*The Fascist anthem*

HITLER's decline, historians of the future may well decide, began with the "diaper revolution," as the American war correspondent Robert St. John termed the children's revolt that preceded Yugoslavia's breach with the Axis. Not since the medieval children's crusade have nine- and ten-year-old boys played such a dramatic role in world-shaking events. Indeed, the Serbian schoolboys shook their country out of the complacency that had engulfed it during its eight years of flirtation with Nazism.

Eighty per cent of the adult Yugoslavian population had loathed this flirtation. But they were cowed and mute. Bribed and corrupt governments were able to lure them into the Axis camp. The traitor Stojadinović signed the Pact of Berlin. It was the expression of total submission, embroidered with the usual frills that trim Hitler's bloodless victories. One of these frills was Prime Minister Stojadinović's order to decorate all the Yugoslavian schoolrooms with pictures of the Führer.

The people of Yugoslavia were stunned; they are stubborn, pigheaded people, fighters by tradition, and they did not see how they could comply with the new worship of the pagan deity. But the nine- and ten-year-old boys and girls saw no problem—only a challenge, requiring immediate action. They tore the pictures of the Führer in their classrooms to shreds. They chalked slogans deriding their spineless governments on the blackboards, and soon they smeared the walls of their schoolhouses with caricatures of Hitler and Stojadinović.

The Premier, no less a disciplinarian than his model Hitler, clamped down on the little revolutionaries, ordering all the schools in the kingdom to be closed. The boys and girls laughed mercilessly as only children can laugh, and refused to obey government orders. A sit-down strike broke out. The children barricaded themselves in their schoolhouses. In all seriousness, Stojadinović threatened to have the schools razed. Prince Regent Paul, however, prevailed on him not to do so. It was the only time that the English-educated Prince Regent, who lived in constant fear of, and hence subservience toward, Nazism, exercised his temporary royal prerogative.

The children's courage increased. They sallied out of their strongholds in the schools and distributed handwritten pamphlets, calling on the nation to resist Nazification, on the main thoroughfares of Belgrade, cleverly choosing the rush hour. Stojadinović met them with police. The children had no defense except muddy snowballs, but the policemen refused to use rubber hose and bayonets against babes—most of them having sons and daughters of their own among the little revolutionaries. Instead, they listened to the shrill chorus and gravely nodded their heads.

A few days afterward all Yugoslavia nodded. The children, after all, were merely repeating what they had heard at home.

The only difference was that they were uncorrupted and unfrightened, and dared to speak out openly. Incited by their offspring, the people of Yugoslavia took their stand. Some observers believe that a conspiracy in the officers' corps brought about the undoing of the traitor government. Others credit Colonel Donovan, at that time in Belgrade as President Roosevelt's personal representative, with persuading young King Peter to action. Whatever may have gone on behind the scenes—it was the school children who resisted in full daylight and swept the nation along with them. The Yugoslavs decided not to surrender.

They had to pay dearly for their foolhardiness. A German punitive expedition assailed the country and conquered it, if only for a short time. The Chetniks (guerrillas), it is well known, re-formed the lines of the crushed Yugoslavian army. They are still holding out. The punitive expedition to Yugoslavia upset Hitler's timetable, causing the loss of a few precious weeks which he badly needed for beginning the attack on Russia. He did not, as planned, capture Moscow in October; and then he was confronted by "General Winter." It was his first military setback on a large scale. The avalanche was set rolling—by the children of Belgrade with their snowballs.

In a way, this miniature revolt, unique in history and portentous in its consequences, vindicated Hitler's often expressed belief that youth, and youth alone, counts in remolding the world. On assuming power, he called those who were over thirty the "lost generation." Germans or not, this generation had to be crushed. It was "too sclerotic" (Alfred Rosenberg's word) to be adaptable. One could not expect more from it than compliance on the surface. The fact that Nazism has attracted the has-beens all over the world does not alter its principal aim, which has always been to capture youth.

Nazism's appeal to youth worked miracles in Germany.

Without it, neither the feats of the German army nor the total brutalization of the German nation would have been possible. Hitler was so much the more stunned when, time and again, the youth of oppressed Europe proved to be the biggest stumbling block in his bloodstained path. He found traitors, turncoats, and collaborators in almost every nation, in all walks of life, in every social class; but it is noticeable that they all have worn-out faces, stooped shoulders, trembling hands. The explanation is simple. Nazism aims at the destruction of organized society. Those who despair of finding a place in orderly society commensurate with their ambitions or vanities are Hitler's natural raw material. The Quisling is not only a political type, but also a psychobiological one. Abroad, the counterpart of the immature, twisted, frustrated German Nazi—a fellow calling himself "dynamic"—is the over-aged.

Unfortunately, France has the largest supply of Quislings: with hardly an exception, they are men with colorful, varying, and mostly dishonorable pasts. From the venerable octogenarian who uses the plural *majestatis*—"*We*, Henri Petain" —to repudiate his shameful bondage, down to the various leaders of collaborationist youth movements, former ministers, former deputies, former sport champions, the advocates of what passes as "national rejuvenation" are all bald, or gray at the temples.

The youth of France resists unanimously. The first open revolutionary flare-up in Paris resulted from a students' demonstration. To this day, the Latin Quarter is the most restive part of France. Since last summer, assaults on Nazi bigwigs and the reprisal shooting of students who have "insulted the German uniform" have been a daily—or rather a nightly— occurrence on the *rive gauche*. The Sorbonne was closed more than a year, "to give the young gentlemen time to cool their heads," in the words of Otto Abetz, Hitler's ambassador in Paris. Since the ancient university reopened, Gestapo agents have attended the lectures to prevent patriotic digressions. Thousands of French students have escaped from their enslaved country, every one risking his life to join De Gaulle's forces and imperiling his relatives with arrest in retaliation. Scores of others have shelved their books and abandoned their bistros (perhaps still more of a sacrifice) to roam the land and preach the creed of the tricolor to the plain people. Scarcely a plot, a conspiracy, or a case of sabotage is discovered but a "bolshevist intellectual" is involved—and the bolshevist intellectual, of course, is generally an undergraduate.

French labor youth has time and again refused to admit collaborationists into its ranks. Charles Spinasse, who had the absurd idea of creating a Youth Chapter in the Nazi-patterned Labor Syndicate, was howled down and driven out of meetings in practically every French industrial center. Anonymous speakers, however, who urge labor in factories working for the German army to go slow and who disappear after their two-minute speeches before the omnipresent Gestapo agents have time to recover from the shock, get an enthusiastic reception from their audiences, particularly from those composed of young men.

The French peasant youth are no more cooperative. They have inherited their elders' shrewd business sense, which makes most of the sturdy individualists who till the French soil purveyors for the innumerable black markets. Moreover, most of them listen to the voice of the village curé, and whatever the two collaborationist diplomats in cardinals' purple in Paris say, M. le Curé does not hide his belief that God feeds the sparrows, whereas it is for the soldiers of the army of occupation to look after their own dietetic needs.

Without exaggeration, it may be said that all French young people, except a few poorly paid anti-Semitic hooligans in Paris, despise the boches, who for their part are entirely powerless to turn the tide.

A new and different generation is growing up in Norway.
Children going through the ordeal of their country's desperate struggle for liberty can never become the easy-going, fun-
loving, somewhat detached Scandinavians their fathers and
mothers were. The first lesson the world teaches them is too
bitter for that. But the bitterness of a life in which eight-year-
old urchins must stand up against ruthless tyranny and lads
in their teens are already veteran guerrilla fighters does not
break them. It steels them.

Not one of the thousands of schoolboys, it is a safe assumption, will ever forget February 13, 1940, when they paraded
in their short trousers down Karl Johan Street, the main thoroughfare of Oslo, armed with nothing more deadly than their
rulers. This was the first large-scale demonstration in the capital against the Nazis and Quislings. If it had been difficult to
intimidate Norwegian men, it proved impossible to cow Norwegian minors. Ragnar Skancke, the Nazi-appointed commissioner of education, had decreed that all elementary and
high-school pupils must attend the opening of the Hitler
Youth exhibition. Dutifully, the pupils left their classrooms.
But instead of taking the tramcars to the exposition ground
they congregated spontaneously on the wide white street that
leads to the abandoned Royal Palace. Thousands and thousands of boys with glowing cheeks and high-pitched voices
sang the Royal anthem.

The police dispersed them with clubs and rubber truncheons, but not easily. An elderly woman stopped a small
boy with a scratched face to ask whether he had been in the
fight. "Of course," he answered proudly. "If you grown-ups
do not care for liberty, we youngsters must take matters into
our own hands."

In Czechoslovakia, as elsewhere, the destruction of all intellectual activity was Nazism's foremost aim. "We will smash

the brains out of the Czechs," stated Karl Hermann Frank, Nazi State Secretary in the Protectorate. The Nazi mouthpiece, *Der Neue Tag,* echoed him: "The Czech people have nothing to do but work and produce children. But these children had better not grow up. And let them not get any ideas into their heads about going to college." This is what happened to the Czech students soon after Nazism had taken over:

On October 28, 1939, the anniversary of national liberation, demonstrations took place in all the towns of the Protectorate; in Prague they were especially violent. The University students took a very active part in the processions which formed despite their prohibition by Baron Neurath. There were some dead and wounded. Nearly four thousand people were arrested by the Gestapo. Few of them left the cellars in the Petschek Palace unhurt. A fortnight afterwards the parents of Ján Opletal, a student of medicine who had been arrested on the turbulent October 28, were informed that their son had died. He had succumbed to blows received at the hands of the Gestapo. On Wednesday November 15, the funeral of Ján Opletal took place, the procession starting from the Pathological Institute. The Prague police had originally forbidden the ceremony, demanding that the body of the dead student should be taken to Moravia and privately interred. But the students, desirous of rendering the last honors to their comrade, applied to the Protectorate authorities for permission to hold the funeral. Herr Frank lifted the ban with the intention of provoking tragic incidents such as were in fact to occur.

The dignified funeral took place without disturbing incidents, attended by students in large numbers; but as they were leaving a car drove up, loaded with Germans who engaged in open provocation. The students overturned the car, and at this moment the police intervened with their truncheons. The crowd split into groups, several of which joined again and continued on their way. One group moved toward the Polytechnic College. Another went towards the Philosophical Faculty building, singing the Czechoslovak national anthems and shouting, "We want liberty," "Long live Beneš," and similar slogans. At this moment Herr Frank's chauffeur arrived and assumed the duty of restoring order, jumping out of his car and striking a number of students. These naturally retaliated. The students everywhere were provoked by the German police—but for this, all would have passed off calmly. The alarm was immediately given to the local police; strong cordons of police were thrown round the Václavské Náměstí and the Staroměstské Náměstí, and the students began to disperse. Special German formations continued the provocations throughout the city, and the discontent and excitement spread among the population. Nevertheless, public order was not seriously troubled; the demonstrations were localized, and the German authorities could still have maintained order and calm. But they were aiming at the very opposite.

Thursday night November 16, German military formations occupied all the main intersections and numerous buildings. In complete silence, toward three o'clock on Friday morning, all the University colleges, institutes, and students' hostels were surrounded, and machine guns were trained on them from the streets. At three-thirty sharp a rocket went off and the attack began. Without any explanation the armed Germans forced their way into the buildings, seizing and imprisoning the caretakers and janitors. It was worst in a number of colleges and foundations where the students lived in groups. The barbarians penetrated the dormitories and bedrooms with rifles ready, and took the students in their night apparel. The Svehla Foundation was surrounded at two A.M. by German troops and police, with a cannon, machine guns, and several tanks in position ready to fire. An hour later the troops forced an entry into the building. There were dozens killed; their bodies were removed by the German police on the following day, in sheets.

Everywhere there were scenes of horror it is impossible to describe. One after another, the students were dragged out. Some were shot on the spot—it seems, for attempting to escape.

The prisoners were then crowded into thirty-one municipal busses and taken to the air-force barracks at Ruzýn. In the course of the arrests in the foundations and the colleges and of the transport of the students to Ruzýn, personal belongings of both male and female students were stolen. On their arrival at Ruzýn the students were subjected to sadistic tortures. They were stripped, drenched with icy water, and made to lie on the ground the whole night in the ice-cold November weather. Others were compelled to run around the Ruzýn riding school, urged on by blows from whips and cudgels, until heart and lungs could stand no more. Others again, bound in groups of three, had the lobes of their ears torn, their eyes struck out by blows from whips—all under the amused gaze of German typists sitting there at their machines. When the students had suffered nameless tortures they were forced to cry out in chorus, "Wir danken Ihnen" (We thank you). Certain atrocities cannot be related as they were inspired by a sexual and sadistic pathological strain by which most of the Gestapo agents and German soldiers seem to be affected.

The Germans also brought to Ruzýn a number of girl students, taken especially from their hostel "Budeč" in the same nocturnal raid. Many of the girls were dragged to large open spaces surrounded by tanks and violated, some of them by several men in succession. The German soldiers burned the breasts of their victims with cigarette ends. Others were forced to drink the contents of spittoons filled with urine and fell down, sick with disgust. The male students were powerless spectators of these scenes. Those who cried out in fright or disgust or showed their horror in any way whatsoever were immediately subjected to new tortures; one of them was shot, another had his thighs pierced by a bayonet. The theological students of the Great Seminary of Prague and the scholars of the Catholic College of Archbishop Ernest of Pardubice were also victims of savage excesses.

Students in private lodgings in Prague were arrested at the same time as the others. The German agents, to whom Sudeten German students familiar with the city served as volunteer guides, entered peaceful homes, dragged the young people out of their beds, and took them off to Pankrác prison. Those who attempted to resist were shot. In several cases parents who tried to protect their sons were also shot.

Subsequently, State Secretary Frank ordered the closing, for a period of three years, of the Czech establishments of higher education. The three years are not yet over. To this day the process of strangling Czech education and torturing the would-be students continues. The hatred that has accumulated in the country is indescribable. For Czechoslovakia, above all, the words of an American observer apply: "The Germans will be those who call in an A.E.F. to Europe—to protect them from the wrath of their victims."

CHAPTER FOURTEEN

THE PREY AND THE PRIDE

THE underground struggle is above all a woman's war. The total destruction of family life carried out by the New Order affects women even more deeply than men. European women used to be more secluded than their American sisters. Only in rare cases was beauty an important asset in business. Very few women had spectacular careers. There was neither a Hollywood nor a Broadway to conquer. There were no powerful women's clubs. Women exercised little direct influence on public affairs; they had no equality of opportunity, no fair remuneration for work, no adequate opportunity for study. Of course the individual woman was no less important in Europe than elsewhere. This is a woman's world at least as much as a man's. But, differing from her American sister, the European woman exercised her power to a much greater degree by remote control. Her legitimate realm was the family, the home, the larder, and her privilege was to smile while she toiled.

Hitler has broken up every family in the subjugated countries, disrupted every home, looted every larder, and wiped the smile from the face of Europe. His hordes have enslaved, tortured, and killed millions of civilians, mostly men. Yet the women were, and are, to suffer much more severely. Scarcely one has escaped heartbreak. They have seen their fathers and sons, their husbands and sweethearts devoured by the octopus. They watched the sanctity of their homes, their personal world, being desecrated.

But woman's capacity for endurance is greater than man's. Her hatred, once kindled, burns more fiercely. Throughout history women formed the spearhead of every revolution. Once more they are the advance guard. There are no noncombatant women left in Europe.

Nazism's fifth columns, it is true, had many women in their ranks. There were important "ladies" among them, such as the Countess Hélène de Portes, the nefarious mistress of Paul Reynaud, the last Premier of independent France. She was a tool of the Gestapo, subsequently killed by her employers. And there was an eleven-year-old Luxembourg schoolgirl who, on the day of German invasion, denounced patriotic snipers who were shooting at the invaders from behind their windows; she received a bar of chocolate for every "information." These, and hundreds like them, were the uprooted, or the abused. They are merely bubbles in the boiling caldron that is European womanhood. The women of Europe stand in the front ranks of their countries' defenders. Devotedly, they fight for a cause which they often find difficult to express in words. Moreover, they are fighting for themselves. What abysmal insults and injuries the women of the subjugated nations suffer, can hardly be told.

The ferocious attack on Poland bore all the marks of rape, and its sexual accompaniments were not missing. The German soldiers were promised unlimited license to devastate the country, once it was conquered. Blood-crazed by their rapid victories, the German regiments, most of them carefully trained elite-troops, emerging from years of intensive Nazi-fication, hurled themselves on their prey. Few of the accounts of what happened to the Polish women are fit to print. They would sound unbelievable, had they not been carefully checked by the Polish government in exile.

The Nazis made their usual fine distinction between "isolated actions" and "general measures." The rape of a woman or girl, preferably in the presence of her parents or husband, passed as an isolated action. General measures were carried out in every Polish town. Lorries bearing the inscription "Only for Women and Girls" toured the streets. Female passers-by were picked up and carried away. The German marauders shanghaied women on the country roads, which were crammed with refugees. "We will transport you home," was their ominous approach. Thus carloads of women were brought to German barracks and houses of ill fame; many victims were shipped to Germany.

One of the most horrible cases on record occurred in the town of Chełm, on June 15, 1940. A great many refugees were returning from the then Soviet-occupied parts of Poland, in which living conditions had proved unbearable for the upper classes. The German garrison commander of Chełm, Major von Richteneck, had all the females rounded up. They were examined by German army doctors. The healthy ones had their palms marked with the letters C and L, indicating that they would be dispatched to German concentration and labor camps. In fact, they ended in German bawdyhouses.

Occupied Poland is probably the only country on earth where brothels are listed in the telephone directories. Under Nazi protection, they are mushrooming in Warsaw, Cracow, Lublin. These houses serve the purpose of depraving the Polish nation, as was explained in a previous chapter. Others are reserved for German officers and soldiers. Printed manuals, circulating in the German army, list their addresses. For the town of Krosinia, in Polish Carpathia, to give just one example, the entry reads: "Place: the former girls' lyceum. Number of roomers: 70. Admission: only by card of authorization, available at the garrison's command."

Almost all the thousands of girls in these houses were kidnaped on the streets; many are the daughters of highly respectable families. The nightmare of their lives and deaths is disclosed in a letter which a girl from Kutno, arrested one day in August, 1940, managed to smuggle out to her mother, a refugee in London, who committed suicide after reading the letter and passing it on to the Polish authorities:

Farewell, Mother. I shall never see you again. We are serving as mattresses for German soldiers. We are all contaminated and sick, which means that we are all doomed to execution. No night passes without a few of us being shot. I await this fate. I, too, am sick. I am already only walking with pain. Farewell.

The German military authorities do not trouble to deny such reports. They have publicly stated that the sending of young Polish women to houses of prostitution was a method of national repression, deliberately applied. Moreover, they pride themselves on their rigid sanitary regulations. A decree issued by the *Sicherheitsdirector* (director of public security) in the Government General orders that all contaminated prostitutes shall be put to death lest they endanger the health of the army of occupation. Orally, Sicherheitsdirector Fassen added, "They can always be replaced."

An official note from the Polish government to the Allied nations sums up the situation in the following words:

Polish women are subjected to particularly humiliating and barbarous treatment by German officers, soldiers and officials. The Polish Government is in possession of abundant proof that many cases of collective rape have occurred. The German police have repeatedly organized raids in various towns, for the purpose of abducting young women who have subsequently been placed in brothels frequented by German officers and soldiers. In numerous cases young women have been arrested on the streets or even in their homes, on the pretext that they were needed for agricultural work, and carried off into brothels for the soldiery in Germany. The German authorities themselves have admitted that the placing of young Polish women in the brothels constitutes a measure of repression that they are applying deliberately.

The Polish Government can only guess at the number of young women thus snatched away from their families to be thrown into German brothels and condemned to a life of dishonor and ignominy, but that it is very large is shown by the frequency with which advertisements of parents searching for their daughters who have suddenly vanished, appear in the papers.

In the course of numerous searches carried out in the homes of Polish citizens, German policemen have forced the women to undress, to dance naked, or to scrub, with the underwear torn from their bodies, the stairs or the floors.

The general German laws and regulations clamp down on women as mercilessly as on men. Perhaps they are applied to women with even more malice. It is the old Nazi system. In his own Germany, before the war, Hitler frequently commuted the death sentences of male criminals to life imprisonment, but never was a woman criminal under death sentence saved from the block. In Poland, the music of Chopin is forbidden, as well as that of Paderewski. No mention is permitted of the nation's great artists. In the last week of November, 1941, two individuals were caught trespassing against this order. A man was sentenced to thirty days' hard labor and a two-hundred-fifty-mark fine, when the Gestapo found an engraving of Chopin in his possession. Marie Malik was sentenced to three years' hard labor and the loss of her civic rights—whatever they may be worth in occupied Poland—for playing Paderewski's Minuet on her gramophone. The fact that she had left her window open was declared an aggravating circumstance. Actually, the aggravating circumstance was her sex.

Women are outlaws in Poland, and they behave accordingly. The newly established first Polish Division fighting with the Russian army has a female lieutenant. Her *nom de guerre* is Marusha; her actual name cannot be disclosed because her relatives are still in conquered Poland. Lieutenant Marusha won her promotion, literally, with her own hands. Mingling with the guerrillas behind the German front, she was arrested by two members of the German military police. She had a drink or two with her captors—who, it appears, felt lonesome on the far-away Russian-Polish border; and when both her Lotharios were dead drunk she stabbed them with their own bayonets, making sure, she later reported, that both were "really dead." Then Marusha crossed the Russian lines, to win instant promotion to a lieutenant's rank after her story had been checked by other guerrilla fighters.

There is, unfortunately, no longer any reason to withhold the identity of the twenty-four-year-old Genowefa Dolacka. She was sentenced for some minor offense—probably buying or selling on the black market—and transferred to the German prison of Danzig, where the more recalcitrant Polish prisoners are kept. Genowefa Dolacka organized a jail mutiny which cost the lives of several German wardens. Genowefa was hanged. So were, according to the Nazi *Ostdeutscher Beobachter*, two Polish women, with three men, on December 17, 1941, for insulting members of the German minority of Poznań in—September, 1939.

In Zamość, in central Poland, the haystacks, containing all the food supplies for Infantry Regiment 364, went up in flames. Of course, the guerrillas had done it. Most of them escaped. But their leader was trapped and publicly hanged— a girl of eighteen, Catherina Zbizbk.

One young Polish heroine the Germans never got. The girl was carrying a flag, embroidered with the likeness of the

Madonna of Ostra Brama in Wilno by the mother of a Polish flier in England, to Poland's Avenging Eagles, the Polish squadrons of the R.A.F. Speaking the German language perfectly, she succeeded in reaching Sweden, and from there, Norway. After many adventures she met some Norwegian sailors about to escape to England. They took her across the North Sea in a small fishing boat. Immediately the young girl went to a Polish airdrome somewhere in Scotland. Ceremoniously, the flag with the Madonna symbol was handed over to the Avenging Eagles. General Sikorski, Premier in the Polish government, embraced the heroic girl, and spoke the beautiful words: "Love calls for sacrifice, and sacrifice spells victory."

The treatment of women in Czechoslovakia is orderly, at least according to Reinhard Heydrich's notion of order. Only single girls over seventeen years are sent to Germany for forced labor—"and to provide a little amusement for German soldiers," the Protector added. In order to avoid this fate, Czech girls invariably marry on their seventeenth birthday. However, in Czechoslovakia even more than elsewhere marriage involves certain risks. If the Gestapo accuses a bride of having married in order to dodge labor service in the Reich, she has to bear the consequences of having committed an act of sabotage, and receives a prison term up to several years. The bride's parents also are imprisoned for aiding and abetting a crime against the state. There is, Heydrich decreed, no appeal against such sentences.

Such Czech women and girls as have actually been shipped to Germany are separated from friends from the same town or village, to be utterly alone when they are exposed to the customary ill treatment and insults. The stories of these indignities which have filtered back to Czechoslovakia are so repulsive that they cannot be retold. However, they have aroused the Czech clergy. Masses have been offered up for the Czech women in Germany. In a score of towns and villages, the religious services have been broken up, and the priests arrested.

Equaling those accounts are recent confidential reports about the way in which Norwegian women are treated by the Nazi "guests" of Norway. There was, for example, the widely publicized mass wedding of Norwegian girls to German soldiers which was held in Trondheim Cathedral with great pomp and ceremony in an effort to persuade other girls to do the same. But disillusionment came rapidly to these young brides when they were curtly ordered "home to the Reich" as German citizens. Those who protested quickly learned that a woman's place in the New Order is "to keep still and obey."

Of far more disgusting nature, however, are the tales—regrettably authentic, the Norwegian government adds—of Nazi brutality against women who venture out alone at night. The sheer barbarity of these actions can be understood simply from the fact that all Norwegian policemen have received strict orders "not to interfere" when they hear a woman calling for help in the dark streets. Norwegian women who have become pregnant after association with German soldiers may obtain free care and maintenance one month before and one month after the birth. To qualify, however, the expectant mother must agree to give the child to German authorities to be cared for permanently by them. She must also agree to move to Germany and enter employment there. The number of women to whom this "generous offer" might apply is not believed to be great.

Reports about the display of German chivalry like the following are not infrequent. On the evening of July 26, a dance was being held at the Bratholmen Youth Hostel in the neighborhood of Bergen. About two hundred young Norwegians were there, when in came four German soldiers who wanted to join in the gayety. But when not a single girl would dance with them they tried to force some of them to accompany them outside. At this the Norwegians promptly beat up the unwelcome intruders. Three were knocked unconscious, but the fourth escaped and reported the affair at military headquarters.

A detachment of German troops soon arrived at the youth hostel and arrested every one inside the building and a large number of persons who were camping near by. The two hundred prisoners were then marched under armed guard to a playing field several miles distant where they spent the night. On the following day sixty-seven persons were sent to the concentration camp at Ulven, among them a fourteen-year-old boy who had been asleep in a tent during the fracas at the youth hostel.

Norway's women are boiling with indignation. Their boycott of the Germans is general. There was but one important case of siding with the intruder. Olga Bjoner, the president of the Countrywomen's Association, became a Quisling. Immediately, signatures by the thousands were collected for an open letter, which rejected her further leadership.

It is a great shame you, the President of the Countrywomen's Association, have entered the service of the traitors' "government" against your fatherland [the letter explained], a government which claims to be working for Norway's freedom and independence, but which seeks to crush our people into the same Prussian mold which has transformed the country of Goethe into an Asiatic slave state. Our shipping trade is wound up, our electrical power carried away, our soil given over to German citizens as a traitors' reward, and our people imprisoned physically and mentally under German rule. Never before have Norwegians stood so united as today. By battle and hardship, in company with all other oppressed people, we will create a new Europe, with freedom and equality for all, great and small.

Such frank language against the creatures of Nazism was never before heard. All the signers of the open letter were well aware that they were exposing themselves to the concentration camp. Amazingly, nothing happened. General von Falkenhorst remained silent. Even the mighty commander of the army of occupation, it appears, is powerless against the women's revolution.

"You are worthy to go down in history with Edith Cavell," was the official English welcome Madame Yvonne Roberts received when she arrived in London on January 19, 1942.

The full story of this woman's heroism cannot be told until after the war. It would disclose many valuable secrets which the Gestapo in France has not been able to solve. But Yvonne Roberts shall have her little monument between these covers. Undoubtedly, she is the bravest and, perhaps, the greatest woman to emerge from this war.

Madame Roberts is a native of Brittany, the peninsula from whence came the stanchest patriots of France, the village curés who swing the cross like a sword, the devil-may-care fighters, and a good number of the leaders of the underground movement. Brittany is a land of fishermen and hunters. The fishermen search for lobsters, and the hunters, preferably, for wearers of German uniforms. For her part, Yvonne Roberts, today in her fifties, married to an Englishman, has also been involved in a lifelong running fight against the field gray. During the first three years of the First World War, she was engaged in helping men to cross the border of occupied Belgium and the invaded parts of France. Thus she saved hundreds of lives. But she was caught by the Germans in 1917 and sentenced to death. King Alfonso XIII of Spain interceded for her. (The King, it must not be forgotten, exercised a strong pro-ally influence on his own country throughout the first war, although he was surrounded by pro-Germans. He once told Winston Churchill: "Only two factors in Spain are for the British: the plain people, and myself.") To oblige him Berlin commuted the death sentence of Yvonne Roberts to imprisonment. She was released after the fall of Imperial Germany. Marshal Foch awarded her the Médaille Militaire, a highly prized French decoration which only seventeen women have received.

There are certainly not seventeen women alive who have returned from a rendezvous with death to start the same thing all over again. Yvonne Roberts is, perhaps, the only one to do it. At the outbreak of the second war she joined the Red Cross. In the summer of 1940, when France collapsed, she was in charge of one hundred fifty babies, whom she brought from Paris to safety in Bordeaux. The journey took eight days, during which the little group was under almost constant bombing or machine-gun attack from German planes. Yvonne Roberts did not care that she herself was wounded in the face by a bullet. But she did not understand, she said, why the Germans should kill refugee babies.

A woman of Brittany does not stop with asking questions. She acts. After the safe delivery of the babies, Yvonne Roberts returned to occupied France. She did not, however, go very far. She established her headquarters near the border between the occupied and the unoccupied zones, and engaged in her old trade. Hundreds of French soldiers and civilians whom she helped to escape and to join the Free French forces, owe their freedom, and in many cases their lives, to the courage and resourcefulness of this unique woman. Although very few of her intimate helpers and agents have ever seen her, all France speaks of "Notre Dame Bénigne" (Our Blessed Lady). A harassed, hounded, middle-aged woman, constantly on the run, every second faced with the thousandfold terror of the Gestapo, has become a legend, the symbol of merciful motherhood.

Her task is achieved. But the fight continues. Herr Heinrich Himmler can try to find out for himself whether Yvonne Roberts is engaged on a new assignment, on which, and where.

CHAPTER FIFTEEN

LIFE AND DEATH IN THE GHETTO

We know fully that the war can only end by the extermination of the Germanic people or by the disappearance of
Jewry. Aryan peoples will not be removed from Europe,
and this war will see the destruction of Judaism. For the first
time in history whole peoples will not be bled, but for the
first time the old Judaic law of an eye for an eye and a tooth
for a tooth will be applied. The day will come when the
world's worst enemy of all time will finish playing his part,
perhaps for a thousand years.—HITLER on January 30, 1942,
the ninth anniversary of his assumption of power.

IT IS a grave error, yet one frequently made by well-meaning
people, to regard the persecution and attempted extermination of the Jews by Hitler and his Nazis as an isolated problem. Two and a half years of this war have proved that the
Jews were not merely Hitler's bugbear, but the guinea pigs in
the New Order. A fate similar to theirs has already been
meted out to the Poles, the Slovenians, and other Slavonic
groups. It may befall any captive nation. There are but two
differences: one is the addition of still more malice, venom,
and savagery to the actual work of annihilation; the other lies
in the fact that anti-Semitism is an age-old, worn-out device
that still works with certain groups in parts of Eastern Europe at present incorporated under the New Order. But the
extent to which it works has been a grievous disappointment
to Hitler. Even the less progressive among the downtrodden

peoples realize that there is only a slight disparity between what is happening to them and what happened to their Jewish whipping boys of yore.

The stunned world is witnessing a Jewish tragedy that seems hopeless. But the outlook brightens if one considers that, now and forevermore, anti-Semitism and Nazism are inseparably linked together. The downfall of the latter evil will purge the world of the first. For the second time in their long history, the Jews are marching through the Red, the blood-red, Sea.

This is how Hitlerism and the New Order have affected the European Jews: At the beginning of 1933, there were in the area now under Axis domination about eight and one-half million Jews. Since that time, about six hundred thousand Jews have migrated. Another four hundred thousand are now homeless refugees, interned in concentration camps, building railways in deserts, waiting vainly in one port or another for a ship, rotting on floating prisons, in the heat of the Sahara—human flotsam.

The Jewish birth rate has dropped steadily during this period, while the death rate has risen to a point five to ten times the normal. The Jewish population has fallen further in the death of thousands in concentration camps at the hands of the Gestapo, and of many thousands more at their own hands in hopeless despair.

Health conditions are frightful. Those who work are virtual slaves; those who are forced to remain idle have no means of sustenance—and all are undernourished. The Jew is entitled to one-fourth the bread rations of the "master race" and to almost no other food. Housing conditions are appalling. Great masses of Jews who could not leave Europe have been driven from their homes, their towns, and their villages. This ruthless treatment has destroyed many historic Jewish communities, while others teem with impoverished deportees from "forbidden" towns. At least one-third of the Jews still in

Nazi-dominated Europe have already been torn from their homes, and those who remain have no security.

The Jews have been ousted from their occupations, robbed of their belongings, and reduced to beggary. Excluded from economic life, many of them find enforced idleness a greater tribulation than forced labor for the Nazi overlords.

The Jews have been eliminated and extirpated from the cultural life of the countries in which they live. At the same time, they are denied the spiritual refuge of their own religion and culture. Their schools, their literary and scientific institutions, have been closed down; their synagogues burned or destroyed; the ritual food laws of their religion, suppressed. The great centers of Jewish learning, religious and secular, are no more. Jewish students no longer attend the high schools and universities, and even elementary education is now denied to the majority. Jews may not enter concert halls, theaters, or cinemas. As outlaws and outcasts, they live under extreme psychological strain which must produce a state of constant moral depression.

A hotbed of anti-Semitism, running Nazi Germany itself a close second, is Rumania.

In 1939, the Jews of Rumania numbered about nine hundred thousand, almost 5 per cent of the total population. Their hour of doom struck on September 5, 1940, when Carol II made General Ion Antonescu Premier "with full power." In gratitude, the dictator ousted his King on the following day. Dissensions between the General and his accomplices in the Iron Guard were temporarily assuaged with Jewish blood. But in November, 1940, when Antonescu permitted—nay, invited—the infiltration of Rumania by German troops, the Iron Guard rose against him in open revolt. Of course, the victims of this anti-German revolt were again the Jews.

In all, it is estimated, ten thousand people throughout the country were killed during the revolt, a fourth of them Jews

—none of whom, it goes without saying, had been involved on either side in the fratricidal strife between the Fascist brothers.

With gusto the German soldiers of occupation watched the bloodshed. It was the first since the advent of Nazism in which they could enjoy themselves as kibitzers. Time was working for them. The more Rumania deteriorated, the more inevitably she became the prey of Nazism. On November 23, 1940, when the tide of revolt was rising against him, General Antonescu made his country officially a member of the Axis. A few days later the General invited Heinrich Himmler to Rumania, to direct expropriation measures against the Jews. Again the Jews had to serve as bait. Actually, Antonescu badly needed the backing of Berlin against ferociously anti-Semitic competition, the Iron Guard.

Himmler came, surveyed the situation, blue-printed a few stringent anti-Semitic measures, as he had been asked to do, and finally flashed the green light for the German soldiers of occupation. They went into action and routed the Iron Guard. Their leader, Hore Simia, fled to Germany, where he was killed. Another anti-Semitic leader, the history professor Jorga, was executed in his own apartment. "I hope the Jews will not get big ideas in their heads," said Himmler when his men had liquidated anti-Semites, for a change. "We shall have to discipline them," he added.

The Nürnberg laws were introduced in the then newest Axis country. The Jews were deprived of every means of making a living. The greater part of the four hundred and fifty thousand left in Rumania must now rely on funds from abroad and on the aid of relatives who still retain some of their fast dwindling assets. The outbreak of the Russo-German war brought new hardships. To stimulate a sentiment for war in the Rumanian population, a mass execution of five hundred "Jewish Communists" was staged in Jassy. When Bessarabia fell to Rumania, the first Rumanian ghetto was established in Kishinev. Another ghetto was built in Czernowitz, an ancient center of Jewish culture. The daily food ration of the ghetto inhabitants amounts to one-eighth of the hardly overabundant ration of the Rumanian soldier. "The Jews can give the other people an example of how to live on almost nothing," Himmler declared. Nowhere did the Jews prove to be more useful to Nazism than in Rumania. Their mere existence among a mostly hostile population was a trump card in Hitler's hand. Their persecution was the price of fierce Nazi-inspired rivalry. Their extinction furnished the pretext for Germany to take over the country. Their mass murder was an incentive to war propaganda. Finally, their suffering and slow death set a heroic example for others doomed to die as cannon fodder. Having considered all this, Heinrich Himmler grinned. "God save the Jews—above all from us," he uttered. It was the most surprising of his many salty statements. "If the Jews did not exist already, they would have to be invented."

Hungary is third in the race for the *grand prix* of anti-Semitism.

The first openly anti-Semitic government was formed by Dr. Béla Imrédy. A popular joke had it that Dr. Imrédy always stood up while eating, since he declined to sit down at table with a Jew. Indeed, it came out that the Jewish blood in his own veins far exceeded even what was permitted by the escape clauses of the Nürnberg laws. Imrédy was convicted of having a Jewish grandmother on one side of his family and a Jewish great-grandfather on the other. Amidst the uproarious laughter of all Budapest he resigned. But his time, he believes, is not yet up. At present he is busy courting Hitler, who, it is well known, has overlooked more than one congenital racial defect in his henchmen and lady friends. Imrédy hopes to stage a comeback.

Regulations very much like the Nürnberg laws had to be

introduced under heavy German pressure by Imrédy's successor, Count Teleki. He acted under duress, against the warning of the Catholic Church of Hungary, which is influential and dead set against racial discrimination. But neither the Church's protest nor the stanch opposition of the President of the Upper House, Count Gyula Karolyi, availed. Hitler threatened invasion if Hungary would not follow the Nürnberg example. Count Teleki yielded. He did not, however, yield a second time when Hitler, preparing his Balkan offensive, demanded the right to occupy Hungary. Hitler does not take No for an answer unless it is backed up by a few million bayonets, and Teleki certainly lacked these. The Premier of Hungary, a celebrated savant and professor of geography who had been well known in the United States, too, could find but one solution for his dilemma. He sent a bullet through his head, well aware of the fact that as a deeply believing Christian he was committing a deadly sin. But his helpless and heroic gesture made not the slightest impression. On his white charger, Admiral Horthy, the Regent, a former Royal Admiral, who had a few years previously broken his oath to his King, rode through the streets of Budapest to welcome Ribbentrop.

Budapest has always been a happy hunting ground for champagne agents. Herr von Ribbentrop feels very much at home there and comes as often as he can make it. On one visit, he persuaded the kingdom under a desk-admiral to join in the Russian crusade. The Hungarian contingent suffered cruel losses in Russia. This interlude brought the abused Hungarians to the brink of revolution. On another occasion Herr von Ribbentrop, with an amused twinkle in his fish-eyes, inquired what was happening to the dear Jews. One could, after all, not let them go "unpunished," since Hungary is in the Führer's immediate neighborhood.

In answer to Ribbentrop's question, three batches of anti-Jewish laws were introduced by the Hungarian Nazi lackeys, some more drastic even than the Nürnberg laws, heaping insult on injury.

Not even these regulations satisfied Berlin. But here Nazi-sponsored anti-Semitism suffered its first and, so far, only setback within the realm of the New Order. More liberal-minded members of Parliament strongly opposed further Nazi proposals. Cardinal Seredi, Primate of Hungary, engaged in a one-man campaign against the racial discrimination that swept the country. Moreover, the Upper House rejected extreme measures by an enormous majority.

For the time being Hitler needs his Hungarian cannon fodder. He lives in constant fear of the European revolution. Hence, he is, as Goebbels put it, ever open to arguments. The bill was dropped, and replaced by a law "to protect the Magyar race" by forbidding intermarriage. "Triumph!" Goebbels yelled in a broadcast hailing the victory in reverse. "That's exactly what we wanted from our Aryan Magyar neighbors." The Magyars, of course, are Turanians, descendants of the Mongols and about as Aryan as the Japanese.

Baron von Neurath, the last court marshal of the King of Württemberg and the first Protector of what is left of Czechoslovakia, was much too much of a gentleman of the old stamp to introduce anti-Semitism in the Protectorate. Instead he forced the puppet government to do the dirty work. Under his pressure the Hácha administration issued a decree as early as on July 4, 1939, excluding the Jews from the liberal professions. Not even the wretched Dr. Hácha wanted to go further in view of the general disgust that the persecution of Jews caused in his nation. So poor old Neurath had to strip off his kid gloves. Desiring to keep the "Aryanization" in German hands, the Reichsprotector proceeded to liquidate Jewish property along the lines of Nazi legislation of 1938 and 1939. Jews were thus completely eliminated from economic life; their entire wealth passed into the hands of the

Reich, and they lost their means of subsistence. Jews in the professions, with very few exceptions, were ousted. Jewish property in the Protectorate was estimated by the German authorities at three billion reichsmarks (about eight hundred million dollars). The Nazis grabbed it all.

Mass arrests, murder, execution, deportation to concentration camps, and every other outrage have been perpetrated against Jews in the Protectorate. They are expelled from their homes and forced to move to prescribed districts where they cannot obtain more than one room for an entire family. They must not appear on the streets between eight P.M. and six A.M.; nor are they permitted in the parks. Travel from one locality to another is prohibited, even to attend a funeral in the family. They receive food ration cards, but are allowed to make purchases only at certain hours; and tickets for clothing and shoes are denied to them. They are forbidden to bathe in the rivers or fish in the streams; they may not travel in the front section of streetcars, use taxis, or drive an automobile. All males between seventeen and fifty-five are ordered to register for forced labor. Acts contrary to the decrees of the German authorities and the Gestapo, as well as all alleged criminal offenses, are tried before German courts according to German regulations.

In order to dispose of the Jews as quickly as possible, Eichmann, the Nazi expert in Jewish affairs, himself helped organize illegal emigration to Palestine and other countries overseas. The torments that such emigrants suffered are known to the world. A notorious case was that of the steamship *St. Louis*, loaded with refugees for Cuba. The vessel could not find a port to admit its passengers and remained long at sea without food or water.

The Gestapo plan to transport the remaining Jews to the Polish Reservation at Lublin was carried out only in part, on October 12, 1939, and affected the eight thousand Jews of Moravská Ostrava and a few other cities in Moravia. Each person was permitted to take only a small overnight bag of personal belongings and a sum of money not exceeding three thousand crowns (eighty dollars). At the Moravská Ostrava station, deportees were robbed by the Gestapo of the little they had.

In the autumn of 1941, when Baron von Neurath was replaced as Reichsprotektor by Reinhard Heydrich, a wave of mass arrests began among leaders of the Czech government, the army, and the intelligentsia. Among the offenses with which they were charged was the nonfulfillment of anti-Jewish legislation and continued intercourse with Jews.

A decree issued on September 1, 1941, and effective September 15, ordered all Jews over the age of six in the Protectorate, as well as in Germany, to wear yellow armbands bearing the word "Jew" in black letters.

At the beginning of October, 1941, a drive was launched for the deportation of Jews from Prague to Polish ghettos and to the Nazi-occupied zone in Russia. The Jews marked for deportation were herded together in synagogues. Among them were elderly men, women, and children. Orders to leave were served at night by two Gestapo agents. In many cases the notice given was no more than two hours, or even ten minutes.

Tragic is the fate of Polish Jewry. They are the most deeply humiliated, the worst persecuted, the most recklessly annihilated human group on earth. For the great majority of them there is no other "living space" than the ghettos in which, according to German statistics, six hundred thousand people (actually over a million) are herded.

The establishment of the ghettos provided the Polish Jews with a certain minimum of security. They now had a refuge albeit by no means a secure one. Living conditions in the ghettos are unbearable. They are overcrowded, and the people are starving. The Jews in Warsaw have increased, since the

German occupation, by an influx of one hundred thousand men and women from all over the country. None of the newcomers receives a ration card; and a Jew who receives one is entitled only to one-fourth of the ration of a Pole, or one-eighth of that of a German. The hundred thousand supernumeraries in the Warsaw ghetto are entirely dependent on the mercy of their brothers, themselves famine-stricken.

The German policy is to concentrate the Polish Jews in ever fewer places, the so-called "points of expulsion." All told, there are some twenty ghettos in the Government General. The typhus-infested, disease-ridden ghetto of Łódz bears the ironic Nazi label, "The Jewish Superstate." Its thirty thousand inhabitants are suffering a lingering death. Although the Jews in Warsaw make up nearly half the population, their quarter, the ghetto, is restricted to 1,359 habitable houses out of the 24,832 buildings of the city. This overcrowding leads to frightful social, moral, and sanitary conditions. One consequence is an annual mortality of one hundred and fifty thousand among two million Polish Jews. This, German authorities insist, is only the "normal" mortality. The figure does not take into account the victims of epidemics.

On what do the ghetto people subsist? Trade is virtually dead, since there are no goods to sell. The factories work exclusively for Germany, mostly supplying military needs. A small part of the Jewish population is still living on its capital. But a Jew must deposit all his money in a German-controlled bank, and may only draw up to two hundred zlotys a month. On this sum (about twenty dollars at the official rate of exchange, and not half as much in purchasing power) a "rich" man lives with his family, supporting also a flock of destitute friends.

A little better is the lot of the laboring elements. The Jews are the hardest-working part of the population of Poland. They engage in the most arduous toil, and receive hardly enough to keep body and soul together. Yet this is the largest, if not almost the only, source of income. The entire Jewish population between the ages of fourteen and sixty must perform any kind of work the Germans want them to. Thus, the registration of all Jews was decreed on October 26, 1939. But this order has not been rigidly enforced. Slave labor must have proven little productive, because the Germans are resorting to it more and more rarely.

In the first six months of 1940, Jews in Warsaw put in one million two hundred thousand days of slave labor. The Jewish community of Warsaw paid 25 per cent of all the workers, a total of one million four hundred and twenty-five thousand zlotys in this period. The remaining workers were paid by the Germans, at no higher rates than those paid by the Warsaw Jewish community. The average daily pay of a worker was less than five zlotys—insufficient even for dry bread, since the price of a pound of bread was equal to a day's pay.

The German contractors, who were supplied with forced labor by the Jewish community, were under obligation to give the workers certain food rations. On the eve of the summer harvest there was a scarcity of farm products, and the contractors were unable to fulfill this condition. So they discontinued the camps. On the other hand, Jews beg to be taken into the camps, since hard and degrading work is still preferable to starvation.

There are some seventy-five labor camps, and in the whole Government General about one hundred thousand Jews are employed at forced labor. Besides, there are times when a great many more Jews are drafted for special labor. Thus, Jews were mobilized in scores of cities during the winter to clear the snow from streets, highways, and railroad tracks.

Besides slave labor there is "free" labor. In the ghetto cities, the Jewish community receives orders from the German Labor Office, as well as the necessary raw material, and assigns the work to Jewish artisans or manufacturers. In other cities where there is no ghetto, Jews work also on private orders.

Apparently the shortage of workers is so acute that the Nazi authorities must violate Hitler's gospel and promise Jews good treatment and the prevailing wage and even decent food. Even when they aim at their most miserable targets, the wretched Polish Jews, the poisoned arrows of Nazism miss the mark, and the bloody nonsense of the New Order is destroying itself.

In April, 1939, Léon Degrelle, Belgium's would-be Mussolini, contested the elections on an anti-Semitic platform, whereupon his followers in Parliament dropped from twenty-one to four. The Belgian people had had their say. Of course, the German invaders overruled them. A series of curbs on Jewish activities and civic liberties were introduced. The Jews were barred from public positions, from teaching, and from press and radio activities. When the law also was about to be closed to them, the Belgian bar association protested, refusing to strike the names of Jewish members from its rolls. The German authorities, in retaliation, issued a decree "Concerning Economic Measures Against the Jews," commonly known as the Third Jew Law. This liquidated all Jewish business; but most members of the older Jewish families, including a thousand engaged in the Antwerp diamond industry, had already left the country, many of them illegally, and had found new homes in the Americas. Those who remained succeeded in continuing their essential social and cultural activities in a limited way, with the strong and determined sympathy of their Gentile neighbors. In Belgium, it is dangerous to be an anti-Semite. The nights are black, and the war-weary German military police pay no attention to discussions of racial problems.

The handful of Luxembourgers, on the other hand, cannot well threaten the German giant with revolt, and the Nazi machine works unhampered. One of its achievements was the liquidation of the Jewish community.

On September 18, 1940, the Gestapo transmitted to Dr. Serebrinic, the Chief Rabbi of Luxembourg, an order that all Jews must leave the country within two weeks, taking with them no more than fifteen hundred francs (about thirty dollars) and about sixty pounds of personal luggage.

It was impossible to comply with the Gestapo order. When the time expired, the Gestapo herded hundreds of Jews in freight trains and sent them by way of occupied France and Spain to the Portuguese border. The Portuguese authorities refused to admit them, and they remained for weeks in a No Man's Land betwen Spain and Portugal, living in freight cars amid frightful conditions of cold and hunger. Thanks to the combined efforts of the Grand Duchess of Luxembourg and Jewish relief organizations, some of them succeeded in obtaining ship passage.

Of the remaining Jews of Luxembourg, groups are periodically rounded up by the Gestapo and sent to Polish ghettos.

The pink-cheeked, albino-blond, soft-spoken tiger Seyss-Inquart exacted a heavy price from the Netherlands Jews for his suppression of his instinctive anti-Semitism through forty-five years of life in Vienna. The terror to which the Eastern Jews are subjected by Nazism may be more violent and more bloodthirsty, but nowhere is the anti-Semitic campaign conducted with more gusto, sharper calculation, and colder hatred than in Seyss-Inquart's temporary Dutch realm.

The persecution started in June, 1940, with the looting of Jewish stores and the removal of Jewish judges from the bench. Jewish lawyers, physicians, and dentists were ordered to practice only among Jews. Children's hostels and refugee centers, as well as the famous Home for the Aged in Amsterdam, were confiscated by the authorities, and a number of

social institutions were closed. Nazi assaults on Jews became
frequent. Some three hundred were arrested in Amsterdam
and The Hague and sent to concentration camps. Refugees
were rounded up and returned to Germany.

On July 31, 1940, Seyss-Inquart proscribed ritual slaughter,
with the "tender" pretext of preventing cruelty to animals.
On August 28, he barred all Jews from public office and from
teaching, except in specific Jewish schools. Under the order,
a person with one Jewish grandparent was a Jew.

Jewish business was strangled. The *Reichskommissar* appointed a trustee for every "non-Aryan" shop. The Nazis
boast that some twenty thousand Jewish enterprises are already under Aryan control. It is their familiar process of expropriation: first Jewish officials are dismissed; then Nazi
commissars are appointed; and finally Jewish property is liquidated at forced prices.

Apart from destroying the Jews economically, other decrees bearing Seyss-Inquart's personal stamp aim to humiliate
the Jews. In December, 1940, Jews were prohibited from em-
ploying domestics of German extraction. No new Jewish student is allowed to enroll in a university. On April 2, the
government commissioner for Haarlem barred Jews from restaurants, motion pictures, theaters, public dining rooms and
baths. Later, the Mayor of The Hague excluded them from
hotels and parks. They were also forbidden to appear on the
boulevards and beaches of Scheveningen, Kÿkduin, Monster,
and Wassenaar. On September 5, an order was issued under
which Jewish children were excluded from schools staffed
with non-Jewish teachers, and were segregated in special
schools.

Finally, decrees were issued which had a tragic but also a
grotesque character: In April, 1941, the occupational authorities decreed that Jewish blood was not to be used for transfu-
sion for German patients and wounded. "It would not be
enough, anyway," commented a widely distributed clandes-

tine handbill. "The Germans lose too many men in street brawls and along the water front."

The conception of Frenchmen bearing arms for Hitler silences irony, and puts a check on the sense of humor. Marshal Pétain still pretends that he is fighting for the New Order only with economic and spiritual weapons. Anti-Semitism, of course, belongs to the latter group. It is a fundamental of the Vichy creed and practice. Still, it is not enough for the Hitler stooges in Paris. Several new French-speaking Nazi organizations have sprung up, including the Free Front, the National Collectivist Party, the French League, the National Popular Group, the French Popular Party, and the Social Revolutionary Movement. The leaders of most of these proclaim that Pétain's Revolution is insufficiently revolutionary and anti-Semitic, and that French collaboration with Germany is not close enough.

Nevertheless, it was not easy to convince French people that the Jews were the cause of their misfortunes. They knew only too well that behind these anti-Semitic onslaughts stand the agents of reaction, working hand in glove with the Nazis. There were, of course, some groups ready to capitalize on the anti-Semitic campaign, such as the young Paris lawyers who on July 30, 1940, protested against Jewish and Masonic competition and the crowds who on August 20 and September 5 demonstrated against Jews on the Champs-Elysées and the main boulevards of the Capital; but the attitude of the French people at large toward the Jews was always correct and often distinctly friendly and considerate. Personal liberty was not assailed. Indeed, it is a matter of record that, the stronger the pressure of the Nazis became, the further did the French people recoil from anti-Semitic feelings. Signs in stores and public places forbidding admission to Jews would disappear, while suggestions in the press that France organize an exodus of the Jews from Europe, failed to find appreciable response.

Preliminary propaganda was, however, soon followed by direct action. This began as extralegal confiscation. On August 21 and 27, Gestapo agents in Paris made the rounds of the leading Jewish organizations, including the World Jewish Congress and the Jewish National Fund. A few weeks later the offices of the Alliance Israélite Universelle and the Jewish Telegraphic Agency were raided, and some sixty thousand volumes from the libraries of the Alliance and the Ecole Rabbinique were removed to the Institute for Research on the Jewish Problem in Frankfurt. On September 13 the children's homes run by the ORT in Saint-Denis and Tournelle were confiscated, while in Paris all synagogues, with but one exception—the Rothschild synagogue in the Rue de la Victoire—were closed. Simultaneously, the fortunes of the house of Rothschild were declared forfeit, and five months later, the same fate overtook those of other wealthy Jews, such as the Lazards, Saul Amar, and Louis Dreyfus.

These measures soon were followed by formal anti-Jewish legislation. An initial decree of September 27 prohibited all fugitives Jewish in religion now or formerly, or with more than two Jewish grandparents from returning to the occupied zone. Jews were ordered to register with the authorities before October 20 and have their papers stamped "JEW," and by the end of that month every Jewish-owned business was to be marked distinctly "Jewish Enterprise." Leaders of Jewish communities were required to supply the authorities with all material and documents necessary for the execution of the measure.

This decree was followed on October 18 by one ordering the registration of all Jewish concerns, and on December 12, 1940, by one placing them under the control of "Aryan" commissioners. The hardest blow fell on April 26, 1941, when the "Third Decree" was issued. This forbade Jews to engage in wholesale and retail commerce, restaurant and hotel business, insurance and tourist agencies, carrier services, banking, advertising, real estate, mortgage transactions, and employment bureaus; or to act as commercial travelers or accept any position which might bring them into direct contact with customers or clients. It was further laid down that, even in other forms of employment, Jews were to be replaced by "Aryans" on the demand of the German military authorities.

As early as the spring of 1941, Berlin could claim that eleven thousand Jewish enterprises in Paris were practically under the administration of "Aryan" commissioners.

Although the "Aryanization" in the economic field was ordered and carried out mainly by the German military authorities, the French Government cooperated, establishing a special Control Commission under the chairmanship of the former Governor of the Bank of France, Fournier. The main task of this commission is to make suggestions on the appointment of "Aryan" commissioners and the adjustment of ownership in various enterprises. Nominally the commission is entitled only to make propositions, but the list of commissioners appointed by the German military authorities is published in the *Journal Officiel*.

The fate of the Jews in France depends mainly on four men. Symbolically, two are Germans and two are (one shudders to use the word) French. The Nazi commissioners for Jewish affairs are two lieutenants of the S.S. named Danaker and Lumpe. Their French colleagues are Comte Serpeille de Gobineau—a descendant of Count Gobineau, the father of "scientific" anti-Semitism—and René Gerard. They are chairman and director, respectively, of the newly created Institute for Jewish Studies in Paris. The official motto of this institute is "From Anthropology to Propaganda," and its first achievement was the exhibition "Jews in France." It is recognized by the Vichy government as an "instrument of national defense."

Other French "instruments of national defense" against the Jewish danger are "internment" camps (hardly to be distinguished from concentration camps), curbs on employment, deprivation of citizenship, and finally the Jewish Statute, re-issued in revised and elaborated form on June 2, 1941. In brief, this statute deprives the Jews of all civil and political rights, excludes them from all public services, sharply limits their practice of the professions and their engaging in trade; of course it bars them from the arts, literature, and the radio.

For the enforcement of this statute a Commissariat for Jew-ish Affairs was set up under Xavier Vallat, a Fascist deputy who, before the war, had already coined the phrase: "The Jews have gained control of our ancient Gallo-Roman father-land." After his appointment Vallat declared that he consid-ered Jews as an ethnical minority unwilling to assimilate, but seeking to dominate the French people. Joseph Barthelemy, then Vichy Minister of Justice, declared the statute "cruel, but necessary." Nazi-bribed hoodlums in Marseilles, Nice, and Vichy interpreted these encouraging words in their own fash-ion: they blew up the local synagogues. Marshal Pétain is a little hard of hearing, and missed the din of the bombs explod-ing in his immediate vicinity. When he was told of the out-rage, he said mildly, shaking his wise head: "This nationless Jew!"

CHAPTER SIXTEEN

THE GERMAN AHASUERUS

There is no longer a chance of withdrawal for any of us. The inferno awaits us all should we lose the war.—Dr. Paul Goebbels, over the Berlin radio, November 9, 1941.

WHETHER the responsibility for unloosing this war and conducting it with a degree of cruelty, particularly toward noncombatants, which has been unknown since barbarian days, rests with that man Hitler or with the German nation collectively, is a question frequently asked and will be the supreme problem when the United Nations have achieved victory.

It is not only one of the decisive questions that will determine which role Germany shall have in the new world, but perhaps the most confusing one the peacemakers will have to answer. Obviously, the British and American nations at least will recoil from indicting seventy million people as the perpetrators of the crimes of Nazism, which include every sort of crime it is possible to commit. The subjugated nations, on the other hand, may well display a different attitude. Millions of their people are being robbed, tortured, insulted, and in-

jured by countless little Hitlers, the overwhelming majority
of whom show remarkable gusto in their crimes. As soon as
they have the opportunity and the weapons to strike back,
two hundred million Europeans will forget their historic cul-
tures. To get even with the warden in the concentration camp
(taking one from among a thousand manifestations of the
Nazi beast) will be far more important to them than to make
a fair apportionment of the guilt in the enslaving and ruining
of Europe.

The question, "Hitler or the German people?" indeed appears to be unanswerable. The relation between Hitler and
the Germans forms a vicious circle. Undoubtedly, the Führer
has corrupted, stultified, terrorized, and crazed scores of millions of previously decent people in his own nation. They are
his from the cradle to the grave. He snatches the children of
kindergarten age, and does not even release the dead who, in
ever increasing numbers, are condemned to pagan burial according to Nazi rites.

In this sense the German nation is guilty only of omission—
of failing to resist with determination the return to cannibalism. On the other hand, Hitler, even if he were superman
instead of super-pathological crank, could not possibly have
achieved what he has without the active support of at least
the vocal element in his powerful, thrusting, hard-hitting nation. Although an Austrian, Hitler has many traits highly
characteristic of German psychology and German history.
He reflects the German impulse and the German vices. His
unique strength is not the strength of a single man. It is magnified by seventy million of his kind, and would be formidable
if it were not totally unbalanced. Nazism's rigid discipline is
only the overcompensation of the German insecurity and
wavering. The German delight in being trodden on, the more
to trample on those below, is a mixture of sadism and mas-
ochism—present in other peoples as human afflictions, but in
their close interrelationship a German epidemic. The German

colossus has not only feet of clay, but nerves that shriek. Its people, although shrewd bargainers, live in a sinister, phantasmagorical world. They dream of dominating the globe and have made a nightmare come true: the New Order.

The Germans' profit from the New Order, and all it stands for, is immeasurable. Their living standards are low, compared with those prevailing in the Western world and with their own prewar level. However, beyond the barest necessities of living, whatever goods are available come from the suppressed countries. Every fur coat or pair of silk stockings a German woman wears today was wrested from the French. During the first two years of war and conquest, more than a third of the total German food supply was looted from other countries. Now subjugated Europe is bare of every commodity. The larders of the once richest agricultural countries are empty. Consequently, rationing in Germany is constantly being tightened. But the squeeze of the victims continues unabated. Their manpower is drained off to Germany, their productive capacity is exploited, every possession not screwed down is taken off to the Reich.

The conveyer is the German army. It is the nucleus of the German nation, and its clearest expression. Albeit the most strictly regimented aggregate of human beings in the world, it is a democratic institution in the sense that it contains members of every level of German society, every age group, and every walk of life. According to the best estimates available outside Germany, the army numbers eleven million men among whom seven or eight million form the fighting forces.

At the top of the pyramid are the generals. We hear from all sides that they did not want the present war, or at least tried to prevent its extension. Frequently it is suggested that they might be disposed to make peace on behalf of the German people, sick of blood. This is a delusive hope—the sooner discarded, the better. The monocled Prussian martinets might well become a guarantee of order; but the conduct of their outstanding representatives, in command of the armies of occupation, proves irrefutably that the German generals are the New Order in pure culture.

Hitler has ousted many of the generals and had others murdered. Rumors crop up incessantly that the Führer is at loggerheads with his generals. But have they protested against the assassination of their comrades and seniors? Numerous gentlemen of high rank gathered in officers' casinos and drank a great amount of liquor in honor of the "fallen" friends. Beyond that, there was never the slightest remonstrance. The explanation is simple: German generals have the reputation of dare-devils in the field, but they are entirely lacking in what the Germans themselves call "civilian courage." They neither opposed their Emperor when they saw him leading them into disaster, nor defended him when his people rose. They display the same supreme indifference toward Hitler. Gladly they grab the titles, dignities, and rapid advances in rank with which he bribes them. In their intimate circles they still call him the lance-corporal. But when he lashes out his marshals click their heels and do or die as told.

This mechanized morale at the top is reflected in the entire German army. Among the most successfully spread lies of German war propaganda was the tale of the gentle giant in field gray. Even incorruptible American war correspondents, hard-bitten crack shots with a congenital suspicion of propaganda reported duly the good behavior of the German ranks they had witnessed. Such reports were based on close observation, hard work, and much personal experience.

Unfortunately this experience was gained by observing only one face of the Janus-headed German army. To be sure, the monster is a dancing bear when and where neutral witnesses are admitted. But alone with its victims it rapidly changes its skin. The most shocking thing about the German army is not its duplicity, but the frightful facility with which it changes its mask. Somewhere at the top a button is pressed, and Hitler's legions assume the attitude of conquerors against their own volition, who can raze a town in less than an hour, but could not kill a flea. But when the man at the top flashes the green light—intimate observers believe that Hitler reserves such decisions for himself—the furies are let loose.

They were unloosed in the first campaign of this war—the rape of Poland—and the grand-scale assault on Russia.

The behavior of the German army in martyrized Poland is particularly revealing. For the first eleven months of occupation the soldiers were permitted to exert "individual law." Suddenly this unbridled terror was stopped. A single order from Berlin sufficed to turn the looting hordes into disciplined forces. To the Polish population this change did not bring much relief. The Gestapo continued where the troops had to leave off. But the change was highly characteristic of the army, in the limitation of its power of decision as well as in its pliant adaptability to Nazi law.

The troops who first entered Warsaw in October, 1939, showed few of the signs of weariness which are expected after a military campaign. They had been transported in motor trucks and even in passenger cars during the campaign, and even the artillery was almost entirely motorized. Troops arriving later looked different—infantry exhausted by long marches, trains and artillery drawn by horses.

It was surprising that despite every effort to maintain a regular food supply, and the presence of a large number of field kitchens, German soldiers rushed to the few Warsaw restaurants still open—but serving only soups of doubtful quality with at best a bit of horse meat.

This German hunt for food in the half-destroyed and starving city reached such proportions that the military authorities had to forbid the sale of foodstuffs to the troops. Finally the soldiers were forbidden, after many cases of looting, to enter food shops.

The Nazi army seems to regard plunder as normal. During

the first days of occupation robbery was conducted under the pretense of searching for arms. All sharp instruments, including even penknives, were seized. Watches, money, and other valuables were taken at the same time. In Warsaw and other large cities whole blocks of houses were surrounded by troops while a general search was carried out under the direction of officers.

Raids in Jewish quarters resulted in the expropriation of food as well as every other kind of portable property. Receipts were seldom given to the owners. A Warsaw jeweler, seventy years old, was shot for "possessing arms." Actually, he had no weapons. His crime was to argue with the soldiers who seized his stock of jewelry.

Often a German soldier entering a Jewish shop with a woman—many German women have entered Poland—would leave it with bunches of gowns on his arms. Sometimes the Jewish saleswoman would shout and argue, only to be "brought to her senses" by the fists of the plunderer, who put his prize into a car and went off with his companion. Sometimes, again, German soldiers entered a shop and chose goods worth many hundred marks, for which they paid by leaving two or three marks on the counter. Many merchants have closed their shops and passed their remaining goods over to street venders, who run smaller risks.

Soldiers frightened by threats of complaint to their officers have sometimes returned stolen money. More often the German authorities have merely ill-treated the people who complained.

Hitler's army advances with propaganda. Even official announcements about such matters as foreign exchange regulations are filled up with propaganda slogans. So are the anti-Jewish proclamations published under the guise of anti-profiteering measures.

Sometimes, especially early in the occupation, propaganda took different forms. A soldier would tear a fur coat from a lady's shoulder and throw it to a poor woman standing in a shop queue. Another would knock down a Jew selling onions in the street, take the Jew's place, and sell them for a cheaper price. Of course he himself pocketed the money paid for the merchandise. Such efforts to win the sympathy of the mob had no success and were not continued.

Restrictions imposed on the German soldiers' relations with the population were strictly observed, on the whole. But there are many facts which show that the morale of the army is by no means conspicuously good. Some of the soldiers, completely convinced by their propaganda, believe that Germany can defeat the whole world; but a German soldier quartered in a Polish flat expressed the following opinion: "We have surrounded you, that is true, but we ourselves are still much more surrounded, and ruin is what we expect, and all this because of the fault of one man." Another soldier living at a farmer's house looked at the portrait of a Polish leader and said: "Yes, these are the people that wanted war, neither you nor we wanted it."

Some elements in the army persecuted the Jews with conviction and enthusiasm, throwing them out of trains, busses, and queues. There were exceptions, however. A German stopped a passing Jew and asked him, "Are you a Jew?"—usually the prelude to an insult. But this soldier warned the Jew not to go farther as a general raid on the Jews was in progress in the neighborhood. A Warsaw lawyer of Jewish origin, officer of the reserve, handed over his revolver to German soldiers who were searching his flat, but forgot some cartridges in his desk which were found. The Germans left the flat with threats. An hour later the officer who had conducted the raid visited the frightened man and told him privately what to say in order to avoid difficulties. There have been many similar exceptions.

Occasionally the German minority also has been persecuted. In a village with a mixed German-Polish population soldiers were requisitioning timber from a German colonist. The latter protested violently and argued that, being *Volks-deutsch*, he was free from requisitions. The answer was that, being a German, he ought to be only too glad to know that his timber would be burned by the German army.

Soldiers requisitioned pigs at a German farm in spite of violent protests by the farmer's wife. They gave her a receipt for the pigs, remarking that Mr. Churchill would pay for them. The woman, inexpert in foreign affairs, read the receipt and asked whether the man was in the nearest town. The soldiers told her that this was so, and the woman duly appeared at the office asking for Mr. Churchill.

At a time when part of Poland under German occupation was handed over to the U.S.S.R., the Nazis explained that the Soviets would repay their debt by helping Germany on the Western Front. This helped to quiet discontent amongst troops who were destined for the Western Front.

The fear of Bolshevization of the German troops probably explains the tightening of rules and reintroduction of discipline in September, 1940. The German army on the Eastern Front in 1918 was permeated by Communist propaganda. The possibility that this may happen again gives Hitler anguish today. On the whole the German army in Poland obeyed orders. But as the war drags on the soldiers are again becoming more licentious and dissolute. Competing with the Gestapo, they organize their own pogroms and persecute the population. In an ever increasing stream, information is coming through from Poland about the renewed barbarous practices of the German army. In a town in Silesia a crowd of drunken German soldiers recently went to the cemetery, profaned the graves, and turned the crosses and statues upside down. This was later explained as an anti-Polish demonstration; but it is just as much a proof that the discontented soldiery is getting out of hand.

Business relations between the civil population and the German troops are a two-way proposition. The soldiers are not only purchasing civilian clothes but selling anything. To accumulate something against the rainy day every German knows is coming, they even offer military equipment, including machine guns. Polish guerrilla bands were ferreted out that had German tanks. Investigation brought to light the surprising fact that they had been purchased for cash in a German arsenal.

An enormous trade, of course, is done in alcohol. In order to deprave the Polish people the Germans encouraged the sale of alcohol, reducing the price to Polish buyers. But on the black liquor markets, busy in every town, German soldiers are the best customers. Dead-drunk German officers, soldiers, and party functionaries are no longer an uncommon sight in Polish towns. The elder generation, remembering the German occupation during the last war, insists that the consumption of alcohol by German troops has increased three or four times.

Despite this evident deterioration in the army morale the German system in Poland has lost nothing of its arrogance. The division between the Polish "minus-man" and the German superman is emphasized more and more strongly as time goes on. Toward the end of 1941, Governor General Frank ordered all Polish citizens of German extraction to register. This order caused grave misgivings among the newcomers from the Reich, who claim the monopoly of true Germanism. Violent dissension ensued between Polish Germans and "German Germans," the latter having the better of it. "When the show is over," they say, "we will return to Germany, whereas you *Volksdeutsche* will have to remain here to be killed by the Poles."

That the end of the show approaches is the general conviction. The Germans realize that it will not be an easy end. Their press is constantly clamoring about the ingratitude of the Polish people. The *Ostdeutscher Beobachter* in Poznań, an edition for Poland of Hitler's own mouthpiece *Völkischer Beobachter*, commented on heavy sentences that had been imposed on local people for insulting the German police and listening to foreign broadcasts: "These cases reflect the deep-seated, the ineradicable opposition to German law in our eastern provinces." The *Goniec Krakowski*, a fake Polish paper, translated from the German, complains: "The population throws dirt on those Poles who are inclined to cooperate."

Dr. Frank in December, 1941, receiving Polish local functionaries at Cracow, addressed them with the words: "I am fully aware of your feeling of slumbering hatred. The fact that you are dissatisfied is no secret to us. The fight against Polish criminals has caused heavy losses among our S.S. Yet I will continue my endeavor to cooperate."

Recently, the Governor General put the Weichselsender, the German radio station for western Poland, into the service of this cooperation. The station, which thus far had only broadcast insults of the Poles and thinly disguised encouragements to persecute them, now tries to explain why Germany was "compelled" to invade Poland. Hitler's policy, it is explained, would have taken a different form had independent Poland agreed to march with the Reich against Russia. This is the first time such a tone has been adopted toward Poland. It shows that the Germans would like to make the Poles believe that a new era of prosperity is opening for them with the conquest of Russian territory, and that the time has come to "bury the hatchet." To the same purpose a few churches have been reopened, and even presented with gifts from the German authorities, which proved to be silk and embroidery from France, mostly stolen in Lyons.

Finally, a formal peace offer was extended by the official Nazi *Kurier Czenstochowski*:

On the basis of what the German occupation authorities have accomplished in Poland up to now, it is obvious that the Poles, if in full measure only after the war, will be given an opportunity for free economic and cultural development with a guarantee of internal and external security, provided, of course, that they steer clear of all political activity.

The same issue of the same paper carried also a different kind of news: House-to-house searches for warm clothing were starting in the small towns and villages. A "League of German Witnesses" was constituted, whose members would make it their business to supply the necessary evidence in trials against enemies of the state. Polish prisoners of war would serve as human guinea pigs, being infected with typhus bacilli to try out new remedies for use in the German armies in Russia.

The general response of the Polish people to the wooing and the threats of their German masters can be guessed from their answer to Dr. Frank's latest decree. He ordered that Germans and Poles should be buried in different cemeteries. The Poles entirely agreed. The general consent was expressed by their adoption of the hated slogan: "More space for the Germans." It was found smeared on the walls of every German cemetery.

The ultimate aim of Nazi policy in Czechoslovakia is the extermination of the Czechoslovak nation. Within one generation, Secretary of State Karl Hermann Frank stated with remarkable frankness, not a single Czech will remain in Bohemia-Moravia. The natives of whole towns, villages, and districts are driven from their homes, and everywhere labor is drained off to Germany. On the other hand enormous numbers of German newcomers are settled in the depopulated areas, and are crowding the big cities. Prague alone has had an influx of two hundred and fifty thousand Germans, and this, according to Nazi plans, is just a beginning. The capital of Bohemia is to be developed into the capital of Central Europe, with an increase in the population from the present one million to three or four millions—all Germans of course.

The measures were carried out on the largest possible scale, and with Nazism's habitual ruthless methods. Yet they brought only one result: At present, the Germans in the Protectorate are on the run, and even Sudetenland, incorporated with the Reich, is dangerously restive. The lot of the Germans in Czechoslovakia is a sample of the fate that awaits them everywhere in Europe. Everywhere the intruders adopted an attitude best expressed in American by "Scram, I'm muscling in!" But everywhere they wish they had never left their homes in Germany which, in spite of increasing shortages and accelerated R.A.F. raids, are still considerably safer.

The influx of Germans followed a grand strategy. The German border was to be methodically expanded, and, by the same token, German "language islands" (German minorities within Czech territory) were to be magnified. Accordingly, the Czech population of twenty-nine villages in the Elbe valley, near the Saxon frontier, were first ordered to make room for German colonists, not from the Reich, but from Bessarabia. For the benefit of the same group of newly arrived Germans forty-two villages in Moravia were evacuated, the expelled farmers receiving about a tenth of the actual worth of their property as compensation.

Strangely, the Bessarabian peasants filtering in proved to have no aptitude for tilling the good soil. They were completely baffled by the beautiful new plows with which the German authorities equipped them and they could not discern any difference between the seeds of rye and of wheat. By the same token, an epidemic of horse stealing broke out, spreading rapidly from the Germanized districts all over the country, and arson cases were numerous. Soon the explanation was found. The "German" racial comrades from Bessarabia were in fact gypsies who had profited from the German "liberation" of their country to satisfy their insatiable wanderlust, and see another part of this beautiful world.

Despite this false start, the evacuation of Czech peasants continues unabated. They have lost hundreds of villages to genuine Germans—not to farmers, of whom there is a shortage in Germany proper, but to deserving party members, mostly parents and widows of soldiers who have fallen on the Russian front, people who are just as unfit for farm life as the Bessarabian gypsies. Thus some of the most fertile soil of Bohemia and Moravia remains untilled and the crops shrink. The Nazis rage.

Another method of Germanization is to transplant numerous armament plants from the heavily bombed industrial areas in the German west to the comparative safety of Bohemia. The factories were moved with their personnel. But again a hitch occurred. German workers became quickly easily infected with the anti-Nazi spirit of their new neighbors. In many cases veteran members of Dr. Ley's Labor Front not only failed to accelerate the faltering speed of Czech production, but even adopted the go-slow attitude of their Czech comrades. Thus Pilsen, once the most violently nationalist Czech town, the site of the gigantic Skoda armament works and of a hardly less important brewery industry, today wears a German face. The local administration is German, and so are the signposts on the streets. But beer is getting scarce, and the production of Skoda, according to reliable reports reaching the Czech government in London, dropped radically in the last half-year, in spite or perhaps on account of the addition of twenty-five thousand German workmen to the plant's personnel.

Similar decreases in production are occurring in all the big Czech plants. The output of the Poldihütte in Kladno, the largest steel works in the country, fell so catastrophically that its general manager, a German named Bazinek, was called to Berlin. He had a long talk with Göring, in which the Marshal probably did most of the talking. Herr Bazinek returned to Kladno and committed suicide, without any explanation. The

strain is telling on the Göring family, too. The Marshal's
brother, Albert Göring, was appointed Director General of
the Hermann Göring works in Czechoslovakia and neighboring countries. He took up residence in Prague. His wife soon
became Czechoslovakia's self-styled first lady. At Christmas,
1941, she left for Switzerland, after liquidating her palatial
home. She could no longer bear hostility around her, her husband bluntly admitted.

Mrs. Albert Göring, it appears, is a particularly sensitive
German woman. Two million German women and children
evacuees are less so. They have, on the contrary, staged another invasion of Czechoslovakia. At least two hundred thousand German children had to be supported throughout the
winter by wretched Slovakia alone. They were forbidden to
disclose from which parts of the Reich they come. By checking their mail from home, however, the unwilling hosts found
out that the majority were from the heavily bombed areas in
the west and north of the Reich. They were most unwelcome
guests, since the local authorities must provide food and shelter when these were already sorely lacking for the native population. Ration cards for Czechs were revoked to increase the
German visitors' rations. Czech schools were used for German
children. The supply of milk for Czech children was radically
cut so that no little Gretchen might go short. The result was
that, after a few months of enforced hospitality, all the German children in the Protectorate, according to the statistics of
the Medizinisches Reichsamt (medical department) in Berlin,
had gained between ten and twenty pounds. Not all of them
needed to put on weight. Without exception the German refugee children in Czechoslovakia came from families of party
functionaries and state officials, officers and black-shirt leaders,
the wealthy ruling class of Nazidom. Not one was a child of
the working class. However, the sweep of the youthful German locusts on Czechoslovakia was a success, only slightly
marred by the disclosure of the Nazi-controlled authorities

in Prague that, in the same time, child mortality among the Czechs had increased 11.6 per cent.

Germanization backfired again in the appropriation of Czech property. Nazis with sufficient pull at home seized first all the state, provincial, and municipal property, then the holdings and belongings of various public and private corporations and foundations, particularly of those with Jewish stockholders. The number of German shareholders was gradually extended, without any contributions to the stock or capital. A great deal of Czech real property has been bought by Germans in the last three years very advantageously. It was only necessary to accuse the Czech owner of being a Beneš adherent to obtain his property at a tenth of its value, or less. The Gestapo was always ready to supply middlemen for a modest consideration. In many cases Czech property owners were arrested and forced to sign receipts for sums they had never received. Moreover, the Nazis were extraordinarily inventive of legal blinds. Thus scores of villages in agricultural areas were expropriated, lock, stock, and barrel, on the claim that the German army had vital interests in their region. The execution of these claims was based on the State Defense Law of the (according to Nazism) defunct Czechoslovakian Republic.

But now these enormous surreptitiously gained holdings are only an embarrassment to their German proprietors. Panic is increasing among the Germans who have moved to the Protectorate. This panic is caused by several reasons, one of them Berlin-manufactured. Bohemia-Moravia has long been the dumping ground for the families of German soldiers, who were considered only as supernumerary bread eaters in Germany. Their situation caused apprehension in the Nazi government when the death toll on the Eastern Front rose to unforeseen heights. Would not the families of the men who had lost their lives in the Russian campaign become so depressed and critical as to be easily affected by the democratic bacillus of democracy, rampant in Czechoslovakia? Numerous incidents proved that it would, indeed, be safer to keep the war widows and orphans under control at home. Instead of messages of condolence, they simply received orders to return to Germany if they wanted to draw their pensions. For similar reasons German firms which had opened branches in the Protectorate were told to send their German staffs back to the Reich. This order reached two hundred business enterprises on a single day, August 1, 1941. Finally, the Czech people did their better than best to inform the German newcomers how little enviable their lot would be on the day of the nation's liberation. They did not need to elaborate much.

The process of Germanization was precipitately interrupted. At present thousands of Germans are frantically withdrawing their bank accounts in Prague and transferring them to German banking institutions. Practically every German locust is trying to sell the Czech real estate which he came by so cheaply. But there are no buyers, because the Czechoslovak government in London broadcast a warning not to purchase looted goods from German holders as the Czechoslovak State would seize them all after victory and recompense the owners from whom they had been taken.

The panic-stricken departure of the German birds of passage has left its strongest mark on Prague. Czech families by the thousands had been forced to vacate apartments in the most desirable sections of the city, in Dejvice, Letna, and the Smichov Embankment. They could now have back their flats for a pittance. But even those Czechs who once were wealthy have lost their aristocratic tastes, it seems. They prefer to dwell among the plain people in the crowded suburbs, and to fight the battle of Czech brotherhood by their side to a glorious finish.

It is impossible that even the dull Nazis should not see the writing on the wall. They see their efforts wrecked. They have failed to Germanize the Czech lands and fields, the houses, or even business and industry. Only three last lines of attack are left: the administration, the German-inhabited Sudetenland, and the armed forces.

Consequently, the Czech puppet government has been forced to accept a German member, "entrusting" him with the portfolios for industry, trade, and labor. The name of this worthy is Bertsch. Since he cannot speak a single word of Czech, the so-called Czech government is now forced to deliberate in German. Another Nazi, named Schubert, was appointed Vice President of Bohemia, and two hundred Germans obtained local offices. They are well aware that they represent the last enrollment for the German service in Czechoslovakia. Following their appointments, a thousand additional Gestapo agents had to be dispatched to the Protectorate. They figure on the pay rolls as bodyguards.

Without their bodyguards the Nazi functionaries no longer venture even into Sudetenland. The awakening of this part of the country, once the hotbed of Nazism, is best exemplified by the fact that a recent purge of the Nazi cell in the Skoda works resulted in 1,221 exclusions and 184 "suspensions for life," a sentence from which it can be inferred that the very lives of the 184 were suspended.

The hope of the Sudeten Germans that they would receive better treatment from Hitler than the Czechs has evaporated. Konrad Henlein, who made international headlines before and shortly after Munich, has been shelved. In vain he appealed recently in a letter to Hitler (published in the *Der Neue Tag*, the Nazi mouthpiece) that his services should be recognized:

I have been lying for you to all the world. I deceived the English until they sent Lord Runciman who returned with his famous report on the Sudeten question. I told them that we were not National Socialists. Of course we were. But our political task was the smashing of Czechoslovakia as the spearhead of the anti-Reich system of alliances, and that could only be achieved by the deception of the democracies.

The abandoned traitor's outcry went unanswered. Henlein must fade into complete anonymity, lest he share the fate of his former opponents, the anti-Nazi Sudeten leaders Senator Stark and Heger who were tortured by the Gestapo, and of the former member of Parliament Franz Kaufmann, who committed suicide to end the torture.

Recruiting of Sudeten Germans is very strict, many men having been called up who held essential offices in the administration and in industry. Some villages have had to produce as many as one hundred seventy recruits at once, which meant taking practically all the men from the farms.

In order to train these men as fast as possible, kicking, beating and other brutal means are resorted to. Any complaints are severely punished.

One result of these policies is that in Schumberk, northern Moravia, handbills were circulated titled "We Want to Rejoin Moravia." These were printed in German, and two hundred Germans were arrested for circulating them.

One hundred and eighty Sudeten business leaders have signed a memorandum to the Berlin government, asking economic autonomy for their area, which indicates the difficulty of doing business under the Nazi regime. By way of a reply, the one hundred and eighty were ordered arrested. Outstanding in the group is Herr Brass of Zabreh, who was one of Henlein's most vociferous supporters. A number of the signers committed suicide to avoid arrest and what was sure to follow arrest.

German soldiers, especially older ones, have confessed to the Czechs that they are tired of the excessive travel across Europe to which they have been subjected. They were promised a short, victorious war, but the early victory did not materialize. They complained of the constant turmoil and of their inability to see their families for years. They blame the Gestapo, the S.A., and the S.S. men for the war, the oppression, and the terrorism which will finally bring a terrible retribution from the peoples now subjugated.

Unrest broke out among the Sudeten German population of the widely separated towns of Aussig, Trautenau, and Schumberk. One of the main causes of unrest was fear about the fate of Austrian and Sudeten soldiers in the German army sent as reinforcements to Norway, occasioned by the reports broadcast from London of the sinking of numerous large transports in the Kattegat. The families receive no word from their men. "Show us the casualty lists," has been chalked up on walls in many Sudeten German cities. These complaints are accentuated by the presence in the cities of large numbers of Reich Germans, young men in Gestapo and S.S. uniforms, who, the people complain, ought to be at the front. So many Sudeten Germans have been conscripted that in many villages only the aged are left to do the farm work.

The uprising in Schumberk was joined even by some German troops who had long complained about food and supplies. The revolt was put down by troops from Olomouc, but the Nazi mayor of Schumberk shot himself in fear of the consequences.

All the Germans in Czechoslovakia are awaiting retribution. Their authorities help them as well as they can. The Protector issued a decree, in December, 1941, according to which every German in Bohemia and Moravia automatically becomes a deputy sheriff. They are authorized to carry arms without any kind of permit, and to arrest any "suspicious Czech" on the spot, using weapons if necessary. On the other hand no Czech is allowed to possess firearms. In spite of this all Germans were ordered on January 15, 1942, to move into closed settlements, in order to help one another in case of trouble.

Norway as well is flooded with two groups of Germans: wounded soldiers and refugees from the R.A.F., mostly women. However, a third group of invaders is decreasing—the most important one, the army. General von Falkenhausen, the commander in chief, has left his Norwegian domain, "temporarily," to have a breath of fresh air on the Finnish front. The Norwegian labor leader Konrad Nordahl stated on his arrival in London after escaping from his country, that Falkenhausen took with him three-quarters of his army of occupation: three hundred thousand out of four hundred thousand. They were replaced by half-trained and less well equipped troops from Austria and the Sudetenland, who show little fighting enthusiasm when they see the human wrecks who have returned from Russia.

Norway had to make room for eighty thousand German wounded. The number is constantly increasing. At Oslo alone at least one hospital train of thirty-five cars arrives daily. The wounded are taken off the train at Grefsen station on the outskirts of the city, lest both the population and the German garrison be shocked by their appearance.

By all accounts the morale of the German army of occupation is constantly getting worse. A mutiny in Bergen was brought about by a soldier, returning from furlough in Germany, who told his comrades that his family at home had vanished without leaving a trace. He was shot for rumor-mongering. But his execution aroused further discontent. A few German soldiers in Bergen attacked their officers, and several additional executions followed. Now the German barracks are heavily guarded by military police. Of course the local municipalities have to foot the bills. The town of Lillehammer alone must contribute twenty-four hundred kroner a week for maintaining the guard in charge of the German barracks.

Schools are being converted into German hospitals, and

every hospital bed for the civilian population is being requisitioned. In addition the Nazis are now seizing private living quarters, not only in Oslo and Trondheim but all along the coast, to make room for scores of thousands of German women and children, "vacationists" who have deserted constantly bombed Hamburg, Bremen, Kiel, and Cologne. The newest and finest apartment houses in the cities have been emptied for this purpose. Like the wicked and heartless landlord of the old melodrama, Hitler's henchmen in Norway are evicting families from their homes with sometimes less than a day's notice. German guests of distinction are assured of particularly careful treatment. On December 15 Heinrich Himmler, whose every casual visit is a marauding expedition, arrived in Oslo with an empty handbag. When he left a few days later, his suitcases bulged with two hundred pounds of the best flour, one hundred twenty-five pounds of coffee, and one thousand bars of chocolate.

Yet the Nazis are at a loss to understand why the Norwegian people show so little liking for their German guests. S.S. Squad Leader Rediess, Gestapo chief for Norway, summoned the Norwegian editors of the controlled press, and unbosomed himself: "We simply do not understand why our friendly attitude and our magnanimity meet with churlish impudence and the throwing of mud at the uniformed German personnel."

This question was asked one day after Himmler had banged the door of the Oslo Grand Hotel behind his back, and exactly one week after three Norwegians had been executed by order of Gauleiter Terboven, as spies for England.

The same incapacity to understand why they are so generally loathed and despised prevails among the Germans and their lackeys in Denmark. It is true that neither are having a good time. The Danes have developed to a fine art the cold-shouldering of the German uniform. They do not assassinate

officers of the army of invasion, like the French. But they
have a way of looking through them as if they were nonexistent. The home-grown Nazis, on the other hand, are
roughly dealt with.

The Danish Nazi paper *Fädrelandet* whines:

Any one who expresses hope of a German victory is spat upon
and called a traitor. Those who collaborate with the Germans are
boycotted and treated with contempt. It will take generations to
wipe out the anti-German feeling in this country, which began
on the 9th of April, 1940. The army of occupation behave correctly, but all their attempts to establish contacts with the people
are rejected. Whatever the German "foreigners" try in the way
of battery, temptation or threats, the Danish passive resistance remains insurmountable. And everywhere we hear: "We detest the
small clique of Danish Nazis." Is there really no solution?

In the same vein the *Nordschleswigsche Zeitung*, a German-language sheet, confessed:

We do not understand why the Danes hate everything that is
German. A fierce hatred of Hitler and the German army is the
dominant feeling among the people of Copenhagen.

A German officer summed it up in the following words:
"I have volunteered for the Russian front. I know it is hell.
But I would rather fight than continue living in this intol-
erable atmosphere of refined hatred."

Many of his comrades, it appears, feel the same way. But
only a few prefer the Russian front as an avenue of escape.
A good number of German officers and officials in Denmark
have committed suicide.

France is more heavily infested with German locusts than
any other occupied country. The opportunities for stealing
and looting are, of course, more tempting than elsewhere
and, strangely, the French atmosphere still keeps the German

tourists spellbound. German soldiers are frequent visitors in French churches, although they come as sight-seers rather than as worshipers. German officers pride themselves on calling the waiters in the boulevard cafés "garçon." It is the only word of the French language they can pronounce faultlessly after almost two years of residence in France, but it gives them a glorious feeling of being civilized which, in their own homeland, is strictly forbidden. It took them, incidentally, a few months to acquire a taste for civilization. On August 31, 1940, the then Nazi Commander-in-Chief von Brauchitsch felt compelled to issue an order denouncing the behavior of his own officers in France. This order was not published until more than a year later, when Mr. Lozovsky, the Soviet spokesman, made its contents known. The order had been found among the belongings of numerous German officers taken prisoner on the Eastern Front. Sentences like "Some of my officers behaved like bandits, others, I regret to say, like heels" make unflattering reading. None but a German would keep them as souvenirs. The German upstarts, however, like to have documentary proof that they were once the lords in God's own garden, France. A general belief permeates the German army that not much more than sweet memory will remain.

Rightly, German officers fear the French people. Take the experience of Colonel Paul Friedrich Hotz, commander of the German military police in Nantes. He took over the command in July, 1940, but for a long time no one saw him. He was suspicious of the people entrusted to his care, and hardly dared to go onto the streets. When he did go, he was always closely surrounded by his bodyguards.

He made his first public appearance in an aircraft factory, to which he went in person to announce that he was dissatisfied with the output, and that the entire personnel had to leave their jobs and evacuate their homes within six hours. They would be replaced by German workers, who of course would move into their apartments as well. But neither unemployment, nor lack of shelter would result: the highly skilled French mechanics would be shipped to Africa when the Sahara road wanted a little paving.

The workers, thus condemned to chain-gang labor in the desert, received the order in perfect silence. Their spokesman only ventured to ask whether they might not have twenty-four hours instead of six to take leave of their families and arrange their affairs.

"I have given my orders," replied the Colonel. "I never cancel or modify them."

Hotz was the typical Prussian bully. Under his heel Nantes had come to be the most heavily fined city in occupied France. A fine of seventy thousand dollars was about his minimum. That was the amount levied for a low-hanging telegraph wire which, the Nazis insisted, had been cut. The culprit proved to have been a cow, but the fine was not remitted. All Nantes knew the reason: Hotz was in the habit of pocketing a part of the levies he exacted.

The much-tried people of Nantes did not lose their patience. Not much more happened than that some women trod heavily on German toes in the crowded busses, always excusing themselves profusely. Furthermore, the overcoats German guests took off in cafés were frequently stolen. This form of resistance was poor enough. Yet the Germans began to feel uneasy. They abandoned the cafés, and opened a clubhouse for themselves. On the day of the ceremonious opening a small, handmade bomb sailed, as it were, through a window. The damage was not great. It was considerably worse, however, when a few days afterward some one tossed a regular bomb into Colonel Hotz's office. No one was hurt, but the whole building had to be evacuated.

The retribution was terrible. A crushing fine was imposed on Nantes, hostages were rounded up right and left, guns were installed at all the strategically important places in town.

"If the people of Nantes will not desist from making themselves a nuisance," read a poster signed by Colonel Paul Friedrich Hotz, commander of the military police, "I shall be obliged to raze Nantes."

Instead, a fire broke out in the stables of the Nazi cavalry. The Nantes fire brigade was summoned, and went into action immediately. But the engines took such a roundabout route through the town that the fire had burned itself out before the brigade arrived.

All these were acts of sabotage on a minor scale. But finally in March, 1941, the people lost their patience, and the show of tolerance ended. A British bomber crashed near Nantes, and the crew was killed. Colonel Hotz ordered a secret burial to avoid the demonstrations he rightly foresaw. Yet, when the German platoon with the coffins came to the hidden spot, miles from town, that had been chosen for the unconsecrated burial, they were met by a crowd of four thousand from Nantes, singing the "Marseillaise" and "God Save the King," and demanding a Christian burial for "our heroic allies."

"Fire!" was Colonel Hotz's answer.

It has not been established how many were killed.

One casualty, however, was Paul Friedrich Hotz. The next morning, he was stabbed in the back while walking to his office. He succumbed immediately. The perpetrator was never found. And no answer was given as to the whereabouts of the Colonel's bodyguards. It might be inferred that they did not care to risk their own necks for the bully.

As an epilogue the commander of the army of occupation in France, General von Stülpnagel, appeared personally in Nantes. But he did not leave his armored train. He gave his orders from the railroad station. One hundred hostages were taken. Fifty of these were instantly executed. The other fifty were brought to Paris, where they are still kept in the Santé, agonizing, hounded day and night by the expectation of death.

Marshal Pétain expressed his deepest grief over the incident of Nantes, which heralded a series of similar outbreaks all over occupied France, speaking of "irresponsible hotheads." On October 25, 1941, Colonel Paul Friedrich Hotz was buried in military splendor, with swastika banners flying at half-mast, after a procession through Nantes between silent lines of onlookers. Among the mourners walked Admiral Darlan, who is said to have remarked, "Nantes, I fear, is lost to the collaborationist cause." The Admiral returned by airplane to Vichy. That very evening the Pétain cabinet voted stringent new measures for the repression of attacks against German soldiers.

One of the best of these measures has been introduced by the Germans themselves. General von Stülpnagel announced publicly that he would either use his influence for the release of French prisoners of war, or pay an adequate sum, as the informers chose, for any information leading to the capture and conviction of French saboteurs and assassins. The announcement was published on October 30, 1941. It worked miracles. On the next day Stülpnagel could already inform the Paris press that two French prisoners in the camp near Breslau had been released, the sons of a butcher who had given valuable information. His name, however, was not disclosed in order to protect him against possible acts of revenge. On November 2, three Frenchmen, acting as guards on the railroads near Paris, received a money award for preventing sabotage on the lines. They had foiled an attempt to place bombs on the tracks. One of them also had a son in the German camp. But he preferred his reward in cash. Stülpnagel delivered one of his rare public orations, lauding the French population for coming to their senses. He expressed the hope that the French would increase their cooperation with the German authorities in the discovery and capture of offenders who had committed acts of aggression against the troops of occupation. In answer, the butcher and the three railway guards were assassinated within the next week. The bribing of informers was discontinued, since not even the French traitors were willing any longer to talk their necks into a noose.

Wearers of the German uniform do not feel safe in France. In the war of nerves, the tide is definitely turning against them. Their arrogant, overbearing behavior no longer goes unpunished. In December, 1941, a street fight broke out between German customs officials and members of the French War Veterans Legion in Annemasse, on the Swiss border. The fracas occurred when a Nazi official failed to doff his hat to a passing legion funeral cortège. A French legionary demanded an explanation: instead, he got a kick in the stomach. At the end of 1940 such a response from a Nazi would have been accepted. Today conditions have changed. Two Frenchmen beat up the aggressive German, breaking his jaw, and when his colleagues interfered, the whole German customs post received a good hiding from the legionaries.

The amazing thing about this otherwise insignificant brawl is the fact that no fine was levied, no hostages were taken, and the German guard tried assiduously to hush up the event. They were obviously afraid of losing their jobs on the comfortable French-Swiss border, and being transferred to a less cozy station, somewhere in Russia.

That dilemma confronts every German in France. Life in the occupied country is getting constantly more unbearable for the conqueror. Yet it is still better than returning to active fighting. Troops from three divisions, in the Besançon region for a rest from the horrors of the Russian front, mutinied when they were ordered back. Sixty-two of them were executed on January 12, 1942. But the mutiny spread to neighboring garrisons. The soldiers, incidentally, were no slackers—they were willing to return if they were equipped with adequate winter clothing. The German authorities showed their understanding and called on the population of Besançon to sacrifice their own warm clothing. The sacrifice would not go unrewarded. It could be inferred that Besançon, by a generous response, could rid itself of the troops of occupation. Yet only two woolen sweaters and one pair of ski trousers were handed over. An effort to confiscate additional clothing was of no avail. Besançon, for a long time, has worn nothing but rags. Once more the New Order of looting and robbery had worked too efficiently for its own good.

How the German army has worked, and behaved, in occupied Russia was disclosed in one of the most terrible indictments in the history of warfare, released by the Russian Foreign Minister Viacheslav M. Molotov to the envoys of all countries with which Russia has diplomatic relations. Mr. Molotov charged the German armies and the German government with crimes ranging from the stealing of children's toys through rape to mass murder and mass destruction.

Mr. Molotov used approximately seven thousand words to describe incidents of "pillage, ruination of the people, and monstrous brutalities perpetrated by the German authorities everywhere on Russian territories they captured."

In an ominous reminder of the ensuing march of the Red Army toward Germany he detailed the German manner of war as it had been revealed by reports of troops who had retaken villages and towns. It was not, he said, the mere excesses of isolated and undisciplined military units or individual German officers and soldiers:

Abundant documentary material at the disposal of the Soviet Government testifies to the fact that plunder and ruination of the population accompanied by bestial outrages and massacres are widespread in all districts that fell under the heel of the German Nazis.

Irrefutable facts prove that the regime of plunder and sanguinary terrorism against the noncombatant population of occupied villages and towns represents a definite system devised beforehand and encouraged by the German Government and the German command, who consciously let loose in their army among officers and soldiers the basest bestial instincts.

The Soviet Government and its organs keep a detailed record of all the villainous crimes of Hitler's armies, for which the indignant Soviet people justly demand retribution and for which they will obtain it.

Mr. Molotov's note said further that over the entire front, from Finland to the Black Sea, the German armies "and their allies" had wreaked destruction and devastation. It told of entire towns utterly wiped out, such as Istra, Klin, and Rogachev on the Moscow front; it detailed the number of homes burned in villages, "in Baklanovo, sixty-six out of sixty-nine." It told how the Germans shot a seventy-year-old man because he pleaded, "Don't destroy my house!"

Next the note detailed individual and mass executions by the Germans and their display of bodies of their victims. "In the village of Volovo, in the Kursk region, a German officer hit the head of the two-year-old son of peasant Boikova against a wall and killed him because he was crying," the note said. "The base outraging of women and girls takes place everywhere in occupied districts." It went on to relate how German soldiers, officers and men, drunk and sober, had raped women and young girls before the eyes of their relatives, how girls had been dragged through the streets for mass rape, how an old priest holding the cross before his breast as he tried to save one group of girls had had his beard set on fire and then had been bayoneted to death.

The note charged that at Tikhvin on the Leningrad front a fifteen-year-old girl named Kolodetskaya wounded by a shell fragment and taken to a hospital, was raped by soldiers there until she died. Then it told of massacres in villages and the following cities: Kiev, more than 52,000 victims; Lvov, 6,000; Odessa, more than 8,000; Kamenets Podolsk, more than 8,500; Dnepropetrovsk, more than 10,500; Mariupol, more than 3,000, and Kerch, 7,000. For ten days, the Germans murdered on a mass scale at Rostov.

Finally the note related how the Germans had used women, children, and old men as shields for their "shock troops" against Russian fire.

Mr. Molotov concluded with the remark that the Russian people would never forget and never pardon what the Germans had done. Highly characteristic was his constant use of the word "Germans" in this important state document. It was never "Nazis" or "Hitlerite Germans" (the term previously used in Russian propaganda). This change of language tallies with reports from Polish sources about an interview between Stalin and General Sikorski, Premier of the Polish government in exile. When conversation between the two statesmen came to the point of reorganizing the world after victory, Stalin, the Polish Premier observed, showed not the slightest inclination to bolshevize the German nation. The Russian dictator believes that the Germans since their Nazification are beyond salvation. They cannot be reeducated, either to his own doctrine or to any other. They must be dealt with according to their own behavior.

In these words of one of the men who will certainly exercise profound influence on the shaping of things to come, the death knell is ringing for the German nation. It is true that Stalin only speaks and decides for himself, whereas the Atlantic Charter, our own magna charta of the freedom to come, knows no annihilation and extermination of nations.

But with their New Order of tyranny, slavery, and abject suppression, with the cannibalism they have introduced into warfare and civil life alike, with their offenses against God and their contempt for humankind, the Germans have piled up sin on sin, none of which will be forgotten. Today, they are still marching in formidable rows, they are still lording it over Europe, perhaps they are even still expanding for a while longer. But wherever they come, they come as fugitives from justice. They are restless, hounded by the millions who cry for vengeance. Every attack they make is but an escape into new uncertainties and perils. But there is no escape from the thing they have themselves wrought. Peace will come, but no peace is bestowed on them. Ahasuerus was a German.

PART III

REVOLT

CHAPTER SEVENTEEN

FRANCE

We have been vanquished. Do we wish to be despised also?
Do we wish to add the loss of honor to all our other losses?
This depends upon ourselves, and upon ourselves alone.
—JOHANN GOTTLIEB FICHTE, the German philosopher, in his
Speeches to the German Nation, during the period of Prussian humiliation at the hands of Napoleon.

WHEREAS the other occupied countries are fighting for their
freedom, France is still engaged in a struggle for her soul.
This statement, it is true, must be conditioned. It goes only
for Vichy-France. In the occupied three-fifths of the country
there is no division of opinion. With the exception of a thin
layer of *hommes vendues* (men for sale) hatred against the
Germans is unanimous, even if love for England, the European spearhead of the United Nations, is less general, because
of a deeply justified inferiority complex. Occupied France is
teeming with unrest. Germans in uniform venture onto the
streets at their own peril. Some provinces, particularly Normandy and Brittany, are on the brink of open revolution.

Unfortunately, this encouraging picture, heralding the rebirth of the *grande nation*, is offset by the complacency, the
apathy, the lethargy strangling the ironically called *zone libre*,
the liberty of which consists exclusively in the fact that the

Germans prefer wearing mufti when they cross the demarcation line.

Vichy-France is at this writing still formally represented by Marshal Henri Pétain, although he is now only the subservient front man. As in the case of Hitler and the German nation it is futile to ask whether the Marshal or his nation promoted the abysmal moral decay. They are bidding one another down. In the opinion of most people in the unoccupied zone Pétain can do no wrong. Strangely, this opinion is shared by many Frenchmen who vigorously oppose Nazism and collaboration. "On lui sert une mauvaise tasse de café" (They serve him a bad cup of coffee—that is, the venerable old man is being double-crossed), is an almost universal excuse given for him. A still stronger argument for Pétain is the legend of the unbreakable die-hard, the resolute grandfather, around whom the children, having lost father and mother, are gratefully gathering. Finally, many Frenchmen cling to Pétain as a drowning man clutches at any stray bit of wreckage.

Pétain, indeed, worked hard to enhance his prestige. His photographs are displayed everywhere. Every Vichy-controlled newspaper carries his likeness daily on the front page. Any shop in the "free zone" which does not want to incur the tax collector's wrath or get into trouble over its license, puts his picture in the middle of its show window; not much pressure need be exercised, since French shops now have few other goods to display. All messages dealing with the well-being of France are issued in Pétain's name. Christmas parcels for starving children, provided for by the taxpayers, are distributed with his greetings. When the Vatican persuaded the Nazis to delay the execution of one hundred French hostages, Vichy gave all the credit to Pétain. Since in the ensuing controversy, conducted most ceremoniously on both sides, the claim had to be dropped, Vichy resorted to the version that the Holy See had acted on Pétain's behalf.

No king of France has received more homage, and no politician more publicity. The Marshal shuns neither glory nor showmanship. "We, Henri Pétain . . ." is the form in which he addresses his people on more solemn occasions.

Is it all due to the Marshal's senile vanity? Pétain can plead that his transformation into a legendary character is necessary to keep intact the shabby remnants of Vichy even after the complete sell-out of April 15, 1942.

The affection and the esteem of France went to the man Pétain, but not to his government, nor to his regime—least of all to his philosophy. To the war-weary people of unoccupied France he was the trustee who kept them out of the war. To history Henri Pétain will be known as a lifelong defeatist, whose hatred of the republican and democratic system has, for decades, overridden even the semblance of patriotism.

The first fifty-seven years of his life passed all but unnoticed. His life in public began when his career seemed at an end. In 1912 Colonel Henri Pétain was retired to the fate of a disgruntled Colonel Blimp, French style. The First World War offered him a new opportunity. He emerged from this war as the hero of Verdun. It was the first Pétain legend. Actually, the record proves that Joffre had to exercise all his tenacity to keep Pétain from giving up Verdun. The correspondence and memoirs of the men who at that time worked intimately with Pétain testify to his having been a congenital defeatist throughout that war. As early as 1916 he was pressing France to betray her allies and conclude a separate peace. In 1918, when Ludendorff launched his big offensive, threatening to sever the British army from the French, Pétain lost his head entirely. The only solution he could see was to leave the British in the lurch and retreat to Paris. All Clemenceau's energy and Foch's stout heart were necessary to keep him in line. After the meeting at Doullens, where it was decided to replace Pétain with Foch in order to keep on fighting, Clemenceau said: "I found two men: Pétain, who told me all was up with us, and Foch, who was striding about like a madman, all agog to fight. Let's try Foch, I thought. We shall at least die gun in hand."

The opinion of all, both French and English, who knew Pétain during the first war, was equally low. Weygand hated him. Neither Joffre nor Foch, neither Lloyd George nor Field Marshal Haig went to great pains to conceal his contempt. Winston Churchill, then Minister of Munitions, refused to avail himself of Clemenceau's invitation to have dinner with Pétain. In his memories of that war, written many years afterward, he called him a "cold, frigid, scientific soldier." Still, this characterization was, in Churchill's well known friendly manner, a slight overstatement. Pétain displayed his scientific soldiery only in obstinately sticking to obsolete strategical views, opposing aviation, and rejecting the use of tanks when, after 1919, as a member of the Supreme War Council he played an important and unfortunate role in the reshaping of the French army.

General de Gaulle was perfectly justified in expressing the following opinion: "The explanation for Pétain must be looked for in his personality. I have known him for a long time. Let's not forget that he belongs to the old French school, and that he is still observing the traditions of the Franco-Prussian War of 1870. He employed the methods of this war in 1914, and had not the slightest understanding that the mechanized warfare of 1939 was a totally different proposition. He tried to wage war with the mentality of a man of eighty. Nothing but catastrophe could possibly result. Moreover, he was always a pessimist, only seeing the bad side of things and events."

Nevertheless, Pétain has always seen on which side his bread is buttered. After the Fascist upflare of February 6, 1934, the overaged war horse made a tardy appearance in politics. He entered the Doumergue cabinet as Minister for War. Political power came late to him, and tasted doubly sweet. Soon he was spoken of in reactionary salons as the "savior of France." He was introduced and interpreted as the possible opposite number to Germany's Führer, minus Hitler's regrettable vices. To stress his simon-pure quality Pétain, already in his seventies, made it his habit to attend the Holy Mass regularly. The defeat of the plotting reactionaries at the elections of 1936 was a blessing for France; but the Front Populaire came into power, which was considerably less of a blessing. In the ensuing general turmoil a rightist plot was slowly hatched for the downfall of the Republic and a fascist coup d'état. Laval was the brains and heart of this conspiracy; but Pétain, who has always disclaimed active co-operation, did not object to being the standard-bearer.

When the war broke out Daladier sent the aged Marshal as ambassador to General Franco; he had seen through the intrigue, and preferred to keep for himself the chance of establishing a dictatorship—some observers believe, even at the price of a separate peace. But Daladier, too, was swept overboard. Paul Reynaud took the helm and Pétain, who during his stay in Madrid had gone entirely fascist, became his Vice Premier. The day of this appointment was May 18, 1940. It was the day of France's downfall. The treason and surrender of Bordeaux was nothing more than an epilogue.

Pétain launched his defeatist campaign on his first day in office. Working openly in the Council of Ministers, and secretly through agents in parliament and press, he helped Laval poison the whole country with the theory that the war was lost, France already beaten, Hitler the master of Europe, and the British Empire in its death struggle. French morale, already at its lowest ebb, fell away entirely. The world saw the macabre spectacle of a ghost triumphantly hoisting his flag on the grave of his country.

The shameful behavior of the Vichy government, even as long as it was Pétain's one-man show, is on the record. Step by step the Marshal bent back before the boche, the more ruthlessly to cement his domestic dictatorship. His every conference with Hitler or Göring was another milestone on France's way to servitude. The French people, however, were made to believe that the Marshal was simply playing for time. Pétain liked to appear as the man who had saved them from catastrophe and who was keeping France on the path of honor, after his predecessors had betrayed her and England had abandoned her—which, incidentally, did not cause him to renounce the annuity of twenty-four hundred dollars which he still receives from the Canada Life Association through its London branch. Prostrate with grief, France began to think: Perhaps he is right. After all, a Marshal of France does not lie. He cannot be deceiving us . . . Thus the Pétain legend gained substance once more.

This double game continued until Pétain was confronted with facts he could no longer dodge. Until a short time ago, at least, he was convinced that Hitler would win the war. He repeated this conviction even to the then American ambassador in Vichy, Admiral Leahy. Hence Pétain's consent to the Nazi penetration of Morocco and the French colonies in Africa, which serve as supply bases and route of transportation for General Rommel's army in Libya; hence his handing over Indo-China to the Japanese, contrasting amazingly with the fratricidal resistance he ordered against the liberation of Syria by the joint Free French and British contingents. Pétain is an undisguised adherent of the Axis system. The reforms his own "National Revolution" tried to introduce, primarily his constitution and his labor charter, are undiluted New Order.

Throughout his shabby shadow rule Pétain was cornered, the prisoner of his own treason. In mid-April, 1942, Hitler put on the heat. He did not even allow the aged Marshal to resign. For the time being Pétain has to continue as the legendary figure, still with the title of Chief of State. But he is shorn of every influence. All the power, meaning the complete and absolute right to lick the Führer's boots, rests with Laval. A desperate ruse of expiring Vichy tries to sell the world Admiral Darlan, who, thus far, remains Pétain's heir apparent and commander in chief of France's armed forces, as a sort of corrective. But the democracies would have to be still much more gullible than they, alas, have been throughout long years to accept the archenemy of yesterday as the white hope of tomorrow. In fact, it makes not the slightest difference to the world who of the Unholy Trinity will make the asthmatic race for Hitler's grace. All three, Pétain, Darlan, and Laval, have sold out France, lock, stock, and barrel. The physical life of all the three depends on a Nazi victory. They do not object to Vichy being no longer even a shadow state, but simply a Nazi fiction. Vichy burst like a soap bubble—with the difference that soap, after all, is clean.

Sharply contrasting with the confusion—to use the mildest expression—prevailing among most of the people of Vichy, is the resolution of the occupied zone to rid itself of the jack boot. This statement involves no moral judgment. Paris is no holier than Vichy. In fact, all France with a few outstanding exceptions (all of whom are today in De Gaulle's camp) has to shoulder a collective guilt which, for charity's sake, shall not be analyzed. The burden of defeat, however, weighs more heavily on the occupied zone which, from invasion day to this moment, has been in an absurdly anomalous position. The occupied zone is ruled jointly by a refugee government which must feed the people, and by occupation authorities who tax, pillage, and do their best to annihilate them. This very condition stultified from the outset the application of Pétain's National Revolution in occupied France. The strongest and most honest rule could not have established a stable order in a country separated from the world, almost two-thirds occupied, and entirely dependent for its future on the outcome of the war. The effort to give emergency measures (the only ones applicable) a deeper and ideologic sense would have miscarried even if these measures had expressed honest conviction instead of double crossing and desperate compromise.

For occupied France the situation has been clear ever since that day of national shame, June 16, 1940—the surrender at Bordeaux. The nation, which had viciously thrown away its chance in an open fight, now had to choose between shutting up, with gradual strangulation, and infinitely self-sacrificing, seemingly hopeless resistance of bare fists against tanks and Stuka divers, to say nothing of cannibal cruelty and cunning, Nazism's sharpest weapon.

Three elements decided the French people's stand. The first was the glory that is England. By her singlehanded fight against crushing odds from the summer of 1940 to the summer of 1941 Great Britain, indeed, saved the world. The example she set kindled the flame of freedom throughout the realm of civilization. The light from across the Channel illuminated even the darkness that blacked out France. When the R.A.F. beat off the Luftwaffe and Hitler's invasion failed to materialize, hope returned everywhere to human hearts; the subjugated European continent was electrified, and France had again a reasonable expectation of revival; at least she could see a distant aim, well worth fighting for.

The second element, undoubtedly, was the thousand years of proud French history, which a single abject generation, the French people before and during the war, could mar, but not destroy. The sell-out, brought about by the leadership of almost every political camp, aided and abetted by almost all the people, could not deliver the goods: the soul of France.

The third element inviting, nay, enforcing resistance was Herr Adolf Hitler himself. His insatiable greed is always his undoing. France is a test case. Had he not overreached himself, he would have stood a good chance of compromising with the people when most of them were ready to compromise with the devil if only he would let them *gagner sa vie* (make a living)—the slogan of the French war generation. But Adolf Hitler is congenitally unable to let other people make a living, after his own people have abandoned human living for the mechanical function of cogs. In Paris, the Führer's field-gray and brown-shirted hordes instituted what Berlin called the "organization of misery." The locusts swept the garden of France.

The students' demonstration on Armistice Day, 1940, not quite three months after the surrender of Bordeaux, was the first indication of deep-seated unrest, the French answer to German tyranny. But the shooting on this occasion was all done from the German side. Although the best French elements were already willing to sacrifice themselves, the nation was not yet in a revolutionary mood. Five months later large French crowds appeared more determined. Two hundred thousand citizens of Marseilles demonstrated on the anniversary of the day King Alexander of Yugoslavia and Louis Barthou, France's Foreign Minister and elder statesman, were killed by Fascist assassins in the city. Marseilles, on that day, was teeming with Gestapo. The German and Italian members of the Armistice commission had called out their platoons. Yet some flowers weighing six hundred pounds were placed at the foot of the memorial to the victims of the Fascist crime, in front of the Town Hall. At seven A.M. a delegation from the university and representatives of the railroad workers brought magnificent bouquets tied with ribbons in the colors of the tricolor. By midday traffic had to be stopped around the Town Hall. Large groups of shopgirls arrived singing the strictly forbidden "Marseillaise." At four P.M. all the students of the university gathered there. They were wearing in their lapels the Cross of Lorraine (the symbol of Free France) and deposited another huge bunch of flowers with the inscription: "From the students of a grateful France to their Serbian brothers." Toward six o'clock the police, by order of the infuriated Germans, tried to disperse the crowds. They could not break up the wall of human bodies. All night the "Marseillaise" rose to the darkened skies.

Hitler refused to see the writing on the wall. His pressure on France increased. Of course he chose to apply it at the point of least resistance. The noose around Pétain's neck was drawn tighter. France went through an uneasy spring and early summer of 1941, while Pétain breathed with increasing difficulty. The aged Marshal, however, had enough breath left to deliver a speech on August 13, 1941, declaring total submission. He appointed Darlan his heir apparent, and vested him with almost limitless powers. Pétain had crossed the bridge. France was to become part and parcel of the New Order.

The country answered with an outcry. The favorable impression made by Laval's dismissal on December 13, which had helped Pétain to regain much lost ground among his people, was now entirely offset. A network of secret organizations sprang up throughout France. The theory of direct action became popular. Activists went systematically to work. The people, feeling abandoned, realized that everything rested on them. Plain men and women rose to leadership of incipient revolutionary movements. Forgetting their old struggles, the socialist and the Catholic parties—both outlawed, but both maintaining their organizations underground—agreed on common action. They decided on two points. They would appeal to the French civilians and soldiers in the colonies, and they would call on the more militant forces in France itself.

Vichy adopted violent countermeasures. One of Darlan's first ukases replaced all the officers on General Nogues's staff in Morocco by reactionaries from the Action Française. Simultaneously a thin voice from Morocco came to his aid. Henri, Comte de Paris, pretender to the nonexistent Lilac banner throne, sent an appeal from his North African exile: "I urge all Frenchmen to rally around the Marshal's colors." This appeal, further developments have proved, has definitely ruined the always slim chance of a royal restoration in France.

Confusion at the top, explosiveness at the bottom—Hitler enjoyed the spectacle. The French, it seemed to him, were about to devour one another. They would save him a good deal of work. The German army of occupation was ordered to maintain strict neutrality in the fight between the "legal authorities" and the "Jewish-Communist-Freemason, pro-British and De Gaullist mob." But this order was of no avail. Hitler can rightly complain, as indeed he does, that democracy has always forced the struggle on him. On the evening of August 23, 1941, a "neutral" German soldier was shot on the streets of Paris. For the first time German blood stained the pavement of the boulevards. On the same day the railway station at Juvisy-sur-Orge, near Paris, where an important German garrison was stationed, was dynamited, and railwaymen in Lyons refused to load cars for Germany.

Terrified of Hitler, Vichy mustered all the forces of punishment and persuasion for a counterblow. All the public buildings in Lyons were occupied by police, the Garde Publique (the National Guard), and Pétain's semiprivate Légion de Combattants. Minister of Justice Berthelot disclosed that repeated acts of sabotage had already occurred; he announced that energetic measures would now be taken. Fernand de Brinon, Laval's chief agent and, by the same token, Pétain's ambassador in Paris, pleaded on the radio with the saboteurs. He was about the last man to whom the French people would listen. The troops returning from Syria to Paris were received at the Gare Saint-Lazare by crowds howling "A bas Vichy!" (Down with Vichy!) The uproar turned into a hunger demonstration. "Give us bread!" shouted thousands of women. The police gave them bullets instead. Six demonstrators were killed at the Gare Saint-Lazare and twenty-four wounded. But no informer was found for the prize of one and one-half million francs which Vichy offered for denunciation of the "rabble rousers" who had staged the demonstration.

Despite the assassination of a German soldier, the situation in Paris still looked like mere French civil war. However, events in the country soon proved that Hitler had once more triumphed too early. Startling news came from Brittany, always the spearhead in the French struggle for freedom. The village curés, it appeared, had organized a moral offensive under the parole: The troops of occupation are entitled to the quarters in which they are billeted, but to no kind of comfort! It was a roundabout way to introduce passive resistance, which spread like wildfire throughout the "forbidden" zone. The port of Le Havre, which is a center of this forbidden zone, is, next to Brest, Germany's most important U-boat base in France. Major von Bartenwerffer, the local German commander, ruled the town with an iron fist. Suddenly, his tactics did not work any longer. On August 25, at dawn, a few hundred houses bore revolutionary inscriptions and caricatures of a Teutonic type impudently resembling the local tyrant. The Nazified local evening paper, the *Petit Havre*, tried to gloss over the incident: "It is just a sign of the small mentality of a small band of small vanquished." But Major von Bartenwerffer accepted no excuse. Nor did he trouble to search out the malefactors. "The whole population of Havre is responsible," he stated, thus introducing the principle of collective responsibility in France that was immediately adopted by all the Nazi authorities in the occupied country. Indiscriminately, twenty citizens of Le Havre were shot on the same day, at dusk.

Three days later, on August 28, another twenty-eight Frenchmen were executed in the fortress at Besançon, for alleged conspiracy against the power of occupation. Among them was the painter André Geuziec and an officer named De Tremel. There was one other man among the victims of Besançon whose blood, it can be assumed, will be avenged on the men of Vichy. His name was Marius Vallet. He came from Marseilles, and led one of the first bands of activists in

France. The Gestapo caught him. His life was spared for a
few weeks, since the German authorities wanted him for a
show trial before their military tribunal. Marius profited from
this respite. On April 23, he broke jail. He had a hairbreadth
escape across the demarcation line. Exhausted, he surrendered
to the French police. Vichy was embarrassed. The people,
hearing via grapevine of Marius Vallet's good luck, were jubilant. All Marseilles drank his good health in public. Marius,
hitherto a beached sailor, was on his way to becoming a
national hero.

But Herr Krug von Nidda, then recently appointed German consul general in Vichy, who had established his office
a stone's throw away from the American embassy, had a talk
with Pucheu, then Vichy Minister of the Interior and Public
Security. Pucheu proved on this occasion that he was about to
become the most sinister character of Vichy. He delivered
Marius Vallet to the German bloodhounds. Another life ended
before the firing squad in the square of the Besançon fortress.

The Germans now carried out their executions as if on the
assembly line. Between August 23 and October 3, seventy-
one men were shot in the occupied zone. The names of only
sixty of them were announced. Simultaneously the Gestapo
enlisted a group of youthful hoodlums to commit anti-Semitic
outrages such as until then had been entirely unknown in
France. The French people did not conceal their disgust. But
their attention was diverted by a much more sensational event.
Paul Collette, a young man from Brittany, enlisted as a volunteer for the antibolshevist crusade. On August 27, when
Pierre Laval came to inspect the recruits, Collette drew a gun,
and riddled Laval with six bullets.

Laval got away with his life. The gun of the would-be
avenger had been an old, obsolete model, and the bullets inflicted only minor wounds on the traitor, which seemed
symbolic for this revolution of stout hearts and miserable
weapons. Yet the assault on Laval brought a showdown. Col-

lette was immediately condemned to death. But the people made ready for another storming of the bastille. They would, of course, have been mowed down by German machine guns. Among other consequences, large-scale bloodshed would have meant the instantaneous collapse of the Pétain regime. So the Marshal displayed his mercy. Collette was asked why he had not fired on the German officer accompanying Laval. He answered: "Why, this man was only doing his duty. It was the traitor I wanted to get." This sentence offered a good talking point with the Nazi authorities. Otto Abetz, German ambassador in Paris and a veteran propagandist, immediately grasped the value of having a French martyr at hand who attested that German officers in France were only doing their duty. He decided that the assault had been an internal French affair, thus permitting Pétain to commute Collette's death sentence to life imprisonment. Very cautiously, Laval himself had pleaded for this act of mercy. He wanted, obviously, to escape renewed assaults by making a grand gesture.

Paris had tasted blood; now it wanted more. No longer were the incessant provocations of the German bullies answered with a docile shrug. A colonel of the army of occupation, riding in the subway, protested noisily when his fellow riders lifted their hats or got up from their seats as the car stopped at the King George station. His face flushed purple in the best manner of a Teuton beer addict. Two minutes later it was very pale. A cut artery leads to rapid loss of blood. At the next station the car was empty. The colonel's body was not found before the terminus was reached.

A German noncommissioned officer wanted to force a French girl—his "fiancée," he claimed boisterously—to enter a hotel in the Rue de Strasbourg with him. Passers-by beat him up so badly that his body could not be identified.

Both cases were of the same character, both were impulse-murder, swift punishment for the provocative behavior of the German swaggerers. However, these two eruptions of spontaneous indignation gave General Ernst von Schaumburg the welcome pretext to declare war, not exactly on France, but on the French people. He issued a decree containing but two sentences: All the French people arrested by German authorities would henceforth be considered as hostages. On the renewal of criminal acts, hostages corresponding in number to the gravity of the acts would be shot.

This decree was published on the same front pages of September 1, which also contained an announcement by the Health Council of the Seine Department:

Child mortality in Paris has risen more than 50 per cent above prewar level. The cause is armistice skinniness. Mortality among the newborn is higher than 9 per cent. Every tenth child born in this year will die in its infancy.

Thus began what Herr Otto Abetz called "the electric days." The people got out of hand. The Nazis tightened their grip, with Vichy obediently trailing the masters. Stroke and counterstroke, events succeeded one another so rapidly that soon they were inextricably mingled. Chaos replaced causality.

The army of occupation was spread thin all over the occupied zone. Even the tiniest village was now garrisoned. The slightest sign of resentment brought a punishment that soon became customary: the people were deprived of food. Theoretically, the meat ration in the autumn of 1941 was still thirteen ounces a week; since then it has been reduced by half. But this ration existed only on paper. The Germans seized 80 per cent of all available foodstuffs. Fat and grinning, they walked into the shops—in front of which the civilian customers, particularly the housewives, had been queueing up since dawn—and left with large parcels under their arms. Some German soldiers acquired the habit of biting into large pieces of butter as if it were bread, preferably before famine-stricken onlookers. Everywhere new devices for humiliating the civilian population were introduced. In Paris, for instance, the Opéra was reserved for the Germans. French theatergoers were crammed into the top gallery.

Yet it was impossible to cow the people. Numerous German enunciations proved it. One of the most amusing was printed in the *Dépêche* of Brest, by order of the German *Kommandantur:*

> The people are forbidden to wear the tricolor emblem in public. They are strictly forbidden to insult the Italians, in particular the Italian Vice Consul in Brest, Signor Vittori Job. If the Vice Consul should be insulted anew, the city of Brest will be forced to pay a fine of 50,000 francs for each insult. Acts such as throwing stones and debris on German soldiers will be repressed with extreme severity. If the culprits are not discovered, the community will be subject to considerable punishment.

The gravest menace to the German tyranny arose on the labor front. French industry plays an important role in the German war effort. Renault and Citroën produce trucks, tanks, and cars; Latil and the seized French Ford works, trucks; the Somma Company, tanks; Hispano-Suiza and Gnome et Rhône, aero engines—all, of course, with the full consent of Vichy. But the workers did not consent. The go-slow movement spread rapidly, production dropped. In some cases the Germans resorted to punitive measures. In the Toulouse Cartridge Factory, newly equipped with German machinery for the production of bombers, the entire personnel was arrested and taken to a concentration camp. It was replaced by Indo-Chinese workers under the supervision of German overseers.

Such ruthless acts only provoked renewed repercussions. An important plant in the suburb of Paris, producing electric parts for the German army, was set on fire on September 2. Three men were caught in this sabotage. But they were armed. They shot at the police who showed no wish for a fight, and escaped. Immediately afterwards another mysterious fire destroyed the Graff factory in Versailles, causing a loss of ten million francs. In a forest ten miles away from Vichy a cache of bombs and large quantities of cheddite, used for explosives, was discovered. Was the danger approaching as near as that? "I feel an ill wind rising in many parts of France," Pétain said on the radio. Simultaneously, his government promised a reward of one million francs for the discovery of saboteurs of the Paris railway system.

Prizes for informers were rising. The Gestapo spread word among the apaches of Paris that assassination of well known enemies of the state, particularly of notorious Jews, was a paying proposition. The Socialist Senator, Marx Dormoy, former Minister of the Interior in the Popular Front Cabinet, had a long black beard; his complexion was dark; his first name Marx, suspicious. Vichy had confined him to home arrest, which he spent in a small hotel, pending his trial by the Court of Riom. Here was the obvious victim for an anti-Semitic plot. One morning his shabby hotel room was a ruin, and the body of Marx Dormoy, terribly mangled. He had been killed by an infernal machine.

No other crime aroused the French people quite so much. Marx Dormoy—incidentally as good an Aryan as any one, scion of a long line of French peasants, and bearing his suspicious first name only because his father had been an admirer of Karl Marx—was among the most popular leaders of French labor. Vichy hurried to disapprove of the crime. For the first and so far the last time its police hunted Fascist killers. They were found in Nice two weeks after they had committed their murder. Ives Moynier, aged twenty-seven, was the leader of the gang. The others were Louis Guyon, twenty-six, a mechanic from Marseilles; Horace Vaillant, twenty-one, a driver; Maurice Marbach, twenty-eight, student; Ludovic Guichard, twenty-seven, traveling salesman; and, adding a romantic touch, Françoise Salisette, a colored belle from French Guiana. All had been members of Doriot's Popular party; but all were dead when the police found them. They had been dabbling negligently with their own infernal machines—at least, this was the official version. All France, of course, was convinced that the Gestapo once more had found a way to do away with blunted tools.

Indiscriminately the Gestapo was ravaging the country to break down the increasing resistance. No one was sure of his life. French convents were forced to release three hundred English and Canadian nuns, who subsequently were dumped in the concentration camp at Vittel, near the Alsatian border. At present this camp "shelters" another thousand British women, a hundred aged Englishmen, fifteen children of British parents, and, to be on the safe side, all the English pupils from an exclusive finishing school in Rouen. Father Price, a British Catholic priest, was arrested at Tarbes, and sent to a concentration camp. A score of his French brothers, accused of having worked for Pétain's overthrow, were interned at Vals-les-Bains.

The German-Vichy collaboration in persecution was revealed by Joseph Barthelemy, Vichy Minister of the Interior, who announced on September 11 that thirty-four thousand French political offenders were held in French prisons, a large part of them by the Gestapo, in addition to those in concentration camps. This information, he hoped, would serve as a warning.

It did not serve as a warning. An hour after Barthelemy had spoken to his betrayed nation a German officer, leaving the Théâtre des Ambassadeurs on the Champs Elysées in Paris, was struck from behind with a bludgeon, and gravely injured. Four days later a German noncommissioned officer was shot at the subway station Boulevard Sébastopol. Among the hostages immediately executed in retaliation, was a boy of seventeen, and an old man of seventy-two. Colonel Alfred Heurteaux, vice president of Pétain's Legion of Combatants,

delivered a speech of protest, not against the shooting of innocent hostages but against the patriotic assassins who forced
the Germans to take "severe but justified" measures. When
he returned home from the protest meeting, he missed his
boy. The French underground movement works fast. The
traitor's son had been kidnaped while his father was still
spreading his poison at the gathering of the Legion. No trace
of young Heurteaux was ever found.

On September 11, according to a German communiqué,
terrorist headquarters were discovered in the very heart of
Paris, between the Place de la République and the Place de la
Bastille. The Gestapo followed up this discovery with a house-
to-house search, covering all Paris. General von Schaumburg
announced that any one might now be shot as a hostage. No
longer would only Jews, Freemasons, and Communists be
liquidated. On the next day the fortress square of the Château
de Vincennes, where Mata Hari was executed, was "reopened" by the Germans and baptized with the blood of
twelve hostages. Almost every day of September was marked
with red letters. On the 19th two cases of sabotage on the
grand scale occurred. In the rich rural district around Char-
tres, fifty-five miles southwest of Paris, five big barns containing wheat for the German army burned down, and field
fires destroyed most of the unharvested crop. On the same
evening ten men wrecked several German troop transport
cars in a garage on the Boulevard Gouvion-Saint-Cyr near
the Porte de Champerret, in Paris. The perpetrators escaped,
but eight hostages were shot.

The R.A.F. raided Bordeaux heavily on September 24. A
few hours after the raiders had left, new explosions occurred
in two plants, a furniture factory working for the German
barracks and an alcohol distillery serving the German officers'
mess. These explosions, investigation proved, were not caused
by delayed bombs, but by sabotage. Word spread that some
of the inhabitants of Bordeaux, mostly women, had helped

two downed R.A.F. fliers to escape. This time General von Stülpnagel, the commander in chief of the army of occupation, went into action himself. His announcement to the French public was the habitual German mixture of threats and bribes. He warned women who helped R.A.F. pilots that they would have to spend the rest of their lives in German concentration camps. By the same token he offered ten thousand francs to any civilian who would deliver an English pilot, dead or alive.

On September 28, twenty-eight French patriots were arrested in Arras, and dispatched to a concentration camp. Two days later the Gestapo raided the sanatorium at Champrosay near Paris, and took away nine patients. The centers of resistance, in these days, proved to be Paris and Lille. In the latter city German military trains were dynamited. In retribution twenty railroad employees were arrested and executed as "Communists," although none could be convicted of ever having belonged to the party, and despite the fact that none was living in Lille itself. They all could prove that they had been sleeping soundly in their little home towns in the mining and textile region near the Belgian border in the night the German military trains were blown up.

To purge Paris, two hundred policemen "whose attitude was not in accord with the national revolution," were dropped from the ranks. The dismissals were ordered by the then Minister of the Interior Pucheu; he termed it the first measure of French self-defense. Another of these measures was the establishment of a civic guard whose members had to watch the railway tracks day and night. If there were any further cases of sabotage, the members of the detachment in whose beat the damage occurred would be held responsible. The result was that on the first night in which the newly established guard was on duty a German troop train ran into a steel cable stretched across the tracks at Puteaux, the industrial suburb of Paris. The train was derailed and wrecked. Hundreds of German soldiers were gravely injured. The civic guard of Puteaux was to be arrested, but the Paris police let them escape. Pucheu raged. He dismissed the Prefect of the Paris Police, replacing him with René Bard, another of Darlan's desk admirals, and an abject creature of the Nazis.

The unrest prevailing in early autumn was analyzed in a report made by several prefects of occupied departments to the Vichy delegation in Paris. Although it was confidential a copy of it reached the United States. The authors are, of course, all collaborationists, subservient to the power of occupation; and a testimony from them to the extent of the people's resistance should carry particular weight. The report states:

Fifteen death sentences in the last fortnight must unfortunately be registered, nearly all in Paris and the northern departments. In most cases the sentences are for spying or help given in crossing the demarcation line. Also in the north fifteen sentences of hard labor were imposed for participation in strikes. Two hundred persons have been interned in Germany for the same reasons and four hundred and fifty detentions were invoked in Pas-de-Calais. In this same Department M. Devin, a teacher of physical education, has been sentenced to eighteen months' imprisonment for beating a German officer. At Calais four pupils of the Teachers School have been sentenced to two, five, and twelve months for listening to foreign broadcasts. Mlle. le Gall, a teacher at La Rochelle, has been sentenced to four months in prison for having said that Brest had been bombed by the Germans. At Lisieux, young Didelot was sentenced to two months in prison after he was found in possession of a copy book in which he had written injurious things about Germany. At Nogent-le-Rotrou, several young men have been sentenced to from six months' to two years' imprisonment for booing a German propaganda film. In Meurthe-et-Moselle, the Mayor of Hannonville has been sentenced to one month of prison for harboring the intention of helping evading prisoners. The prefect of Vienne reports that the military tribunal in his Department continues to inflict numerous and frequent sentences varying from fines to imprisonment, and that the inhabitants react very strongly against this. At Vire, a director of a school has been arrested for having proffered insults against the German army. In the Cher, M. Jacquet, a railway inspector and Mayor of Marmagne, has been imprisoned for listening to a British broadcast. At Lille, M. Pauce, Professor at the University of Medicine, has been arrested. At Saint-Martin all the teachers have been arrested because the pupils had sung the "Marche Lorraine" when leaving school. In the Aisne Department thirty detentions have been invoked during June. The Prefect of Calvados reports that more than four hundred persons are actually in the town prison. This town was fined one million francs after a telephonic cable had been cut and various acts of sabotage had been reported.

This report, probably, caused the otherwise unexplained outcry of the official Vichy news agency on September 30: "We can expect to see street fighting multiply." The Germans certainly did their best to provoke it. The streets of Paris were patrolled by motorcyclists with orders to shoot on sight at the smallest incident. Suspects were subjected to the worst indignities. They had, for instance, to spend their nights shining the shoes of the German soldiers. Measures of retaliation increased in severity. The mere writing of an anti-Nazi slogan on a wall was now punished by death. So was the harboring of fugitives from German "justice." Martin Poirier was shot for helping a few French prisoners of war who had escaped to cross the Vichy border. Women too were put to death. Mme. Henriette Schmidt of Belfort, and Mme. Marie Theresa Fleury, wife of a former Paris Municipal Councilor, were executed for harboring the Communist ex-deputy Emile Dutilleul. Whereupon a Vichy tribunal in Clermont-Ferrand, not to be bested, sentenced eleven persons to prison terms of ten to twenty years for alleged Communist activities. Gabriel Peri, one of the former chiefs of the Communist party, was tried and sentenced by a specially established "Communist Court" in Paris. In Amiens, forty-five other alleged Communists were interned in the concentration camp. Meanwhile the purge of the Paris police continued. Twenty high police officials were discharged. Collaborators got their jobs. One of those, Commissioner Depit, was seriously wounded by two shots as he entered his new office for the first time. In Roubaix two business agents of the German High Command were shot. The town was fined five million francs.

All this happened during the last days of September. *Regime Fascista*, Mussolini's mouthpiece, reviewing the situation in neighboring France, had to admit:

A vast clandestine struggle is developing against German organizations and individuals. During the last week alone twelve acts of sabotage were committed in some of the largest factories of Paris. Wholesale arrests are becoming increasingly frequent. During the same week 1,570 people were arrested. Yet no abatement of resistance is discernible.

It is impossible to list even a small part of the bloody incidents that followed in October. René Darreau, of Vendôme, was executed on a charge of illegally possessing a revolver and ten cartridges. Léon Albert Liust was shot for "aiding the enemy through activity against the forces of occupation." Charles Darrell had stolen a German rifle and 196 bullets at the railway station at Vayres, near Paris. The commander of the local German garrison displayed his sense of humor by shooting the culprit, without troubling the courts, with the very rifle that had been stolen. In a house near the Austerlitz station in Paris, Marie Meslar, mother of four children, had hidden stacks of a tract called "France Is Being Pillaged." Being a woman, she was not shot, but hanged.

The gallows and the firing squads worked overtime. On October 7, the German High Command in Paris boastfully disclosed that the seventy-third execution in the month had just been carried out—that of Alfred Bartin, Belgian, in reprisal for an attack on a German soldier. For three days the High Command was silent on the score. On October 10, red posters announced: "*Number 84*, Gaston Pinot of Courmelles,

Aisne Department, was shot for having hidden a machine gun." The next day the Germans divulged that in raids and police operations in Paris alone seventy-six thousand five hundred persons had been searched and questioned—eleven hundred of them arrested for various violations.

But this time the teamwork between the Nazis and the French serfs was not so well coordinated. The Paris police prefecture, a stronghold of collaborationism, published different statistics. According to Admiral Bard, no fewer than 8,849 persons had been arrested during the past few days: 7,749 for possessing arms, 1,100 for Communist and De Gaulle activities.

A short but heated argument between the brothers in crime ensued, in which the Nazis did most of the talking. They accused the French police of "misdirecting orders, muddling commands, and giving loose instructions." These charges were printed in the Nazi-controlled press, obviously under German direction. "Is there a new kind of sabotage going on?" the super-Nazi *Œuvre* asked. "Are there still Marxists, De Gaullists, democrats, or Christians influenced by Jews left in our service?"

Admiral Darlan hurried to Paris to assure that no one belonging to those despicable groups was left. He did not find much credence. The Paris police force was still riddled with Communists, he was told, in spite of both the preceding purges. Darlan was urgently in need of an alibi. He conferred with his creatures. On October 16, a plot to dynamite the entire Paris underground system was discovered. If this sensational plot was not manufactured by Darlan's police, it was at least largely exaggerated by them in order to get a clean bill of health from the Nazis. The facts were these: One of the numerous Free French cells, spread all over the country, had its headquarters in a subway station. Lucien Noël, the stationmaster, was the head of this particular group. Like

all Free Frenchmen who are arming themselves against the day
of revolution, Noël and his group had stored arms, including,
ironically, German Mauser rifles and submachine guns and revolvers bought from mercenary German officers and soldiers.
(In France, where all trade is done on the black bourse, there
is also a black market for German arms. A machine gun
embezzled from the army of occupation will bring 1,100
francs on the average, and a rifle or revolver with a hundred
rounds of ammunition 450 to 660 francs.) In addition, Noël's
cache contained a hundred pounds of dynamite from a German-owned quarry near Chantilly, twenty miles north of
Paris. The trapped men admitted frankly that they had
amassed the weapons for the day of glory. But they denied
persistently the alleged plot to dynamite Paris. This accusation was certainly a product of Darlan's fertile imagination,
and of his panicky fear of being dropped, or even liquidated,
by his German paymasters. Darlan is perfectly aware that he
is surrounded by enemies, even in his own camp. Now the Admiral had his reassuring success. He was quick to make the
most of it. The Paris dynamite plot became his *cause célèbre*.

On his return to Vichy he persuaded Pétain to press the
campaign against the political enemies of the regime. The
Marshal did not need much persuasion. In an effort to halt
anti-German terrorism and sabotage—this was the official version—Pétain established special courts, which went to work
with lightning speed. Immediately the special court in Toulouse handed down twenty-five convictions for illegal political activities, with sentences ranging up to fifteen years of
hard labor. Another court at Marseilles sent six persons to an
undisclosed penal colony. Six others were sentenced by a
Pétain court at Douai, in the occupied zone. Indeed, the Marshal's tribunals stepped on the gas. They sat in court in day-
and-night shifts. Their deliberations took five minutes. On
October 17, Vichy could proudly announce that more than

thirty thousand persons in France had been sentenced to death or imprisonment since the establishing of the courts by the Chief of State, Marshal Henri Pétain.

The only trouble was that most of the convicted men and women were small fry. Another *cause célèbre* was badly needed. This led to the arrest of six famous French scientists who had never concealed their hatred for the Nazis and their contempt for the latter's French lackeys. All six were members of the Academy of Sciences. The first victim was Paul Langevin, Nobel prize winner for physics, whom the Gestapo had already arrested a few months previously, but released on parole after a storm of protests. Next came Professor Jean Villey of the Paris Faculty of Science, a brother of the former Prefect of the Seine Department. He was charged with spreading De Gaullist propaganda. His son and daughter were arrested on the same charge. The others were Emile Borel, aged seventy, professor of mathematics at the University of Paris, and once French Minister of the Navy; further Aimé Cotton, the celebrated discoverer of magnetic birefringence; Charles Mauguin, the most prominent crystallographer in France, and Louis Lapique, emeritus professor of physiology at the University of Paris.

Educated and scientific circles all over the world were outraged by the arrest of these savants whose only crime consisted of refusing to share in the sell-out of France. From every quarter of the globe protests flowed into Vichy. None of them was answered. Pétain's government had no time for diplomatic niceties. There is never a dull moment in France. Two days after the arrest of the six professors in Paris, Colonel Hotz was killed in Nantes while Dr. Hans Gottfried Reimers, a German military lawyer, was slain in Bordeaux, and a French traitor named Auguste Jourany, director of the Ratier factories working on German war orders, was found shot through the head on a sidewalk outside his factory on the Seine.

This was the death crop the incipient French revolution harvested on a single October day. But the success exacted a terrible price. Besides the fifty hostages immediately executed in Nantes, another fifty were shot in Bordeaux.

Others shot were four executives of the branch of the former Communist party at Ivry, industrial suburb of Paris; eight men of the Paris region, all dubbed Communists; and sixteen men of Nantes charged with having "acted in favor of the enemy."

Theirs was a guiltless death, for they had no connection with the crime that was so terribly avenged. They were chosen at random from prisons and jails. The Germans offered fifteen million francs in blood money for information leading to capture of the assassins—a sum unheard of in the criminal annals of France and one that might tempt the loyalty even of close confederates.

Marshal Henri Philippe Pétain, Chief of State, and Admiral François Darlan, Vice Premier, made statements to the French people. The killing of German officers, they declared, was the effect of foreign instigation and foreign propaganda. Both Marshal Pétain, who talked from Vichy, and Admiral Darlan, who spoke from Paris, spoke in anxious tones. Both speeches were rebroadcast throughout the day, pleading with the French people not only to refrain from violence but to aid the authorities, French and German, in capturing the assassins and in giving information to prevent further assaults.

"A stream of blood is flowing again over France," declared the Marshal. "The ransom is a frightful one. It does not affect the guilty ones. Frenchmen, your duty is clear—put an end to this butchery. Do not let more evil be done to France."

Admiral Darlan's appeal was the same. He ascribed the killings to foreign agents whose interests were "to retard the hour of peace in Europe," and told the French: "You must act. It is your duty to aid us in capturing those who prepare and execute these aggressions."

While the Marshal and Admiral Darlan mentioned only foreign inspiration, General von Stülpnagel, the commander of the German occupying forces, spoke directly of Britain and Soviet Russia. "Cowardly criminals in the pay of England and Moscow," he said, "have shot German officers in the back."

The General, however, could not produce any foreign instigators or perpetrators of the assassinations. Only Frenchmen fell before the German firing squads. In the next two or three days they fell in droves. Four had been charged with illegal possession of arms, and one, Hubert Tuffery of Beaugency, near Orléans, was also said to have had nine sticks of dynamite. The others were identified as Jules Steinmetz of Bayonne, Henry Tyrole of Saint-Hippolyte, and Georges Bourotte of Troyes. Among many others, François Blanchot, once socialist mayor of the shipyard city of Saint-Nazaire and a former Undersecretary of State, was killed; and Philibert Dupard, acting prefect of Loire-Inférieure, where the shipping and industrial center of Nantes is located, was grilled by the Gestapo. Four French officers, Colonel Naudin, and Captains Le Compte, Pertin, and Colonna, were arrested by the Germans for neglect of duty.

While the wave of arrests and executions rose even higher, Pierre Pucheu betook himself to Paris to express Vichy's regret at the death of the two German officers. On behalf of Marshal Pétain he deplored the horrible crimes, and promised General von Stülpnagel that he, Pucheu, would himself see to it that the assassins were brought to justice. The investigation, he asserted, was under the efficient direction of M. Paringaux, director of the secret service in the Ministry of the Interior.

Everything went according to plan. M. Paringaux produced the killer of Nantes in a short time—a Polish Jew, aged sixty, a derelict, incapable of squeezing a louse. His wrinkled, bearded face hung down, as if he wanted to hide in shame.

One could well take this humble attitude for a confession of guilt, the more easily as the old Jew spoke not one word of French, and hence could not answer questions.

But Herr Schwertfeger, Gestapo boss in Nantes, was suspicious. Was this fellow Paringaux trying to put one over on the Gestapo? Before executing the old Jew, he sought information. Indeed, he discovered that the derelict had been lent to Paringaux by the commander of concentration camps Gours to substitute for the unknown murderer of Nantes. Schwertfeger kicked the alleged assassin out of his office. It is the only case on record of the Gestapo saving the life of a Jew.

Messrs. Pucheu and Paringaux were forced to try their luck once more. On November 7 they announced that they had uncovered a terrorist organization in Paris, which they charged with the assassination of the German officers in Nantes and Bordeaux. Adopting General von Stülpnagel's point of view, they, too, now realized clearly that the plot was on an international scale, involving enemies of the Reich abroad. The identification of the guilty men could only be a matter of hours. But the hours went and the days passed, and no killer of German officers was brought forth. General von Stülpnagel showed distinct impatience. He felt his responsibility toward two hundred more hostages, who were still held for the shootings in Nantes and Bordeaux. The kind-hearted German general could not keep them waiting indefinitely. If the real criminals were not found, he would, much to his regret, have to call out the firing squads and have the innocent hostages shot, to relieve them from a fate worse than death—expectation of death.

The war of nerves became unbearable for every one involved: the Germans were on the point of losing their temper; the hostages counted the hours they had left; Vichy shivered in anguish. Only the French people displayed supreme indifference. Their resistance stiffened from day to day. Chain letters in increasing numbers were circulated by underground organizations. Although strictly forbidden, these letters passed from family to family throughout occupied France, reminding loyal citizens that there is a world outside Nazism actively working to destroy Hitler's system. "Do not break this chain," the letters concluded. "Copy this text as many times as you can and distribute it among your friends, asking them to do the same. Little streams make great rivers. Faith. Hope. Charity."

Trains were derailed with amazing regularity. The traffic on the strategically important line between Rouen and Havre had to be interrupted for two weeks. Ever more frequently German customs officers at the boundary between the occupied and the unoccupied zones were attacked. The most resolute resistance came from the farmers. Their slow-down of production reached such dimensions that Vichy Minister for Agriculture, Pierre Caziot, addressing them at a meeting in Lyons, had to warn them against "perfidious voices inciting you to reduce your production. You have enough common sense to see what the consequences would be," he added. "It would mean famine with all its tragic repercussions."

"Have the hostages set free!" the farmers answered stubbornly.

At this, Pétain decided to make a grand gesture. He declared in his cabinet council that he was willing to go to the occupied zone and offer himself as hostage to the Germans in order to bring about the release of those who were kept. "I have promised to give my life to France," he said, melodramatically. "Now is the moment to fulfill my promise. Will any one of you accompany me?" he asked his colleagues.

Pierre Pucheu was the first to jump up. But it was only to excuse himself on the score of an urgent telephone call to Berlin he could no longer delay. His colleagues have never forgiven him this ruse. Two or three members of the government said reluctantly: "Marshal, lead us to Paris! We follow." But Herr von Stülpnagel showed not the slightest interest in arresting Pétain and his crew. He must have been aware that he could not find any better collaborators in France. Pétain alone is worthy forty divisions to Hitler.

Moreover, there were enough other people to be arrested. A new wave of violence swept the occupied zone toward the end of November. An upheaval occurred in Nantes, where the people seemed by no means disheartened by the punishment they had received after the slaying of Colonel Hotz. The power station at Arras, in the heart of the northeastern industrial region, was dynamited. Near Abbeville and near Noyelles, both in the northeastern coastal region, the "forbidden zone" controlled rigidly by the Germans, troop trains were derailed. A house-to-house search at Nancy netted more than a hundred hidden firearms, and two of the owners were shot. But thousands of rifles and revolvers are still tucked away in Nancy. The Gestapo knows it, and cannot find them.

The unrest during November reached its peak on the 29th, when two German soldiers were killed and several others wounded in the bombing of a Paris restaurant on Montmartre. It was a particularly daring act, since it came two days after General von Schaumburg had warned Parisians of the "gravity of the consequences of continued bombings, especially if, for example, a German soldier should be killed." Every one expected a new mass round-up of hostages—no fewer than eighty-nine innocent people having been executed after the last assassination of a German soldier in Paris. To the general astonishment, Schaumburg this time confined himself to fining Paris ten million francs and imposing a 5:30 P.M. curfew for restaurants, cafés, night clubs, theaters and motion picture houses in the Quartier Latin and the Rive Gauche. The worst sufferers from this measure were the German officers, the steadiest patrons of Paris *boîtes*. Even the hostesses of the night clubs and the barmaids were now unapproachable. "Curfew!" they answered at gallant approaches.

Schaumburg set December 10 as the time limit for the discovery of the perpetrators of the bombing on Montmartre. Five days before the dead line a man on a bicycle rode up to a German officer ambling down Rue de Seine, in the heart of the Latin Quarter, fired several pistol shots, and rode quietly away. The officer died in a hospital. On the same day a major of the German air corps was shot near Versailles.

Amazingly, the German High Command again kept silent. The Nazi authorities simply invited Darlan to Paris. Before he could arrive, his creature, Admiral René Bard, Police Prefect of Paris, had already delivered a diatribe. Appealing to the population of Paris, he violently reproved "cowardly acts, always committed in the dark and from behind," although both the last shootings had occurred in full daylight, the assailants facing their victims. He added: "The police are waging merciless war on these criminals. They have already discovered several, and they will catch them all." (Thousands of innocent Frenchmen have been killed by the Nazi-Vichy butchers, but not a single killer of Nazis had yet been found.) "But action must be swift and calls for the aid of all the population," Admiral Bard continued. "You must send me every indication, notify me of every suspicion, join your efforts to ours to track down and denounce all those who murder for the benefit of the foreigner without regard for the consequences to the French." In the next days Admiral Bard received thousands of letters, all abusing and insulting him, but no help such as he had requested. He complained of this in public.

His chief, Darlan, had been invited to a conference with Göring in which the arch-collaborators Pierre Laval and Marcel Déat took part. Göring issued an ultimatum: Either Vichy must end the acts of violence, or Pétain's government would cease to be regarded as a partner in the New Order. At this threat Darlan, Laval, and Marcel Déat chuckled: none of them minded the downfall of Pétain. Each felt capable of replacing him at the head of a serf government for which partnership in the New Order was of no importance—permission to lick the Nazi boot was enough. The smiles faded, however, when the conference was interrupted by a telephone message: a German medical officer had been shot down on the Boulevard Haussmann. "I am afraid," Göring said enigmatically, "that no representative of the French people was sitting in at our conference."

Again one hundred hostages were executed, bringing the total in Paris alone to three hundred and three. The Jews, of course, were not forgotten. Although already they had been squeezed to the last sou, another astronomic fine of one billion francs was imposed on them. Jews who could not pay were condemned to forced labor in the Ukraine. Soon ten thousand French gentiles had to follow them into lingering death in Russia. Yet General von Stülpnagel clung to the anti-Semitic pretext.

He issued a decree announcing that he would "mercilessly suppress Judaeo-Bolshevists whose purpose is to sabotage reconciliation between Germany and France." Recalling recent cases of shooting and bombing in the occupied zone, and ascribing them to "elements, some young, in the pay of Anglo-Saxons, Jews, and Bolshevists, and acting on their infamous incitement," General von Stülpnagel proceeded to accuse Vichy directly. "In no case," he wrote, "have the murderers been arrested." Hence, he continued, by implication putting the blame for his own cruelty on Vichy's shoulders, the German authorities were forced to take their own appropriate measures. With obvious relish the note enumerated them: the billion-franc fine, imposed on the Jews in the occupied zone; the deportation "eastward" of a large number of "Judaeo-Bolshevists" for forced labor, with the threat of large-scale deportations should further outrages be committed; and the execution of one hundred "Jews, Communists, and Anarchists certainly connected with the authors of the outrages." The note concluded: "These measures do not hit the French people, but solely individuals who, in the pay of enemies of Germany, seek to precipitate France into misfortune and whose aim is to sabotage reconciliation between Germany and France." At the same time Stülpnagel announced that he had imposed further curfew restrictions on Paris, and that the members of the army of occupation had been ordered to shoot on sight persons behaving suspiciously.

His note was delivered on December 13. On the next day Pétain answered. The official Vichy agency called this answer the most important document since the armistice of June, 1940. It was released early enough for the evening broadcast from all official stations, which may be picked up all over the world. In fact, it was the first time that Vichy had publicly made a complaint against the Germans. But even this studied show of "resistance" was couched in tones of abject submission. Pétain declared:

(1) "The French government has always affirmed its reprobation, as well as that of the French people, for the outrages committed."

(2) "In fact through its police it has been able to arrest those guilty of several of these outrages."

(3) This week, in the course of anguishing and repeated demarches, it had solicited and thought it might expect a notable reduction in the number of men to be shot. "Although on this occasion the men concerned are not hostages but offenders, the very high number of those condemned nevertheless causes deep uneasiness among all the French people. The government has made known to the German authorities its sentiments regarding such massive repressions."

On the third day of the controversy, December 15, the French people had their say. A dynamite bomb hidden in an artichoke exploded with terrific force in a restaurant on the Rue de la Victoire, requisitioned for the exclusive use of German officers. Three officers were killed and considerable damage was done. The Gestapo, always at loggerheads with the officers' corps, regretted that no trace of the evildoers could be found. On the next day, however, the Gestapo was less complacent after two of its own buildings were blasted: the headquarters in the southern suburb, Ville Juif, where six Gestapo agents were killed, and the Gestapo's mess hall, just as the German gentlemen were making merry at dinner. The number of casualties was never disclosed, but a roundup of Jews followed immediately. Six thousand were singled out, taken to the local police stations and then put behind the high walls of the War College pending deportation to Poland and Russia. In the group were some of the most wealthy and influential Jews in Paris—among others, Eugène Dreyfus, former President of the Court of Appeals, Judge Laemlé, former president of the Seine Court, and the two Bollack brothers, well known members of the Bourse.

Undoubtedly, this was another case of "mass repression." It evoked differing reactions. Cardinal Tisserant personally in behalf of the Pope protested against the German hostage system in occupied France. Jean Luchaire, editor of the *Nouveaux Temps,* chief spokesman of the French Quislings, celebrated the latest measure of repression as a further step on the road to collaboration, since the German authority was taking action against Judaeo-Bolshevists who had been outlawed by Vichy itself. Fernand de Brinon, as Delegate General of Pétain's government in the occupied zone, laid a wreath on the tomb of L'Aiglon, Napoleon's son, whose ashes Hitler had ordered returned to Paris as his first demonstration of collaboration.

It remained for the students of the Quartier Latin to protest this new gesture of subservience. They gathered under the leadership of Professor Holweck, the chief assistant of the Curie laboratory and a well known authority on radioactivity. The students' meeting was undisturbed, but Professor Holweck was subsequently arrested and killed by the Germans.

The eventful year 1941 closed with pagan funeral rites for the soldiers and party comrades who had fallen on French soil during the twelve months, for which the Germans requisitioned Père-Lachaise, Paris' most venerable cemetery. The dark night was dimly lit by torches, the symbol of the Nordic New Year. Out of the dark came a salvo, and a second later, another. Many Germans stumbled, and collapsed. This assault, too, was duly punished. Sixty De Gaullists and sixty alleged Communists were held responsible—none of them in any way connected with the attack. The French had a word for the assailants. "With us," they said, "even corpses fight the invaders."

Marshal Pétain delivered a New Year's message, bitterly complaining about the "deserters inside France and abroad." As usual, his words were ambiguous. They could be taken as an attack on the Nazi-bribed press and politicians in Paris as well as on the Free French patriots. But the aged Marshal has no longer the right even to ambiguity, his last and favorite weapon. The Paris press told him in so many words where to get off. Marcel Déat, whom Goebbels frequently uses as a French spokesman, pointed out in a broadcast the dire consequences should collaboration be abandoned. Other pro-Nazi extremists demanded Pétain's replacement by a government of genuine collaborators who would have no objections to the outright incorporation of large parts of France with the Reich.

It was the moment for the arch-traitors of Vichy, Pierre Pucheu and his right-hand man Paringaux, to come to Paris and resume their connections with the German masters. The pretext was that both the Minister of the Interior and his Director of Security wanted to accelerate the investigation into the assailants of the Germans. M. Pucheu, however, did not find the Paris atmosphere to his taste and returned to Vichy the next day, after issuing a misleading statement of his traveling plans, obviously to conceal his whereabouts. The air was thick, and he did not care to challenge his fate. M. Paringaux stayed on in Paris—how long is not known. When his body

was found on the railway tracks near Melun, between Paris
and Troyes, the doctor conducting the autopsy assumed that
it had been lying three days on the ground, which makes
January 5 the probable day of his assassination.

With Yves Paringaux the most sinister villain in the French
tragedy disappeared from the scene. He was forty-three years
old, more than six feet tall, and of powerful physique. Seeing
him for the first time, Göring paid him the compliment: "You
look exactly like one of us." He also acted accordingly. Paringaux was Breton by birth, but Nazi by blood. On the Place
de la Concorde in Paris, February 6, 1934, he was in the front
line of the Fascist Croix de Feu uprising that tried to storm
the Chamber of Deputies. He received a blow on his skull
from a police truncheon, and stumbled into the arms of a fellow demonstrator—Pierre Pucheu. Their embrace did not end
until death parted them.

Not even the Croix de Feu was reactionary enough for the
newly formed team Paringaux and Pucheu. They left it after
a time, and founded their own short-lived "labor movement,"
Pucheu already being on the pay roll of the Comité de Forges,
the organization of the French steel and iron industry, as a
"legal counselor." French labor refused to accept such self-
styled leaders, and they switched over to the French Popu-
list party of Jacques Doriot, the renegade Communist who was
the first French traitor to get Hitler money on the grand
scale. The inevitable struggle for the spoils ensued. Pucheu
and Paringaux abandoned Doriot in 1938, to become an independent firm of business agents. In fact, both men conducted
the negotiations of French industry with Berlin, the strongest
single factor contributing to the downfall, surrender and sell-
out of France. For the team Pucheu-Paringaux the collapse
of their country was a windfall. The Nazis forced Pétain to
accept them in his government, and to invest them with large
powers. Characteristically, the Marshal yielded to this pressure, satisfying himself with one of his habitual feeble com-

promises. Only Pucheu was to receive cabinet rank—first as industrial adviser, then, when his name became more familiar in France, as Minister of the Interior. Paringaux, as Director of Public Security, was to boss the secret service and command the brigades of specialists engaged in hunting down anti-Nazi terrorists in both the French zones.

The team worked, Pucheu as the brains, Paringaux as the slugger. Boisterously he declared that he was prepared to meet force with force. Severe repression of terrorism, he said, was a logical necessity, and his basic policy was "to inflict maximum punishment for its psychological effect in preventing the spread of anarchy."

He did not prevent anything. With all the power of Vichy's vicious secret service, and the help of the Gestapo, he failed to ferret out a single patriotic murderer. Activism, which he termed "anarchy," spread. All that was determined about his own death was that his head was mashed to pieces, and his oversized body was literally sliced by knife-slashings. Various Paris churches refused to hold funeral services for him. In the end the Church of Saint-Philippe-du-Roule was forced by the Gestapo to pay the dead traitor his last honors. Archbishop Emanuel Célestin, Cardinal of Paris, received an unmistakable invitation to attend the ceremony. The prince of the Church duly attended, but did not officiate. In Brittany, Paringaux's home country, the strictly forbidden tricolor waved from every house on January 8, the day of the traitor's burial, and the people danced in the streets.

The murder of Paringaux tremendously encouraged the patriot activists. It even crazed some of them with joy. A razor-wielding terrorist raided the headquarters of Marcel Déat in Paris, badly hacking the only man he found there, since Déat, who had already once been shot at and wounded in the company of Laval, was absent, making a radio speech for all-out collaboration. Returning to his office and hearing of his lucky escape, Déat took the air once more and uttered

a precedent-breaking blast against Vichy, warning that France
would lose North Africa if she continued to avoid full collaboration with the Axis. He ridiculed the American war effort,
declaring that the gangster nation could only commit individual crimes such as the assassination of Paringaux. Of course
the killer of this poor fellow had been an American. Did not
the whole press report that Paringaux had been mishandled
with *poings Américains?* (The phrase, incidentally, is French
for "brass knuckles.")

Déat's harangue backfired. The people of Paris answered
on the same evening, with two more bombings. A club for
German soldiers on Rue d'Hauteville, just off the Boulevard
Bonne-Nouvelle, was blown up. So was the German Library,
Rue Bassano, just north of the Avenue George-V, in the fash-
ionable Champs Elysées quarter.

Paris was fined one million francs, officially twenty thousand dollars, for the recurrent bombings, and General von
Stülpnagel appointed a special commission to study "means
of putting an end to these outrages." The commission consisted of three German officers, three S.S. specialists, and, with
Pétain's consent, three French police officials. One of these,
Louis Lecureuil, was prevented from attending the commission's meeting. He was shot and killed in front of his garage
on the Boulevard de Magenta.

In the general turmoil sounded the voice of Berlin. An official spokesman shouted through the radio that the atmosphere
in Paris during the last forty-eight hours had reached a tension
comparable only to that existing in Belgrade early in April.
The inference was obvious. Early in April the Luftwaffe
razed the town of Belgrade in an effort to suppress the Yugoslav revolt.

Would the people of Paris, who during the war had declared their town an open city and had accepted invasion in
preference to endangering historic buildings, be deterred by
such a threat? Their reaction proved how much the French

nation has changed in the interim. The broadcast from Berlin was answered by a bomb explosion, during a meeting of German officers in the Salle Wagram sports arena, the Madison Square Garden of Paris. Two time bombs went off at the same moment, one in the heating plant and the other in the hall itself. Five German officers were killed, fourteen seriously injured, and all the others were cut and bruised in a scramble to get out of the hall. On the same evening a German staff car was shot at in the Boulevard des Batignolles, near the Saint-Lazare station. The car went over the edge of the railway cut, and collided with a moving train. Its three occupants, a colonel and two majors, were killed.

At the same time, the war of nerves increased rapidly in severity. Paris suffered a plague of stench bombs. The Germans found them everywhere with notes attached, remarking that it would be easy to replace them with explosive bombs. Acts of "petty sabotage," like puncturing the tires and drawing ribald pictures in the dust on German automobiles, occurred by the thousands.

The terroristic outbreaks were not confined to Paris. On January 4 occurred what the German garrison commander termed a "serious incident" in the port of Brest, where two damaged German battleships had been in hiding for many months. The incident must, indeed, have been serious. It involved the entire city government from the mayor, Senator Le Gorgeu, down. All the aldermen and the mayor's aides were arrested at their banqueting table, as they were holding an inaugural ceremony for the Council.

The German firing squads worked overtime. Mass arrests in Toulouse, six executions of alleged Communists in Bordeaux, the shooting of Lucien Gourlot in an undisclosed German prison square, the murder of ninety-five Jewish hostages (after five had been released) in a camp near the Swiss border, and sentences either of death or of life imprisonment at hard labor imposed on twenty-eight "enemies of the German state" by the military tribunal at Douai—all this, and Heaven knows what else, during the second week of January. The worst was the aftermath of the students' demonstration in the Paris Quartier Latin in the afternoon of January 3. This demonstration was particularly odious to the German authorities, who well remembered that a similar gathering of students on Armistice Day, 1940, had presaged the upheaval of France. This time, General von Stülpnagel decided, the unrest should be nipped in the bud. The first signs of restiveness were in various cafés on the Boulevard Saint-Michel where Gestapo agents mingled with the patrons from the Quartier Latin. The time was three o'clock. An hour later the venerable Boul Mich was thronged with shouting, gesticulating students and passers-by who soon turned into active sympathizers. At 4:15 German patrol cars roared along, and immediately went into action. Stülpnagel declared later that the first volley was fired, as a warning, over the heads of the crowd. Thousands of witnesses denied this. Unanimously they testified that the cars began to shoot at once, machine-gunning the masses. According to the German communiqué thirty-two were killed and a hundred wounded before the demonstrators were dispersed. There is no doubt that the actual number of casualties was many times greater.

But in the same week a large death toll was exacted from the German side as well. Fifty soldiers were killed, and many more injured when a troop train collided with a freight train near Hazebrouck, in the "forbidden" frontier zone. A few days later a firedamp explosion in a coal mine near Saint-Etienne, the only important coal-mining town in unoccupied France, killed thirty-three and injured thirty more miners—all German workers who had been brought to the "free" zone because the German authorities considered the productive effort of the French miners unsatisfactory. The unoccupied zone produces less than 8 per cent of her own coal needs. Yet even this pittance is looted for Germany.

All France stands in flames. Nevertheless, the terrific life-and-death struggle of the people is not reflected in the political relations with Germany which finally succeeded in establishing Laval's undisguised serf-government. The reason is that Fascism, both Nazi and Vichy, conducts its policy in a vacuum, with utter disregard for the people. Neither Hitler nor Pétain nor Laval really cares whether his followers assassinate one another. The tyrant and the would-be-tyrants are, to a degree, dependent on each other. Hitler, wanting France's fleet and colonies to back up his planned push across the seas, needs his French slaves to a degree, whereas these must pray for the victory of the New Order that humiliates them every day, because the restoration of democracy in France would be more dangerous for them than even Pétain's arteriosclerosis.

It is, in consequence, the Marshal of defeat who, robbed of his last semblance of influence, frantically tries to hush up as "incidents caused by hotheads" the outbursts and acts of French patriotism. The punishment which disturbers of the harmony with Nazism in unoccupied France suffer is no less severe than that inflicted on the occupied zone by the German army.

Worried by the innumerable acts of sabotage directed against him as much as against the Nazis, Pétain, while still in official power, announced the creation of a "Council of Political Justice" and asked his nation to send him "names and recommendations for punishment." Trailing Hitler under the heroic slogan, "Me, too!" he imposed the death penalty for sabotage acts in a series of decrees to bring the unoccupied zone into line with the German measures against the growing ferment. Even the Vichy press buried these decrees on their back pages. Only Doriot's rabidly anti-Semitic *Cri du Peuple* blessed Pétain for his cooperation against Jews, Freemasons, and De Gaullists.

In the first days of January the police at Clermont-Ferrand, in the unoccupied zone, arrested fifty-one members of a "secret organization with anti-German aims." A few days later Radio-Vichy pointed out that persons in the free zone could also earn the premium of two hundred thousand francs which the prefecture of the Paris police was offering for information about those responsible for the derailment of sixty German freight cars at Epinay-sur-Seine, near Paris, an important junction for traffic with Germany. Declaring that "fines were too lenient a punishment" for listening to the London and Boston broadcasts, the Vichy courts recently increased the penalties to long prison terms. The Germans decreed the death sentence for such offenses.

In Vichy as well as in the occupied territory government officials are immediately removed on discovery of any previous connection with the Freemasons. The papers had to publish this sanction under the headline "National Renovation—the Purge Continues." Commissioners were named in both zones with power to suspend politically suspicious civil servants. Policemen are wearing new uniforms with armlets bearing the words "National Police—National Revolution." The first duty of the new police is to suppress attacks on the occupying forces. A law passed by the cabinet provides for severe punishment for eyewitnesses, accomplices, or others who have information about acts of terrorism, and fail to make them known to officials. All France is to be a huge army of stool pigeons and informers. On January 11, Vichy triumphantly announced that "French persons" had furnished the authorities with clues to the assassins in two recent slayings of German officers. These persons, Vichy said, were rewarded by the release of their relatives in prison camps in Germany.

The general release of the French prisoners of war is, Pétain and Laval lose no opportunity of affirming, their prime concern. They frequently become positively lyrical in describing the prisoners' martyrdom. It is the crux of all their conversations and negotiations with the Germans. Unfortunately, the parties cannot come to terms. Suffering acute shortage of labor, the Germans cannot set free the million and a half French serfs still working in German plants and farms, and in the better Berlin hotels and cafés. The Nazis claim to have already released five hundred thousand of the original two million. Actually the number released is one hundred and fifty thousand; the other three hundred and fifty thousand have managed to escape from the Reich since the armistice. On the other hand the French prisoners of war retained in Germany have developed into a factor gravely disturbing the Nazi system. They have evolved a sort of agreement with German workmen—an agreement directed against Hitler's regime. German factory workers, it is reported, are willing to trust the French prisoners and are openly discussing with them their grievances against a government which is leading them ever deeper into a seemingly endless war.

The German workers and French prisoners are making all kinds of deals. In some cases the Germans have provided the prisoners with civilian clothes and maps to facilitate their escape. Developments of this sort are occurring much more frequently now than three months ago.

The French private held prisoner in Germany thoroughly dislikes the Hitler regime and opposes collaboration, while the French officer, who has no contact with the German people and is exempted from all work, is more likely to favor collaboration.

The Nazis would like to rid themselves of this "ferment of decomposition," but they are obliged to hang on to every pair of hands. Vichy professes its heartfelt desire to receive them in France's bosom, but it is well aware that this would mean inviting a million determined and hard-bitten enemies of the regime. The complete hypocrisy of Nazi-Vichy relations is in no case so clearly exposed as in the continuous bickering over the French prisoners of war, unwanted by both sides, and yet "desired" by both.

One point, however, about which Hitler and Vichy agree perfectly is detestation of the United States. American policy, if continuing the abortive effort to appease Vichy, must swallow a good deal of pride. Last October, months before America's entry into the war, huge French government propaganda posters connected President Roosevelt by implication with the terror wave in France. These posters were put up in Vichy on the very day that German authorities in Paris executed their seventy-seventh French victim for acts against the occupying forces. One poster, issued by the Information Secretariat, said that "aboard the *Potomac* Europe was knocked down to the Soviets and their agents, the Communists!" (President Roosevelt had used the yacht *Potomac* for part of the trip to his Atlantic conference with Churchill.) Another poster showed an American gangster, as known in Hollywood pictures, with a smoking gun, his hand directed by Stalin.

When two hundred of the most prominent American expatriates were seized by the Germans in Paris and carried off to the crude wooden barracks at Besançon to be held as hostages for the good treatment of Nazi criminals in the United States, Vichy solemnly refused to intervene on their behalf. Again Pétain's government refused intervention when it was informed that American foodstuffs, a gift of charity for the starving children of Marseilles, were redirected to Germany by the Nazi members of the Armistice Commission in the port.

The Vichy government is not so silent in all cases. At the height of the furious Japanese attack in the Western Pacific it assured Tokyo that there was no need to worry about Indo-China. France, the message declared, is quite content with the settlement which transformed the French colony into a Japanese advance base. Although most of the French Pacific islands have gone over to De Gaulle, a few are still under Vichy control. Darlan recently designated his friend, Vice-Admiral Jean Decoux, a notorious collaborator, High Com-

missioner for the French possessions in the Pacific. Decoux
scored the only success France has had in the international
field for years. The dusky King of the Wallis Islands, southwest of Hawaii, pledged his loyalty to Vichy. Japanese submarines, one may assume, will receive a friendly welcome in
the Wallis Islands, as well as in the Society Islands, the other
Vichy-French holding in the Pacific.

Vichy's sell-out in the Far East is about to be repeated on
a much larger scale, threatening American interests still more
directly, by the bargain involving the French possessions in
Africa. This bargain has been in the making for months. It
was the main topic of conversations in Saint-Florentin between Göring and Pétain, at which, it is rumored, the aged
Marshal repeatedly fainted under the impact of Göring's
bullying. Although the existence of an agreement concerning
the French Empire was never officially admitted, semioffi-
cially both Radio-Algiers and Radio-Vichy let the cat out of
the bag. On December 3, Radio-Algiers struck this note:
"When we remember that France, before she came under
English tutelage, always attached extreme importance to European problems, that Europe needs to keep Africa, and that
Africa is largely French, we can only emphasize the historical
character of the meeting. The Saint-Florentin meeting is only
a starting point, but one which opens a new road."

On the return of Admiral Platon, Secretary of State for
Colonies, from an inspection of African defenses, Radio-
Vichy said, also on December 3: "From the military point of
view much has been done in French West Africa, and the results we have achieved are of a nature to discourage those
who would wish to attack us." Paris associated Platon's visit
with defense against an Anglo-Saxon coup. America was represented by the Paris stations as advancing toward French
Africa, whether by means of lend-lease support granted to
De Gaullist colonies there, or by beginning construction work
on military bases in Liberia, West Africa, and Massawa. The

listeners were warned that the only way of protecting their colonies was in effect to be prepared to fight England and America for them. Europe was represented as impregnable to those who hope for great things from entrance of the United States in the war. The idea that France will have to fight America as well as England is steadily instilled in the minds of French listeners. Here is what Jean Luchaire, chief advocate of Nazism in the Paris press, has to say on the subject:

> The decisive hour has struck for France. Against John Bull's tyranny of many centuries and the young tyranny of Uncle Sam, all the young peoples have now banded themselves together. Unless our country wishes to adopt a policy of abdication, like a dog dying of thirst on the banks of a rivulet, it owes it to itself, without any further delay, to take its side.

Since the Saint-Florentin meeting, an increase in German activities has been noted in unoccupied France as well as in North Africa as far as Dakar. The well known German tourists have appeared in numbers at Lyons, Marseilles, Tunis, etc. Also French troops formerly in Syria, and now refitted, were sent to Dakar in order "to protect the integrity of the French Empire," to the defense of which the Germans were called in Pétain's speech of January 1. It is now generally admitted that General Erwin Rommel expects to regroup and refit his forces on the Tunisian fortified lines, not only to check General Auchinleck's forces but eventually to find support there for a new drive toward the Nile and Iran. A new German campaign is in the making in this part of the world by means of which Germany seems to have decided to force her way to the oil wells. The German need for French cooperation is evident. All this may explain Pétain's final surrender to Hitler since the French army and navy officers—particularly those with the African forces—cannot be called "safe" from the point of view of collaboration.

There is obviously strong potential opposition to a German

invasion in French Morocco, and the De Gaulle supporters are increasing. French North Africa has apparently undergone an important change, passing from an apathetic desire for peace at any price after the collapse of France to the prevalent adverse criticism of Vichy which became noticeable during the Syrian campaign. Next, it is believed, will come hostility toward the Laval regime—for whatever hostility of French officials and officers is worth today.

The number of Vichy adherents in North Africa has dwindled since General Maxime Weygand's dismissal as proconsul, which was especially resented in the army. But it is still doubtful whether this animosity toward Vichy will or can soon be translated into acts, in case the French overseas territories are forced into collaboration with Germany.

The appalling condition of occupied France and the humiliation of unoccupied France are still insufficiently comprehended in the colonies, where German propaganda has the ascendancy.

Also, in the French colonial army a discipline making for rigidity is paramount. The native troops are nothing if not obedient. It is hard to imagine them joining any movement of revolt while the top officers remain loyal to Vichy.

While it is unlikely that there will be in the near future any general movement to back General Charles de Gaulle, probably many officers in North Africa, who have hitherto justified their adherence to Vichy on the ground that Marshal Philippe Pétain stuck to the terms of the Franco-German armistice, may become practicing converts to the Free French cause.

However, the German "tourist-technician" army already in West Africa is more powerful and better equipped than any French force there. The German force could be augmented quickly by German effectives sent into North Africa through arrangement with Vichy.

At the same time the German forces surreptitiously present

in West Africa can without much delay reinforce garrisons at Sfax and Bizerte, Tunisia. The presence of a large, well equipped Axis force in Tunisia, on the Libyan frontier, is ominous.

It could use the "Maginot Line of Africa," supposed to be strong enough not only to discourage all Italian challenges but to provide the French General Staff with a springboard for an offensive which, as General Maurice Gustave Gamelin saw it, would have swept the Italian colony.

Incidentally, General Gamelin always expressed the conviction that the war would be decided in North Africa. It would be a strange reversal, but no longer an unexpected one, if in 1942 the elaborate fortifications in southern Tunisia came into the conflict to the advantage of the enemy against which they were directed.

Were the German command to appropriate those fortifications, it could perhaps avoid the difficult advance of armies through Spain and Morocco. Tunis and Bizerte might fall within the grasp of the bodies of troops driven away from the Egyptian frontier by the British.

On December 27 the Vichy Government was reported to have concluded with Italy an agreement linked to Article 10 of the armistice convention of June 24, 1940. The text of that article is well worth quoting:

To guarantee the enforcement of the convention, Italy reserves the right to ask for the delivery, wholly or in part, of the collective arms of infantry, artillery, armored cars, motor, horse-drawn vehicles and ammunition, which were engaged or put in position in any way against the armed forces of Italy.

Was that text drafted to include the fortified lines? And was it rendered still more definite in the supplementary understanding reached a short time ago?

It was certainly one of Vichy's habitual compromises. To say the least, it endangered France's African Empire in return for the release of the French prisoners in Italy—all of one hundred and thirty-four men.

The question arises whether the French commanders in North Africa, on whose attitude so much depends, will follow the new set-up. Unfortunately, among the French generals in North Africa only one, General de Lattre de Tassigny, with headquarters in Tunis, has the strength of character required for bold resistance. The others are weaklings or "safe men," in the sense of Admiral Darlan, who has assumed the functions of commander in chief of the Army. But General de Lattre de Tassigny was promoted last August at the very moment when the Vichy trend toward the Axis was most determined, and it must be inferred that he also was deemed a "safe man."

The two top men—General Alphonse Pierre Juin, commander of the French forces in North Africa, who recently inspected the fortifications along the Tripolitanian frontier, and the Resident-General, Admiral Jean Esteva—are dyed-in-the-wool collaborators. Since Weygand's dismissal they have allowed German and Italian supply ships to hug the coast of Tunisia, where they are less vulnerable to British naval and aerial attacks. Neither objects to the activities of German military experts and fifth columnists in French Africa. The German military chieftains are the infantry colonels Klauber and Pitrie.

In Larache, in Spanish Morocco, incidentally, German activities are directed by Herr Reschnaunsen, well known among the tribes of eastern Djebala, whose influence extends to Tangiers.

Another Nazi spy-master, named Lanhenmain, is an intimate friend of General Beigbeder, former Spanish High Commissioner in Morocco and former Minister of Foreign Affairs in the Franco Government. He too is very influential in Spanish Morocco. Angelo Girelli, an Italian mining engineer, also works for the Germans. Girelli lived in the Balearic Islands, where he acquired some land. He was formerly on the pay roll of the Italian intelligence service and enjoys the confidence of the Spanish authorities.

The German Secret Service in Morocco has been very active for many years. One of the leaders of this organization is a certain Ritter Franz von Goss, captain in the German army, known in Madrid under the name of "Paco." From 1936 to 1939 von Goss directed the activities of the German secret agents, and played an important part in the formation of the German Labor Front in Morocco and in establishing an insurance company for Arab farmers, wtih headquarters in Tetuan and branches in Xauen and Riff.

In southern Spain and Morocco, this work is directed by Guillermo Burbach, German military attaché in Paris, Madrid, and Lisbon between 1936 and 1939. Burbach, who was very close to General Beigbeder, accompanying him through Spain and Morocco in 1928, founded several Nazi centers in Morocco. Local party groups were established in Ceuta, Tetuan, Larache, and Tangiers.

The bulk of the task of preparing the ground in Africa for Nazification, however, is entrusted to the officers of the various armistice commissions. How these gentlemen work can be guessed from an order released to them on October 9, 1941 —"strictly personal and confidential"—of which a few copies fell into the hands of the Free French. It reads, in part:

The commissions must by all means, legal as well as illegal, intensify their control in order to be informed about every event and movement. Every German and Italian officer must always be aware of his role as an informer. He must endeavor to establish intimate relations with French officers to make them speak freely. To gain the Frenchmen's confidence it will be advisable to display chilly feelings toward the Nazi regime, and to admit that a total Axis victory is not to be wished for. Most important are all and any information about the state of mind of the French sailors, and about what reaction is to expected from them in case the French government should be forced by the Axis powers to join their naval warfare.

Thus the German moles were undermining what was left of France: her navy and her empire. Now Laval has to deliver the goods. In the end, he will not lack pretexts for Vichy-France's full participation in the war under the direction of the German High Command.

The leaders of resistance in France, on the other hand, prepare the revolution. They recognize, however, that a revolution needs general consent to be effective. To win, it must furthermore tally with military action from abroad. The moment for such action has not yet come. Yet millions of Frenchmen prepare for the day with unfaltering persistence. If complacency is dangerous to a belligerent nation, its spread would be suicidal to an oppressed people. Without stubborn and ever increasing resistance, the occupied countries would add dangerously to the economic and military potential of the Axis. Hence resistance on the European continent is of cardinal importance for America too. The oppressed nations still hold the key to victory in their clenched fists.

How do the French carry themselves in this crucial situation? The answer is: In spite of numerous individual defections, they bear their lot heroically, in general.

Despite censorship French people are well informed of world events, even those which are not mentioned on the Paris and Vichy radios. This applies, naturally, to those who have taken upon themselves the job of keeping the French people keenly aware of the penalties of collaboration.

The general optimism is based on two new factors: the Russian stubbornness and the magnitude of American war effort, and the sense of confidence which this instills.

There is as yet no well coordinated movement. It is only recently that Frenchmen have tried anything like an organized campaign except small groups of trusted friends. In general, up to now "Down with Hitler!" is the only watchword —that has united all Frenchmen. But in the humming armament factories in Alsace and in the South at Tarbes, sabotage

is becoming more and more common. The general principle
is, "Work Slowly."

The morale of the population is marvelous, particularly in
Alsace and Lorraine, in the forbidden areas, the mining districts in the North of France and the occupied zone. The
pressure applied by the army of occupation is appalling.
However, it creates a will to survive and a greater determination to resist. A few months ago this spirit was practically
nonexistent. But now the avalanche starts rolling.

In the unoccupied zone, however, a pronounced passivity
still prevails, a proneness to await liberation through a Revolution in Germany, or a Russian success, rather than to take
an active part in working toward this goal of freedom.

As long as possible, life in Paris went on undisturbed. Since
the Revolution of 1789 Paris has set the pace for all great
French movements. This time, the city of blacked-out lights
followed the example of the country. The capital is, after all,
the invader's headquarters and the nerve center of collaboration. The general dislocation resulting from the defeat and
the partition of the country has forced the entire nation to
examine critically all policies and opinions that emanate from
Paris. Resistance was already in full swing in the provinces
when Paris awoke. It was a gradual awakening, but now it has
gathered full momentum. Paris is a battlefield shaken by explosions every day and all night.

On the surface it is still gay Paree. "The reign of gold is
over," according to the Nazis. But money floats in streams.
People are having plenty of good times. Never before were
there in Paris so many night clubs, bars, speakeasies, taverns,
and other places where money can be spent for amusement—
only glance at *La Semaine à Paris* (the equivalent of *Cue*)
and its German edition, or at the amusement sections of the
dailies. Many liquidated places are reopening and are decorated more luxuriously than ever. And new ones are constantly springing up all over the city. In these places the fifty-

franc maximum menu is not obligatory; rationing cards are unknown. Bands, gypsy or Russian, international singers and performers contribute to the excitement of the atmosphere, which does not at all remind the Frenchmen of their national mourning, or the Nazis of their Spartan spirit, so much exalted by Hitler. Well after midnight, when the rest of Paris is asleep, the new Paris, made up of Germans and those few French of both sexes who get along with the Germans well, comes to life and has a "good time."

Leaving the night clubs the revelers see the first queues being formed outside the stores, where the sale of potatoes will begin several hours later. They will encounter a shadowlike apparition, the vender of a clandestine newspaper, or a man distributing leaflets like this one:

Frenchmen: If nickel coins are being withdrawn from circulation, it is because nickel is a supply indispensable to the German war machine.

If every Frenchman holds onto two francs in twenty-five-centime, forty-gram coins, the French people will deprive Hitler of sixteen hundred tons of nickel needed for his armament.

Don't say, "If I alone do it," but act quickly and get those around you to act.

If you recopy this pamphlet five times and distribute the copies within twenty-four hours instead of ten days, a million of the pamphlets will be distributed.

Frenchmen, act quickly.

Drunken German officers roam the streets of Paris at dawn. Invariably "Vive De Gaulle" is lipsticked on the back of their coats, or perhaps the letter *V* in chalk. When they empty their pockets, they are sure to find that a calling card has been slipped in: "Compliments of the B.B.C.," or "Churchill wants to see you." They can fill the air of a morning in Paris with their tipsy laughter and guttural din as much as they please. No one cares. Paris is a city of shadows—of German shadows. One looks through them, one does not answer their

requests for street directions, one does not even recoil when
they bump into one. Necessary conversations with them assume aphoristic shape. "Our German soldiers have strict orders to behave like gentlemen," a Nazi colonel bragged. "I
served during the occupation of the Rhineland," a Frenchman answered. "We did not need to issue any orders about
our soldiers' behavior." This answer brought the speaker six
weeks in jail, and local fame all over Paris. Another much
quoted Parisian is the old lady who replied to two German
officers, thanking her with Prussian politeness including much
heel clicking and bowing from the waist for her kindness
in billeting them: "You do not have to thank me. I am
thankful. For the first time in my life I thank God that I am
blind."

In daytime Paris appears almost medieval. There are no cars
on the streets. Only the Germans and prominent collaborators
ride in automobiles—the latter reluctantly, for they are well
aware that their cars will be smashed or overturned in the first
unguarded moment. A few horses and buggies have been sal-
vaged. But the poor animals are so underfed that they pull
their loads slowly, neighing miserably. The great majority of
the students also are underfed. Yet they have found it profitable to take the place of the horse. By carrying passengers on
their bicycles, they work their way through college. But no
one can say that Paris students have lost any of their dignity.
On the contrary, the unbreakable spirit of independence they
display amazes even German observers. As in the old days
students and professors of the Sorbonne prefer to stroll along
the *rive gauche*, where the *bouquinistes'* stalls offer second-
and twentieth-hand volumes. The arrangement of these books
is artful. The book venders exhibit, as prescribed, Hitler's and
Mussolini's memoirs. Sandwiched between is *Les Miserables*,
Victor Hugo's classic.

The battle of wits, of course, is confined to Paris proper.
The suburbs prefer direct action. The "red belt," they have

long been called, because they were Communist. They are still more or less so today. The Germans insist that they are more so. Indiscriminately, all opposition was labeled communistic, at least until the end of 1941 when resistance had reached such dimensions that the Communist blind was no longer of any avail. In fact there is evidence of a distinct Communist drift among the French working class. Underground red cells are increasingly active, and the Russian military successes have brought back many into the bolshevist camp. But the drift is by no means as general as might appear. The French workers cannot quite forget the Russo-German pact. Of course they strongly sympathize with Stalin in his duel with Hitler, but they will no longer act as his seconds, as they unfortunately did at the outbreak of the war.

Sabotage, in particular, is by no means a Communist monopoly. It is spreading everywhere, and affects particularly the armament factories working for the Nazi military machine. The idea is to work slowly, and to be extremely finicky about the safety regulations. Despite the ban on the C.G.T., the trade unions' underground activities are very intense. In the majority of the factories the former delegates continue to represent the unions and are recognized by the owners. If the latter did not acknowledge them, they might easily incur severe consequences. But wages are all inadequate to meet the cost of living, even among skilled workers.

In the plants machines are not oiled, transmission belts snap, short circuits develop, and boilers explode. Sabotage of finished products is very prevalent. The German authorities have to examine every rivet and every screw: there have been too many accidents. At the aviation plant of Toulouse the Germans stipulated that the factory manager and a man elected by the workers be taken along on every test flight. Moreover, only parts are now produced in this particular factory. The planes are assembled in Paris. At the Tarbes arsenal several sit-down strikes occurred. The workers were trying to prevent munitions from being delivered to the Germans.

There is no communism at all among the French peasants. Yet the peasants are putting up the stiffest possible opposition.

The farmers are beginning to hide their produce and to slaughter small livestock. They feel they are being plundered because they can buy very little with the money they collect: the disparity between industrial and farm prices is very wide.

The assassinations and sabotage now being committed in the occupied zone, as well as the repressions that have followed, are creating a great stir in France, in all France. This wide official publicity is entirely new. The assassinations and the sabotage are an old story compared to it.

France is not yet in a state of open revolution, but she is only one step short of it. Vichy knows, and so do the German masters, that all their talk about "Communist propaganda" is so much nonsense. Among the shot or arrested "Communists" are men belonging to every party and class. Several score of deputies and senators have been imprisoned—democrats, liberals, republicans of every shade, and even royalists. More than a hundred of their colleagues who lost their positions when Pétain abolished parliament are meeting frequently in secret and are organizing resistance to Vichy. Pétain, Darlan, and Laval depend on the loyalty of the *gardes mobiles* and other mercenaries who alone enable Vichy to do Hitler's dirty business in France.

In some parts of France this regime is today already practically nonexistent. The Somme department, bordering the English Channel in northeastern France, is the center of sabotage and terrorism, including the dynamiting of railroads. Amiens, its local capital, was called by the German garrison commander "the seething city." Naval stores from the French naval arsenal in Cherbourg were looted by "partisans" under the eyes of indifferent *gardes mobiles*. The population of the

Calvados department in Normandy has simply banned all Vichy functionaries from the district. The line of demarcation is not respected. Thousands of people cross it illegally every day, guided by peasants who know every blade of grass and every stone in the road. Yet it is a difficult trip. One leaves at dawn, makes stops in ditches and thickets, wades through puddles, and jumps barriers.

People cross by secret paths in the rural districts in forced marches, in market wagons behind sacks of potatoes or coal, in vehicles with double bottoms, with false passports, or by bribing German soldiers. All ways are good when they succeed. If they don't succeed, it means a more or less lengthy jail sentence, a heavy fine, or sometimes death, if the guards have fired.

Frequently the "passers" fire back. Hundreds of German soldiers have been killed along the demarcation line. In Chalon-sur-Saône the service is so dangerous that the local garrison refused to man the posts.

The French are not the only ones to cross. There also are many English who are escaping, and even some Germans trying to hide in the free zone and desert in order to avoid being sent to the Russian front.

There is much to be said on the subject of German desertions. There is the fear of leaving France for some dangerous front in Russia, Asia, or Africa. The charm of the country has worked.

Officers and soldiers would give anything to remain here even as civilians after the war. Many housewives who have been obliged to quarter them relate how at the time of departing for new and unknown destinations their guests wept, cursed, and even stamped on their uniforms or their flags. They had to be convinced by arguments and threats or, if words failed, by punishment. And the punishments are terrible. The occupying authorities are quick to shoot French hostages, and they are just as quick to shoot German soldiers who refuse to stay in the service. Then their coffins are shown to their comrades, and the lesson is effective.

All German industrialists in contact with the French display great anxiety regarding the fate of Germany.

Although the discipline of the German army remains unbelievably severe, most German soldiers commit the crime of listening to the English radio when no one except their French hosts is watching them. They do not relish the executions which they must carry out. To spare their tender feelings the German High Command recently ordered that the French Mobile Guard itself should shoot some of the people who had attacked field-gray uniforms. With one stroke the whole Mobile Guard became fiercely anti-German. If the imbecile authorities of occupation believed that by not picking the members of the firing squads from among their own men they had placed the odium of their terror on the French, they certainly miscalculated once again.

There is one large group that no longer believes in organized discipline until a distant hour strikes. The underground organizations have no time to wait. Everywhere under-cover resistance is beginning to be organized. It menaces both the Germans and, still more, the traitors. Today no *journaliste vendu* can sign his infamous articles without being threatened by the secret associations. Many turncoats have disappeared.

That groups of activists exist is known and admitted by both French and German authority. Painstaking searches and long questioning of the few small-fry suspects so far caught have done nothing to unearth the central organization.

One of the most important of these groups, "Les Chevaliers de Coup de Balai" (Knights of the Broom), began making itself heard throughout the country recently with a powerful mobile short-wave transmitter. Powerful it had to be to get over the jamming as it does; and mobile it most certainly is, since its broadcasts have continued, with one break of two days, for more than three months.

The material for the evening broadcasts consists largely of rather ribald comment on editorials in the evening papers of the capital, while the morning session is exclusively devoted to pertinent remarks from the morning press of the same day. Subsequent checks with copies of the newspapers cited have so far failed to reveal any discrepancy in dates for citation.

Opening and closing each program with the ominous six notes of "Aux armes, citoyens" from the "Marseillaise," notes heard so often on French national hook-ups, during the last few days before the armistice. The Chevaliers show some inside knowledge of the comings and goings of officialdom between France and Germany. They exhort their listeners, however, to further patience, invariably citing the futility, as shown by reprisals so far, of any unorganized attempt at fighting the Germans' grip on the country.

That one is being prepared, however, is guaranteed, and some of these alleged "preparations" are cited. Invariably the next day there is a swoop of the police on the basis of information given in the broadcast—and, according to many reports, not infrequently the police arrive only in time to save from further punishment some prominent pro-Nazi who has been kidnaped—not infrequently surrounded with large "plants" of Communist literature and other embarrassingly incriminating material.

It is the considered opinion of competent observers after long residence in France that an Allied offensive on the coast would bring the country to its feet in forty-eight hours.

On the other hand, the "gestures" of "collaboration" with its mass executions, have come so close to breaking the patience of the cruelly suffering population that a spontaneous outbreak is possible at any moment.

A secret French society made itself felt in the Béthune mining basin of northern France by demanding the withdrawal of the troops of occupation. The Germans answered that they would shoot at any demonstration. The same evening meetings gathered in all three halls of Béthune. The garrison commander ordered his troops to remain in their barracks. He had received a letter, signed by the secretary general of the "party," and containing a single sentence. "At the first shot our miners will flood the mines, which would put them out of commission for six months."

An organization was uncovered, but not disbanded, which delivered secret packages, leaflets, and papers by an underground postal system throughout France. Motorcycles with trailers made deliveries to a network of depots from which other motorcycles relayed the material.

Behind the murder of Bordeaux the Germans themselves believe there was "a real terrorist organization." The same group was made responsible for the assassination of two German officers in Paris. Along the demarcation line between the two zones a highly organized "underground railway" is operating; the Germans, unable to stop it, complain bitterly. They regard a man whose picture hangs on the walls of all French railway stations and public buildings as their most dangerous enemy. The legend says: "Sought by police and gendarmerie is Gilbert André Brulstein, born March 20, 1919, in Paris." It continues with a detailed description of the fugitive, mentioning that he walks with "head bent and with a distinct stoop of the shoulders," and promises both a reward of a million francs for his capture and the release of the informer's relatives who may happen to be in German captivity. Thus young Brulstein has been sought for more than six months. He is still at liberty, and constant assaults on the Germans mark his way.

More important than even the heroism of this lone wolf fighting singlehanded the destroyers of his country, is the fact that the spontaneous movement of resistance, formerly haphazard and disunited, is solidifying and coordinating all its activities into a common effort.

Since the wave of resistance first began to rise in France,

three underground organizations have developed as the most important and most active rallying forces. These are:

(1) The "National Liberation" group, which expresses itself through its publication, *Vérité* (Truth), formerly appearing as *Les Petites Ailes* (Fledgling Wings).

(2) The "Liberté" (Liberty) group, which publishes a paper with the same name as the organization.

(3) The "Liberation" group, which publishes a paper with the same name as the organization.

At the outset these groups were autonomous, but they have now merged their efforts to a great extent. They retain their initial independence and self-administration, but are working together to promote a program of common action; and they are operating in complete unity.

These three groups work in the unoccupied zone. They publish a joint paper called *Résistance*, which has a circulation of thirty-five thousand. They are in sharp contrast to the old political parties. They accept members of any political faith who share the militant determination to fight the invader and the Vichy Government, and that government's collaborationism. This obviously excludes all fascist-inclined nationalists and pro-authoritarians. These groups have refused to work with the Communist organizations, which therefore retain their own set-up and employ totally different methods. The groups do, however, maintain contact with socialist organizations which have secretly reconstituted.

These groups, in which French youths are active, that already have established numerous contacts throughout France, include, in addition to the militants who carry on the work, thousands of tacit adherents from every walk of life. The organization is secret and follows the pattern of the outlaw societies that have sprung up throughout Europe since the advent of Hitlerism.

Most of the members don't know who the leaders are and, in fact, are acquainted with only a few members of their group. As they now stand, they represent the cream of moral and political rebirth since France's defeat.

The intellectuals have done much to encourage the formation of these groups. The underground groups also are in more or less close contact with army officers and members of the police force who aid and abet them *sub rosa*. These groups compose, in fact, the backbone of a "Sixth Column" which will reveal itself in its full strength at the moment when the Nazi army has to face invading armies. The cardinal immediate aim of the groups which reach out directly or indirectly to all the living forces in France, is the preparation and organization of a people's army which will begin marching the instant the Nazi armies betray signs of weakness.

At present their principal role is to spread propaganda and unrest. But they are fundamentally organized with a view to sterner missions.

Headache number one of the power of occupation, and its Vichy satellites is, of course, the De Gaulle movement. One is disclosing no anxiously guarded secret in pointing out the organization known both as Free France and as Friends of De Gaulle which maintains branches throughout France. These branches keep lists of traitors, all of whom will be seized at one and the same moment—the very moment the General crosses the Channel. Whether he will have smooth going on his return depends on the general situation prevailing on the *jour de gloire*, and on whether the Germans will be able to carry out their diabolical plans for the split-second annihilation of those occupied countries from which they will be forced to flee. But everywhere friendly hands will be stretched out to welcome home the man who did not quit. De Gaullist organizations of sailors, railway employees, policemen, and ex-soldiers keen on resuming the fight are already in being.

Close ties link the Free French forces battling valiantly on three continents and on the seven seas, with their adherents inside France. De Gaullist parachutists frequently descend on French soil carrying instructions for the agents at home, and equipping the General's followers with arms and ammunition. The worst danger, these parachutists admit, is the jubilant reception they are getting from the population—a most heartening demonstration, but not one that makes for the discretion on which a parachutist's life in enemy-occupied land depends. Indeed, in a few cases De Gaullist parachutists have been seized. One of these incidents occurred at Villamblard, between Bergerac and Périgueux, after the British plane, in which the Free French pilots had traveled, made a forced landing. A patrol of gendarmes hurried to the scene. They saluted stiffly, and clicked their heels, aping their German superiors. Then they volunteered to repair the damage on condition that they were taken along. The return flight, the pilot reported, was terrible. They were so crowded in the plane that they could scarcely make it. Moreover, they had to shoot three "bandits"—R.A.F. slang for their German colleagues—out of their way.

They will have to shoot many more bandits out of their way: their own traitors. The importance of both Free France and Vichy increases rapidly as the war engulfs the whole world. In the Pacific theater, for instance, Vichy servilely handed over Indo-China, whereas Free France holds most of the French Pacific islands, all of which are in a highly strategic position, and could be used as important air and naval bases for the Allied forces.

In the Atlantic theater Admiral Muselier's brilliant coup on the islands of Saint-Pierre and Miquelon, although it embarrassed slightly some incurable appeasers, freed the Western Hemisphere from the menace of a pistol in the hands of the Axis, pointing right at the U-boat-infested Canadian waters. Martinique is at this writing still under Vichy control, a control exercised by Admiral Robert, a notorious pro-Nazi. American authorities are satisfied that Admiral Robert can do no mischief under the rigid control to which he is subject. Unfortunately, the control only surrounds Martinique from outsiders. Domestically, the islanders, all clamoring to be recognized as Americans, are subject to the worst chicanes in the Nazi style. They must read a controlled local press and listen to the nauseating "French" broadcast. Cut off from all trade and traffic, they are dependent on American magnanimity for their living. As long as the Vichy banner "protects" them they cannot earn their bread.

Vichy lets the people starve, but not the troops of the German masters. In spite of denials manufactured in Vichy, the world's biggest lie producer, it is revealed that two French ships a week provided supplies for General Rommel's *Afrikakorps*, whatever the consequences. It was, obviously, an effort to drag France through the back door into the war on the German side, another step in that grand strategy which condemns some ten thousand former inmates of French concentration camps, both Frenchmen and anti-Fascist refugees, the chain-gang labor in the desert, to build another of Germany's famous strategic roads—to Dakar, the jumping-off point for Hitler's planned attack on South America.

General de Gaulle retaliates with deeds. Word comes of the completion of two important roads through French Equatorial Africa. The roads will play an important part in the transportation of American and British supplies across Africa to Cairo, whence they could be sent to the British forces in the Western Desert, to the Russian armies, or even to the forces of the United Nations in the Far East. The importance and magnitude of this latest Free French contribution to the Allied war effort has not yet been quite grasped in America.

Vichy understood it at once. True to type, the traitor government tries to fight off both De Gaulle's splendid share in the war and the coming revolution in France, with every sort of blackmail.

Even this country was flooded with Vichy-manufactured

pamphlets in the best Nazi style. One of these pamphlets, printed in color on both sides of a thin piece of paper that could easily be folded and slipped into a pocket, bore the official imprint, "Publication of the General Secretariat of Information, Vichy." At the top was a reproduction of a Free French poster, "These Free French leaders have only one aim—victory!" showing the likeness of De Gaulle and his lieutenants. Beneath appeared Vichy's message: "Their victory would be the victory of Anglo-Saxon finance, the Jews, the Masons, the victory of Bolshevism with all its horrors."

Can such propaganda be bettered by Laval, now he is back in power? It cannot. It is the real thing. It is Vichy at its most vicious: the system of the jellyfish, flabby, slimy, with a poisonous sting. If one thing is more contemptible than Nazism itself, it is Nazism's treacherous copy.

CHAPTER EIGHTEEN

BELGIUM

Can one bury Ulenspiegel, the wit, or Nele, the heart, of Mother Flanders? She, too, can sleep. But die? Never!
—CHARLES DE COSTER in *Ulenspiegel.*

THE father of the "V for Victory" campaign is not by mere coincidence a Belgian. Remembering that his own initial, *V*, stood for "victory" in English, *victoire* in French, and *vrijeid* ("liberty") in Flemish and Dutch, Victor De Laveleye launched his great idea on January 14, 1941, in his Belgian program at the B.B.C. Today, from the South Pacific to the Arctic Circle, *V* is by far the most popular letter in the alphabet.

It was a typical Belgian idea, a product of the spiritual heritage of a grand little nation that has never learned to accept defeat. At present, as a quarter of a century ago, the Belgians are again suffering all the misery of enemy occupation. After the Greeks, the Poles, and the Czechs, they are, perhaps, the worst treated among the oppressed nations. But they are undaunted.

Their epic resistance sprang above all from two incidents. The arrest of the burgomaster of Brussels and the bloody day of Tournai has kindled a flame that no German terror can extinguish. F. J. Vandemeulebroeck, Mayor of Brussels, was, after the King, the most popular man in Belgium. Loyally and proudly he followed in the footsteps of his great predecessor Adolphe Max, the indomitable Mayor of Brussels who had strongly opposed the system of terror applied by the army of the invaders during the first war.

In view of his immense popularity, the Germans let Vandemeulebroeck alone for more than a year after the occupation of Brussels. On June 30, 1941, however, word spread that the Mayor would be "prevented from fulfilling his duties." Immediately the City Council held a meeting to express homage to the Burgomaster. In the name of his colleagues, Alderman Jules Coelst declared that M. Vandemeulebroeck was a worthy successor of Burgomaster Max and said: "In our turn, we will follow the example offered to us by our Burgomasters. Here before you we solemnly undertake never to give in either to the occupying powers or to the traitors who consent to collaborate with him."

M. Vandemeulebroeck, answering, said that the City Hall symbolized the indomitable tenacity, energy, and courage of their nation. He added: "I have the feeling that my absence will not be long. I believe that our liberation is not far off."

While the council meeting was still in session, Gestapo agents entered and arrested the Mayor. The news spread like wildfire through Brussels. Crowds jammed the Grande Place in front of the City Hall. Goose-stepping German troops appeared. But they found no pretext for firing. The crowds were armed only with huge bunches of flowers which soon piled up around the City Hall.

In the evening posters appeared on the walls of important buildings. The Burgomaster was bidding farewell to his fellow citizens in restrained and noble terms:

My dear Fellow Citizens:

The German Authorities have just informed me that I must relinquish my office.

I have no option but to conform to this order, although legally it is a violation of the Hague Convention and, in fact, nothing justifies such a decision against me.

I feel that I have loyally and usefully accomplished the multiple duties, often so hard, which fall to the chiefs of towns and communities occupied by the enemy.

I have been asked to remain in office, but under circumstances that would imply my participation in the execution of the Decrees of April 16 and May 26, 1941.

Consent would have meant giving up my honor and my duty; would have meant disobedience to the fundamental laws of our country, the laws to which I have sworn fidelity. I refused.

Contrary to what is being said, I have not left my post and I have not resigned. I am, I remain, I shall remain the only legitimate Burgomaster of Brussels.

I am not bidding you adieu, but au revoir.

In taking leave of you temporarily, I ask you to bear your material and moral hardships with calm, courage, and confidence.

You will face your fate with a strong soul and a proud heart.

Those who really belong to our nation fear nothing nor anybody in this world. They have but one fear: failure in their duty and in their honor.

Remain united. Union will be our strength and will assure us a happier future.

God will protect Belgium and her King.

Fr. J. Vandemeulebroeck

Brussels Town Hall
June 30, 1941

Police Commissioner Gilta and the municipal printer were arrested for helping in the distribution of this proclamation. The Germans had every reason to fear an open outbreak. But none came. The underground paper *Libre Belgique* commented: "Thus far, we were united in an idea—now we are united in a man." The sentence expressed the resolution of a nation.

The Germans did not understand it. Indiscriminately they

arrested burgomaster after burgomaster, throughout the country, replacing them with abject collaborators. They had valid reasons. From one end of bleeding Belgium to the other, municipal authorities were waging an ardent struggle against the ruthless German occupation. This struggle remained true to the best tradition of Belgium, whose cities and towns have always been strongholds of independence. Local administration concerned the average Belgian much more intimately than the national government. It was, after all, the burgomaster and not the premier who married him off, baptized his children, accompanied him from the cradle to the grave.

Lovely and picturesque little Verviers, but a few miles from the German border, was the first Belgian city to be occupied by the invaders. But it held its head high. With characteristic lack of psychology, the Germans thought that they could make Verviers bow by appointing as its mayor one of their kind, an unknown Rexist named Simon. On the day he assumed office Aldermen Burguet, Gaspar, and Tiberghien read to him a protest as moving as it is noble:

"M. Simon, in order to avoid all misunderstanding between us, we feel that we should express ourselves clearly and openly. . . . Therefore we make the following declaration, and in order that a proof of this may subsist we ask the town clerk to put it on record in the proceedings.

"We are bound by our oath of fidelity to the King, by our loyalty to the Constitution and to the laws of the Belgian people, and if we should officially receive among us one who tried to seize communal authority in an illegal way, we should betray the authority of which our Board constitutes the last rampart. Since your appointment cannot be approved by the King, we feel that it does not give you any legal authority. . . .

"We know that we now live under foreign occupation; that the occupant reigns supreme according to the principle 'Might is right.' He imposes on us new conditions, he disrupts our social order and our age-old traditions. . . . But it is inadmissible that, at the time when the sufferings of our people command a fraternal union of all Belgians, there should be Belgian subjects in our

Fatherland who would contribute to the destruction of the great work of national unity. It would be a crime to give them our collaboration. We may lose everything, except honor. . . . To serve our King and our Country is and will always be our object."

Needless to say that this lofty attitude made no impression on the mercenary Simon, whose sole interest was in his pay envelope. But it had a most happy effect on the entire population of Verviers and on the Belgian people at large. It is very likely that, at the present hour, MM. Burguet, Gaspar, and Tiberghien have already paid with their liberty for this timely reminder of duty to those whom their fellow citizens had trusted with governing their cities. But their example is not in vain. The spirit of defiance rose rapidly. Traitors were no longer safe on the streets. In the city of Tournai the Rexist leader, whom the Germans later described as a "well known attorney," was shot under cover of darkness. The murder occurred during the night of September 29, 1941. The date is memorable, since it marked the beginning of a period of terror and anti-terror which has not yet ended.

Three German police officers heard the shots and hurried to the scene. Two were killed, the third seriously wounded. The slayers escaped into the night. On the next day, they shot two more traitors in the neighborhood of Tournai.

General von Falkenhausen, commander in chief of the army of occupation in Belgium, came personally to Tournai, arrested twenty-five hostages, and had them shot on the following day. For four weeks nothing more happened. Then Falkenhausen announced that the murderer's identity was known. He posted a reward of two hundred thousand francs for the capture of two men named Lelong and Talboom. A man hunt was on, extending into the forbidden zone of France. For another three weeks the search was in vain. In the meantime fifteen more citizens of Tournai were shot as hostages. On November 24, the German police trapped the two patriotic assassins in a farmhouse near the French border. They fought for their lives. Five more German policemen fell in the attempt to capture them. When Lelong finally realized that he was cornered, he put his last bullet through his temple. But Talboom escaped. At present he is said to lead a band of activists in northern France. To the Belgian people he remains a national hero.

The bloodshed at Tournai did not deter the people. The whole country was now teeming with unrest. A German sentinel was shot in Dieghem. Three German soldiers fell in a street in Liége as they were leaving a barroom. In reprisal the town was fined two million francs and ten hostages were executed. Twenty-five more hostages were arrested and brought to trial before the German military court in Liége after the railroad tracks had been ripped up in several places in the vicinity. This was one of the rare cases in which the hostage blackmail worked. Seven students gave themselves up as the perpetrators. They could not endure to see innocent people killed for their acts. The students were sentenced to life terms at hard labor and the hostages were duly released. But most of these—leading citizens—were arrested again two weeks later, after an explosion in the local railway station. The students had sacrificed themselves in vain, and their example was not followed.

The sabotage of railways and waterways is favored by Belgian activism. This hurts the Germans most. Within three months, from October to December, 1941, one hundred twenty-five trains, transporting material for the Germans, were derailed, and wires were cut four hundred and five times. Sabotage, of course, is not confined to the railways. It interferes with all the lines of communication. The Germans are building a magnificent express highway from Berlin to Paris —one of those famous strategic roads which allow Hitler to throw his armies rapidly in any direction. Unfortunately for the German High Command the Paris-Berlin road crosses Belgian soil, passing through Liége. The work, in the hands of Belgian labor, does not proceed. Every time a piece is completed, one may be sure that mysterious explosions will tear it up again.

All the important buildings on the beach of Ostend, the world famous resort, were blown up, and not by British raiders. Only the Kursaal still stands in solitude and glory. Ostend is an important German naval base, and the civilian population has been evacuated; yet even in their military stronghold the Germans cannot maintain order. The haystack of the German cavalry garrison at Bressoux near Liége was burned down—again an assault on a German military objective. But Belgian sabotage scored its biggest success on German soil. A batch of Belgian labor conscripts, all highly skilled workers, was forcibly transferred to the Krupp works in Essen. Two days after their arrival a a gigantic explosion devastated one of the most important Krupp plants. One hundred twelve persons were killed—by the grace of God not a single Belgian among them.

The output of Belgian mines dropped. At the end of 1941 there were thirty thousand fewer workers in Belgian mines than a year previously. This decline was due to inadequate food, British air raids, and, above all, to the slow-down tactics applied in the pits. Partly the Germans themselves are responsible for the decrease of the industrial output in Belgium, since they are stopping supplies of raw materials and coal. Hence, the textile industry which should be working at full speed to equip the German army in Russia, is half shut down: of thirty-two large textile factories producing in July, 1941, only sixteen are operating at present; fifty-nine smaller factories ceased work in October owing to lack of coal, and at least as many more have stopped since.

Sabotage extends to every economic field and affects every person every day. The Nazis called in the coins containing nickel, which they need badly for military purposes. The population, understanding the reason, withheld the coins.

School children hid their savings, and the peasants' stockings —their "banks"—disappeared. Against "reluctant" farmers exemplary measures are being taken. They are accused of promoting the prevailing famine. But hunger is rampant in Belgium, only due to the well known German pillaging.

Famine looks out of the eyes of the Belgian people. Most of the men are pitiful. Their belts can go twice round their middles. Their necks have shrunk so that they seem to be wearing collars much too large. Many faces are marked with the deadly pallor of starvation. In the schools, the children faint with hunger. Switzerland magnanimously organized a campaign to help the children in the occupied countries which opened with a convoy of four hundred fifty-six children from Belgium. Thirty-three of them arrived too late: they were no longer able to eat, and died of undernourishment.

There is only one way to escape the pangs of hunger. One must have "pull" with some of the madams operating hospitable salons in the red-light district of downtown Brussels. These kind-hearted ladies act as go-betweens for the German authorities, officers, and Gestapo agents—and the population. Name your price, and you can get anything through their intervention: travel permits, visas, identification cards for another name, and even a full-sized T-bone steak. "Don't hesitate," Madam encourages her customers. "Whatever you wish, I can get for you. With those German gentlemen everything can be arranged with cash."

Here is an illuminating incident: A German officer, selling additional ration cards for heavy workers, made the mistake of not sharing his booty generously enough with the controller from the Gestapo. He was denounced, and received the customary worst punishment. He was transferred to the Russian front. A monocled, spur-clanking captain replaced him. Three days after assuming his job as food controller of Brussels the new man visited a Belgian merchant who had been a good customer of his predecessor, suggesting that they should continue the pleasant relations at the same prices and under the same conditions.

For the rest, relations between the invaders and the Belgians continue to be unpleasant. The undeclared war between patriotic Belgians and their Nazi overlords goes on with unabated fury and bitterness, despite the "official" total of fifty-four executed and four hundred imprisoned—which is only a fraction of the number of German victims, a spokesman for the Free Belgian government declared.

"The Belgians at this moment are carrying on merciless sabotage against occupation authorities," he said. "We blame the Germans for nearly six thousand deaths among Belgian workmen carted off by Germany to work in the coastal industrial areas, which are frequently bombed by the R.A.F.; and every day another Belgian disappears on some undefined charge, sent to prison or to a concentration camp.

"Supply depots of the German army have been set afire repeatedly. Several factories have been destroyed by flames or explosions. Trains are constantly derailed, and one day the Germans discovered that fifteen million cartridges manufactured by the Fabrique Nationale d'Armes de Guerre had been left unfilled. Twenty men were shot recently near the French border for setting fire to a train and destroying it. Yet all this underground activity continues despite the Germans' hiring Belgian spies at a salary of twelve hundred francs a month.

"Hand-drawn fingers of scorn decorate the walls of our cities, pointing to the houses of these spies. They are well known to all patriotic Belgians. German soldiers continue to be thrown into the Mons Canal each night, or into the Meuse River near Liége. The Nazis have repeatedly warned that the perpetrators of such acts will face firing squads; but their soldiers still get ducked and drowned.

"Belgian officers, airmen, and soldiers every day try to join the free forces to fight the Germans. Hand-to-hand fighting between Belgians and Germans has taken place in the streets of Brussels on numerous occasions, as the vicious but necessary campaign continues.

"Among the more important jobs of sabotage may be included the complete destruction by fire of the Roeselare warehouses, gutting of the Gosselies-Bossière grain depot, and the burning of the Aalst shoe plant. The R.A.F. blasted a factory at Antwerp, after it had been lit up by 'neglectful' workers. The Hoboken Oil Refinery and the Avantin Rubber factory also were burned up by saboteurs among the personnel.

"We have eliminated some of our internal enemies. Justice will come to all of them."

"To assure protection against political acts of violence" (actually to protect his beloved Quislings), General von Falkenhausen had the following notice posted:

Loyal collaboration by most of the population with the army of occupation has made it possible, up to now, for order to be maintained and for business and civic life to continue as usual. In the interests of the country, it is absolutely necessary to fight with everything in our power against those who wish to end this collaboration. To accomplish this, I hereby announce that in the future any one who commits a political act of violence against any collaborator, or against any one speaking in favor of loyal collaboration with the army of occupation, will be tried before a military court and may be sentenced to death, according to the law as enacted. Any violence against relatives of these persons will be punished in a like manner.

General von Falkenhausen did not stop at words. He ordered the National League of War Veterans to be dissolved and had sixty-one of their leaders court-martialed for refusal to tolerate collaborators in their ranks. All sixty-one could have saved their necks by a volte-face, accepting collaboration and collaborators. They preferred death to treason. Immediately afterward ninety Belgian prisoners of war, recently released, were rounded up in Liége, and sent back to their camps in Germany for having sabotaged the "collaborationist spirit" in their town.

The persecution of local mayors who did not allow individual collaborators in their communities enough "latitude of propaganda" increased. Mayor Gerite of Ressaix, a stubborn foe of Degrelle, was arrested and deported to Germany after anti-Nazi placards had been posted during the night. M. Maistriau, Mayor of Mons and a former Minister of Justice, was also arrested for his anticollaborationist attitude. Mayor Dessain of Malines was arrested for his heroic behavior —during the first war.

The Germans announced the execution of fifty Belgian journalists, civil servants, and priests collectively, without disclosing their names.

At the beginning of 1942 the German terror ran riot. The military courts were working day and night. Every morning execution squads riddled blindfolded victims with twelve bullets—which, as General von Falkenhausen expressed it, was an excellent way of training young soldiers for the Russian campaign. He did not, however, convince his own men of the advantages gained from this training. The morale of German airmen and soldiers stationed in Belgium deteriorated visibly. Desertions increased. Some German soldiers asked not to be detailed to the execution squads any longer. It had been great fun, they admitted, but in the long run it became unsupportable.

The campaign to protect the collaborators reached its climax in the case of the "phantom train." The military court in Brussels indicted those officers and officials who had escorted a bunch of notorious Quislings, among them Degrelle, to France, after they had been rounded up, very belatedly, on May 10, 1940. Lieutenant Dubois, commander of the prison train, was sentenced to fifteen years' hard labor. The president of the court expressed regret at his inability to sentence Lieutenant Dubois to death—Falkenhausen's order being, unfortunately, not retroactive. Four noncommissioned officers under Dubois's command received ten-year terms. The Belgian Quislings smiled. But their smiles faded within the next twenty-four hours.

Aroused by the phantom-train trial, the Bar of Brussels decided to strike from its rolls all members known to be collaborators. The Quislings are outcasts in their own country. They have lost practically all their following, and their shameless licking of the invaders' boots has resulted in a definite rapprochement between Flemings and Walloons, hitherto antagonistic groups, in the interests of the independent spirit of the nation. Understanding between the two sections of the population has never been so close as it is today. Excluded from this great union are thirty thousand people out of eight and a half million. Twenty-five thousand are Rexists, and five thousand, including wives and children, are members of the Flemish Nazi party.

The Quislings are perfectly conscious of their isolation. To counteract it they formulate desperate plans, not always devoid of involuntary humor. Thus Staf Declercq, the Flemish extremist leader, suggested to his German masters in all seriousness that they should deport the majority of the Flemish people to France. France, he argued, has seven million hectares of uncultivated land, whereas Flanders has the densest population per square mile in Europe. It was Hitler's "geopolitics" in a nutshell. "We are confident," Declercq stated, "that the Führer of the German people whom we recognize as the Leader of the whole Germanic race, will put an end to the ordeal that has weighed on our people for three centuries: the fact that Germanic blood runs to waste in the arteries of Latins."

On hearing this gibberish, Dr. Corneel Heymans, Nobel prize winner and professor at the University of Ghent, the only reputable member of the Nazi-appointed Flemish Cultural Council, resigned without giving any reasons. Even the Flemish National Socialist legionaries, who never reached the Russian battlefields but showed a distinct preference for a Polish camp, did not relish their boss's speech which was sent to them in pamphlets. They expressed their opinion distinctly, and a solemn brawl with their German comrades ensued. When the German High Command brought Declercq by airplane to the camp in Poland, to preach submission to his men, he was received with a Bronx cheer and the question: "What is happening to our families at home?"

This was, indeed, a painful question. The families of the members of the "Black Brigade" (as the handful of volunteers for Russia call themselves) are ostracized in their own homes. Women especially refuse to deal with them. The wife of a Black Brigand (popular name for a member of the Brigade) is not tolerated in any food line. She is excluded from neighborhood meetings, sewing circles, and all charitable activities. In a village in the Campine some recruits for the Black Brigade were besieged in a house for three hours by a hostile crowd. When the Combat Formation of the Brigade, wearing the original Nazi brown shirt, took their oath in Brussels, Commander Simoens addressed his troops: "You are soldiers and will be treated as such. There will be victims among you, martyrs of the Nazi revolution. But be assured that every drop of your blood that is shed shall be paid for a hundred times by your enemies. We will finish off the pro-British traitors." He was carefully preparing the men for civil warfare. The idea that they were to march against Russia did not strike him. Indeed, even the members of the Combat Formation are slow to march. When a group of them was attacked in Liége, and Degrelle's personal bodyguard was overpowered by the outraged population, the German garrison did not interfere. "It serves them right," commented the local German commander. "As long as they feel more comfortable at home than in the Russian winter we shall never get them to the front."

Wherever the Rexists, the Flemish Extremists, the Black Brigands, show up singly or in groups, they get a merciless beating. The chief of Rex-Walloonia, Joseph Pevenasse, had the nerve to appear in Rexist uniform in the court of Charleroi. Immediately two lawyers, MM. Gailly and Dubuisson, took exception to his appearance, declaring that his uniform was an outrage, and that any one wearing it was an enemy agent. Pevenasse tried to bully them, and received an unforgettable flogging. He shouted for the gendarmes, but when they came they appraised the situation, said "Nothing wrong, it seems," and strolled away again.

On the other hand, the German military police intervened to protect Rexists leaving a Degrelle meeting in the Brussels Royal Circus in small groups. It was too spectacular an occasion to allow any uproar. But the commander of the military police said, "I am sorry," when he ordered his men to disperse the crowds jostling the traitors. Contrary to the German custom, the clubs and rubber truncheons were applied mildly. The German police themselves despise the Rexists, a good number of whom received "erroneously misdirected" blows from their German protectors.

On a single occasion Léon Degrelle ventured to carry his apostolate of treason into the mining district. He spoke in Thuin, violently attacking Cardinal van Roey—whom Belgian miners revere as a saintly man and love as a son of their own soil—and calling him a "servant of the interests of plutocracy." Beau Léon had to recall tricks of the time when he was a celebrated athlete in order to get away alive.

Awaking in the hospital after his speech to the miners, he found he had lost both rows of pearl-white teeth. He did not spill his blood for his Führer, but he never forgets to mention that he lost his teeth in Adolf Hitler's service.

The dentist who replaced the teeth had a sad experience. His name was put on the blacklist including all doctors treating Quislings, and he lost all his patients overnight.

Another blacklist contains the names of all contributors to Quislingite publications. It begins with "a Dutchman of doubtful morality" who went bankrupt a few months before the German invasion, but recouped his fortune by taking over the old established Catholic *Gazet van Antwerpen* and transforming it into an anti-Semitic Nazi sheet. The Liége newspaper *Le Legia* was taken over by an F. C. Desmet who had entered journalism by writing for *Chaînes Brisées* (Broken Chains), the magazine published by the inmates of the state prison at Hoogstraeten. Later he published a series of articles on the fight against crime in Belgium, a problem concerning which he certainly was an expert. Then he repeatedly served time for swindling and embezzling. Finally he advanced to become publisher of *Le Legia* and editor of the Nazified *Le Soir*, interrupting his activities for four months to do time once more for cheating five young girls in Brussels. The *Vooruit*, the blacklist continues, still pretends to cling to its honorable Socialist past; but its editor, G. Crommen, burgomaster of Ledeberg near Ghent, was arrested, and replaced with a turncoat. A new collaborationist sheet *Notre Terre Wallonne* also uses a patriotic disguise to spread Nazi poison. The notary Paul Gérard contributed under a pen name to the Nazi *Nouveau Journal*. One day in the autumn Gérard ceased sending in his articles. Toward the middle of December the fact became known that he had been the "well known attorney" whose assassination in Tournai, during the night of September 17th was the signal fire of revolution. "This is only the first in a long list," commented a former Catholic cabinet minister.

The blacklists circulate everywhere in Belgium. Every town has its own list of doomed men. In Louvain, for instance, three hundred names are included, with addresses, occupations, telephone numbers, and the reasons for their indictment. They appear under an identical banner head: "The vermin must be exterminated."

The Belgians, like all peoples of occupied countries, hate their own traitors more ferociously than the invaders. Yet there is not much love lost between the population and the field-gray uniforms, either.

On the Belgian national holiday huge throngs in Antwerp clashed with the German military police. Evidently, the masses were beaten off. After nearly two months' imprisonment seventy-five people came before the military court, charged with rioting, and were condemned to long prison terms. Similar demonstrations were staged in Brussels. The city was heavily fined, curfew advanced to five P.M. and, as an additional irritation, the Bois de la Cambre, the park of the capital, was closed to the civilian population.

The Germans issued a warning to the people to avoid the streets on November 15, King Leopold's name day. Consequently, the streets were crowded on this day, and people were arrested in practically every Belgian town.

Mass demonstrations led nowhere. The people resorted to roundabout measures. Inscriptions were chalked on Brussels streets: "A bas les Boches!" and "Vive l'Angleterre!" and most frequently "Gloire à la R.A.F.!" A few weeks later the preferred inscription was "Death to the tyrants!"

It was not a Platonic declaration. Since the Bois de la Cambre was closed to civilians, Belgian patriots decided to make the other public garden, Laeken Park, hot soil for ambling German uniforms. A number of soldiers were assaulted in the park, and killed. As a rule former service men were arrested in retribution, or former politicians whose anti-German activities were held responsible for the feelings that inspired the assaults. A few young Belgians dropped a bomb in front of the German Kommandantur in Malines, damaging the house. Because they escaped, ten released prisoners of war were sent back to the German camp. In the blood-soaked town of Ypres, scene of a great battle in the first war, a Nazi sentry was attacked and beaten up by three civilians. Finding a hat with the initials "A. E. D." near the Hotel Grand' Place, where the incident had taken place, the Germans immediately summoned for interrogation every one in the town whose initials corresponded to the three ominous letters. Four citizens were arrested and shot.

General von Falkenhausen issued two more decrees: Every town or village in or near which German telegraph wires were cut would be instantly evacuated, and the entire civil population would be dispatched to concentration camps. Furthermore, the punishment for attack on German soldiers would no longer be arrest, but the execution of ten hostages in each case.

The General soon saw himself confronted by another problem. A series of organized thefts of military documents, cameras, weapons, and other army material broke out. The thefts became so numerous that he threatened to punish them with death. But he was up against an enemy whom it was not easy to intimidate. The thievery was organized on a country-wide scale by a former Gestapo man who had himself been imprisoned for his refusal to participate in an anti-Jewish action. He broke jail, escaped to Belgium, and there found a new field of activities to his liking, and in line with the education he had received from Heinrich Himmler.

Another Gestapo man in Brussels, a warden in the notorious prison cellar, startled an inmate, from whom this story comes since his release, with a remark. "Fundamentally," the inmate had remarked, "you are just as poor a devil as we are here." "Yes," replied the jailer after clearing his throat. "The difference is only that with us it has already lasted too long."

If any individual groups may be singled out as the pillars

of a whole Belgian nation's seething resistance, they are the returned prisoners of war, organized labor, the women, and the Church.

A classic witness to the attitude of the released prisoners is Léon Degrelle's own *Pays Réel*, which stated:

The prisoners returned from German camps still keep a feeling of hatred against the enemy. As soon as they reach home they join the opponents of the New Order. They are of weak character, they have understood nothing before the liberation of our country by Hitler, and they will again be deceived in the future.

For the time being, however, it appears that it is the Nazis who are deceived in Belgium. Their authorities complain incessantly of an underground organization of released prisoners of war which they accuse of most of the anti-Nazi outrages committed. If such an organization, indeed, is in existence it is well concealed. Thus far, no member has been ferreted out.

There is no doubt that the underground resistance of Belgian labor is organized. This is a very delicate matter, since one cannot tell more than the Nazis themselves know already. However, both Nazis and Belgian patriots know the coal-mining region of Beaurivage is the center of violent agitation against the invaders and their creatures, particularly against their abject "labor leader" Henri de Man. His sheet is officially declared "must" reading for all trade-union members. But out of their number (over one million) only ten thousand subscribe to it, all under duress. On the other hand the clandestine periodical *Clarté*, printed by the revived syndical movement, is distributed to every miner's house. It is remarkable that not only the Walloon but the Flemish part of labor joins in active opposition. The Flemish seamen, who were once regarded as the natural raw material for Nazism, are now issuing their own illegal newspaper in a bootleg printing office in Antwerp.

Belgian labor is involved in a life-and-death struggle. Its ranks are the first targets of the Nazi attack. Germany is suffering from a grave lack of man power for the preparation of the "industrial offensive" which, according to Hitler, is to outbalance the rapidly increasing American war production and equip the German armies on the Eastern Front with new weapons for the counterattack against Russia. Although the Germans are well aware of the fact that enforced labor's productive capacity and willingness cannot be compared with those of free labor, they envisage, as this is written, the introduction of general labor service throughout occupied Europe. Belgium is to be the testing ground for this measure. Hence the whole world is vitally interested in the outcome of the desperate and heroic struggle Belgian labor is putting up to resist enslavement.

To a much greater degree than Adolf Hitler has ever realized, women influence, and perhaps decide, the psychological attitude of a nation. In Belgium, at present, every woman is a belligerent. She has to cope with almost unsurmountable difficulties. Food is becoming scarcer and scarcer. Another hardship of the women of Belgium is the recently decreed introduction of compulsory female labor—a measure, incidentally, for which the Germans did not dare to assume the responsibility, and which, therefore, they had M. Romsée, their puppet, sign. To add their customary vulgar touch the German authorities have reintroduced prostitution, banned in most Belgian cities for many years.

Small wonder that the women are the most violent demonstrators in the upflares that occur regularly. When the news spread that the heavy pounding of Cologne by the R.A.F. had killed six thousand workers from Brussels, dispatched to the well known target of enemy air raids and forbidden by the German regulations to take to the shelters while the raids were on, thousands of widows demonstrated on the Grand' Place in Brussels. In the provinces of Charleroi and Namur women carrying black banners paraded in front of the German labor exchanges, until German motorized squads, driving at full speed into the crowds, dispersed them.

In Antwerp the housewives staged a hunger demonstration as a protest against the insufficient food supplies. Preceded by banners with the inscription "We want coal and potatoes, more bread, milk and fat," they marched to the Town Hall, where their delegation tried to hand in a petition. The women composing the delegation were arrested. Against the demonstrating groups platoons of German soldiers were set in motion. Most of the fleeing women sought refuge in the churches.

The church is the only place in which the average Belgian can still breathe. There he breathes the air of independence. Despite the incessant vicious attacks by the Nazi officials and their lackeys on hierarchy and clergy, as "scoundrels in cassocks," "cassocked accomplices of the British murderers," and "valets of Churchill," the Church in Belgium maintains, and strengthens everywhere, the spirit of resistance.

In the Flemish extremist press curious articles were to be found in which the Church of Rome was ranked among the international conspirators, and its activity was compared with that of Freemasonry and international Bolshevism. Following such denunciations, Catholic social organizations were dissolved, and through the "coordination" of the trade unions an effort was made to destroy the whole structure of the Christian-Social movement in Belgium. Several priests at Namur were forbidden to officiate at church services. A Catholic priest in Antwerp was sent to a concentration camp because he had encouraged his parishioners to resist the Nazi looting. All Catholic schools in Brussels and Antwerp were closed. In Ghent, the Bishop was ordered to kill three of the six hens he had in his coop, since his palace was inhabited by only three people, and according to a German regulation each person may only possess a single hen.

The clergy has shown great courage in defying the Nazi rule. The Bishop of Bruges and the Dean of Sainte-Gudule refused to celebrate High Mass in memory of the traitors shot at Abbeville, since they knew well that this holy service would be used as an anti-Belgian, pro-Nazi demonstration. The Rexists and Flemish Nationalist storm troopers are refused Holy Communion. Revengeful, the Quisling rabble threw paving stones into the windows of the Bishop's palace at Bruges, and smeared the Archbishop's palace in Malines with the words "Down with the Pope!" In both towns the citizens immediately chased away the mob. All over the country the religious spirit is reviving. Services, courses for adult instruction in religious matters, and pilgrimages are crowded. The village churches were never as heavily attended as now. Is it a spiritual revival alone? Without, of course, attempting to minimize the religious urge of the people, brought about by the anti-Christian and antihumane behavior of the invaders, another reason may explain the packing of the churches. They are the only places where the Belgian people can hear the "Brabançonne" and "God Save the King."

Countless Belgians, men and women alike, were sentenced to death for harboring British pilots and helping them to escape. Young people among them accompany the British in their escapes, to serve with the Belgian forces in England.

Among the proudest escape stories is the tale of two young Belgian mechanics who stole a German plane and crossed the border, saluted by the Luftwaffe's air police. A similar story involves two young patriots, one a hairdresser and the other an office apprentice, who took thirteen months to get from Brussels to London, traveling the roundabout way through occupied France, Spain, Africa, the Red Sea, the Indian Ocean, China, and finally via Canada to England. "Here we are," they reported, arriving at the London Belgian recruiting office. "Forgive us the delay." All escape stories include accounts of smuggling, exhausting marches at night over stony hillsides or along river beds, descriptions of disguises which must be assumed in order to pass safely through enemy-occupied countries, and finally the hazards of stowing away on shipboard.

Such escapes are not isolated cases. Thousands of young Belgians have devised schemes for breaking the jail into which their country has been transformed by the Germans. Some steal boats at night and cross the North Sea at the risk of foundering or being caught by some U-boat. Others walk for days and weeks, tramping the highways of France, risking denunciation and concentration camps, entering Spain by swimming the Bidassoa River near Hendaye or crossing the Pyrenees at night, and arriving at last in Portugal, where they find passage in a ship. The French arrest them whenever they can, and so do the Spaniards, for Madrid like Vichy takes instructions from Berlin. But most of the Belgians somehow work their way out of the French and Spanish jails, give the slip to the Portuguese international police and reach their goal.

What was perhaps the most glorious escape story was reported by an elderly woman, who, together with her son and three other young men managed to escape the country by the shortest route, across the North Sea, to England. Here is her story—a proof that a nation of such people cannot be Germanized, nor annihilated within the promised Nazi millennium, of which it appears the first nine hundred and ninety-eight years are already over. The widow said that her son and his friends had dreamed for a long time of joining the Belgian Army in Great Britain:

"We had a summer cottage on the coast. In 1940 we tried to get to Great Britain, but after a fruitless trip to France we had to come back. My son was terribly disappointed, and day and night he tried to work out some plan practical enough for us to risk.

"Finally, some months ago, in spite of the fact that every kind of boat had been requisitioned by the Germans or registered with them, we secured a dinghy—twenty feet long and five feet wide.

"To row across the North Sea was, of course, unthinkable. We needed a motor for our boat—a well-nigh impossible item in an occupied country. However, nothing daunted, my son scoured the neighboring villages and after a long search succeeded in securing a four-horsepower motor which had not been used for four years, and whose battery was naturally dead. My son, who was desperate by this time, took a chance and carried the motor to a near-by city for repairs—right under the noses of the Germans! They even helped him lift the crate onto the streetcar!

"However, a short time later we had a chance to buy a more powerful, nine-horsepower motor. This we installed in the dinghy, and it seemed in such good shape that we discarded the four-horsepower motor. And now for the fuel. We couldn't buy it, but we could steal it from the Germans who had some reserves (colored red to prevent Belgians from using it without permission) in their truck garages. With the help of some friends we finally stole about twenty-four gallons, and this we stored in a near-by deserted cottage.

"My son, his three friends, and I had agreed that we must leave at low tide, on a calm night with no moon. The date was fixed and everything in readiness. At three o'clock in the morning, after placing the fuel cans and spare parts for the motor in the boat, we pulled it onto the beach with a small rubber-wheeled wagon. There the wagon got bogged down in the sand, and we were forced to unload the boat and carry it about seven hundred feet to the water, where the waves lifted it up and nearly carried it away. Clinging to it for dear life, we placed our supplies on board.

"We were ready to leave. Fearful of the noise it might make, we nevertheless tried the motor for a minute, and turned it off as soon as we heard it running well. Then we took out our oars and rowed away from the shore. A half-hour out from land we felt a little safer. We got out our compass, checked the course our dinghy was to take, and turned over the motor. It ran a minute on two cylinders, sputtered, and died. Again and again we tried to start it, but with no success. However, having come this far, there was nothing to do but go on, and we started to row.

"At daybreak my son tried to fix the motor, but again with no success. Everything was soaked with salt water. So we began to row again. Late in the afternoon we spied a buoy, but the current prevented us from reaching it. For several hours we turned round and round it, and finally managed to reach it and anchor ourselves to wait for low tide to help us on again toward England.

"Suddenly, as we were clinging to the buoy, two Messerschmitt-109's passed over us. They must have seen us for they swooped down only sixty feet above us. We threw ourselves onto the floor of the boat, expecting every minute to be machine-gunned, and as soon as they had passed on toward Ostend, we unhitched ourselves from the buoy and started rowing as hard as we could. We were in despair, believing that German speedboats would soon be after us and we should be captured and thrown into concentration camps. The boys wanted to drop everything in the boat overboard, but I finally dissuaded them, pointing out that we should have plenty of time for that when the speedboat appeared. The tide was with us now, and we rowed all night, taking turns.

"The next day, at about nine o'clock, we had a very disagreeable surprise. We were nearly caught in the middle of a German convoy which was heading for the Belgian coast accompanied by six Messerschmitt-109's. We got out of their way as quickly as possible, but an hour later our hearts fell again when four bombers and six pursuit planes appeared on the horizon. With what relief we discovered they were English cannot be imagined! We shouted and signaled in every conceivable way to attract their attention, and were sure that one of the pursuit planes had seen us since it turned and flew back to England. We were overjoyed at the prospect of being rescued and kept our eyes glued to the horizon for its return. After hours of fruitless waiting we turned wearily to our oars and rowed until night. About seven o'clock a seaplane, with seven other English planes, flew over us, followed by four Spitfires. Again we waved and tried to attract their attention; but they seemed to take no notice of us. During the night we made up a kind of bed roll and took turns sleeping and rowing.

"At twelve-thirty a ship suddenly appeared out of the darkness only a hundred and fifty feet from us. It was moving so silently that we didn't hear it. It came straight toward us and we were nearly overturned as it passed. Another narrow escape! It appeared as silently as it had come, and we never knew whether it was German or English.

"The next morning we were about forty-five miles from the English coast. We had already been rowing for hours when about eleven o'clock four planes appeared to the west. They apparently checked our location, and while two of them flew back toward England, the two others circled over us and dropped us life belts. Half an hour later two destroyers appeared and bore down upon us full speed. We had one final fright when, in their zeal, they almost cut our boat in two.

"We were brought to Dover and after we had told our stories, the authorities explained our rescue. It seemed that, as soon as our boat had been spotted at sea by the first airplane, a report was made and rescue planes sent out to find us. This turned out to be extremely difficult, and planes had even flown as far as Ostend trying to locate our little boat. And so it was twenty-four hours before we were sighted.

"I still have the white napkin which we waved as a signal to our rescuers, and on which I drew a huge S.O.S. with lipstick. I guess I'll keep it with me always as a souvenir of the most exciting journey I ever hope to take."

CHAPTER NINETEEN

NORWAY

Let us not forget that the guerrillas in, say, Norway and Serbia are helping us.—PRESIDENT ROOSEVELT.

NORWAY is girded for the decisive fight. The battle stations are manned. Three million patriots are eagerly awaiting the combat signal: the counter invasion by the Free Nations. They know that the forces of liberation will not come tomorrow, nor the next day. But come they will—about that Norwegians have no doubt. Two years of agony have not broken their spirit, nor shattered their confidence. Perhaps the greatest glory of the Norwegians, and other oppressed peoples, is the fact that they have not even grown cynical in this world for sale; a world of double dealing and of bartering honor for profit; Hitler's world. Their countries are blacked out. Sometimes it seems as if life itself were dwindling. Many, indeed, have fallen, and passed away. But as the Catholic does not fear purgatory, so the Norwegian does not fear the New Order. It is a nuisance. It is an insult. It is a criminal assault. It is, however, not the end. The bugles will blow again. Grinning English, American, Canadian boys will plunge through the surf. Their parachutists will drop from the skies. Even if, at first, they should only be a handful— three million Norwegian men, women, and children are ready to join them. Each is already at his post.

The enemy is warned. He, too, is preparing. In itself the elevation of Quisling to the rank of Premier on February 1, 1942, was an empty formality, by no means indicating even a strengthening of the puppet dictator's shaky position with his own masters. But it clearly presaged Nazism's plan to deal the deathblow to Norway.

Hitler is attacking because he cannot escape. We shall see this strategy of his as long as he lasts in this war. We shall see it applied on larger fronts than the Norwegian side line. But the case of Norway, as it unfolds at present, is a test case. Preparing for his spring drive against Russia, and probably also for his push across the Mediterranean, Hitler, it appears, needs no additional trouble with a "colonial" war. But he cannot avoid it. His troubles in Norway have become so grave and so pressing that he must once more resort to the age-old German adage: To strike first is the best defense.

Conditions in Norway have become almost unbearable both for the downtrodden people and for the invaders with their Quislingite appendix. The people are on the brink of starvation, robbed of—literally—even their shirts, which they must deliver to the German army in Russia, and squeezed by the Gestapo, their best men executed by the score. The army of occupation, on the other hand, is visibly deteriorating, and not entirely on account of the shift of most of the troops to the Eastern Front. Quisling, on his side, is confronted with one unsurmountable obstacle: a total lack of following. Not one in a hundred of the Norwegian people is in his camp. The small number of traitors is sufficient to replace the seven members of the Supreme Court, and to find a few henchmen for the administration, or to replace those editors and writers who would not comply with Goebbels' perversion of the Norwegian press. But Quisling cannot refill the cadres of the restive police with men he can trust, although most of the professional criminals have been enlisted in the newly established secret police and in the ranks of the *Hirdmen*, the Norwegian brown-shirts. Quisling has dismissed teachers and professors by the hundreds. But only one professor at the Oslo University, Dr. Klaus Hansen, belongs to the Nasjonal Samling, the single permitted party. Even the Nazification of the theater and the arts—in Norway an extremely important branch of public life—has proved impossible because of the absence of Hitler-inspired artists and, strangely enough for Norway, the silence of Wagner singers.

The gravest handicap the Quisling system incurs is the lack of cooperation by the municipal administration. An order issued by the Nazi-appointed Minister of the Interior, for municipal employees to take an active part in work of the Nazi party, has met with this response: fifteen civil service men replied that they were members of the party; fifty-one merely acknowledged receipt of the circular order without making any comment, and three thousand nine hundred and eighty-two answered categorically that they could not understand what the order from the Interior Department had to do with their duties as municipal and county employees.

In spite of the arrival of an ever-increasing number of German "specialists" in Norway, Quisling and his real boss, Gauleiter Terboven, simply have not enough men to organize Norway in the totalitarian style. It has proved quite impossible to find an adequate number of Quislingists for mayors of villages, and where "reliable" men could be found they have shown themselves so completely incompetent that half of the Norwegian countryside is in a state of complete administrative chaos.

The labor situation presents the same picture. Last September, Quisling had a few of the most popular labor leaders executed. Others were sent to the Grini concentration camp, where twenty-two died of "heart disease." The trade unions were "new-ordered." But not enough traitors were available to run the complicated and widespread organization of the unions. At present, most of these unions are functioning underground or have simply ceased to exist. The workers are not paying their membership dues and are sabotaging all instructions from their appointed head men.

Forty-three of the most important Norwegian labor and professional organizations sent a sharp protest to Reichskommissar Terboven against the conditions which have dominated Norway since Quisling was put into power. In bold words this protest blamed the German and puppet authorities for the brutal behavior of storm troopers, for threats and acts of violence against loyal Norwegians, for the thousands of arrests that have taken place, and for heedless destruction of law and order in general.

The German administration's answer was to introduce general labor conscription on a nation-wide scale. The Social Department of the puppet government, with the approval of Terboven, issued an order providing for the registration of industrial and construction workers. This order, in its own words, "creates a legal basis for requiring able-bodied persons to carry on their work in a designated place." Whether this designated place lies inside Norway or outside is not specified. Norwegian youths in the labor camp at Trögstad, however, received an inkling of the plans in the making. They were informed that they should all "volunteer" to go to Finland and do work behind the lines. All protested bitterly against the suggestion. For though drafted into the German-style work camps, these Norwegian lads were wholeheartedly anti-Nazi. On the following day the request was repeated, but again the boys shouted, "No!" Whereupon all were called together in a meeting to hear the following pronouncement from the camp leader: "We have asked you whether you will go to Finland voluntarily, but next time we won't ask. You will just go!"

Advertisements in all the Norwegian papers, soliciting labor for Germany, particularly for the heavily bombed cities, evoked no response. Since lack of man power is Germany's most pressing immediate problem, and ruthless compulsion is applied everywhere—with Norway only representing a small sector of the German labor battle front—Norwegian labor has good reason to fear the severest pressure. Whether such pressure can be exerted without open resistance is, to say the least, doubtful. The Norwegian workers have time and again shown their opposition to German rule and their contempt for the Quislings in word and deed.

Also the attitude of the Norwegian police, on whose shoulders has fallen the difficult task of cooperating with enemy authorities while at the same time trying to protect their fellow countrymen from crime and violence, is doubtful, from Quisling's point of view. Many policemen resigned when they were ordered not to interfere with anything the Hirdmen chose to do, and to give the Nazi salute on duty. In Kristiansund, fifty-nine out of a force of sixty-two resigned for this reason. In Oslo, one hundred police officers refused to accept orders from their new Quisling chief. Many of them were sent to a German concentration camp. In the traffic division of the Oslo police fourteen men who at first tried to comply with the New Order canceled their membership in the Nasjonal Samling. A letter written to the Gestapo by the Nazi-appointed mayor of Alta was found in which the traitor complained: "The whole population is decidedly pro-English, and the same holds true for the local police."

The task of maintaining the system in the country rests entirely with the army of occupation. Feverishly the Germans endeavor to entrench themselves in Norway. The repeated raids by British and Free Norwegian commandos have proved that their hold on the country is no longer uncontested. To repel further commando raids, a heavily fortified "Falkenhorst line" has just been completed, extending from Kristiansand on the Skagerrak, the southernmost point of Norway, as far north as Trondheim. The fact that this line is being extended up to Kirkenes shows, however, that the Nazis do not yet consider Norway invasion-proof. At Laksevaag a new German submarine base is under construction. Work proceeds in strictest secrecy. But with the evacuation of fifty-seven families the news, of course, spread as far as London. The neuralgic border of Norway is the northern coast. On account of the heavy losses the Germans suffered along these shores at the hands of the British, all sea traffic and fishing has been stopped. Mechanized units of the army of occupation are pouring into northern Norway. Military law has been established. Persons accused of derogatory remarks about German soldiers are arrested in great numbers. Among the prisoners of this district are Mr. Björnstad of Narvik, the former British Vice Consul, and two Norwegian officers, Port Captain Holgh and Major Hagemann. In spite of the most stringent measures, however, the large munition dump at Elvenes near Narvik was blown up, seriously wounding all the German guards. The ensuing investigation brought to light a remarkable fact. This explosion was not the work of Norwegian patriots. It happened when the German guard were engaged in a free-for-all among themselves. Stray bullets set the ammunition stores on fire. Such incidents are by no means isolated. In the arctic solitude of northern Norway the German jailers themselves develop the mentality of prisoners. Most of them suffer from what is known as barbed-wire disease.

Not all the German heroes, however, are losing their senses. There are still some endowed with a keen business sense. One day in December an officer was shipping from Oslo to Germany four hundred coffins which, he said, contained the bodies of soldiers fallen in Norway. While cranes were loading them on the ship, however, a chain broke, a load of coffins crashed to the dock and broke open. People closed their eyes in horror—but then a laugh broke out. Out of the broken coffins had tumbled dressed hogs, quarters of beef, and quantities of veal. No one was shot: the conqueror has the right to steal. As a rule, his appearance is overlooked, but his name is well remembered.

Not all the generally despised soldiers of the army of occupation take their ostracism with equanimity. Particularly among the elder men, who are now generally replacing the younger classes dispatched to Russia, deterioration of morale is steady—a widespread phenomenon among the armies of occupation. From Norway alone, and in the last two months alone, the following incidents are on record: The German commander in Flekkerfjord on the southern coast issued a stern warning to the citizens against appearing on the streets during aerial attacks. While Allied planes attack their city the townspeople congregate on the streets, singing "God Save Our King" (the Norwegian royal anthem). This shameless behavior must necessarily demoralize the German garrison, the commander admitted bluntly.

Recently, the German authorities have had warning sirens installed at Harstad, Tromsö, and several other places along the coast. On hearing them, the order said, the garrison must march in formation to the shelters. "Soldiers using an alert to stray away will be punished as deserters."

The inhabitants of Bergen were awakened by a terrific explosion. Rushing to their windows, they saw a column of fire rising from a German patrol boat in the harbor. The ship, totally wrecked, was removed as speedily as possible. Later some German sailors admitted to the Norwegian families with whom they were billeted that the patrol boat had been sabotaged by its own crew.

In the Stavanger district extensive robberies of German

military armories and warehouses occurred. Seven soldiers were shot as the culprits. After the raid on Maalöy panic spread among the German troops. A great number of them fled into the trackless mountains. Six of the deserters were caught wearing civilian clothes, but still carrying their rifles. They had joined the Norwegian guerrilla band led by Ingvald Garbo. He too was trapped, and executed. But most of his mixed German-Norwegian band is still at large.

Records of membership of the Nasjonal Samling chapters in Asker and Baerum mysteriously disappeared. Instantly, a score of members, fearing the consequences now that their belonging to the Quisling party was known, resigned from the party. Some had to pay heavy fines for their revocation, others lost their official appointments. But they hope that they have saved their lives. Sverre Riisnaes, Quisling's Minister of Justice, has not much hope on this score. This was made perfectly clear to him when he told an anti-Nazi lawyer in Oslo: "It is my duty to inform you that your license to practice law has been revoked for life!" "For whose life?" the lawyer countered.

In the world of sports there has been a nation-wide rebellion against the enforced Nazi reorganization of the formerly democratic associations of skiers and of other sports groups. When the duly elected leaders were replaced by minor puppets of the Quisling regime, thousands upon thousands of young Norwegians showed their displeasure and contempt by refusing to participate in athletic competitions.

The most recent example of unbending resistance to the Nazis on the sports front comes from the Lyn Athletic Club in Oslo, one of Norway's best equipped clubs. When the newly established Nazi "Sports Ministry" recently appointed a Norwegian Nazi, Harald Schjölberg, as director of the Lyn Club, seven hundred and sixty-four of its eight hundred members immediately resigned in a body. In retaliation the Nazi sports leader proclaimed that henceforth none of those who resigned would be permitted to set foot in the club's quarters or on any of its tennis courts or playing fields. They also had pictures of Sonja Henie and Birger Ruud, the international ski-jumping champion, removed from the Normanna Exhibition, since both Sonja and Birger are regarded as enemies of the state.

As everywhere, the Nazis wage a ferocious battle against literature, which is to be replaced with Nazi propaganda. In Norway, a thorough clean-up of bookstores and libraries was ordered. Books by three hundred foreign authors were confiscated, as well as the writings of such national authors as Sigrid Undset and the memoirs of former Foreign Minister Halvdan Koht and the Speaker of the Storting, C. J. Hambro. Suppressed also was a volume describing Crown Prince Olav's visit to America in 1939. On a recent ransacking of a large publishing house in Oslo by Nazi censors, one of them spoke as follows: "I see you have published a great many books by this fellow Maxim Gorki. Give us his address!" As Gorki, the world-famous Russian writer, had died in 1936, the publisher, with a chuckle, complied readily.

The actors went on strike in protest against the Quisling administration's effort to coerce them into appearing in Nazi propaganda shows. For six months all Norwegian theaters remained closed. Only the introduction of martial law, which punishes every sort of strike with death, could compel them to reopen.

But it is still difficult to cow the movie fans. Since only German pictures are shown, the boycott of cinemas by the Norwegian people is so effective that it has reduced the income of theaters by 65 per cent. Every night posters are put up in Oslo urging loyal Norwegians to continue the strike against German and Italian moving pictures.

A similar boycott is now effectively in force against theaters in many parts of Norway. Citizens of Stavanger, Trondheim, and Lillehammer have for weeks refused to attend any movies, while popular indignation against the storm troopers' practice of entering theaters without paying has even found printed expression in the newspapers.

When Norwegians in other towns go to the movies, their behavior during German "enlightenment films" is so deplorable that the puppet regime has seen fit to issue strict orders forbidding all demonstrations in theaters. "Demonstration" is defined explicitly as including these points of behavior: laughter; "meaningless applause" (i.e., clapping at the wrong place in a film); stamping with the feet; whistling; coughing; clearing the throat. Nothing has been decreed as to sneezing. It has however, been ordered in the Oslo district that three uniformed policemen shall be present at every performance to insure proper public decorum.

The Nazis recently ran a film of the unloading of German ships at a dock in Oslo, to convey the impression that the Germans were bringing their own supplies to Norway. Suddenly a man in the audience rose and shouted: "Stop! You're running the film in reverse." The audience was collectively fined.

These are, of course, only minor incidents. But they illustrate perhaps better than resounding resolutions how deeply the spirit of resistance permeates a nation, 99 per cent of whom have refused to submit to the Nazis' New Order and are carrying on a grim, unyielding opposition which has forced the Germans to maintain a larger army of occupation in Norway, in proportion to population, than in any other occupied country. The killing of many Norwegians by German firing squads in recent months has failed to stem the tide of resistance. Lined up solidly in their contempt for the German "overlords" and in their resistance to Nazification are the country's churches, labor unions, employers' organizations, farmers and fisherfolk, professional and scientific groups, sports organizations, youth associations and even school children. Frequently the opposition is by sabotage, espionage, and street fights. Resistance cannot remain forever passive where there is so much deep-seated hate among so many; and that is why prisons and concentration camps are jammed with persons arrested by the Nazis, why executions continue to mount.

The system of espionage developed in Norway has been of constant and considerable aid to Great Britain. Information is regularly supplied to London on the land activities of the German troops in Norway, such as the construction of airports and submarine bases, or the shifting of troops and the size of the occupational forces. Information is also steadily sent to London on the movement of German ships along the Norwegian coast. In this way the British first learned that the new German battleship *Bismarck* was heading out to sea. Numerous other German ships have been sunk by the British along the Norwegian coast as the result of "tips" supplied by the espionage service in Norway, which has its own ways and means of communicating with London. It is an important phase of the battle which Norwegians are carrying out on the home front.

With the news of the United States' entry into the war the oppressed people of Norway took new heart, confident that the day was now not far off when they could rise to help drive the enemy from their country and to settle accounts with those of the Quisling ilk who had betrayed them.

The news was celebrated by a large gathering around Abraham Lincoln's statue in the Frogner Park of Oslo in order to pay homage to American democracy and American ideas of freedom. Speeches were made eulogizing the spirit of the United States, so cherished by the people of all Nazi-occupied countries, and wreaths were placed on the statue of Abraham Lincoln amid the singing of patriotic songs.

A clash occurred when members of the Norwegian storm troopers tried to take away these wreaths. The crowd attacked the storm troopers, who got the hottest reception of their lives and howled for protection. After the skirmish had gone on for some time about fifty policemen arrived in motor cars and made a few arrests. However, the Norwegian patriots had already effectively commented on America's entry into the war.

Norwegian labor was so heartened by the good news from America that it staged a small rebellion. It began with a strike involving some forty thousand metal workers. The Nazi Commissar, Josef Terboven, promptly clamped martial law upon Oslo and the surrounding districts, following it with mass arrests.

All other classes of the population keep in tune. The resentment of Norwegian farmers against all attempts to Nazify their organizations has now become so bitter that it is openly stated the German authorities will ask Quisling to leave the farmers alone, although he is now Premier. Members of the Quisling party have been chased away from farmers' meetings, and Quislingites who had gained a foothold in agricultural organizations with the backing of storm troopers, have been forced to resign.

The professions are no less steadfast in their resistance than the working people. The teachers demonstrated their courage when Quisling's Department of Education attempted to bring them within the fold of Nazidom by demanding that they sign a pledge on their "honor and conscience" to work for the "New Order" in Norway and "to counteract any attempt on the part of pupils or colleagues to oppose cooperation with the new [Nazi] government." Teachers were also invited to sign a declaration that they would resign from their jobs if they ever hindered the progress of the "New Order."

But instead of signing these declarations, the members of the five teachers' organizations in Norway drew up a counter pledge:

I hereby declare that I will remain loyal to my profession as a teacher and to my conscience, and that I will carry on my work as before and follow those instructions which are rightfully given me by my superiors.

Even more outspoken was the answer of the principals of all the Oslo schools when they were ordered by decree to set aside class time for Nazi lectures:

Regarding the new law, it is our duty to declare to the Department of Education that we look upon obligatory propaganda meetings as very harmful and as directly contrary to what should be the most important part of higher education: the leading of our pupils, as far as possible, towards independent thinking.

One of the many attempts by the Nazi-appointed Minister of the Interior to force civil servants into the so-called National Union party took the form of a circular postulating that the only way to freedom was the Nasjonal Samling, and that consequently all government and municipal employees must cooperate with it. "The slightest deviation or failure to do so will be looked upon as an action hostile to the state," this document declared; and it threatened further that "drastic punishment will be imposed on every one who is an enemy of the state."

Here again the answer quickly came in the shape of a counter declaration drawn up by patriotic leaders of these employees, a declaration enthusiastically received on all sides:

We advise all civil servants and private officials to stand firm and not submit to threats made by the Nazi party. If we will stand together, no one can force us to abandon our position. Influence your colleagues to resist in order that there may be a strong wall against all threats.

The resignation of the entire Supreme Court on December 12, 1940, has proved that the Judiciary was the first group to challenge the system. The glorious protest of the Church is on the record. It led to the arrest of Bishop Berggrav, Primate of Norway, on February 24, 1942. Now Norway has its patron saint.

Last December by a decree of the Nazi authorities in Norway the duly elected town and county councils were shorn of their authority, and it was declared that from now on the city and county administration would be handled by council presidents appointed by the Department of the Interior in conjunction with the district governor and the district Nazi leader. This scheme to gain control of the internal municipal affairs is, however, meeting serious difficulties. A number of appointed council presidents have declined the honor, declaring that they would not serve and that they had not been approached by the Nazis before their appointment was made public. One such "appointee," Mr. Einar Tveten of Tjölling, has stated that not only has he handed in his resignation but he will refuse to open any letters addressed to him as president of the county council.

Violations of the law protecting Norwegian physicians and high-handed attempts to Nazify the Doctors' Guild created such bitter resentment that the few remaining medical men of Norway declared a strike.

Also the nurses went on strike. When the well known president of the Norwegian Nurses' Association, Miss Berta Helgestad, was removed from office by the Nazis a short time ago, the directors, the office staff and almost all of the Association's thirty-seven hundred members immediately resigned in protest. Miss Helgestad has been replaced by a Nazi president, a woman who formerly was refused membership in the Nurses' Association because of lack of proper training. The Nazi has taken over the nurses' vacation home in Asker (near Oslo), along with funds of the Association amounting to nearly $200,000.

Outraged, but smiling, a white-haired Norwegian professor commented, "I now go to bed an hour earlier than usual, and

I drink milk instead of my beloved red wine, for I must live to see the day when Norway is again free and happy."

The people no longer hide their feeling in public. Hardly a day passes without some new attack against Quislingites or without a new complaint by the "persecuted" followers of Vidkun, confirming the general impression that both the traitor and his German masters are fighting a losing battle. They can still fine a town like Skien fifty thousand kroner for anti-Quisling demonstrations, but they cannot prevent a renewal of these demonstrations on the following day.

Apparently driven by increasing nervousness over Norwegian resistance and by rising fear of an Allied invasion, the German Reichskommissar for Norway published an order which gave him full power to declare a "state of civil emergency" in any or all parts of Norway. This decree fanned Norwegian opposition to an open flame.

The *Deutsche Zeitung* in Norway, commenting editorially on Terboven's decree, said that "regrettable episodes" had now reached such a point that the German powers could no longer regard them with the "toleration and magnanimity" hitherto displayed.

The flow of escapes across the North Sea to England is steadily rising. Norwegians are slipping away by boatloads to join the Free Norwegian forces in England and Canada. One day a two-hundred-ton ship sailed out of a remote harbor on the west coast with two hundred persons aboard, including some sought by the Gestapo for political "crimes." On the next day another steamship with ninety passengers made a similar get-away. Within a short period, it is estimated, 10 per cent of the remaining Norwegian fishing fleet succeeded in escaping to Great Britain; so did numerous small steamers. Early in January, 1942, all police chiefs of Norwegian towns were instructed that the family of every citizen believed to have fled should be "examined," and their property confiscated. Yet the Norwegian Crown Prince, speaking

at a gathering in New York City, could express his reasoned
opinion that at least two thousand Norwegians had found
their way to England in small boats. Most of them enlist in
the gallant Norwegian navy, sixty units of which, including
destroyers, submarines, mine sweepers and other craft, are assisting the naval effort of the United Nations.

Equal admiration is due to those who continue the underground fight at home. The number of sabotage acts is persistently and dangerously increasing.

At Holmestrand, a mysterious and violent explosion on the
water front cost the lives of five imported German workmen.
At Trondheim a large factory caught fire; controlled Norwegian newspapers attributed it to "gross carelessness," but
the real cause was sabotage. Saboteurs burned the famous
Gladtvedt Hotel at Hönefoss and the Strömmens timber factory near Hamar. One wing of the hotel, dating from the
eighteenth century and containing valuable paintings, was
destroyed. Authorities of the Quisling regime and German
officials had taken over the hotel before the fire. Extensive
stocks of lumber were destroyed in the other fire.

"Accidents" have so often broken the power lines to German airports in western Norway that Nazi authorities have
resorted to wholesale fining of the communities nearest the
scene of sabotage.

The city of Trondheim was recently fined sixty thousand
crowns because an unidentified assailant threw acid in the
face of a German sailor; while Stavanger had to pay a levy
of fifty thousand crowns for a "power failure" in that town.

The destruction by fire of two large gasoline storage tanks,
also in Trondheim, was attributed to sabotage. One man was
arrested. Another fire, which destroyed a number of Trondheim warehouses containing food and ammunition destined
for German forces in Finland, has also been blamed on saboteurs.

Finally, about a million gallons of gasoline were recently

destroyed by a fire. This storage represented the entire fuel supply of the army of occupation, which had been careless enough to store its most valuable goods in the neighborhood of—Trondheim.

Similarly railway lines in increasing numbers were damaged.

Slow-down strikes followed, and indiscriminate destruction not only of German goods but even of the Norwegian people's own belongings, which were to be handed over. The Norwegians practice not only the scorched earth, but even the scorched cupboard and larder. Peasants destroy their foodstuffs. Many people burned their haversacks rather than turn them over. All woolen clothes were burned before the German collectors came to confiscate them for the army in Russia.

At the end of February, Joseph Terboven, a little breathless, took the air. "Recently," he said over the radio, "Norwegians have assisted the British in different ways and on several occasions. These acts were so grave that the German Supreme Court Martial was obliged to order the death penalty. I am afraid this obligation persists in ever increasing measure. He who conspires against Führer Hitler and Premier Quisling is forsaking his life."

The Norwegian insurance companies, however, although amalgamated with German combines, take a different view. In Norway life insurance is issued only after a thorough investigation of the applicant's political record as well as his health. If the authorities confirm that the man who wants to buy life insurance is simon-pure, a well known follower of the New Order, the companies, to their regret, forgo the business. They find a thousand excuses to explain why they are not interested in the proposition.

CHAPTER TWENTY

CZECHOSLOVAKIA

The serfs of today will be the masters of tomorrow.—
PRESIDENT BENEŠ *addressing his nation.*

EXIT the Protectorate. On February 1, 1942, the word disappeared from the German vocabulary. The country in the center of Europe, indeed the heart of the continent, is now officially labeled "what is left of Czechia." The supreme contempt the Nazis put into this term is the expression of their supreme failure. Bad losers, as always, they cock a snook when they are dealt a blow. It is one way of demonstrating their invincibility.

Hitler's decision to liquidate the Protectorate and to incorporate "what is left of Czechia" with the Reich, as a sort of domestic colony, may be explained in two ways. The first is simply his greediness, the driving motive of all Germany. The Führer is no longer satisfied with controlling rich, fertile, productive Bohemia-Moravia—he wants it in the bag, and no nonsense about "protection." Seyss-Inquart recently announced to the Netherlanders that the same fate, annexation by the Reich, is in prospect for them. Quisling's advance to titular Premier presages an identical future for Norway, too. No one doubts that Belgium and Denmark are destined to become German provinces, as well. Hitler is about to cash in on the countries he has, up to the present, mortgaged to the last drop of blood.

The second explanation for the outright annexation of countries so far only occupied or "protected' is Nazism's total failure to coerce them into collaboration. In Czechoslovakia, for instance, there are, according to the estimate of President Beneš, two hundred to three hundred genuine Quislings out of ten million people. The oppressed peoples prefer terror, torture, and mass executions to selling their souls.

Both these explanations, whether seen from Hitler's point of view or from that of the captive nations, still fighting in their agony, lead to the same conclusion. Hitler's mask of Europeanism is torn to shreds and tatters. His is the simple, time-worn game of annexation which the Teutons have been playing for two thousand years. The New Order, now about to be abandoned even as a pretext, was the revival of the oldest form of the cave man's war.

The Czechs, to be sure, do not mourn the loss of their protection. They were not the ones to pretend a nonexistent community of interests between Germany and themselves. With their last breath they insisted, and they continue to insist, that there can be nothing but hostility between themselves, a stubborn, pigheaded, self-sufficient race, and the intruders. Czechoslovakia, to the shame of international democracy then at its lowest ebb, was the next victim after Austria to fall prey to Nazism's world revolution. But up to this very moment they have not abandoned their resistance, nor interrupted it for a single second. Their splendid army was disarmed. But their two mightiest weapons remained invasion-proof. Not even Hitler could alter the geographic position of the country; nor could he write off his dependence, to a large extent, on the Czechs' productive capacity.

Both these weapons have been relentlessly used against the invader. The railway lines, the roads, the rivers and waterways of Czechoslovakia connect Germany with eastern and southern Europe, her foremost target of aggression. But they have served rather to separate Nazism from its aim. In Czechoslovakia, the means of transportation are in a chaotic condition. Sabotage is rampant, as the wave of indictments by German military tribunals and the warrants of arrest issued by the Gestapo disclose.

The average Czech saboteur by no means corresponds to the old romantic picture of a conspirator—foreign-looking, sinister, a bomb hidden in his coat, hunched furtively in some shady joint. The typical modern plotter is a respected citizen, perhaps a prominent public figure, the last person whose integrity would be questioned. Secret societies are led by well known burgesses operating in very small circles. But their work is made easier by the "understanding" attitude of 99 per cent of the Czech people. In fact, all ten million Czechs are a close-knit band of plotters. Many maintain underground connections abroad, above all with America. In Chicago alone nearly two hundred thousand citizens are of Czechoslovak origin, few of whom lack ties with the old country.

The Nazis are, rightly, so distrustful of the Czechs that, within the last few months, as many as fifty-four thousand Czechs have been packed into concentration camps or imprisoned for no other reason than for their "suspicious" attitude. Nevertheless, all the terror of the Gestapo cannot stamp out the secret societies.

Ján Masaryk, Foreign Minister and Vice Premier of the Czechoslovak government, incidentally, explains the terror of the Gestapo in his country by the strained relations existing between the Nazi secret police and the German army, which, in his opinion, is dissatisfied with Heinrich Himmler's organization. The army, he thinks, will soon take over the policing of the occupied countries. He, like all his countrymen, is unperturbed by this prospect. The Czechs are terror-proof.

Neither the Czechs nor the Germans in Czechoslovakia believe that Hitler will win this war. The Czechs have never believed that he could win. Even Allied reverses like the Greek campaign and Hitler's success in Crete were only a momentary shock to them, never shaking their faith in ultimate victory. At the time of the attack on Yugoslavia a general feeling spread through Czechoslovakia that Hitler was overreaching himself. Before the Balkan campaign started, President Beneš said at a press conference in London that Hitler was about to undertake something which would commit him to more than Germany could possibly achieve, and which would in the long run be disastrous to the Nazi cause. Even gains in food and ores would not be worth the price of occupation and endless guerrilla warfare. These prophetic words have, in the meantime, come true.

The uninterrupted exchange of information between patriotic Czechs at home and abroad provides not only the Czech government, but all interested agencies and departments of the United Nations with valuable inside material. Actually Prague, cut off from the rest of the world, as the Germans would have it, is, next to Vichy, the most important listening post on the European continent. In some cases the information obtained from the Czechs is confined to highlighting the German morale, particularly the army morale. Thus a Czech patriot reported the following experience. He was riding in a train with a German captain, and the third passenger in the compartment was an S.S. man (of whom one hundred and twenty thousand are now on duty in Czechoslovakia). When this fellow left he stiffly saluted the officer, with a loud "Heil Hitler." The captain replied with the perfunctory "Heitler," which is common among German officers making the prescribed salute, and surprised his Czech fellow passenger as soon as the door closed by saying: "Excuse me for that. You see, we have to return their greeting." He also disclosed, as a sign of the bad feeling between the army and the semimilitary services, that they cannot even use the same hospitals in Prague. Podol Sanitarium is reserved for German officers, Bulovka Hospital for S.S. and Gestapo men. The many wounded German soldiers, returning from the Russian front, are carefully segregated from the brown-shirts in hospitals, schools, and hotels requisitioned for their benefit.

Such signs of deterioration of the united Nazi front should, of course, not be overestimated. There are many flaws in the machine, but as yet no proof of its cracking. The Czechs, however, observe the flaws that are manifest in everyday life, and are greatly heartened. Every street in the cities and every village has its group of Czech patriots, closely organized to resist the invader. Jews, foreigners, and any persons already prominent in political life are excluded from the organization, in order to reduce the risk of detection by Gestapo. These patriots keep watch on every German home, on local offices and army points, on stocks of army gasoline, food, and ammunition, on barracks and air fields. They report to secret headquarters every change of troops, officials, every delivery and truck. They have helped hundreds of former Czech public leaders, army officers, and aviators to escape.

Sabotage is going on all the time in factories, especially in munition works where it hurts most, for the steel industry of Czechoslovakia is larger than that of Italy and has been almost completely converted to serve German needs. When Germany attacked Russia, army telephone communications were cut and paralyzed, bridges blown up, and railways brought almost to a standstill. Materials and products were damaged in factories almost under the eyes of guards and Gestapo agents.

Germany has to keep three hundred thousand troops and S.S. men in Bohemia and Moravia. The Czechs say that even though their army and fortifications were sacrificed by the

Powers, they will keep twenty divisions of Nazis from fighting by active resistance in the Protectorate.

The press is muzzled, of course, and recently two reporters were executed by the Nazis for reporting troop movements through Moravská Ostrava. Listening to broadcasts from abroad is punishable by death, but members of the underground organization have a regular service listening in by turns. They take down news items and speeches of foreign statesmen in shorthand, and by next morning these are translated, mimeographed, and passed from hand to hand by thousands all over the country. Several of President Beneš's speeches have appeared word for word. The Czechs at home had no advance notice when Beneš spoke on the London radio and called on the nation to fight Nazism, but the speech was taken down in shorthand by many listeners and electrified the nation in hundreds of thousands of mimeographed copies next day. Photographs and clippings from foreign papers are smuggled in, reproduced by offset, and passed from hand to hand. A Prague policeman had such photographs in his pocket one day showing them to every one he knew to be a loyal Czech.

Because of ever increasing sabotage, the German authorities in the "Protectorate" have issued a series of posters depicting the results of, and the reasons against, sabotage. A typical poster portrays a woman and child weeping because of the irresponsible act of the father of the family. The caption below advises, "Don't ruin your family by sabotage."

But the wave of sabotage in the territory of Bohemia-Moravia is assuming such proportions that the Germans are forced to guard all industrial enterprises. In the Skoda Works, a guard has been placed at every fifth machine.

Yet the go-slow campaign continues undisturbed by the Germans, who dare not proclaim a state of emergency in the red-hot district of Pilsen, the site of the Skoda Works. Similarly, in the mining districts of Moravská Ostrava and Kladno —where the first German soldier was killed and his assailant, although known to the Gestapo, never found—high tension is evident. In the coal district of Rosice near Oslavany, output has fallen 65 per cent since summer.

The flame of resistance was fanned by the following appeal from President Beneš to his people at home:

"Oppressed people of Europe: Events have made you key men in the German war machine.

"German soldiers are dying in their thousands on the Eastern Front. They were unable to take Moscow and could not take Leningrad. They are retreating in the Ukraine—numbers are against them. They leave their guns and ammunition behind them as they retreat.

"And so, forced laborers, the Germans look to you to replenish their stocks. Unless you give them the armor, the steel and the food they need, they cannot go on fighting.

"Their new ally in the Far East will not save them. On the contrary, our new ally, the United States, will begin with her real war production only now.

"And therefore the German war machine must be fed day and night more than before—otherwise the might of Germany will perish.

"That is why you are key men in the German war machine. A shortage in German man power has made you vitally important to their successes.

"You must fail them—for this is your hour of opportunity.

"You, the slaves of today, will be the masters of tomorrow."

Immediately strikes broke out in many Czech factories with redoubled determination. Workers at the Avia aircraft factory, near Prague, downed tools, as did the personnel of the Walter aircraft engine factory in Prague and labor in a number of other concerns.

Every night explosions occurred in munition plants. The night is a valuable ally in the stubborn and unceasing underground struggle between the Czech people and their German oppressors. The Czechs are fighting with their bare fists. It is a warfare calling for special weapons, and the Czechs have been extremely clever and thorough in their discovery and use.

Acts of sabotage are committed under cover of darkness. The commonest attacks are against the railways, which have become a preferred object of sabotage since the Nazis began moving large bodies of troops into the Balkans.

Secret organizations in Bohemia and Moravia are very well informed as to the movement of transports. They know when trains will be passing certain points, and whence and whither they are bound. Hence the many accidents on the Czech railways. Quite recently there was a collision near Opava between a troop train and an express. Two days later another troop train collided with a workmen's train at Plán, in western Bohemia. At the end of January a train full of soldiers was derailed at Suchdol, Bohemia, because of an impaired track. In a similar accident, near Tabor in southern Bohemia, a signal box was destroyed and the signalman killed. All these accidents resulted in loss of many German lives and interrupted traffic for days.

Not far from Ceské Budéjovice false semaphore signals stopped a trainload of German tanks one night and kept it standing a long time on the permanent way. Meanwhile the soldiers accompanying the transport alighted to stretch their legs. In their absence, unknown persons cut the wires in the tanks, putting their engines out of action. Although the entire station staff at Ceské Budéjovice was closely questioned, the perpetrators were never discovered.

As in Belgium, Holland, and Norway, German soldiers are afraid to walk by night in the streets of the smaller towns or in the suburbs of the capital. Darkness is the ally of men whose only weapons against machine guns, tanks, and the great might of the German army are fists, sticks, knives, and, occasionally, revolvers—the last are rarely used, for shooting makes too much noise. Unaccompanied German soldiers are set upon, as part of this unrelenting warfare against the hated tyrant, and are seriously injured or killed. In some towns conditions have become so bad that the military authorities have suspended night passes to soldiers, and ordered their men to walk about only in groups after dark.

The anti-Nazi organizations in the defunct Protectorate work secretly and by night. Under cover of darkness, a fierce and deadly fight is going on all the time. It is a war without mercy. At night, and especially toward early morning, the agents of the Gestapo carry out their lightning raids and house searches, knowing that their victims are most likely to be at home at four or five o'clock in the morning. At night, too, arrested men are locked in jails and thrown into Gestapo cellars. At night they are submitted to cross-examination and torture. Trucks carrying the bodies of those who have succumbed leave police headquarters for the crematory at night. At night, finally, men are transported, alive or half dead, to the concentration camps.

The black-out, however, had to be canceled because the darkness only helped the patriots. Walls in the cities and fences in the villages blossomed out each night with paint or tar: "Down with Hitler! Bring back Beneš," or "We thank the Führer—for hunger." Even in the once violently Nazi Sudeten area, walls have been painted and crowds of German workmen have shouted: *"Hitler nieder! Beneš wieder!"* ("Down with Hitler!—come back, Beneš!") In the darkness of black-outs German proclamations on public bulletin boards have been torn down or pasted over with the underground news sheets.

A particular feature of the Czechs' restiveness is their unquenchable humor. Political jokes help to keep up their courage. It is said that a man was arrested for declaring on the street that Goebbels' father was a Jew. He was convicted in court on three counts for the one remark: first, for attracting a crowd and disturbing the peace; secondly, for inciting to riot; thirdly, for divulging a state secret.

A Czech constable in Prague surprised a group of people at night in the act of writing upon some wall in Czech, "May Hitler perish!" He admonished them earnestly: "Don't you know that under the law all inscriptions in the Protectorate have to be written in German first?"

Because of black-out regulations, it was impossible for people in Czechoslovakia to place lighted lamps on the graves of their relatives, as is the custom on All Souls' at the end of November. Some one took advantage of the darkness to paste printed sheets on the headstones in the Central Cemetery of Brno: "ARISE, YOU CZECHS, AND MAKE WAY FOR GERMANS."

But these are only sidelights. The seriousness of the situation is emphasized by the fact that during the last few months the number of actions threatening the efficiency of the German war machine and the contact between the German arsenals and the Eastern Front greatly increased. The Germans had to increase to three thousand marks the reward for catching offenders who were constantly damaging the telephone and telegraph connections in the Protectorate used for military purposes. Accidents on the railways were ingeniously managed with German troop trains at important junctions, so that connections were blocked for days at a time. A military transport was destroyed by an explosion in Vlára Pass, an important railway connection between Moravia and Slovakia. Weeks after week it was announced that the gasoline had leaked out of the drums of the German or Rumanian transports passing through the Protectorate. Two million shells had to be returned to one munition factory because of faults in sorting. The munition workers made the excuse that the factory was badly lighted. At an airplane factory the order to cease manufacturing certain parts was mysteriously lost. The result was that for two months parts were manufactured which were of no use at all to the German Army.

This Czech war against the Germans is different from the English war, different from the Russian war. But all the reports, whether they announce fresh shootings and atrocities, the reduction of Czech industrial output by 40 per cent, or an explosion in a powder factory, are all really war communiqués from the front behind the lines. On this front the Germans have to fight, as Heydrich is fighting in Prague, with a great expenditure of energy. The terrible thing about this war is that the most powerful military and police organization in Europe is faced by the heroic Czech nation with bare hands. For three years they have been carrying on active warfare against the Germans, with no weapon but their inventiveness, cunning, courage, and patriotic spirit.

The reports of the shootings are astonishing in the number of classes and professions included in Heydrich's terror. In front of his firing squads there stood side by side a general, a workman from a munition factory, a butcher, a tailor, a doctor, a farmer, a bank manager, the Mayor of Prague, and a Jew without occuption. Could Heydrich give the world better proof of the way in which all classes of the nation are fighting actively against the Germans than by giving orders for the arrest of the Premier Eliáš and three of his ministers? It was the Germans themselves who chose Eliáš, and they have condemned their own docile Premier to death. They have not carried out the sentence yet, because they wish to force from Eliáš by threats and torture more and more confessions in more and more trials. *Der Neue Tag,* the German paper in Prague, accuses Eliáš of knowing about and supporting the widespread network of spying in Czechoslovakia, helping the enemy, and being in touch with the present War Minister in the Czechoslovak Government in London, General Ingr.

The manner in which active resistance to the Germans expresses itself is apparent from the reasons given for some recent death sentences. Three persons were executed for sabotage in which "they had unjustifiedly masqueraded as Gestapo agents while committing acts of sabotage." Another group in Brno was condemned to death for "concealing persons for whom the German police were searching and for assisting them with money and clothes." Others were condemned for "maintaining a courier service between Prague and other places and circulating, in thousands, leaflets calling for sabotage." The boycott of the "Protectorate" press continues.

"The Czech nation still wanders in an intellectual and political crisis, and has not recovered from its former political orientation," said State Secretary Frank. "A large stratum of Czech intellectuals still hope that Germany will be defeated, and that Czechoslovakia will be restored. *It is impossible to come to an understanding with this stratum, and it must disappear. The Czechs must realize that Europe can live very well without them,* but that they cannot get along without the German Reich. *The seven million Czechs must recognize the privileged position of eighty-five million Germans and subordinate their interests to ours.*"

Speaking at the celebration of Hitler's birthday, the State Secretary—the true power behind the transient protectors, Neurath and Heydrich—coined the ominous phrase: "Work is not enough."

The implication is clear. The upper class is to be annihilated so that the masses of Czechs may be driven into full, armed participation in the war. Probably this will be a by-product of the annexation of their country. The Czechs can conceive nothing better. Let Hitler give them guns. Every single bullet will backfire.

CHAPTER TWENTY-ONE

POLAND

The Polish government will ask severe punishment for those responsible for the present war; that is, for Germany and her allies. They must be made to suffer merited chastisement for the injustices, crimes and destruction they have committed and, at the same time, render full moral and material satisfaction to those who have been wronged.—WŁA-DISŁAW SIKORSKI, Premier of Poland, February 24, 1942.

IN CRUCIFIED Poland, the world's most fervently Catholic country, the Ten Commandments have been altered, and the new text circulates secretly throughout the country. It is printed in very small type on pages one and one-half by one and one-quarter inches:

I am Poland, thy Motherland, the land of thy forefathers where thou hast grown up. Thy entire existence thou owest after God to me.

1. Thou shalt have no other earthly love above me.
2. Thou shalt not take the name of Poland for thine own glory, career, or reward.
3. Remember that thou shalt give without hesitation unto Poland thy possessions, thy personal happiness, and thy life.
4. Honor Poland, thy Motherland, and thine own Mother.
5. Fight persistently with Poland's enemies to thy last breath, to the last drop of blood in thy veins.

6. Struggle with thine own complacency and cowardice. Behold, a skunk cannot be a Pole.

7. Be without mercy to them that betray the Polish name.

8. Always and everywhere, boldly admit that thou art a Pole.

9. Suffer none to have doubt as to Poland.

10. Let no one insult Poland, belittle her merits and greatness, her achievements and majesty. Thou shalt love Poland above all else, save only God. Thou shalt love her more than thyself.

Another secret document, less pious, but equally freely distributed, advises the Polish people how to behave toward Germans:

1. You should not voluntarily render any services to the army of occupation. Officials should not be zealous. The businessman, the shopkeeper, or the man in the street should not be polite, not even in such small things as giving Germans information in the street. You can always pretend that you don't understand German. Treat everything officially, and let the Germans feel how strong is the hatred that divides us from them.

2. Do not go to the cinemas. Every ticket you buy contains a contribution to the German war fund. You thus help to destroy your freedom and the freedom of other nations.

3. Never go to places of amusement (music halls, night clubs, gambling casinos). It is not fitting to amuse ourselves while the Germans destroy our country and torture hundreds of thousands of our brethren in concentration camps and prisons.

4. Reduce as much as possible the purchase and consumption of all goods from which the occupiers draw profits: boycott their papers, their vodka, and their tobacco.

5. It is our sacred duty, whenever possible, to harm the oppressor: in executing his orders, in industrial production, everywhere and always.

These documents show how both the spiritual and the secular life of the Polish nation is imbued with a hatred of the oppressor, impossible to describe in words. It is by no means a sterile, impotent hatred. No country on earth, perhaps no people in history, has had to endure what Poland has suffered under the German heel. But despite the Gestapo terror, despite the necessity for the strictest secrecy and the difficulties of communication, some time ago delegates from all the underground groups gathered "somewhere in Poland." They represented two thousand organizations of workers, peasants, and white-collar men. Every one of them knew that the slightest slip, any failure to take precautions, would mean his life. Nevertheless, all the expected delegates appeared at the catacomb congress which voted to start the all-out battle immediately.

A part of their declaration reads:

We were the first to resist the barbarous force when it began to subjugate free peoples. We were the first victims of the superiority of brute force and its military machine. But we were also the first to begin underground resistance against the invader whose iron heel tramples our country and the other countries of Europe. All who fight against tyranny and crimes of Nazi totalitarianism are our natural allies. It is to them that we turn to tell of our struggles, our suffering, and our life today.

. . . Deep faith in the victory of justice and freedom, and profound conviction that despite its apparent strength today aggressive barbarism must lose in the end, have endowed the Polish people, its working masses in cities and villages, with indomitable courage in the face of the invader.

We have been forced underground. Every moment the bloody terror finds victims among us. Despite the fact that the slightest connection with the work of liberation—even the reading or possession of an illegal newspaper—is punished by execution or by slow death in a concentration camp, a far-flung net of freedom has come into being in the darkness of conspiracy. An invincible tide has arisen which steadily undermines the conqueror, surrounding him with the implacable hatred of all Poles. This hatred will never permit the oppressor to take root and solidify his power in our country. . . .

. . . Our struggle, like those of the other oppressed nations, is being waged through united effort for a common end: for freedom and social justice in our country, and for a new and better order in a Europe reconstructed as a Union of Free Peoples.

We are firmly convinced that the enemy will be overthrown in the end. At the first opportunity the conquered peoples will arise to strike the deathblow to the invader. Therefore, in the name of the Polish people, working and fighting in underground conspiracy, we call to the peoples of Europe and of the world. . . .

. . . No truth in history is as clear and evident as that the war of today, the war against the aims of its instigators, is above all a defense of the very foundations of civilization, a defense of the most elementary human rights. No one can remain neutral. In the struggle against the new tyranny, the working people of the world must unite under the slogan:

For our freedom and yours!

The Polish underground fighters do not regard their action as an isolated incident. They are well aware that they are taking part in a world war. This war cannot end in a way satisfactory for democracy, they argue, without an outright defeat of Nazi Germany. The mere staving off of democratic defeat would lead to a "negotiated peace" which would leave the Nazis with all their conquests on the European continent. Such a peace would really be a Nazi victory. But the defeat of the Nazis requires an armed invasion of the continent. How can such an invasion be successful? The answer is supplied by the existence of the antifascist underground movements. The invasion of the continent by the Allied armies must be combined and coordinated with the assistance of these movements. Already some of these movements have made themselves a considerable nuisance to the German armies. They sabotage production and transport, and compel the Nazis to keep in the conquered countries more military and police power than otherwise would be necessary. Of course, by themselves they cannot overthrow Nazi domination, and it would be fallacious to rely upon the antifascist movements alone to bring about the end of Nazism, without a military defeat of Germany. But, supplementing military action, the guerrillas may be of decisive importance at a critical moment when blockade and aerial warfare have sufficiently "softened up" the Axis powers. Cooperation of the Allied armies with these underground movements implies of course a full realization of the "civil war" aspect of the present international conflict. The realization of this aspect was the source of the strength of Nazi and Fascist strategy which culminated in the technique of the "fifth column." The organized underground movements are the "fifth column" of international democracy.

It is remarkable that the Polish underground movement, involved in a life-and-death struggle, still finds time and energy to tackle an additional problem the shadow of which has loomed over Eastern and Central Europe throughout the ages. If anti-Semitism is the scourge of Hitler, it was the curse of Poland and many neighboring countries. The Polish underground movement wages war also against this relic of the dark days.

In one of the most important towns of eastern Poland a "League to Fight Anti-Semitism" has been organized by prominent Polish democratic intellectuals. The work of the League has met with full approval and sympathy from the Polish population.

Several secret meetings were devoted to formulation of the program and discussion of methods to combat anti-Semitism. The speakers emphasized that friendship among the nationalities of Poland is fundamental to the successful prosecution of the struggle against German domination, and declared that full collaboration between Gentiles and Jews will provide one of the basic conditions toward the solution of their common problem.

The organizers of the League made provisions to spread the movement among the Polish intelligentsia. Simultaneously other groups of the same character have been started in execution of the first group's program.

Several conferences have been organized with representatives of the Polish democratic and labor movement to the end of coordinating all the activities which are directly or indirectly concerned with the struggle against anti-Semitism. Informative talks took place with representatives of Jewish labor organizations.

The German occupation, of course, remains the principal concern of the Polish underground movement. For their part, the Germans are anxious to suppress all information concerning Polish armed resistance. In spite of themselves, however, they have officially admitted its existence. Late in 1941, the *Warschauer Zeitung* published an article reviewing the work of the German police and the S.S. The article stressed that "fighting various gangs is a major task of the German police. The Polish forests have always been a favorite hide-out for all sorts of bandits and criminal gangs. Gangsterism has become especially prevalent in wartime." The German newspaper further stated that the "bandits" had machine guns, hand grenades, and other firearms. German mounted and foot police operated throughout the winter and spring, attempting to wipe out the *Untermenschtum* ("human scum").

On the day following the publication of the above article, the special war-press bulletin of the Nazi party, *Die Innere Front*, published an interview with Moder, the Warsaw chief of the S.S., who declared openly that *"50 per cent of the terrorist raids which have occurred during the last winter were politically motivated."*

German papers have recently referred to at least three such bands operating in western Poland alone. Frequent raids on post offices are reported (by which the guerrillas get money with which to keep themselves alive). The Nazi *Krakauer Zeitung* admitted that "several German military objectives were attacked in one night by the bandits."

Another German-controlled paper announced a high reward for the delivery—alive or dead—of one Emmanuel Labus, a bank clerk, who was said to be the leader of a "gang" operating in Upper Silesia. This "gang" was described as engaging in sabotage, and as being responsible for the death of a high German police official.

These "bandits," as the Nazis described them, carry on a grim and terrible guerrilla warfare which no efforts of the Gestapo and the S.S. can crush.

Polish guerrillas are often armed with machine guns and automatic pistols. In a fight described by a Gestapo officer to the *Kurjer Krakowski*, fifty-six Poles were killed. Even the German praised the Poles' courage, saying they fought to the last man. When their ammunition was getting scarce, they sought refuge in a house from which they continued firing until it was destroyed by fire. In the ruins the Germans found the charred remains of the last defenders, some still holding their guns in clenched hands.

Some idea of the intensity of Polish guerrilla warfare may be obtained from the surprised indignation to which the German-controlled press in Poland gives vent. The *Krakauer Zeitung* comments bitterly on the fact that Germany is having to wage a "war in Poland." Telephone and telegraph wires are continually cut, warehouses set on fire, railway tracks torn up, and trains derailed.

In addition more than a hundred clandestine papers are published in Poland. The patriotic editors, reporters, and printers always go armed. When discovered, they do not hesitate to shoot in order to escape. The printing plant is seized, but most of the staff manages to get away.

Evidence that Polish patriots are conducting guerrilla activities behind the German lines on the Russo-German front was also seen in a warning by Governor General Frank that the death penalty would be imposed on all persons wearing or availing themselves of any and all uniforms, including that of the Polish police, without specific authorization from the Nazi authorities.

The warning, given in a proclamation which opened with a stirring description of the Nazis as defenders of civilization against Bolshevism, complained that the Poles are allying themselves even with Stalin in their desire to destroy Hitler.

Such warnings are common, and are little heeded by the population. At Sochaczew, near Warsaw, the German authorities put up special posters concerning insults to German soldiers. The posters threatened that ten Poles would be shot if any person who insulted a German soldier or picked a quarrel with him was not delivered within three hours.

But the casualty lists in the underground war are by no means all on the side of the oppressed. Turning over the leaves of the *Ostdeutscher Beobachter*, only one of the Nazi papers in Poland, if the most important one, the attentive reader will find the following obituaries in one week's issues:

S.S. Rottenführer Walter Buchner died unexpectedly.

S.S. Scharführer Wilhelm Bruring died unexpectedly.

Owing to an unfortunate accident, our colleague, Reinhard Zelm, an agronomist, was lost to our ranks.

In the loyal fulfillment of his duty to the Führer and to the Fatherland, Obersturmbannführer Egon Schulz died in a hospital.

Truppenführer Helmut Dymke perished in a fatal accident as he was returning home from duty.

These sudden German fatalities were obviously the result of clashes between the Germans and Polish armed guerrilla bands.

It is very significant that a fortnight after the appearance of these notices, the *Ostdeutscher Beobachter* reported that the senior teacher and party comrade Kurt Schattkovsky had died suddenly. Two days later the unexpected death of the teacher Oscar Gellert was announced.

The Nazis mentioned were probably the victims of snipers. But the Polish guerrillas attack whole groups of German soldiers as well. Among recent events the following incidents came to the knowledge of the Polish government in exile,

which maintains—particularly by the use of parachutists—
close relations with the leaders of the underground war at
home. Near Siedlce, east of Warsaw, Polish guerrillas attacked
and killed a platoon of thirty German soldiers. Another band
of twenty-five men in the Opole district shot down "every
German soldier and official in the district" they met. Five
guerrillas attacked the German police station at Slupia, killing the post commander and making a good haul of arms and
ammunition. In Gostynow, site of the ominous concentration camp, six Poles attacked a Gestapo detachment that had
just been relieved from "duty" in the camp. Two of the
assailants fell, four got away. Of the Gestapo detachment not
one man survived to tell the tale. The *Gauleiter* of Silesia immediately betook himself to Warsaw to confer with the Governor General about means to check banditry in his district.
But nothing resulted from the conference except a pompous
communiqué.

Guerrilla warfare, of course, is an anonymous business.
Only those whom German courts sentence to death receive
publicity. Thus the peasant leader Ranowicz is now the hero
of songs and legends. He destroyed a number of Nazi tanks
and dozens of convoys, and was active twenty-two months
before his fate was sealed. The German tribunals do not
speak of "guerrilla activities," but condemn their victims for
"armed resistance against the army of occupation." Many
names which the Poles honor appear on these sad lists. There
is so far only one case on record in which German authorities have admitted continuous Polish resistance: "A little war
is going on along the Warsaw-Lublin railway," the Governor
General announced, warning his officials not to travel on the
embattled line. Reports received abroad confirm that guerrillas
armed with rifles and machine guns are, indeed, regularly interrupting traffic on this route—one of the main arteries of
communication in Poland. The special railroad patrol recently
established by the German army does not deter them in the

least. The guerrillas attack police and gendarmerie on guard, and mostly get away with the arms of their victims. In a forest near Gdynia they even attacked a German cavalry detachment, killing fourteen of the famous German elite Death's Head Hussars.

The railroads have become the main battlefields in the underground war, since practically all German supplies and reinforcements to the Russian front must cross Poland. Not all freight cars and troop transports arrive safely. The guerrillas have a habit of shooting at tanker trains transporting oil from Rumania. They claim that at least 20 per cent of the tankers arrive empty at their destination. The German garrison at Smolensk was starving for two weeks because Polish "bandits" succeeded in derailing every food train sent to them.

Who are these mysterious fighters, growing out of the dark, and swallowed up by the night? They are the Polish people, all of them. The latest list of executions for "armed resistance" includes a professor of the now closed Cracow University, aged sixty-nine, a housemaid from Poznań, and the errand boy Karl Gryza, born in Warsaw on February 14, 1929.

CHAPTER TWENTY-TWO

THE BURNING BALKANS

We are accustomed to dying.—Old Serbian saying.

THE Yugoslav war (for it is no longer an underground fight, nor civilian resistance alone) will be remembered in history for many reasons. It will survive as Hitler's first military defeat; as a glorious example of a fight for liberty, and, above all, as a drama of the logic and pathos of ancient Greek tragedy. None of its elements was missing in the tragedy the Yugoslavs staged in 1941. There was original guilt, accessory treason, the great atoning, the pitiable yet titanic struggle of human beings against the dark forces, the merciless, sacrificial battle, and, through streams of their own blood, the march of the people toward liberation.

The Yugoslavs were guilty of no greater sin than most democratic nations, big and small, have been at one time or another. They did not recognize the enemy of the world. They permitted their leaders to pick up the crumbs that fell from the dictators' table for seven years. This complacency had to lead to surrender to the Axis.

The Yugoslav people were shocked by the pact of surrender. Popular uproar overthrew the traitorous government. Two days after Zvetković had signed away Yugoslavia's independence, he was replaced by the chief of the air force—courageous, erudite General Dusan Simović. A volte-face brought Yugoslavia back into the camp of the liberty-loving peoples which only a few traitors in power, but never the nation itself, had deserted.

The moment chosen by General Simović to resist the Axis was anything but propitious. The country was surrounded by enemies. The army was not prepared for a great struggle. Although Simović did not lose a moment in putting his troops into a state of readiness, he had no time to complete the mobilization. Hitler struck with his habitual lightning speed. On April 6 at dawn the Germans bombarded Belgrade. The Nazis attacked simultaneously from three directions. Three days later they broke through the Yugoslav army at Skoplje. On the 14th of April, it seemed as if the war was over.

Pretending to be fatigued from the eight-day war, two Yugoslav military leaders returned to German-occupied Belgrade. One of them was Zvetković. His exhaustion, however, did not prevent him from putting himself at the disposal of the German High Command. He was entrusted with maintaining order in Nish, Serbia's second biggest town. He still holds this local command, serving the Nazi army as a mercenary. It was not a rich compensation for having sold out the fatherland. The prize of treason was won by the other martinet who returned after the inglorious defeat. Milan Nedić, the brilliant military attaché, rose from a position of comparative unimportance to form a puppet government. He insisted that he was not a Quisling, but a Pétain, a Marshal—indeed, Colonel Nedić assumed the title of Field Marshal—who wanted to collaborate with the victors in order to stop the bloodshed. His idea of stopping the bloodshed was revealed when he formed an army of fifteen thousand men to put down what he termed the "remnants of resistance" and what was actually the first upflare of the great revolution. Nedić's fifteen thousand antirevolutionary "Yugoslav" troops were, in fact, Italian and German soldiers in disguise.

For the revolutionaries there was no return to Belgrade. On the contrary, they went into the mountains and formed out of the scattered remnants of a beaten army the nucleus of a new force. This is how the Chetniks, the most heroic fighters of this war, came into being. They are the heirs to an old and proud tradition. Their predecessors were the Serbian Haiduks, guerrillas during the time of the Turkish oppression in the eighteenth century.

In 1939, under the shadow of the impending war, the Yugoslav Military Command re-created the Chetnik battalions. They were organized as peacetime units. To each army was added one battalion of Chetniks—altogether five battalions, fewer than three thousand men. They were volunteers, selected from among the recruits. They had to be in perfect health and particularly tough.

Their main duty was to conduct guerrilla warfare behind any enemy motorized and panzer columns which succeeded in breaking the defense lines. Besides, they were to be used in all independent actions which required special courage and sacrifice.

The Chetniks are supplied with special equipment. Their uniform is light to permit easy movement in difficult terrain; it resembles the uniforms of Alpine troops. Their footwear, the *opanki*, are moccasins. Their emblem is the skull with crossed bones. Their armament consists of rifles, bombs, knives, and hand grenades to deal with tanks.

The Chetnik battalions are under the command of the "Commander of the Chetnik Detachment." They rank as a division, with its own general staff. They are commanded by

Division General Mihailo Mihailović, already a well known Chetnik during the Balkan wars.

When the end of Yugoslav resistance was announced, some troops were partly mobilized, others stayed in mountainous regions where the enemy's aviation and mechanized columns were ineffective. The Yugoslav soldiers had entered the fight for the liberty of their country with enthusiasm. The end came too soon for them. Enthusiasm still permeated their ranks. The soldiers refused to believe that they ought to surrender after such a short time. The spring had just begun. Young, green leaves provided a thick shadow under the trees in the forests. They heard that the enemy had ruthlessly bombarded open, undefended cities, killing thousands of helpless women, children, and old people. They heard that the enemy brutally and ruthlessly mistreated the populace, plundering their homes. The soldiers felt they must avenge and protect the helpless and unprotected. Spontaneously, groups of soldiers, acting independently, defied the order to surrender, and remained in the woods and mountains.

Thus, groups of Yugoslav soldiers, led by their commanders and officers, continued the fight in Serbia, Montenegro, Bosnia, and Herzegovina, enthusiastic "Haiduks," defending their people from the tyrant. With them are all the regular Chetnik battalions trained for such actions. They were gradually joined by those whom the ruthless regime of oppressors animated to resistance. To date the three thousand men of the original five battalions have expanded into a fully equipped army of one hundred thousand.

The Chetniks went into battle on the first day of German aggression, April 6, 1941. They were at first assigned to special duties: combating parachutists, saboteurs, and fifth columnists. Gradually they took over all the duties of the regular army, without, however, being properly equipped for the job. But this lack of arms and supplies did not prove an unsurmountable obstacle: they learned how to arm and equip them-

selves from the enemy columns which they attacked and
routed. Most of their arms are still of German and Italian
origin; but the Russians, and the British, too, managed to send
them weapons by airplane. Unfortunately, this source of supplies dried up as the war spread to other theaters. The constant rearming of the unconquered fighters in Serbia is among
the most difficult problems, but also the most vital, of the European war. Fortunately, both Washington and London fully
realize the necessity of solving it.

After almost a year of guerrilla warfare the Chetniks hold
more than two-thirds of their country. They had to abandon
the undefendable northernmost part, Slovenia, where the Germans established a rule of terror unparalleled even in this war.
But the Chetniks are fighting on in every other part of Yugoslavia. North, in the plains of the Voivodina, they are sniping
at the Hungarian hyenas that follow in the wake of the German army. This part of Yugoslavia has been for some time
a no man's land. The Germans promised it alternately to the
Hungarians and Rumanians, evidently intending to use it as
a bait for both. Recently they offered it to a third party, the
traitor government in Belgrade, as compensation for Marshal
Nedić's willingness to appoint a German Vice Premier. In the
meantime the Chetniks disrupt the whole country. They
wreck trains by the score and commit every sort of sabotage.
The local population must pay the price. They are held responsible for guarding railroads, and are executed in bunches
after every "accident." Yet the peasants of the Banat—Voivodina—enthusiastically follow the Chetniks. Many farmers have
left their homes to join the fighters in the dense forests. Various appeals to them to return, the Germans and their Hungarian, Croatian, and Rumanian puppets complain, have only
been answered by renewed "destructive activities, attempts at
murder, and other crimes." On a single day in December the
deserters sabotaged the railway line between Mokrin and
Velika Kikinda. They blew up the house of a German at

Mokrin. They cut the telephone lines at Torda. They derailed a Hungarian troop train between Veliki Bečkerek and Pančevo.

These stanchly Catholic peasants under the guidance of a handful of Chetnik leaders, are, of course, labeled "communists" by the Nazis, and treated accordingly. After an assault on a Hungarian troop train near Veliki Bečkerek twelve inhabitants of the town were indiscriminately arrested. They were shot, and their bodies hung in the market place for twenty-four hours as a deterrent. To simplify the procedure in the future the German garrison commander announced that all the men in the town would be executed as hostages, if one more "accident" occurred in the neighborhood.

This part of Yugoslavia, the Voivodina, is at one end of the battlefield. Next to it is a wide stretch of land the control of which changes hands day and night. At night, the Chetniks have the upper hand: under cover of darkness they destroy the crops, always with the assistance of the farmers; they interrupt rail traffic; they sweep through the towns and the open country. Sometimes they burn the harvest—if the opportunity allows, they hoard it for themselves. Telephone lines, railroad switches, electric wires, and bridges are damaged; wells are poisoned (consequently, the Germans make it a rule to have the local mayor drink out of a well before they themselves drink). All this goes on in spite of the strict curfew which the Germans have decreed for the whole country. "Curfew," said a Chetnik interpreting this decree, "means the right to shoot immediately, without warning, after dark."

But at the hour the people in the northern, embattled districts of Yugoslavia call "hell dawn" the Chetniks disappear into the woods. The days are filled with horror for the population. German patrols are on the prowl. They search houses and homes.

The atrocities committed by the Nazis in Yugoslavia are comparable only with their barbarities in Poland and the oc-

cupied parts of Russia. According to Milan Grol, Minister in
the Yugoslavian government in exile, the Germans massacred,
imprisoned, or tortured into insanity one hundred and eighty
thousand Yugoslavs up to the end of August, 1941. This was
merely a beginning. When General of Aviation Dunkelmann,
intimate friend of Göring, succeeded General von Schroeder,
a savage Nazi warrior but an officer of the old stamp, as commander in chief of the army of occupation, the razing of
towns from the air supplemented the use of firing squads and
the gallows. Unspeakable crimes such as the German assault
on the town of Sabac were committed, which profoundly
shocked President Roosevelt when it was reported to him.

The best report on the annihilation of Sabac came from a
German source. Nazi War Correspondent Gruber wrote it.
Advancing with the German assault troops upon Sabac, seventy miles west of Belgrade, he witnessed the German attack,
led by dive bombers and preceded by heavy shelling. Herr
Gruber's written account describes the Serbian defense of
"the Verdun of Serbia," where the Serbian Army wiped out
an entire Austro-Hungarian army corps in the First World
War.

With the fall of the city, according to the German report,
"Sabac was reduced virtually to ashes, so great was the destructive ferocity of the attack." The report then states that
more than twenty other Serbian villages and communities
along the Sabac-Valjevo line were "utterly destroyed" by
the Germans either during attacks or afterward in reprisals
for resistance by Chetniks in the village populations.

"In some villages," wrote Herr Gruber, "the population
met us with white flags; in some cases we respected them. In
others we found unflattering slogans chalked on the walls,
posters insulting the Führer. In those cases we sometimes shot
one man out of ten in the entire village and sometimes burned
the villages to the ground."

Women and children were shot, Herr Gruber stated, when

they resisted the Germans or when they were found in possession of "illegal newspapers." He recounted the shooting of a small child because allegedly Communist pamphlets were found in the child's pocket. In another case, he reported, the German troops "were forced to shoot a young girl who asked to surrender but who was discovered hiding a homemade hand grenade."

"The entire country," wrote Herr Gruber, "was infested with Chetniks and peasants with arms."

Describing the Chetnik and peasant defenses and arms—mines, hand grenades, dynamite, bottles of gasoline, and even light artillery—the German war correspondent passed on to the punishment meted out to Chetniks, and townspeople suspected of aiding them. "All such persons," said Herr Gruber, "were shot out of hand."

The laurels the German army won in this fashion apparently made the traitor Premier Nedič, envious. He, too, decided to play a part in the mopping up of resistance. He summoned a small force of bribed mercenaries. His assistant, Dmitri Lyotić, head of the Zbor (Fascist) party, passed these troops in review before they were dispatched into western Serbia to fight the Chetniks.

The Serbian punitive expedition advanced, but failed utterly to disclose the Chetniks; after one or two inconclusive brushes with guerrillas, the expedition was abandoned. The German army division that Herr Gruber accompanied was even then rolling into western Serbia to carry on the fighting.

General Nedić wrote a stinging article for the *Novo Vreme* attacking Serbian officers for "lack of discipline and failure to carry out orders" to fire on the fighting Serbs.

In the meantime, in Kučevo, a mining town sixty miles southeast of Belgrade, the Germans shot twenty Serbian miners who had prevailed upon Chetniks not to dynamite the mines—the charge being that the miners "fraternized" with the Serbian guerrillas.

Turkish diplomatic couriers were instructed not to travel by rail through Yugoslavia because dynamiting and other sabotage against the railroads were so common.

The Germans advanced into the mountainous region of inner Serbia. Stukas preceded their infantry which was equipped with flame throwers. But small bands of Chetniks, up to five hundred men, resisted them everywhere. At Javenika a battalion of German flame throwers was routed after a seven day's fight. Not one of them survived. Ferocious battles raged everywhere. The outcome, to this day, is a glory for the Chetniks. They are holding firm throughout Serbia, from the suburbs of Belgrade to the far south. All Montenegro is in their hands. The Dalmatian coast, annexed by Mussolini, has frequently been shelled by Fascism's hit-and-run navy, but never subdued. Only a few key positions, scattered throughout the country, are in German hands. But the invaders' hold on them is tenuous. Even in Belgrade, the capital, and the refuge of all Serbian Quislings—estimated at fifty thousand persons—unrest increased so dangerously that Milan Nedić preferred to escape "somewhere to the north." His present residence has never been disclosed.

The Chetnik revolt has grown into full-fledged war. No longer do single units operate independently, without communication with one another. All operations are conducted from a single center. Mobile radio stations enable the general staff of the "invisible army" to maintain communications, which are so well coordinated that, for instance, small riots flare up in the extreme north to divert the Germans from operations that they are preparing somewhere in the south. The invisible army became such a dangerous foe that the Germans decided to negotiate for peace. They sent Yugoslav Quisling No. 2, General Dokić, in the company of two ranking officers from the German General Staff to the Chetniks' headquarters. The emissaries were received at a specified place, blindfolded, and led, crisscrossing the hills and valleys, to

Mihailović. The conference lasted two hours. For one hour and fifty-five minutes the German officers, arrogant despite the bandages over their eyes, tried to bully the Chetnik chief into surrender, while the traitor Dokić sat uncomfortably at at the peace conference, contributing an occasional "er—er." Mihailović spoke for five minutes. Perhaps it did not even take him as long as that to say: "We are ready for peace—but only on the day that Germany surrenders unconditionally to the Allies or on the day the last German soldier dies. Until then it is useless to speak of peace terms."

Blindfolded again, the three emissaries left for Belgrade. The answer they brought caused Hitler to give way to a fit of rage, as bad news usually does. The Führer's fits of rage have a way of ending in wholesale murder. Three weeks after the conference in Mihailović's secret headquarters, the Yugoslavian government in exile had to announce that the number of German executions of Yugoslavs had mounted to three hundred thousand. The names of one hundred and eighty thousand victims were registered in London. Stephen Early, President Roosevelt's secretary, disclosed news from reliable sources according to which the Nazis were planning to mete out to Belgrade the fate of Sabac. They were about to raze the subjugated capital in revenge on the mountain fighters.

But even this threat, perhaps the worst blackmail in contemporary history, failed against the Serbs. The Yugoslav government promoted Colonel Mihailović to the rank of general, and made him Minister of War.

Mihailović, indeed, is an unusual man, one of the outstanding soldiers of this war, yet in appearance almost civilian. He is forty-eight, and has five children. He is a famous mandolin player and is well known for his singing of popular Serbian folk songs. But he is better known for his military achievements. His life has been a constant struggle: in 1912, against the Turks; in 1913, against the Bulgars; during the First World War, against the Central Powers; and now, against the Germans and their assorted following of Italians, Bulgars, and Hungarians, Croatians and native traitors. His two lieutenants are equally remarkable men. Dragisha Vassich, also the father of a large family, in civil life a lawyer, is holding eastern Serbia, while Colonel Kovacević controls large areas in Bosnia and Herzegovina, as well as Montenegro—where the Italians command only a few of the bigger towns—and much of the Dalmatian coast.

The battle song of the Chetniks resounds over two-thirds of the unconquerable country. It is a thrilling anthem, regarded by many as surpassing other revolutionary hymns like the "International" and the "Marseillaise." Its refrain goes:

> Spremite se, spremite, Czetnice!
> Syuta tache borba da bude
> Vojvoda Jovan Babunski
> Frlyate bombe, Czetnice!

(In English: Get ready, Chetniks! A fierce battle will take place. Our old leader, John Babunski, reminds you: Hurl your bombs, Chetniks!)

The song, they insist, helps greatly in attacking. Moreover, attacks on German tanks and flame throwers hold no terror for them. Their leader explained, "We are accustomed to death." Thus, and only thus, they save the life of their nation.

Almost a year has passed since the Germans completed the conquest of Greece. But in spite of the strict control to which they are subject, and notwithstanding the famine rampant among them—a famine imposed upon them as a means of keeping them down—the Greeks, according to their Crown Prince Paul, still immobilize about two hundred thousand Italians (fifteen divisions) and at least seventy thousand Germans. This contribution of a people in chains to the cause of the United Nations will tell even more when Hitler is forced to summon every man for his push across the Mediterranean.

In terms of atrocities committed by Hitler's Huns in all the ravaged countries, it is difficult to compare the countries. Moreover, Americans who have still to familiarize themselves with Nazism before their normal brains can fully grasp its abnormality, will naturally feel inclined to consider as exaggeration what is, indeed, an understatement. All that being said, the fact may be stated that Grece is, at present, undoubtedly the chief sufferer on the globe. Starvation, typhus, and the German occupation have brought about the complete undoing of the country. Rats, lice, and Italians all add their nuisance value. The only thing of value that is not destroyed is the Hellenic spirit.

The Greek War Minister, S. Dimitrakakis, reported to Winston Churchill from Cairo:

The Germans looted every single house and store in towns and villages, leaving them empty of every single object. They proceeded to innumerable murders of people flying for safety in the open country, of children and old people asleep in their homes, and to collective executions following upon summary parodies of trials. Condemned people were forced to dig a common grave before their executions.

Three men wounded during executions at Kystomadon were buried while they were yet alive and

their families were forced to offer dinner to the murderers of their own husbands, fathers and brothers and to suffer mocking jests of the feasting Germans.

In lower Cydonia, War Minister Dimitrakakis continued, eight hundred women and children were expelled from their homes and marched through Canea.

In the village of Crises, in the Rethymnon district, one police sergeant was tortured to death, his limbs being wrenched off one by one in an attempt to force him to reveal the names of persons possessing German rifles. Citing executions of peo-

ple in the villages of Perivolia and Sellia in the presence of
their relatives, after they had dug their own graves, the War
Minister went on to say:

According to the first available information the number of executions in Canea amounts to 506; in Rethymnon, 130, and Herak-
lion (Candia), 50.

A Greek patriot in Athens sent to the government in exile
in London a list of food prices in Athens which shows that
meat—obtainable only in the "black market"—costs ten times
as much as before the invasion; fish, five times as much; olive
oil, three times; sugar—when obtainable—six times; and potatoes fifteen to twenty. Flour and butter are unobtainable.
He continues:

The daily ration of bread has been cut to about a sixth of the
normal consumption. Workmen complain that they cannot do
heavy work on this ration, and many people faint from hunger.
Yet German ships loaded with Greek wheat have been seen to
leave the Peiraeus—destination unknown.

The Germans say, "You have no cause to complain—in Poland
six hundred people die every day from starvation." The Italians
have at least sent food from Italy for their own troops. They also
sent several hundred cases of milk for Greek children. The Greek
children got as much as was needed to make pictures of Italian
soldiers distributing the milk; the Germans took the rest. Two
incidents, described to me by people who actually saw them,
illustrate the particular meannesses of the Germans and the Italians, and the differences between them:

German officers on the balcony of a large house in Patissia
showed a large loaf of white bread to people in the street waiting
in a bread queue. Each German took a large piece and began to
eat it. Occasionally one broke off a small morsel and tantalized
the women and children below with it, finally throwing it down
and laughing at the scramble for the crusts.

Italian soldiers drove up in a lorry to a group of Greek civilians
in Canning Square. Some of the soldiers surrounded the Greeks
so that they could not get away; then the other soldiers distrib-

uted bread while a cinema picture was taken of the touching scene. When the picture had been taken the soldiers gathered up the bread and departed.

The Germans do not concentrate their troops in camps, but scatter them through the city in requisitioned houses or rooms. Many of these houses have been thoroughly looted by the soldiers. One woman complained to the Germans that her belongings had been stolen, and was told, "Don't dare to say such things again. You must realize that this is a conquered country and everything in it belongs to the German Army."

Here is, finally, a document that recently arrived in Washington. It paints a somber picture of the Greek capital. The once vivacious, elegant city wears a lugubrious aspect. One sees Athens in gloom, dilapidation, and depression. The Germans enforced the evacuation of all the wounded soldiers from the Athenian hospitals to make room for their own wounded. The streets of Athens are now full of wounded Greek soldiers still bandaged and often begging bread. The horrors of the German occupation are aggravated by the humiliation felt by the Greeks at sight of the defeated Italians replacing the German troops.

The looting by the Germans, either openly or by means of spurious marks, was so complete that it left very little for their successors. Moreover, the Gestapo remains the supreme master. Some well educated and cultured Greeks felt the German tyranny so cruelly that they committed suicide.

Although Italians replaced the Germans in Athens, it is not possible to say that the occupation is completely Italian. The Germans continue to hold the upper hand there by means of the Gestapo and some more or less influential German officials. They take no notice of the so-called "Greek Government" they themselves instituted.

The food situation becomes daily worse and worse. Communications remain chaotic. The bridge across the Corinth Canal, destroyed during the campaign, has been replaced by a temporary wooden bridge which is so weak that only the smallest locomotives with one or two cars can pass over it. The railway communications beyond the pass of Thermopylae are still disrupted. Thus, when the International Red Cross decided to send supplies of concentrated food extracts for the use of the wounded of all armies in Greece, they were forced to send them by air. These supplies will have to be large if they are to be of real help to thousands and thousands of wounded Greek soldiers and starving people.

Peiraeus and the districts around were severely damaged by the explosion of a ship loaded with munitions. The Germans compelled many Greek shipowners to order their agents in America and elsewhere to withdraw their ships from the Allied service. These orders were communicated to the Greek agents in New York by the German Consul General shortly before he was ousted. The Greek agents, of course, refused to comply with these evidently enemy-dictated orders. The Gestapo thereupon, through the Italians, turned its wrath against the owners in Athens and compelled them to work in Peiraeus to clean up the wreckage, demolish wrecked buildings, and sweep up the streets.

The Gestapo terror reached its climax in a series of wholesale executions throughout Greece, intended to crush resistance. Forty Athenian students were shot on charges of sabotage. Greek uniforms are no longer permitted in public, although ex-soldiers cannot obtain civilian clothing. The shortage of textiles and leather is so extreme that thousands of people walk the streets of Athens and other towns barefoot, in pajamas. Food is so scarce that many people are too weak to work. In the Athens area alone some twenty-five hundred people are starving to death every week. Under such appalling conditions the British Cabinet is considering the feasibility of sending food through the blockade to Greece, although it is well aware that the Greeks have been brought to their present plight by Nazi blackmail. It is estimated that Greece needs thirty thousand tons of grain a month. But will the famine-stricken people receive it, even if the British, setting a dubious precedent, decide to drop their strongest weapon, the blockade, for the benefit of stricken friends? The American Undersecretary of State, Sumner Welles, expressed the hope that the Greeks would receive it, in answer to a question at a press conference. Let us hope that the government does not underestimate the healthy German appetite.

Jean Pipinellis, Greek Minister in Russia, submitted in an official note to the Foreign Commissar, M. Molotov, a detailed report on outrages committed by German and Bulgarian forces in occupied Greece.

According to this note about thirty-five thousand Greeks have been slaughtered in occupied areas since the late October outbreaks arising from the proposed German appropriation of the tobacco crop and the later seizure of other crops. Two thousand of these were slain at Doxato, a town reduced to ashes by German bombing raids. It is estimated that fifteen hundred others were slain in isolated areas, but full details are not available.

The note states specifically that at Messovounies women and children under sixteen years of age were evacuated; the rest of the population was executed, and the village destroyed. At the village of Stavros the entire population of one hundred fifty was slaughtered. Mass executions took place at Katoproia, Anoproia, Hagionpneuma, Prosotani, and Pentalofos, "where Germans and Bulgarians rivaled each other in savagery." As a result of these massacres armed peasants sought refuge in the mountains, especially around Mount Veles. The note asserts that Bulgarians excused the massacres by saying the villages harbored bands of guerrillas.

On the basis of cables from official sources, the note states that atrocities in Kavalla resulted in a revolt in the entire district. The revolt spread to the department of Drama.

A conservative official estimate based on a statement by eyewitnesses places the victims of Bulgarian savagery in Drama, Kavalla, and Zikne at fifteen thousand. Nevertheless, the practically unarmed Greeks put up a fight and killed three hundred thirty Bulgarians and seven Germans.

The Bulgarians, acting on German instructions, arrested many personages in three districts and kept them as "hostages to be shot if clashes occurred." They arrested thirty Greeks and Jews of Kavalla in the night of September 10, and later shot them.

Discontent increased when the Germans commandeered all tobacco in the area without payment.

"A Bulgarian major deliberately exploited the discontent of tobacco-growing villagers by sending out *agents provocateurs* to foment trouble, which soon broke out in minor disturbances," in the words of the official Greek statement. "This was what the Bulgars desired, and they lost no time in carrying out a series of brutal massacres."

A mass uprising followed, in the Bulgarian-occupied territory. Greeks crossed the Struma to seize what was left of the town of Kavalla, killed nineteen Bulgarian soldiers and a number of officers, burned down the Bulgarian police headquarters, and blew up the Struma bridge. After skirmishes in which hundreds of Greeks from the neighboring villages, armed with rifles and machine guns, participated, they were beaten. With a terseness appropriated from the German masters, the Bulgarian communiqué concluded: "In retaliation, the town of Kavalla was razed."

It seems that the Germans do not care to be copied too closely by their little allies. The victors of Kavalla did not enjoy the fruits of conquest very long. Five German infantry regiments muscled in, and the Bulgarian killers had to disappear.

Today, the seething revolution is primarily directed against the German masters. Its central theater is the island of Crete, policed by no fewer than three hundred thousand German soldiers who would otherwise be available for the Libyan front. The Germans are enraged because the villagers of Crete will not denounce the Anzac bands who are still holding out in the mountains, almost a year after the loss of the island by the British. Jointly with the native population, the Anzacs are raiding German military storehouses and air fields, appearing with lightning speed and disappearing again into the pathless highlands just as rapidly after having achieved their task of destruction. The latest report about such raids reveals that a German foraging detachment of thirty-eight men was annihilated near Herakleion. Baffled by such mysterious and deadly attacks, the joint German-Italian command of Crete offered rewards of a thousand drachmas for information leading to the arrest of an Australian soldier. No man or woman in Crete showed any desire to earn the bribe.

British soldiers who were not captured when the Germans arrived, or who were taken prisoner and escaped, are protected and sheltered all over Greece. The penalty for helping them is death, and the rewards for denouncing them are high. Yet the people hide and feed them. Even the poor, who are themselves starving, share their last potato with British fugitives and will not let them give themselves up. A girl from a remote village told a patriot, whose report reached London, that the British hiding in the mountains were "a little bit better fed" than the villagers who are looking after them. She explained, "They were fighting for us, and they still are fighting for us." Aiding the stray Britishers is carried out by a conspiracy which unites the whole Greek nation. In one town an English soldier who had an infected hand went to the hospital for treatment every day for two weeks. All the doctors, nurses, and patients knew that he was British. And all risked their necks rather than give him away.

Greece, indeed, has not lost her age-old humanitarian tradition. But there is more to it than four thousand years of

history alone. It is the undaunted hope of the future, the outlook into a brighter tomorrow that keeps the suffering heroic
Greeks alive, and fighting in line with their allies.

But what have the peoples in the vassal state to look for? The
overwhelming majority fear the victory of the cause to which
they have been sold by their traitors.

The destiny of the vassals will be among the major problems of peacemaking. It will be a most difficult problem. It
will not be possible to give, for instance, Rumanians, Bulgarians, and Hungarians who have contributed so much to
Nazism's atrocities, a clean bill of health. On the other hand,
their case is very different from the German case. Hitler was
made by Herr Schmidt and Herr Müller just as much as
Franklin Delano Roosevelt was produced by America, and
Winston Churchill is English breed. Herr Schmidt and Herr
Müller, average Germans, either instinctively craved for a
Hitler or else found his barbarism not important enough to
resist. Even if a large part of the German nation is only guilty
of the crime of indifference—indifference, as some democracies also have learned and others would almost have learned
but for their great leaders, is the worst sin a nation can possibly commit. This war arose from indifference: first, from
the indifference (to put it mildly) toward humanism and
civilization that the Germans displayed; then, from the indifference of the civilized nations who almost failed to understand that the fate of each was the fate of all.

Where, in this alignment, do the nations actively cooperating with Nazism stand? Not exactly where they would prefer to be. But, on the other hand, they are where they had to
end up since they refused to fight for values more sacred than
complacency, shrugging, and compliance. Are these sinful
weaknesses now vanishing? Do even the mercenaries hear
the call?

The following report on unrest in the collaborationist countries does not attempt to answer any questions definitely. Its aim is exclusively to analyze the mounting tide of dissatisfaction which may, but by no means necessarily must, lead to defections from the Axis camp.

The Rumanians had to bear the brunt of the Russian war. The siege of Odessa devoured whole Rumanian army corps. How their mass-slaughter affected the morale of the Rumanian troops can be concluded from documents of General Resin, captured by the Russians in the second rout of the General's 13th Rumanian infantry division. He called his own troops "unfaithful to their duty and reluctant to fight":

One soldier only slightly wounded was quite able to get to the field dressing station himself. But two soldiers on their own initiative rushed to escort him. As a rule these "escorts" return to their posts only when the fighting is over. Thus in certain companies there were at times not more than thirty men in action when the fighting was at its peak.

General Resin also mentioned the creation of special police detachments armed with machine guns in companies and battalions with orders to shoot men attempting to desert while in action. Despite these innovations, most of the 13th Rumanian division surrendered on the Odessa front.

Heavy Rumanian losses in men and armament at the approaches to Odessa were also revealed in letters and diaries of dead officers. In a letter he had no time to dispatch, the Rumanian officer Todorescu wrote:

In the last engagement we were continuously battered for twenty-four hours by heavy artillery and mortar fire. Only five men of my ill fated platoon survived.

The diary of the Rumanian officer Kazaku contains the following description of the destruction of one company:

The enemy shelled us incessantly. The men could not stand this hurricane of fire, and fled. I shouted and brandished my revolver at them; otherwise I might be accused of having done nothing. At dawn the Russians completely wiped out our anti-tank company.

Demoralization of Rumanian troops is revealed in a confidential memorandum signed by General Masarini, Chief of the Rumanian General Staff, "Deductions and Lessons of Operations in the War Against Russia," and found by Red Army men in the captured headquarters of the 3rd Rumanian infantry division. It reads in part:

The Russians resort to various ruses to trap and demoralize our units. Indicative is the case of a column of three infantry battalions and one artillery regiment advancing to the field of action. Its vanguard, falling into a trap set by Soviet troops and residents of a Bessarabian village, was attacked and became disorganized. This vanguard, without protection of artillery and the main forces of the column which were following, suffered heavy losses.

Other cases should be mentioned. A German unit, entering a village after the first wave of troops had passed, ran into fire of Russian automatic weapons from houses, trees, and culverts. A large reconnoitering detachment of our troops was allowed to approach within several meters of a garden wall behind which Russians had camouflaged themselves. The Russians opened fire unexpectedly and inflicted heavy losses on the German detachment. Most of our losses are due to the enemy's exploitation of the inexperience of our troops.

General Antonescu, inspecting the front, noted the complete lack of organization and discipline behind the lines of our troops. Horse and automobile transport functioned in a disorderly manner. For example, vehicles traveled incessantly in all directions, and it was impossible to ascertain who sent them or why. Small units of our troops wandered about the fields and roads without specific purpose. Carts and motor trucks were seen loaded with articles having no relation to war operations: civilian clothes, furniture, pots, crockery, and other household articles secured from the local population.

Owing to bad organization of transport and endless traveling from place to place, our troops and animals are so exhausted as to be unfit for service. During air raids and artillery bombardments, regular columns and auxiliary troops succumbed to panic and fell victim to guerrilla sabotage.

In many units our men do not receive rations for days on end. In some troop columns and formations one comes across dirty, unwashed, unshaven privates with the most untidy appearance imaginable. When admonished they reply: "We are starving, we are getting nothing to eat, we have no soap."

There is lack of initiative everywhere. Inertia is to be observed in many commanders. Nobody thinks of attempting to obtain things he needs himself by his own efforts. The army's requirements must be satisfied from local resources. Everything needed must be taken on the spot without compunction. Rumanian troops believe the Russian war is over as far as they are concerned.

High Rumanian authorities said the main Rumanian advance had ended at the west bank of the Bug River. Their statement was interpreted to mean that Rumanian territorial ambitions had been realized. Now many of the occupation troops expect to return home. Among them are General Mircea Dimitriu and his forces, who, after participating in the two-month siege of Odessa, are "resting."

One Rumanian cavalry corps operating in the Crimean zone, however, is expected to remain in the field, as a "contribution to Europe's common front against bolshevism." Otherwise, the troops anticipate a discharge shortly.

Small wonder that Rumanian soldiers did not return as conquering heroes from the front, from which scores of thousands already had to be withdrawn, but as a deeply dissatisfied and disappointed mob. They were ordered to deliver their arms, but they entirely failed to comply with this order. The Rumanian broadcast finally had to transmit the following order: "As many Rumanian soldiers who have returned from occupied territory beyond the Dniester River have not yet handed back their arms, ammunition and explosives, twelve o'clock on January 20 has been fixed as the new date by which they must have surrendered military arms in their possession if they wish to escape punishment. All those in whose possession arms are found after this date will be sentenced to death, even if the reason for the neglected surrender was not a political one."

The reason, however, for the execution of twelve Rumanian generals on October 3, 1941, was clearly and simply political. They were recalled from the Odessa front and summarily shot for signing an appeal to puppet dictator Antonescu, stating that Rumania, after recovering the provinces of Bessarabia and Bukovina, was now only "fighting Germany's war." The executed generals, among them General Ciuperek, Commander of the Rumanian forces in Russia, it appears, were the leaders of a widespread plot. Twelve days after their murder, the Nazi-controlled Rumanian authorities announced that, in the meantime, another 1,628 executions among the followers of the "treacherous defeatists in uniform" had been carried out.

Toward the end of January, 1942, widespread unrest led to the arrest of at least 150 persons of "high Rumanian society." Those arrested were accused of "conduct unbecoming Rumanians desirous of safeguarding the honor and dignity of the country in time of war." The group was said to disapprove of continued military support of the Russian campaign and Premier Antonescu's "ruinous" policy toward Britain and her Allies. That it would have attempted a coup d'état to overthrow the Antonescu regime was believed likely.

Subsequently fourteen Rumanians have been sent to a concentration camp on the orders of Premier General Ion Antonescu for "leading a dissolute life of pleasure at a time when the Rumanian Army is fighting for justice and honor, and a united country is making sacrifices." Perfumed "beau Jean" Antonescu is certainly a competent judge of what constitutes a "dissolute life of pleasure."

Rumanian prisons are crowded. The Jews are still the preferred scapegoats. Rumanian sources estimate that eighty-six hundred Jews have been killed for alleged pro-Russian activities. But among the Bucharest hostages are eighty of the most distinguished Jews, and some of the once wealthiest, whom it would be ridiculous to identify with bolshevist leanings.

State prisoner number one is not in prison. King Michael, who was twenty years old last October, lives under Gestapo surveillance in a villa in the country after an attempt to spirit him out of Rumania had failed. Although the youthful King never refused any act of collaboration required of him, and although he never interfered with Antonescu's dictatorship, his ghastly suffering under the conditions imposed on him and on the country is well known. The young ruler, of course, never had a chance to show his mettle. But the Germans, for their part, prefer to have him on the safe side: educated by a tutor, escorted by an aide-de-camp, and served by a valet who answer to the melodious names of Kruppstein, Vollbach, and Holz. All three are Gestapo agents of long standing.

The King is silent. His more or less loyal subjects are not. A wave of rioting, sabotage, and bitter resistance is sweeping Rumania's northern and eastern provinces.

The Gestapo is facing a new crisis in Rumania, with popular resistance rapidly growing against further participation in the Russian campaign, in which two hundred and fifty thousand have been lost in dead and wounded.

The Gestapo, in a new effort to cope with the sabotage, rioting, and army desertions that have swept Rumania's eastern provinces, has augmented its Rumanian staff with hundreds of former Iron Guards who engage in counter espionage and the suppression of anti-German feeling. The Gestapo now has a larger organization in Rumania than in any other country outside the Reich and occupied France, because of the growing discontent and disorders, and a spy scare which is sweeping the capital and the provinces.

Former Guardsmen, now Gestapo agents, are denouncing

their former personal and political enemies by hundreds. Rumania's three large concentration camps are crowded to capacity.

Rumanian discontent is inspired by growing anti-German feeling, by fears of an Allied victory and possible annexation of eastern Rumania by the Soviet, by German infiltration into all state offices, the Gestapo campaign, the serious lack of food and fuel, and a dangerous shortage of physicians and surgeons.

Rumanian authorities and the Germans are reported to be seriously alarmed by the growth of the Seventh Day Adventist sect in Rumania. The Gestapo arrested several leaders of the sect upon charges of "Communist activity."

Sabotage increases by leaps and bounds. Considerable damage was done recently by saboteurs to armament factories, ironworks, and other plants. The threatening attitude of the workers forced the Germans to send additional armed units into the areas for police duty.

This turbulent state of affairs caused Dr. Juliu Maniu, the veteran peasant leader, and Rumania's elder statesman, to address an open letter to Dictator Ion Antonescu protesting against Rumania's further military cooperation with Germany, which Maniu called the source of all evil in the country. Not only sub-leaders of his former party but spokesmen of the dissolved Liberal party, which for decades ran Rumania, concurred in the protest. Two hundred of them were promptly arrested by the Nazis. The fate of Dr. Maniu is unknown. Antonescu, gravely embarrassed, tried to explain the incident as a "Hungarian intrigue."

Hungary and Rumania, both under the German heel and both comrades in arms on the Russian front, are constantly at loggerheads. The German masters, instead of endeavoring to bring about peace in their camp, pit one vassal against the other, as is their habit. When fighting broke out between Rumanian and Hungarian troops on the Eastern Front, with many casualties on both sides, the German troops were in no hurry to restore order. Let the serfs knock one another's skulls bloody, lest they fraternize and turn against the master: this is the New Order's supreme wisdom, best exemplified in the burning Balkans.

Bulgaria presents the strange picture of a country 85 per cent of whose population—according to George H. Earle, former American minister to Bulgaria, and other reliable experts—hate the Nazis and love the Russians, but are nevertheless involved in an anti-Russian war as the Nazis' slaves. Of course, Bulgaria's alliance with the Third Reich is nonbelligerent, as far as actual battle in Russia is concerned. Every Bulgarian gun and rifle would backfire, if the men were given an opportunity to reach the front. But the Bulgarian soldiers render valuable yeoman service to the Nazi army in doing its dirty work in Serbia and Greece, where they are pitted against the guerrillas, and excel in savage cruelty.

This cruelty is intensified by centuries-old Balkan feuds which today still concern the Bulgarians more closely and deeply than the World War. That the fight against the Serbs has nothing to do with kind feelings for Germany is made evident by every report coming out of the country. Unanimously such reports agree in stating that Bulgaria smolders under the Nazi rule.

Immediately after Bulgaria's invasion by the Germans, a Gestapo organization was created; and the German army soon controlled everything that the Gestapo did not lay hands on. Bulgarian peasants began to feel the pinch when the Germans commandeered staple food, bread and cheese. A poor daily ration helped to revive the traditional Bulgar friendliness toward Russia, leaving only government circles and the upper classes supporting Adolf Hitler's cause.

The mass of the population actively supports the Allied

cause, primarily through sabotage. Fires and explosions occur frequently in such carefully guarded ports as Varna and Burgas, while the Gestapo hunts "Communist" scapegoats in a vain effort to check the widespread derailment of trains, tampering with telephone lines, and other damage.

German propagandists try to explain the reverses suffered in Russia as a deep-laid German plan to keep the Russians moving. They are now minimizing the eastern war theater and declaring the far eastern situation more important.

The Soviet Legation in Sofia has not been closed, apparently because of Bulgaria's fear of the reaction if she should take the initiative and break off relations. But members of the Soviet Legation are badly treated and are spied on by Gestapo agents.

In one case a Gestapo agent followed a member of the Soviet Legation and, when called away for a few minutes, punctured a tire on the diplomat's car to make sure he would not leave before the agent could return. Strong German troop concentrations in Bulgaria, coupled with the establishment of German naval intelligence headquarters in Sofia, point to the undiminished danger of German designs against Turkey.

Bulgars are being told that they must be prepared against any eventuality and that they are threatened by their Turkish neighbors. But pro-Nazi sentiment in Bulgaria, undermined by the Russian victories, was definitely jettisoned by America's entry into the war. Until then the ruling clique had fondly hoped that there would be an early American peace move, preserving the status quo in Europe and thus keeping the Bulgarian Quislings in power. They played their cards badly, since they will be liquidated by their Nazi overlords or crushed by their own countrymen when the time comes.

Although the Bulgarian peasants are largely illiterate, some of them write pungent phrases upon walls for the Nazis and Bulgarian Quislings to read.

Tsar Boris' treacherous regime pretends to see Communist ghosts everywhere in order to find a pretext for ruthlessly persecuting the dissenters from the German course, meaning practically all the people of Bulgaria. Hence the incessant official reports on Russian parachutist activity in Bulgaria.

These reports allege that the parachutists were landed along the Black Sea coast, and that they had been instructed by the Bulgarian Communist leader now in Russia, Georg Dimitroff, to destroy storehouses, factories, railroads, and bridges and kill German and Bulgarian officials. Some saboteurs were landed on the coast between Varna and Burgas from Russian submarines.

Obviously in order to give such reports additional weight, the military tribunal works overtime to indict alleged Communists, available or not.

A general raid was carried out by the police in Varna. While it was in progress—that is, from three A.M. to eleven-thirty P.M.—all traffic in streets was interrupted. All houses were searched, and five hundred and twenty-two men and women were arrested. It was found that six of the arrested persons were "wanted by the police." Seventy-eight men were interned and one hundred and thirty-eight men fined because their identification papers were not in accordance with regulations.

Varna, one must bear in mind, is the most important German U-boat base in the Black Sea. Its garrison commander is Vice Admiral Döberitz, an intimate of the German naval chief, Grand Admiral Raeder. Despite his importance as a naval big shot Vice Admiral Döberitz condescended to use as his flagship the light cruiser *Karlsruhe*. The longshoremen of Varna, it appears, were not impressed by the German commander's modesty. On the night of February 4, 1942, a fire broke out in the port of Varna, gravely damaging the German cruiser. On the same night Tsar Boris dined and wined the German minister in his Sofia castle. The unpleasant news from Varna came just as his Majesty was lifting his glass to toast the eternal friendship between the German and the Bulgarian people. But Dr. Remmerscheidt, the Tsar's German aide-de-camp, and Gestapo-appointed shadow, saw to it that the news was not broken before coffee and brandy had been served.

Relations between the German masters and their well groomed Hungarian valets are of the same barbed friendliness. Admiral Horthy, the Prince Regent who many years ago created the model after which Pétain was patterned, is on the point of throwing up his hands. He introduced in his shadow parliament a law of succession by inheritance, which bequeaths the regency to his elder son Stephen, a Budapest playboy, constantly involved in embarrassing personal affairs. The old Admiral without a fleet thus admits that he can no longer run the kingdom without a king. His policy, for many years, of feeding the Nazi brute without being devoured by it, has become impossible.

The Hungarians, fiery patriots imbued with chivalrous ideas of *Dulce et decorum est pro patria mori*, but also endowed with a shrewd sense of bargaining, are in a mental depression similar to that after the Treaty of Trianon when they lost two thirds of their country. They now realize that in the Nazi embrace they lost the last third. The fact became evident when they duly declared war on Britain and thought it desirable to place Budapest in a state of defense, at least against air raids. On this occasion it was discovered that the entire stock of antiaircraft guns, stored at the Manfred Weiss Works, Hungary's foremost armament plant, had been diverted by the Germans for use in France. Similarly, their shipping industry, which maintains traffic along the Danube, Hungary's life line, was entirely despoiled.

The destruction of Axis shipping by the R.A.F. offensive has made it necessary for Hitler's transport experts to look for ships built at the smaller dockyards of Europe. Thus, the Hungarian dockyards at Csepel received big contracts for new ships. The Csepel works build ships with a special low water line to enable them to steam down the Danube and into the Black Sea.

The Italians also have ordered several tugs and a large steamer to be built in Hungary. To cope with the increasing orders, the Hungarian Government built new dockyards on the lower reaches of the Hungarian section of the Danube. The Germans have promised to send some skilled workers and experts from the bombed areas of Bremen, Hamburg, Rotterdam, and Amsterdam, where work is upset by constant raids.

In return, Hungarian labor is "permitted" to accept jobs in those cities. Many, indeed, avail themselves of this good opportunity to be bombed, since the alternative is to freeze to death on the Russian front. Germany put eighty thousand Hungarian troops in the van of the Donets battle. The Hungarian contingent counted thirty thousand casualties and twenty thousand "missing" (deserters) before its shattered remnants were rescued by the Germans.

Violent agitation increased in favor of the return of troops from the Russian front. Two Hungarian front-line divisions are now along the Donets, and some Budapest newspapers comment that they would be better employed in garrisoning and consolidating Galicia, which is apparently to be annexed by Horthy by permission of Hitler.

This agitation is watched carefully by the Rumanians, and General Antonescu made it clear to the German Minister in Bucharest that if the Hungarian troops return home he will have to recall Rumanian front-line troops as well. Hungary has never given up hope that at some future opportunity she will be able to seize southern Transylvania from Rumania, and Antonescu cannot afford to be left out in the Crimea with the Hungarians threatening his rear on the northeastern border of the country.

Major Francis Szaiasy, the Nazi Arrow-Cross leader, is exploiting the position against the Government by agitating against further adventures in distant Russia, and for a march on Rumania.

Leading members of the Hungarian Nazi party, among them the editor in chief of the official mouthpiece *Magyar-shag,* resigned with the slogan: "Rumania, not Russia, must be beaten." It seemed like a palace revolution of the most trusted Nazi stooges. But soon the fact was disclosed that the political revolt was phony. It had been manufactured in Berlin in order to embarrass the Horthy administration so as to force new concessions.

Ribbentrop himself appeared in Budapest on January 12, 1942, to present the new demands. His aims were twofold. First he demanded that the Hungarian army be kept at maximum strength and be placed under direct orders of the German High Command. He asked that the Army be available for use anywhere, at any time, for any duty the German High Command might desire.

He also demanded that Hungarian agriculture be more efficiently regimented, with stricter rationing to permit sending more supplies to Germany.

In exchange, it was reported, Ribbentrop said Germany would allow Hungary greater independence in internal affairs.

To a Hungarian query about the Transylvania question, Ribbentrop replied reaffirming the present settlement with Rumania.

Yet persistent rumors in Budapest, the gossip capital of Central Europe, speak of an impending deal to strip Hungary of some of the territory recently ceded by Rumania. The Germans keep these rumors going as a means of intimidation.

In the meantime Hungary is hard pressed by increasing

food shortage. The larder of the hitherto richest agrarian country in Europe has been emptied by the Germans. Even Budapest feels the pressure. To a large extent the city used to live on tourist traffic. Budapest prided herself on being the Paris of the East. She is, like Paris, a dead city today. Streams of German uniforms float through the streets. With their practically worthless tourist allowances they are buying up all goods in all the stores. Hungarians from the country and the provinces had to cease their customary shopping trips. They find it easier to hoard food at home. The fact that food hoarding has become the most widespread offense in a land once overflowing with wheat and meat, fruit and vegetables is the clearest indication of Hungary's doom. But the shortage of foodstuffs is not alone due to the Germans' ruthless requisitioning and plunder. It is caused, at least to the same extent, by sabotage. A secret radio station, which up to now has not been found out, incites the peasants to unrest. Hungarian peasants, the Irish of Central Europe, do not need much incitement. By the scores of thousands they burn their crops and destroy their stores, rather than see them fall into German hands. In the second week of February, 1942, two hundred peasants were indicted for sabotage, and two hundred and ninety for food hoarding. Hungary, being an old-fashioned country, still used the gallows for executions. A farmer from the neighborhood of Debrecen mounted them with a grin. "I am in good company," he shouted. "Horthy comes next!" Then he added an unprintable invitation to the Prince Regent, and died cheerfully.

Montenegro, from whence Queen Giovanna of Italy hails, once an independent kingdom and later a part of Yugoslavia, is no longer the favorite scene of Viennese operettas, Ruritania on the Blue Danube. Montenegro was part of Mussolini's grab in the Balkans. But to this day not a single Italian soldier has disgraced its beautiful shores and mountains. The Italian navy has frequently subjected the coast of Montenegro to savage shelling—fairly safe, since the farmers and fishermen have no guns with which to shoot back. But they have cudgels, forks, pickaxes, and clenched fists. Every Italian landing party was beaten off. Prince George of Montenegro was invited to Rome from Paris, where he made his home, in order to accept, from the Duce's hands, the crown of his own country. "I am a Serbian," the prince replied, "and loyal to King Peter"—who, incidentally, is his cousin. Prince George was arrested. Thus Mussolini made his only Montenegrin prisoner of war.

The Duce, it appears, is on the point of losing even Albania, the first Axis conquest on the Balkan peninsula. Zog I, the dethroned king, is, at this writing, setting up an exile government in England. He is counting heavily on the support of the large Albanian colony in America. He expresses the hope that perhaps this country will also sympathize with his cause since his wife, beautiful Queen Geraldine, is half American by descent. But the times are gone in which the captive nations pinned their hopes on miracles from outside. Albania, to quote her king in exile, is teeming with unrest. The country was, he insists, one of the victims, and the first victim at that, of the disunity that prevailed in the Balkans, paralyzing individual efforts. This disunity, King Zog adds, has been burned out by the flames of hatred against the Axis. Albania, although policed by Italian troops, will be the next to join the ranks of the united Balkan front.

Undoubtedly, the King of small Albania has a point to make. Hatred against the New Order sweeps the world. But it is nowhere more violent than in the abused Balkan countries. Their people, although exposed to terrible suffering, view the situation hopefully. Germany's increasing demand

for man power from Hungary, Rumania, and Bulgaria is regarded by them as proof of Hitler's desperate military needs.
His serious reverses in Yugoslavia are signal fires, illuminating
the whole peninsula. The hard-bitten Balkan people regard
even the plague and famine in Greece as an indication that
Hitler started a war against nature.

The Balkan people believe that their lands are destined to
play an important role in the further development of the war.
They are unshakable in their confidence that the Balkans must
become the jumping-off ground for an invasion of the European continent by the United Nations. Hitler will probably
try to anticipate such an invasion by striking first in the direction of Turkey. But it is the common opinion that the
Turks will resist, and will be aided by guerrillas mushrooming everywhere between the plains of the Danube and the
Greek islands. Perhaps Russia will be able to help by advancing through Rumania. The Rumanians would welcome the
Russians. So would the Bulgars, the Serbs, the Greeks, all the
Balkan nations.

This is, of course, all speculation. The only clearly discernible fact, at this moment, is Hitler's gigantic massing of troops
in Sicily and southern Italy, Bulgaria, Greece, Crete, and the
Aegean Islands, and his concentration of vast air power in all
the Axis Mediterranean air bases. The Nazis (the Balkan people believe, knowing the monster better than any one else)
have still the power to strike a heavy blow, perhaps even a
second and a third. But Crete, the key position for the command of the eastern Mediterranean, can be won back just as
the Germans won it: by aerial supremacy and by the use of
parachutists, who would, in addition, have the fighting support of every inhabitant. From Crete the way leads to Salonika, to the Yugoslavian mountains, and up to the plains of the
Danube basin, the heart of continental Europe. It is true that
there are at least half a dozen borders to be crossed. But bor-

ders have lost their meaning. History might well judge some day that the Nazi terror was a blessing in disguise to that part of Europe, traditionally the worst torn by internal strife and dissension. Out of the abyss of the New Order surge—already alive in the hearts of millions of people—the United Balkans.

CHAPTER TWENTY-THREE

THE BALTICS—FORGOTTEN?

The German Reich never had any intention of occupying Lithuania.—ADOLF HITLER, June 21, 1941 (one day before the invasion of the country).

IT IS a regrettable fact that the Baltic States receive scant attention from the Western world, of which they form a valuable part. The fate of Latvia, Lithuania, and Estonia is in danger of being overlooked, although it is a truly tragic fate remarkable, beyond its limited geographical scope, as a test-case of the small nations' destiny in Europe.

The combined area of the Baltic States is about sixty-four thousand square miles—approximately the size of New England, or 9 per cent less than the state of Washington. In 1940 the population of Estonia was 1,200,000; that of Latvia 2,000,-000; and of Lithuania 3,200,000—a total of 6,400,000, or about the equivalent of that of Texas. Under the German rule it has decreased by hundreds of thousands of victims and expelled people.

The Reich did not give the Baltic republics even those

farcical "independent governments" that have been instituted in other parts of the New Order. Remembering the incorporation of the countries with Imperial Germany during the first war, the Nazis relied on the power of their military occupation to keep the Baltic nations in check.

In the case of Lithuania, at least, this was outright double-crossing, for a general rising against the Soviets in Lithuania "coincided" with the German assault on the U.S.S.R.

However, military cooperation with the Germans did not bring the Lithuanians the expected results, nor even the appearance of independence in the form of a German protectorate, like Slovakia. In their disillusionment the Lithuanians began to ask themselves whether it had been really worth while to sacrifice four thousand killed and ten thousand wounded simply for the sake of a general council advising the German commissar, together with the military police formation already mentioned and the dubious benefits of the German military occupation. The last hopes from Germany vanished, when "Ostland" was created, a shadowy country with so far undefined frontiers, including territories from Latvia, Lithuania, Poland, and White Russian parts of the Soviet Union. It is treated as a mere colony.

Of course the German press spares no labor or ingenuity to discover traces of German cultural influence, both real and imaginary, in the Baltic countries; for the German press completely ignores Estonian, Latvian, and Lithuanian culture and the achievements of the Baltic States during their twenty years of independence. The Nazis declare that their people have no civilization, and that only the more fortunate among them will be Germanized, whereas the rest will be removed by force to areas farther east, or possibly to the Arctic regions.

The Nazi rule began with the appointment of Heinrich Lohse (former Gauleiter of Schleswig-Holstein, who had to be removed from this post for irregularities) to the dignity of a protector of Lithuania. His initial proclamation was couched in the language of a condescending conqueror, and referred to the sovereign republic of Lithuania as a former free state without any regard to the rights and feelings of the nation. There were words about order, bread and work, compulsory work, but not one about Freedom.

The originally Provisional Government of Lithuania, with Dr. J. Ambrazevičius at the head, requested Reich Commissar Lohse and Commissar General von Renteln to give an explanation of the situation created by the Reich Commissar's declaration. They were received by both Commissars, and expressed the determined wish of the Lithuanian people to remain masters of their homelands and to reestablish good neighborly relations.

When these efforts failed, Professor Ambrazevičius sent a telegram to Hitler; but his appeal brought no reply. On August 5, 1941, the Provisional Government was forced to resign. Public protest took place on August 10, 1941, when, once again, the people, sorely disappointed over the German attitude, gathered in their Forum, the usual meeting place in front of the National Museum, as though seeking solace or enlightenment on the newly developed situation. The members of the resigned Provisional Government were there—they placed a wreath on the Tomb of the Unknown Soldier while the people sang the national anthem, "Lithuania, Our Fatherland." Then Dr. Ambrazevičius spoke, urging the people not to despair and not to lose faith in the undying ideal of Liberty. The atmosphere was filled with emotion. The gathering then was dispersed, and the Lithuanian flag as well as a plaque commemorating Lithuanian rule of Klaipeda (Memel) was removed from the War Museum by a German soldier. The Lithuanian national anthem was forbidden, and the Lithuanian flag (yellow, green, and red) disappeared.

Three members of the resigned Provisional Government, B. Vitkus, J. Matulionis, M. Mackevičius, were appointed by

Commissar von Renteln to important posts in advisory capacities. They refused, pointing out Hitler's declaration in Berlin on June 21, 1941: "The German Reich never had any intention of occupying Lithuania."

But it was of no avail. Double-crossed Lithuania had to endure all the terror of the New Order. In the German invasion and the ensuing regime, the country has lost approximately two hundred thousand people. Ninety thousand of these disappeared in the Russian-German war. The Freedom Fighters, who materially helped the German troops in wresting Kaunas from the Russians, were disbanded, and their leaders arrested by the Gestapo.

Like every other invaded country, Lithuania, too, was bled white by the economic squeeze. The Germans enforced the delivery of one hundred and fifty thousand tons of grain, about double Lithuania's normal export, and almost the entire crop of potatoes (two hundred and fifty thousand tons), fodder and hay. Finally, they snatched the meat and butter out of the mouths of the Lithuanians. Their method of combating Bolshevism was to confirm the Russian confiscation of Lithuanian farms, houses, and factories, not for collective, communal use as in the Russian system, but for the benefit of deserving German soldiers and party members. The Lithuanian Chamber of Agriculture was dissolved after it had submitted to the Reichskommissar a memorandum stating that the farmers were being ruined by the enforced deliveries at nominal prices. To cloak the system of loot the Reichskommissar, by special decree, has conferred upon Germans in the Baltic States the privilege of extraterritorial jurisdiction, a prerogative which white men no longer enjoy in the darkest Africa. For this law of the New Order, Lithuanians had to abandon the Code Napoléon which prevailed in the country.

Justice is meted out by double standards. Lithuanian courts are overruled by German courts. Arrests are made throughout the country by the Gestapo on the slightest suspicion, with the result that numerous innocent people are imprisoned. Recently one hundred and seventy-eight persons in the towns of Siauliai, Telšiai, and Mažeikiai alone have been released with the curt announcement that they were arrested "by mistake." There was no apology. A number of people were executed publicly. Former Kaunas residents who sought shelter in villages during the Soviet occupation are not permitted to return to the city. Lithuanian refugees in Germany and those of "German descent" who were repatriated to Germany are not permitted to return to Lithuania. Until October 15, 1941, about one hundred and eighty prominent Lithuanians, permanent residents of the Klaipeda district, were banished to remote parts of the Reich and not allowed to settle in Lithuania.

The Catholic religion is restricted in many ways. Enrollment of new students at the Lithuanian universities in Vilna and Kaunas is prohibited. Of twenty-nine high schools in the district of Vilna in 1937–38, only six are now open; and of eighty primary schools, only forty-nine are open—half of them on part time. Compulsory German-language classes were recently started in the Teachers' Institute. Short courses in German are conducted for teachers and officials with the ultimate purpose of Germanizing Lithuania.

A Nazi Propaganda Agency has been organized. It is directed by Walter Zimmermann, who also controls the Kaunas radio station. Most Lithuanian newspapers have suspended publication; those remaining have to be printed partly in German, although two daily newspapers in German are published. No parliament, political party, or other organization is allowed to function. The Lithuanian police force has been abolished or partly incorporated into that of the Reich. Illegal remnants of the Lithuanian army remain the hope of the people. Nevertheless, they are awaiting their day. The Soviet Russians will have no trouble with the Lithuanian people when they enter Kaunas a second time. The whole population is prepared to help them—in the firm conviction, of course, that rebolshevization of their country is not planned. In this firm belief Dr. Povilas Zadeikis, the Lithuanian Minister in Washington, announced that his nation wished to be considered as aligned with the states fighting the Axis and expressed in behalf of his government "deep sympathy as well as full confidence in the victorious exploits of American armed forces."

Dr. Zadeikis said he looked to the Atlantic Charter as a guarantee of the reestablishment of Lithuania as a Republic. The Atlantic Charter of President Roosevelt and Prime Minister Churchill states, he recalled, that "sovereign rights and self-government should be restored to those nations who have been forcibly deprived of them."

"Though Lithuania is a small nation and her geographical situation is unenviable," the Minister concluded, "she refuses to be buried alive or to be sacrificed for the benefit of her great neighbors. Lithuania has rich historical traditions which are a part of her soul, and she has will and ability to lead an independent life in no way interfering with the legitimate interests of her neighbors."

And after all, on the small Lithuanian scale, that is what this war is all about.

Latvia, proudly insisting that she remains a democratic republic, is the largest of the three Baltic States. Her territory, indeed, is bigger than that of Switzerland, Denmark, Holland, or Belgium. The country lies on the eastern shore of the Baltic Sea, where the principal routes of Western and Eastern Europe meet. She is in an important "geopolitic" position, besides being a prosperous and industrious land—meat for Adolf Hitler.

For many months German military authorities have ruled in Latvia. They have blacked the country out, and cut it off from all connection with the outer world. Evidently, they are doing something in occupied Latvia that they prefer to keep hidden. Dark deeds must be done in the dark. The first news received by the Latvian government in exile was that the Latvian Red Cross had been forbidden.

In January, 1942, further information began to filter out. Then the brutal features of the German conqueror appeared in all their horrible slyness and mercilessness. The orders, decrees, and characteristic acts of oppression of the new conquerors followed one another in rapid succession. First of all, the German administration was established. Germans were appointed provincial commissars under the Ostland Reichskommissar Lohse.

Decrees have been issued prohibiting the sale to Latvians of whole categories of commodities—even tooth paste and shoe polish. Only German soldiers may buy them without special permission. Buildings in cities and farms nationalized by the Bolsheviks have not been returned to their Latvian owners, but are held "temporarily" and administered by the German economic organization *Wirtschaftskommando*. The farm land nationalized by the Bolsheviks remains at the disposal of the German authorities, evidently for settling German colonists in place of Latvians.

Simply styled proclamations were issued in which the Germans attempted to convince the Latvians how evil were the former Latvian governments, and even how bad for them was independence, but how "sweet and secure" is life under German military occupation. Then, as if still uncertain of their victory, the German commanders and political commissars began to rush Germanization.

Under German occupation the University of Latvia is not to be reopened. All philosophic faculties are transferred to Tartu, Estonia, and only the technical faculties remain in Riga. This Institute is now named after Alfred Rosenberg, who once started to study there, but finished his studies in Moscow, already under Lenin's rule.

The supply of the German army is placed above all else,

and for that reason meat is rationed even outside the cities. The German administration is the sole purchaser of cattle. Naturally, everything goes to the German army, and the Latvian farmers are left with worthless German slips of paper called money, but good for nothing because there is nothing to be had. Truly, for the Germans "Lettland" is now "Fettland" (land of fats); but a time will come, the Latvians insist, when for them it will become "Deathland."

All schools in Latvia have to teach German three to four times a week. The teachers are imported carpetbaggers. Religion is now replaced by Nordic, pagan "ethics." Many schools have been burned to the ground.

On October 19, 1941, the *Deutsche Zeitung im Ostland*, official organ of the German Reichskommissar, published an authoritative announcement issued by Dr. W. Zimmermann, his chief of press, concerning property rights in the territory occupied by Germany. In this matter the point of view of official Germany is as follows: At the commencement of the German-Soviet war, private property did not exist in the countries under Soviet rule; so nobody could claim to be a legal proprietor. By sacrificing the blood of German soldiers, all these countries were liberated. The German Reich, therefore, becomes the legal heir to the Soviet inheritance. Even the former owners of real estate, buildings, and factories in the Baltic countries now have to pay rent to the German Government. Similarly all industrial enterprises have to pay even for their own raw materials which they had in stock. This same policy also applies to farms and forests. By such acts the Germans indirectly legalize Bolshevik practices and even profit by them. Thus the German forces of occupation are simply "neo-Bolsheviks."

The reichsmark has become the official currency of Estonia, Latvia, Lithuania, and White Russia. The Germans have fixed the rate of exchange at ten roubles to one mark and have flooded these countries with more than fifty million marks to buy up everything of value left undamaged by war. The new province of Ostland is designed purely as a Nazi workshop under strictest German supervision, in which independence is a dangerous and expensive dream. Berlin now declares that Baltic nationalism is a mere phantom, since the republics have always been part of the splendidly elastic German lebensraum and have frequently shown themselves "helpers of England."

The Bolsheviks accused the Baltic peoples of being secretly pro-German and plotting against Soviet Russia. The Germans, in their turn, accused the Baltic governments of being pro-British and plotting against Germany. As a matter of fact, the Latvian Government actually was pro-democratic. The Latvian President, Dr. K. Ulmanis, once professor at the University of Nebraska, and the Cabinet Ministers always placed their faith in the democracies and trusted that the democracies would win and protect Latvia.

"My country," Dr. Alfred Bilmanis, Latvian Minister in Washington, puts it, "is well acquainted with the brutal methods of unrestricted and barbaric force and oppression. Latvia pleads on the basis of law and justice, on the basis of moral rights and humanitarianism. It appeals to the immortal American Declaration of Independence.

"We cannot conceive of national life without family-life, private property, religion. We cannot conceive of International Relations, of economical and cultural intercourse between nations without international justice and law. There can be no existence for small nations until these principles are generally accepted. And the big and powerful countries will not enjoy the blessing of peace until a new order is founded on the basis of universal justice, voluntary cooperation, and equal freedom for all mankind."

Estonia, dangerously close to the Leningrad front, is hermetically sealed. No news of any kind comes from the country. The following report is the only document received since the German invasion by the Estonian government in exile, which valiantly maintains whatever resistance against Nazism it can muster. It speaks for itself:

Germany has given indirect recognition to the Soviet Russian invasion of Estonia as well as to the nationalization of private property by the following general reasoning: "We have not occupied the Republic of Estonia, but a republic of the Union of Soviet Socialist Republics." And from this all other consequences are to be drawn. Private property is not restored, and at the present time it is not even certain whether the property that was not nationalized by Soviet Russia will remain in private hands. What will be done with these properties is not yet clear. However, one thing is certain: the big industries, important for German war production, will be built up; but they will pass into the hands of German industrial enterprises or banks. In the first place the Germans plan to reopen the Krull factory in order to build machines for the shale-oil industry, which they want to start to operate in the coming spring. But much of Krull's machinery has been either taken to Russia or destroyed, and therefore it is doubtful whether the plan will be carried out by spring. The German banks and industrial enterprises are also making competitive rushes for a number of other industries. The former owners are kept away from their properties; in a few cases they have been permitted to come back as employees. With less important industries there is evidently little hurry, as unemployed factory workers are signed up for work in Germany. Because of all this the conditions in cities are very difficult. A large number of the former manufacturers and businessmen are gone, and to those who still remain no enterprises or businesses are being returned. Who still is in possession of his business, has no goods or materials.

There is no sugar or soap in Estonia, and very little salt, clothes, and footwear. Nothing is brought in from Germany, partly for reasons of Nazi principle and partly because of transportation difficulties. The Communists left behind only about a dozen locomotives and about three hundred railway cars. These are used for service on the Leningrad front. Travel of private persons is very restricted. Traveling is possible only with a special permit from the military authorities which allows the holder to purchase a ticket on a certain train.

Transport difficulties also hinder the supply of food to cities. There are practically only women and children left in cities, and the problem of feeding them is difficult. But the most serious problem is health in cities and also in rural districts. There are no medicines available. This may become catastrophic.

In the countryside the situation is not easy either. The harvest this year was not very good. There was evidently not enough seed for the autumn sowing. Part of the harvest has not yet been threshed because of the oil shortage. Oil is not available for tractors either, regardless of the destruction of about 25 per cent of all horses and the lack of men for farm work. It was announced over the radio that farmers should not expect to receive any oil. Nevertheless, the German army has to be fed. Right now compulsory sales to the army have been announced with the warning that if the demanded quantities are not delivered, requisitions will follow. In order to assure full deliveries, it is permitted to sell liquors and tobacco, which are scarce, only to those who have delivered their quotas.

The German army remains in Estonia in winter quarters, as the territory between Narva and Leningrad is completely devastated. This condition adds a new burden to the farmers who have no security, and consequently no reason to work—just like the manufacturers, businessmen, and landlords.

Estonia's pulse beats dangerously slow. The collapse of Nazism alone can revive the ancient little country.

CHAPTER TWENTY-FOUR

RUSSIA

The Hitlers come and go.—STALIN in his order of the day, February 22, 1942 (twenty-fourth anniversary of the Red Army).

AT THE height of their success on the Eastern Front the Germans, according to their official statement of October 31, 1941, had occupied six hundred and fifteen thousand square miles of Russian territory—more than three times the area of Germany in 1937—with a total population of over seventy million inhabitants and endowed, as the Nazis boast, with "unestimable natural wealth." They have lost a good part of their gains since then but continue to hold much Russian soil.

Occupied Russia is by far the biggest and the most important among the subjugated countries, but it may well become a colossal grave of Nazism.

The principal difference between occupied Russia and all the other captive countries except Yugoslavia lies in the fact that the hold of the army of occupation on the downtrodden people of Russia is contested, and in vast regions only nominal. The best proof of this is the Nazi-Tsar's unwillingness to visit his conquered, but not subdued, domain. His second in command, Dr. Alfred Meyer, admitted recently that the administration of "Eastland" will remain centralized in Berlin for the duration.

It may be worth while to take a brief look at the gang controlling the spoils of Russia at some two thousand miles' distance. Alfred Rosenberg has been sketched in a previous chapter. Inside reports from Berlin agree that he received his dignity as *Reichsminister für den Osten* only because Hitler did not want to hurt his feelings, since Alfred has been Nazism's outstanding Bolshevik-eater for over twenty years, ever since he came home to Germany, after a short detour via Paris, from red Leningrad. The power behind his shaky throne is a man, not by coincidence named Meyer, like a few million of his German fellow men. His common name, as well as his nondescript looks, and his inconspicuous bearing form the smokescreen hiding one of the most influential men in the Nazi camp. The Führer, indeed, owes to Herr Meyer his access to power.

At the turn of 1933 Hitler and his party were all washed up. The last elections to the Reichstag had brought Nazism a crushing defeat. Again elections were due, though only in the former principality of Lippe—Germany's tiniest state, about the size of Westchester County, New York. But the little state had a big Nazi boss, Dr. Alfred Meyer, who rushed from house to house, cajoling, threatening, pleading. The huge Nazi propaganda machine and all the money available, millions from Thyssen and millions from Mussolini, as well as a contribution from the Comité de Forges, the French steel cartel, were lavished on Lippe. The local Nazi boss, however, scored the biggest success by his name. No Meyer could resist his namesake's buttonholing: 51 per cent of the electorate were named Meyer, and when the day came 51.6 per cent voted for Hitler. The Führer's waning prestige was restored by this signal triumph. He was back in the race. At the end of the month he landed in the Wilhelmstrasse. His first official act was to make his friend Gauleiter of Lippe.

Herr Meyer moved into the former ruling prince's palace. This was the only act of showmanship he permitted himself. For the rest he remained a modest backbencher in the Nazified Reichstag. His close relations with Hitler, who calls him his mascot, have never been revealed. Indeed, Meyer's benevolently beaming, bespectacled cherub's face spells kindness. Seeing him, one would never guess that this man is responsible for the terror in Kishenev, the razing of Rostov, and similar Nazi pleasantries. The responsibility, it is true, is not Meyer's alone. Meyer's two foremost henchmen are Erich Koch, special commissioner for the Ukraine, and S.S. Sturmbannführer Eichmann, special commissioner for Jewish affairs. Besides, the Nazi government of occupied Russia has a Goebbels of its own, Major Carl Cranz of the air force, who owes his career with Rosenberg to his "dismissal without honor" from the Luftwaffe by Göring. The remarkable feature of this outfit is the absence of a Quisling. With the exception of a handful of Ukrainian veterans of the Russian civil war, who have been living in Berlin for twenty-five years, no Russian Quisling was available. In the many thousands of captured villages—it is a characteristic sidelight—five mayors, all told, showed themselves ready to collaborate with the invaders. All five, according to official Soviet reports, were killed by their own citizens.

Erich Koch, commissioner for the Ukraine, forty-six years old, square-faced, and plump, is a veteran Nazi assassin. He is the typical representative of that by now middle-aged generation of hoodlums who very early pledged their allegiance to Hitler since they were not born, they felt, to slave away at a job. Herr Koch's entire professional career consisted, according to his own proud confession, of the two weeks he worked as a railway clerk, until he was discharged for undisclosed reasons. Subsequently, he joined one of the right-wing Free Corps which, after the last war, fought against the French in the Ruhr rising. André-François Poncet, later French ambassador to Rome and Berlin, was director of the French intelligence service during the Allied occupation of the Rhineland and Ruhr. The well groomed diplomat smiled enigmatically when, many years afterward, the name of Erich Koch came into prominence. M. Poncet remembered the name very well. It had figured on a good many checks which Robert Simon—M. Poncet's nomme de guerre as spy master—had signed.

Unfortunately for Koch the Ruhr rising succeeded. France was persuaded to withdraw her troops. Erich Koch saw freedom restored to home soil, but he lost an excellent job as informer. His last bargain with the French was to have himself imprisoned in order to emerge as an unblemished German patriot and martyr when the occupation was over. M. Poncet did Koch a last little favor by detaining him for six weeks in an idyllic country parsonage. The later ambassador had the true French understanding for the frailties of human nature.

Erich Koch was looking toward the next war. He had only to wait a few months before German bands terrorized the Polish minority in Upper Silesia, prior to the plebiscite. Since the poor Polish farmers and miners had no checks to sign, Herr Koch took his business very seriously. This time there was no double-crossing. This time, cross your heart, he was in earnest.

The real career started back in 1922 when Erich Koch, as one of the earliest disciples of Hitler, joined the Nazi party. Five years later he got into hot water when a fellow Nazi leader accused him of embezzling party funds, and an inquiry revealed that both men had accepted graft. Koch was sent to do the party's work in Germany's remotest corner, East Prussia; but Hitler is not vindictive where the corruption of his accomplices is concerned, and he nominated Koch to the Reichstag.

In September, 1933, Koch shared in the Nazi triumph. He was appointed president of the administration of East Prussia. A year later he was given the lucrative job of Controller of the Reich Post Office. By seizing anti-Nazi newspapers and publishing houses, Koch did very well for himself. His beautiful country estate near Königsberg is one of Germany's finest. He has, in common with Rosenberg, unbounded hatred and contempt for the Slav peoples. When, not long before the war, Lithuania was bullied into surrendering the Memel district to the Reich, it was Koch who organized the war of nerves and the blood purge in Memel that followed.

His next job was to prepare a revolution in the Ukraine which, for a long time, was intended to furnish the pretext for Nazism's attack on the Soviet Union. He enlisted the veteran hetman (tribal head) Skoropadsky, a refugee living in Berlin, who had fought the Bolshevists unsuccessfully during the civil war. An imposing array of other Ukrainians gathered around the two men, attracted both by the Nazi pay roll and by the dream of establishing, as Koch had promised them, an independent Greater Ukraine. However, when the long prepared attack materialized the members of the Ukrainian legion were not even permitted to join the fight. In the heyday of his assault Hitler, obviously, believed that he could do without mercenaries. Koch was instructed to tell them that they had entirely misunderstood him. There was no idea of establishing anything like independence; the Ukrainians would instead be treated as a racial minority in occupied Poland and Russia. It is true that Hitler changed his opinion about the fighting value of mercenaries when he frantically tried to enlist the derelicts and professional criminals in all the occupied countries for his "Christian Crusade." A group of Ukrainians showed that they could forgive. They even volunteered to fight as the spearhead of the German army. Crossing the Don, they immediately joined the Russian defenders. Herr Koch is now busy ferreting out their relatives in the Ukrainian villages.

But the double game the Nazis played with them has entirely alienated even those Ukrainians who considered making common cause with Hitler against the Soviets. Today the whole nation is ferociously anti-German, especially embittered over the "loss" of the main provincial city of Lwów, which under Austrian rule was considered as the spiritual capital of Ukrainian nationalism.

To keep the outraged Ukrainians down, Koch availed himself of the services of the only man to whom he concedes priority in ruthlessness: Wilhelm Kube, who played a prominent part in the earlier stages of the Nazi movement, being known for his aggressiveness in dealing with political opponents, and later was governor of Brandenburg until August, 1936.

One of Herr Kube's first proclamations as assistant in charge of the former Soviet White Russian Republic appeared in the *Minsk Gazette*, in the White Russian dialect, decreeing labor service for boys from fourteen to twenty years and for girls from seventeen to twenty-four years. He also decreed compulsory Nazi-education for children from seven to fourteen years and ordered the opening of all schools except Jewish schools, which must remain closed.

Herr Kube further admonished religious orders to "preserve peace and good relations" and to occupy themselves exclusively with religious questions. "Pastors who interfere with politics will be arrested or expelled from White Russia," his order stated.

The *Minsk Gazette* also published a proclamation of the local police chief establishing the death penalty for hunting and fishing without special license.

The extent of the destruction which Minsk, the capital of White Russia, suffered in military operations may be gauged by the fact, mentioned in the *Minsk Gazette*, that only one of the streetcar lines would resume operations "before long," but that in all fourteen streetcars were available for this purpose. But Kiev, the capital of the Ukraine, was not to be cowed. Here is a brief description, furnished by the government of the U.S.S.R., of the city's "welcome" to the German occupation:

As soon as the Germans entered Kiev they began to look for living quarters. On the Kreschatik, Kiev's main street, they turned a big children's toy shop into the commander's headquarters. In other big houses on the Kreschatik they opened officers' clubs, military headquarters, and offices. A big motion picture theater on the same street was set aside especially for officers.

At first everything was quiet, and the German officers enjoyed German films in their theater. But one evening, a few days after the Germans entered Kiev, the city was shaken by an explosion, which destroyed the headquarters of the German commander. It was followed by another explosion, which blew up the motion picture theater while it was thronged with German officers.

More explosions followed, and in less than two minutes most of the Kreschatik was a heap of smoking ruins. Then the explosions began on Nikolayevskaia Street. Here the Hotel Continental, the circus, the Franko Theater, and neighboring houses, all confiscated by the Germans, flew into the air. Powerful mines had been laid beneath the foundations. The walls of the buildings were ripped clear away from the earth.

Many buildings are now empty. Their bitter experience on the Kreschatik and Nikolayevskaia Street has made the Germans wary. They keep away from Kiev's big buildings. No wonder that every day bodies of dead German officers and soldiers are found in all parts of the city.

The trouble Herr Koch ran into in trying to build up his Ukrainian administration was not confined to Kiev alone. It still permeates the whole country. Much to their disappointment the Nazis are realizing that in conquering a big part of the Ukraine they won an empty bread basket. In normal times this conquered area, roughly half the size of Texas, produced millions of tons of wheat annually, much of which found an outlet through Odessa. Today the bulk of the wheat acreage is idle and not even a fishing smack is navigating out of this once busy Black Sea port. Many difficulties must be overcome before this agricultural region can start feeding Europe again. In the first place, work animals and tractors taken for war purposes, as well as other livestock and implements destroyed or removed under Stalin's scorched-earth policy must be replaced.

To handle the job many *Sonderführer* (special leaders) have been trained in Germany. No matter how well trained he may be, however, the German farm boy, accustomed to the Reich's miniature farms, still must adapt himself to the task of supervising thousands of acres of Russian wheat land.

Two of these leaders are supposed to supervise fifty-four of the Russian collective farm units known as kolkhozes—a total of one hundred and eighty thousand acres.

Russian observers who remained in the Ukraine after the German invasion, or who had the courage to return in disguise, called the impression the occupied country had made on them "a picture of swift destruction and snail-like reconstruction." It is a mistake, they insist, to assume that all the towns from which the Russians have withdrawn have been destroyed completely. Almost invariably the central business section is razed by fire, and factories and public utility plants are burned and blasted or their machinery is removed; but in most places the residential sections, except when they border highways, are left intact. Thus shelter at least remains.

Women and children rummage through burned structures for wood to use as fuel against the rigors of the Russian winter.

In many towns all community life revolves around the public markets. Where the market buildings themselves have been destroyed, temporary stands or tables are set up.

The barter system prevails. A pair of old boots is swapped for a gallon of milk or a sack of sunflower seed. Russian currency is spurned in the conquered area and German coins are accepted reluctantly.

Tobacco will buy almost anything on the market square. In larger transactions, wheat frequently serves as a medium of exchange.

Ukrainians have found many uses for wheat straw. It is used for bedding, for roofing, for padding clothes, for fuel. Branches of the willow trees that flourish along Ukrainian streams are plaited into fences, building material, corn cribs, and wagon beds.

Despite all these makeshifts, there is no evidence of stripping of parts, which peasants conceivably could use, from the thousands of wrecked tanks, trucks, tractors, motor cars and cannon in the area.

This military debris remains along highways on the battlefields until German salvage crews get around to hauling the machines to the nearest concentration point.

These German salvage crews are assisted by the economic commands, or, as Herr Koch prefers to call them, his economic sleuths. Their organization is an idea of his in which he takes particular pride. Their detective duty is to find out every piece of scrap which the Russians have not succeeded in shipping away. If the German army happens to catch up with some of the eastbound machines and other equipment from evacuated factories, the industrial experts from the economic command come into action. It is their task to find out to what industrial plant in the German-occupied territory the machines and apparatus belong. This task, it is stated, requires a high degree of "detective" talent, since the marks that will permit the identification of these machines are lacking or have been purposely destroyed.

Another duty of the army's economic commands is to spot and lay hands on any Soviet stocks and raw materials that are particularly needed by the armament and other industries in the blockaded Reich. If these stocks have not been burned or otherwise destroyed they are often hidden by the Russians in what an eyewitness calls "the most incredible places." The tracing of these stocks is also said to tax the detective abilities of the German Army's economic experts.

Apparently some of the technicians attached to the economic command are also expected to possess an intimate knowledge of Soviet industry and of individual Soviet plants. Thus, when a power station or some other important Russian plant comes within range of German artillery, an eyewitness report states, it is the duty of the economic command attached to the attacking unit to call the attention of the commander to this fact and to ask him, military considerations permitting, to spare the Soviet plant. It seems, however, that these duties are generally rendered futile by the thoroughness with which the Russians themselves destroy all industrial property.

When the German troops move forward, the economic commands have the task of trying to organize work on farms and factories in territory that has been thoroughly depleted of raw materials, equipment, and even workers. Another of Herr Koch's principal preoccupations is revamping the Soviet industry in the conquered parts. His organization has been preparing for this task by engaging the services of the best German industrial experts with a Russian background. Engineers also have followed in the wake of the advancing German armies, taking stock of all industrial property in the occupied area and planning for the resumption of work in mines and factories.

Special bureaus have been set up for exploiting Russian oil fields, although the German vanguards still have to cover long distances before they will come in sight of the first derricks.

In two respects the task of exploiting Soviet industry is different from any that the German industrial "occupation experts" have faced in other territories occupied by the German armed forces: first, Soviet industry is entirely State-owned; and secondly, the destruction and disorganization exceed everything the Germans have experienced so far in their easier "Blitz" campaigns in the north, west, and south of Europe.

The fact that the Soviet industry is State-owned permits the Reich Government to lay hands on it without further ado, as the Germans see it. But this theoretical advantage is probably more than offset by the wholesale destruction of equipment and raw materials and by the evacuation of workers and technical personnel.

The new German managers of conquered Soviet mines and factories, therefore, face a truly herculean task. The plan to sell "conquered" Soviet industrial plants to private interests in Germany and other countries of Europe and, thereby, eventually to cover a substantial part of the Reich's current war expenditures, is still in its theoretical stage. In view of the extent of destruction and of the unsettled conditions in the occupied area, financial experts point out that it will not be easy to arouse business enthusiasm for this scheme.

The conquerors are helpless to profit by their seeming booty. Their high-geared machine runs empty. In Kovno, Lwów, Bialystok, and Minsk new branches of the German Bank (Reichskreditkasse) were opened; but no customers appeared, and the counters had to close again. Industry is dead, and even farm land worthless. Desperately Herr Koch tried, as a last resort, to hand over to individual peasants as personal property the land which under the Soviet scheme they had been only allowed to work as trustees for the community.

The land, Herr Koch promised, would be tax-free and deduction-free. If the peasants brought in a good harvest, their individual holdings might be doubled. The Germans, posters announced, would make sure that the peasants got an adequate number of cattle. The Germans would pay "fixed and just" prices for products delivered both from individual holdings and from collective fields. The German prices were said to exceed greatly those fixed by the Russians. Measures also were taken to assure that capitalist exploitation methods should not be employed in dealing with the peasants. Full freedom of religion was assured into the bargain.

But no bidders came. It was probably the first time in human memory that farmers refused to avail themselves of free soil and cattle. Why this unique stubbornness? There are probably two reasons. Every Ukrainian peasant knows the fate that awaits him after the return of the Soviets if his record is marred by dealings with the Germans. Furthermore, regardless of punishment, Ukrainians do not want to deal with them.

The country remains entirely unresponsive. The people feign not to notice the foreign, hated uniform. Life goes on as well or as bad as possible. For the most part, the collective farming system has been retained to keep the economy going at all. Efforts to install kulaks, Ukrainian expatriates, and other opponents of the Soviet regime as chiefs of these institutions were soon abandoned. The guerrillas saw to it that no candidates should be found for those jobs.

While the Germans may be refraining from any exceptional efforts to get a Nazi political organization going in this temporarily conquered territory, because it is far simpler to maintain the status quo economically and govern solely through military courts and administration, the population's reaction is distinctly disappointing to Berlin, which had hoped for widespread demonstrations of sympathy. During the occupation of the Ukraine more than two decades ago the Germans were similarly disappointed at being forced to keep an exceedingly large garrison there and at failing to receive nearly the size crops, raw materials and other output they had anticipated. The present occupying force includes Finnish troops wearing Reichswehr uniforms and Hungarians.

The Finns are around the Chernigov area, guarding Russian prisoners at the camp of Nejin, and are bitterly hated for their pillaging and brutality. A tremendous game of hide-and-seek is going on in the Ukraine, with the Germans searching for wounded officers and men secretly transported toward the Soviet lines and for guerrilla bases. One wounded officer was carried swiftly through seven cottages as the Germans searched the village for him, and he reported later that the entire population of each village had facilitated his eastward journey, with little boys guiding him through fields.

The Germans have published warnings that any one sheltering partisans, Jews, or Communists will be hanged, and have tried to institute in each village a council of elders that will assist in carrying out these instructions. However, general disinclination by the population to accept these posts, the limited numbers of former kulaks, and the constant threat of punishment by guerrillas make this most difficult.

The Germans made a great to-do in their propaganda about opening new churches, but they have not been able to find enough priests. In some cases, German officers gave sermons on the *Wehrmacht's* advances, after perfunctory religious services, spreading such tales as that the Red Army had already fallen back on the Urals. Economically speaking, escaped refugees said, the Germans have so far gained little. Quantities of sugar beets have been taken over, but machinery for processing has been either safely evacuated or destroyed. Grain stores have usually been burned or distributed to those peasant families remaining behind when the Russians withdrew, and much has been hidden away, although the Germans are trying to regain some by systematic house-to-house searches. Many factories have been entered at Kiev, and the buildings emptied. When the Germans entered Kiev they found the radio station, bridges, and the telephone system all useless. The railway was functioning only along short stretches, while the Germans had forced gangs of Ukrainians to repair the lines. One bridge near Klimovka had been shattered, and the Germans were forcing peasants to provide timber for its reconstruction.

Although the Germans have worked hard on the Ukrainian population with propaganda broadcasts and leaflets for many months—even while the Red Army was there—the Russians continue to maintain contact with them. A Ukrainian patriots' meeting was held at Saratov, where the fraternity in arms of the Ukrainian and the Polish peoples was among the points emphasized. Thousands of the soldiers in the Polish army being formed here are from the western Ukraine.

Thus German efforts to win over the Ukraine have completely failed. There is neither contact nor cooperation between the population and the invaders. Nowhere have the peasants surrendered to the German authorities stray Russian soldiers or "partisans," although the country teems with them. The death penalty imposed even for petty offenses does not intimidate the Ukrainians. The strength of their resistance lies in their indifference to what may happen to them. They take everything in deadly silence. Herr Koch rules a cemetery.

S.S. Sturmbannführer Eichmann supplies the bodies. In Kiev alone, according to the Soviet government, the "Jewish specialist for Ostland" had thirty thousand Jews massacred, among them three thousand children. Such manifestations of insanity demand an explanation which not even psychiatry can furnish. Perhaps Herr Eichmann's personal history offers it. He is a German, ironically born in Palestine among Oriental Jews, where he sucked in his anti-Semitism with his mother's milk. His case is similar to that of Hitler, who acquired his anti-Jewish obsession during the years he spent in a Viennese flophouse, mostly filled with Jews. Perhaps the case of Eichmann parallels still more that of Rudolf Hess, once Nazi Number Two, who invented the "Nordic man" because he was born in Alexandria, Egypt, and looks like an Arab sheik.

Herr Eichmann, undoubtedly, looks like a Zionist. I saw him in the days immediately following the rape of Vienna. An S.S. functionary of long standing, he had assumed the job of purging the city of Jews. I could scarcely conceal a smile when he blew into our government office, asking whether there were any non-Aryans on the staff. A smart Jew boy, it flashed through my mind, can make all sorts of careers.

His own personnel, the hitherto illegal Viennese S.S., was less indulgent. He had summoned them into the square of the Rossauer barracks to take command. Since in these hectic days of pogrom he was a very busy man, he did not don his dress uniform, but showed up in mufti. The Viennese S.S. hoodlums were struck by the appearance of a man with a dark complexion, aquiline nose, and distinctly oriental features. "One-way ticket to Palestine!" they roared—it was a habitual greeting in these days—before he could explain to them that it was now, under his command, open season for Jewish prey.

Of course, the hoodlums could not know that their new, Semitic-looking boss was a German from Palestine. He bore the marks of the land of his birth. They have, I am sure, harassed him throughout his life, and constantly the word "Palestine" pursued him. Hence, a few years later, the carnage among the Jews in the Ukrainian towns and villages had to assume tremendous proportions.

It was Eichmann's scheme to separate the population of every conquered place into two groups—the "Aryans" (meaning the Russians and the Ukrainians) and the Jews. There were no limits as to what German soldiers and storm troopers were permitted to do to the Jews. Hundreds of thousands of Jews throughout the provinces have been interned in forced-labor camps. Many of them get no pay. Where they are paid, the rate is about one cent per hour. The forced-labor decree applies to all men from eighteen to forty-five. No provision is made for their families, and in most cases these are destitute except for the limited aid the Jewish community can give them.

In Kishinev, Jews are not allowed any employment whatever, and the Jewish population is left to die of starvation. Hunger and starvation are rampant among them, and some young girls prostitute themselves for a piece of bread.

Similar atrocities occurred in Galicia, another province in which Herr Eichmann acts as Jewish commissar. The fate of the Galician victims is the more tragic as thousands of them had been deported from Hungary, and dumped across the Galician border to be machine-gunned by German soldiers. The number of murdered Jews in the Kamenets Podolsk region alone was placed at about fifteen thousand, among whom were twenty-five hundred deportees from Hungary. Those who survived found temporary refuge in villages scattered along the Dniester River, which, according to an old local saying, has always carried more blood than water. But also there Jewish deaths were so numerous that bodies floated down the river; no one made an attempt to recover and bury them.

The anti-Jewish horror, instigated and carefully organized by Eichmann, is not an incidental phenomenon. It represents the spirit of the war behind the war in Russia. Equal hatred intoxicates both sides. But all the accounts of the bloodiest battles in history, which are raging at present along Europe's Eastern Front, are outdone by the reports of the atrocities committed by the Germans behind the lines. The Soviet government has collected and published them in Foreign Commissar Molotov's report, mentioned in a previous chapter.

Out of the untold sufferings of the conquered Russian people came the most desperate and dangerous fighter in this war: the Russian guerrilla. The guerrillas, a constant thorn in the side of Hitler's white-bled troops, are now integrated with the Red Army. The scale and intensity of their activities far exceeds the mere harassing of the invaders. The Russian commanders in chief on the three principal fronts, Voroshilov,

Timoshenko, and Budyenny, all have appealed to the guerrilla fighters to extend their activity. These appeals have not
gone unanswered.

In the Latvian Soviet Socialist Republic guerrilla groups,
operating since the outbreak of the war, have merged into
a Latvian regiment of the Red Army. Commanded by the
former head of an agricultural academy, this regiment is
equipped with artillery and tanks capable of giving the visiting Nazi army a first-rate example of Soviet military efficiency.

Regularization of the guerrillas' status has included the
following oath: "I, a Red guerrilla, swear to my comrades-
in-arms that I shall be brave, disciplined, and merciless to the
enemy. To the end of my days I shall remain faithful to my
country, my party, and my leader Stalin. If I break this sacred oath, may severe punishment be meted out to me at the
hands of guerrillas."

Guerrilla fighters who take this oath include men drawn
from every section of the Soviet population. In the southwest,
schoolteachers from the Uman district have joined up. A doctor, head of a hospital in this area, also joined the guerrillas
with his two daughters, who act as nurses for a detachment.

Women are active with various guerrilla groups. An *Izvestia*
war correspondent tells of a young girl, Katya, who acts as
scout for an important detachment and frequently takes part
in fighting. Another girl, Julia, recently conveyed information which enabled her comrades to repulse a Nazi attack on
the village of "N" and capture a rich haul of German equipment in the process. The captured weapons were added to
the guerrilla arsenal.

Veterans of the October Revolution of 1917 often take a
leading part in guerrilla warfare, using the tactics learned in
their youth. A detachment commanded by a civil-war veteran recently attacked an enemy airdrome and captured six
Heinkel planes and other equipment after killing more than

a hundred German soldiers. An amateur air enthusiast among the group named Solin, in civilian life a tractor driver, flew one plane to the Red Army lines. The other five were destroyed. The guerrillas set fire to gasoline tanks, blew holes in runways, set fire to hangars and drove away five trucks, seven motorcycles and a mobile radio station. All this equipment was in good order and served the guerrillas well.

Enemy airdromes are especially vulnerable to guerrilla attack. Near the village of "V," after studying the habits of German fliers and ground crews, guerrillas attacked an airfield one night, killing twenty-two Nazis who tried to defend it. The guerrillas set fire to twelve enemy planes, loaded two trucks with ammunition and drums of gasoline, and drove away.

One hundred guerrillas held back a Nazi attack on the Ukrainian town of "K" for three days recently, ambushing German scouts and compelling the main forces to advance blindly. These guerrillas, collective farmers and workers from machine tractor stations, then held off the advancing Nazis with machine guns captured from the scouts.

Near the town of "O" a guerrilla group armed only with one automatic rifle and seven ordinary rifles stopped fifteen German ammunition trucks one night by placing spiked planks across the road. When the guerrillas opened fire the surprised Nazis fled to the woods.

In the Ukraine guerrillas have ambushed the Nazis whenever they left well guarded highways. A group of Nazi armored cars were brought to a halt on a side road, in one instance, but it proved impossible to rout the Nazi crews with rifle fire. One fighter in the guerrilla group crept close, dragging three sheaves of ripe wheat. Suddenly rising, he shouted: "The robbers wanted our bread. Let's give it to them!" And he hurled the wheat against one of the Nazi cars following it with a flaming bottle of gasoline. The wheat blazed up and quickly converted the Nazi car into a pile of blackened iron.

From the Arctic Ocean to the Black Sea the guerrillas materialize from nowhere, thousands of them, wherever there are German troops. They slash out from ambush, strike in the night, and vanish leaving the Nazis to count their dead. In Byelorussia Guerrilla Commander B, recently decorated by the Soviet Government, wrote the following description of his group:

Our detachment was formed in the first days of the war and numbered eighty men. We began to study military tactics and selected trusted people in neighboring villages with whom we could keep in contact. We obtained explosives with which we mined bridges, and we prepared bottles of gasoline for destroying tanks.

We concealed our ammunition and food in places inaccessible to the enemy. When the Nazis attacked our hiding place, we blew up a bridge before them and met their tanks with machine-gun fire and gasoline bottles. We wrecked fifteen German tanks in this action and an equal number of armored cars.

Another guerrilla commander from the same area wrote of his activities:

We are camped in a virgin forest. Only the people who guard our supplies stay in camp. Our main detachment is constantly on the march. The Nazis worry themselves to death hunting us. The population of the occupied villages loves us as a mother loves her children, and keeps us informed of the enemy's movements.

The German command has honored Soviet guerrilla activity on numerous occasions by issuing specific orders for the extermination of these groups. Recently, special Gestapo punitive expeditions were sent from Berlin to deal with guerrillas and terrorize civilians aiding them. The Gestapo will have its hands full. The Germans must reckon with the guerrillas as a powerful auxiliary of the Red Army as long as the war lasts.

The heroic example set by the Russian guerrillas will be followed by all the conquered people when the bells of Europe sound the hour of liberation. This hour is not yet at hand. Conditions under the New Order will get considerably worse before the monster collapses. Every day and every hour, Hitler is tightening his grip. Some countries are on the point of losing even their mock independence. Others are driven to greater and greater exertion for the German war effort. France is the most vulnerable spot on the continent; the Vichy government is about to force the French into fighting alongside their own destroyers. Two hundred million subjugated people in Europe have nothing with which to oppose tyranny and to stave off annihilation but their morale and their will power. The morale of the captive nations is the miracle of our times. But is will power made of elastic? Can it not be stretched until it snaps? The peoples of Europe are freezing, famine-stricken, prostrated, and exposed to wholesale extermination. If years of war count double, years of enemy occupation count tenfold. How long will their span of life be under such conditions?

The invasion of the European continent by the forces of the United Nations is, unfortunately, not the next point on our agenda. Much else must be achieved before it can materialize. Nevertheless, we cannot forget that every day counts, double for us, and ten times for our shackled allies. It will be no child's play, but the greatest military undertaking in history. It is, however, an inevitable action. Let no one fancy that Nazism can be broken by bombers and blockade. The New Order will fade like a nightmare, once it receives the deadly blow. But this blow must be dealt. Hitler has, at present, the world's mightiest army. But he cannot form a second one. The borders and shores of his subjugated continent bristle with every ingenious device of defense. But he has no second line. The New Order is a colossal patchwork. But it is rotten. Inside Europe, two hundred million slaves are prepared to take up arms. When the end comes, it will come with lightning speed—provided it does not come too late. Time counts above all. Europe's battered but unbeaten and unbroken nations wait, in desperate anxiety, for the signal from across the seas.